CHAMPION OF ENGLISH FREEDOM

CHAMPION OF ENGLISH FREEDOM

THE LIFE OF JOHN WILKES, MP AND LORD MAYOR OF LONDON

ROBIN EAGLES

AMBERLEY

For Bella

First published 2024

Amberley Publishing
The Hill, Stroud
Gloucestershire, GL5 4EP

www.amberley-books.com

Copyright © Robin Eagles, 2024

The right of Robin Eagles to be identified as the Author
of this work has been asserted in accordance with the
Copyright, Designs and Patents Act 1988.

All rights reserved. No part of this book may be reprinted
or reproduced or utilised in any form or by any electronic,
mechanical or other means, now known or hereafter invented,
including photocopying and recording, or in any information
storage or retrieval system, without the permission in writing
from the Publishers.

British Library Cataloguing in Publication Data.
A catalogue record for this book is available from the British Library.

ISBN 978 1 3981 1170 7 (hardback)
ISBN 978 1 3981 1171 4 (ebook)

1 2 3 4 5 6 7 8 9 10

Typeset in 10.5pt on 13pt Sabon.
Typesetting by SJmagic DESIGN SERVICES, India.
Printed in the UK.

Contents

	Acknowledgements	7
	Introduction	9
1	Matthew, Mark, Luke and Joan	13
2	Aylesbury	31
3	Parliament and Hellfire	48
4	The *North Briton*	66
5	Wilkes and Liberty	89
6	Exile	115
7	London and Middlesex	139
8	Parliament and Prison	155
9	An Alderman of London	167
10	Lord Mayor of London, MP for Middlesex and City Chamberlain	191
11	From the Gordon Riots to Respectability	213
12	A Patriot in Retirement	230
	Epilogue	244
	Endnotes	248
	Bibliography	294
	Index	309

Acknowledgements

I have been living with John Wilkes for longer than I care to remember. This book is the result of a somewhat accidental email conversation after I foolishly decided to take another look at the man. I am most grateful to the staff at Amberley for agreeing to take it on, and to Connor Stait, in particular, for seeking me out and being such an encouraging presence in the background.

I am extremely conscious that I am following in the steps of many fine writers who have all made their mark on Wilkes studies. I am particularly indebted to the last three major biographers of Wilkes – Arthur Cash, John Sainsbury and P.D.G. Thomas – whose books were invaluable in producing my own, along with that by Charles Chevenix Trench. The debt should be obvious from what follows.

Wilkes's papers and those of people associated with him are spread around the world and I have benefited from so much material now being available digitally. The staff of a number of libraries, archives and record offices have all been unfailingly helpful whether in person or remotely. I must thank the staff of the Clements Library, Michigan, for making available some of Wilkes's family papers and I am extremely grateful to the Oxfordshire History Centre for allowing me to cite material from the diary of Viscount Villiers. Other archives visited in the course of research include the British Library, Hampshire Archives, London Metropolitan Archives, the National Archives, the Parliamentary Archives and the Public Record Office of Northern Ireland. The National Gallery of Victoria, Melbourne, and the Rijksmuseum, Amsterdam, were extremely generous in permitting me to produce images from their collections, and I must also thank the staff of all the other collections for helping me source pictures, notably Bridgeman Images, on behalf of the British Library, the British Museum, Museum of London, National Portrait Gallery and Parliamentary Art Collection.

I have been quite overwhelmed by the kindness and generosity of friends and colleagues who have been only too happy to help, sharing notes, reading draft chapters, and generally putting up with around three years of Wilkes-related wittering. Sections of the book were tried out at conferences and I am very grateful to the participants for their questions and feedback on those occasions. I must thank Peter Galliver, who invited me to Winchester College to give a brief talk on Wilkes, and for both his and his students' forbearance when I carried on for much longer than planned. Clyve Jones and Graham Townend sent me material related to Wilkes from their own researches into the archives of Scotland some years ago, and I am delighted finally to have been able to put some of it to use; I am also grateful to Kendra Packham for sharing information from her work on ballads from 18th-century elections. I have benefited from conversations with, and the support of, Conrad Brunstrom, Tim Couzens, Coleman Dennehy, Ben Gilding, Freya Gowrley, David Hayton, Matthew Grenby, Peter Moore, Rory Muir, Kate Retford, Guy Rowlands, and Rachel Wilson, who have all helped shape my approach to a range of issues. I am hugely indebted to the output of the brilliant 'ECPPEC' project, based at the University of Newcastle, which made tracing the poll books associated with Wilkes's elections so much easier. I must also thank the trustees and editorial board of the History of Parliament for allowing me two months to work on Wilkes, and many of my colleagues, chief among them Hannes Kleineke, Kathryn Rix, Philip Salmon, Paul Seaward and Martin Spychal for their encouragement and assistance.

Several intrepid friends and colleagues have been generous enough to read all or part of the manuscript as it developed. I have been kept buoyed by the enthusiasm of Perry Gauci, Nick Holland and Max Skjönsberg, who all read chapters and have each of them encouraged me throughout its production. Hillary Burlock has been unfailingly enthusiastic and very generously read sections as well as providing me with material when she was supposed to be working on her own projects. I am enormously grateful to Elaine Chalus, who kindly made time to read the manuscript, and Jonathan Conlin, who sent me a raft of papers from his own research as well as reading the entire book in draft, and even treated me to a drink afterwards rather than the other way around. I am also indebted to Michael Schaich for his thoughtful and detailed comments on several of the chapters. It goes without saying that any remaining mistakes are entirely my own.

Above all, I have to thank my wife Bella, who read the whole thing – parts of it more than once – and has had to live with the spirit of Wilkes for a worryingly large proportion of our married life. It is dedicated to her, with love.

Robin Eagles
Oxford

Introduction

The famous, wicked Wilkes

During the 1760s and 1770s, John Wilkes was probably the most famous man in England. It was hard to open a newspaper without finding something about him in its pages. His striking visage might be seen in print shop windows and pasted onto the walls of taverns and coffee shops. People may not have known who the prime minister was, but they certainly knew all about John Wilkes, renegade MP, journalist and ultimately Lord Mayor of London. From a rather minor member of an aristocratic faction in Parliament, he rose to become a folk hero, willing to take on the establishment and always armed with a ready quip.

Wilkes's ability to reinvent himself, to outwit government and the courts alike never ceased to amaze his contemporaries and later writers. Around the time of his election for Parliament in 1774, one observer commented: 'He is an astonishing Fellow, and will keep his ground in spite of them all.'[1] The historian of Georgian Britain, John Brooke, commented that Wilkes's life was so extraordinary that it might have formed the subject for 'a long, rambling eighteenth-century novel'.[2] Wilkes survived being thrown out of Parliament more than once, as well as stints in prison, to re-emerge time and again at the head of a series of campaigns for reform. Ultimately, the causes with which Wilkes was concerned became bigger than the man himself as his followers 'independently of John Wilkes' went on to take over public meetings agitating for change.[3]

At the heart of Wilkes's story is one of liberty. It was the mantra he adopted for himself and summed up much of what he was about. As was noted at the opening of one of the articles in his paper, the *North Briton*, 'liberty is precious.'[4] It was by no means an original concept and might have been heard in myriad contexts in the period. When the people of

Shropshire gathered to celebrate the marriage of the Princess Royal to the Prince of Orange in 1734, for example, one of the healths drunk was 'liberty and property in spite of the Jacobites'.[5]

Samuel Johnson's Dictionary offered five definitions for the word 'liberty', three of them particularly relevant to Wilkes. The first was 'Freedom, as opposed to slavery'. Wilkes frequently played on fears that hard-won political and religious rights and freedoms secured by the Revolution of 1688 were under threat from an emergent Tory Party, newly readmitted to government by George III. It was a development, he suggested, that should be of concern to all sensible people: 'Every man of common understanding ... very clearly saw what the friends of liberty were to expect, when the *talons* were fully grown.'[6] Next in Johnson's lexicon was 'Privilege; exemption; immunity', again a sense that meant much to Wilkes as he battled to ensure his immunity from prosecution for publishing criticism of the government. The last was 'relaxation of restraint', something that reflected Wilkes's identity as a gentleman libertine.[7]

When he thought of liberty, Wilkes was reflecting in essence the values of 1688. Wilkes saw himself very clearly as a successor to the men who had rebelled against James II and were the upholders of the 'Revolution Settlement'. His political philosophy, such as it was, stemmed largely from this. William III was lauded as the saviour of English liberty and it was the spirit of 'Whig heroes' like the duke of Devonshire ('a true friend of liberty and the constitution') that he professed to be emulating in his various campaigns.[8] His fear was that the Whigs, the upholders of what had been achieved in 1688, were being eclipsed by a resurgent Tory party and that the result of this was an increasing loss of hard-won and inalienable freedoms.[9] The opening line of the *North Briton* stated unequivocally, 'The liberty of the press is the birth-right of a Briton.'[10] Wilkes signed off his controversial 45th issue of the *North Briton* with a quotation from John Dryden: 'Freedom is the English subject's prerogative.'[11] That said, when he spoke of liberty as his career progressed, Wilkes was also aware that he was increasingly looking beyond Britain and, as has been argued recently, was making a conscious effort 'to place English liberty in a European and geopolitical context'.[12]

As well as someone devoted to liberty, Wilkes was also a libertine, defined by Johnson as 'licentious, irreligious', but as John Sainsbury has made clear, there was much more to it than that. Libertines might also present themselves as characters of exquisite taste and fashion.[13] It was, after all, no contradiction to be thought of as a 'man of taste', interested in the latest ideas of the enlightenment, and also to relish the fleshpots of eighteenth-century society. For Wilkes, it was a key part of his identity.[14] He famously embarked on his libertine education while a student at the university of Leiden and then progressed with ever more abandonment under the tutelage of Thomas Potter, the notorious

Introduction

son of the archbishop of Canterbury. Libertinism also had its roots in the bravos of the 17th-century: men like John Wilmot, 2nd earl of Rochester, the scurrilous poet of Charles II's restoration court. By adopting this persona, Wilkes, though, was associating himself with the fashionable men of his own day. For many, it was a reason to view him with suspicion. As one contemporary put it, when reflecting on Wilkes's ejection from Parliament: 'How was it possible for the house of commons to avoid declaring that he was or was not an infamous person unworthy of a share in the legislature of his Countrey?'[15] This was a sentiment shared by the bluestocking Hester Thrale (Mrs Piozzi), who told Samuel Johnson after meeting Wilkes: 'I like him not, he professed himself a Lyar and an Infidel, and I see no Merit in being either.' In 1768, she even contributed an article for the *Public Advertiser* comparing Wilkes with the mythological snake-biting ichneumon.[16] Some have argued that as a consequence of such negative assessments, over time Wilkes felt the need to tone down his libertine persona to make himself more acceptable to a wider public.[17] Certainly, as he aged his more respectable domestic life increasingly overshadowed his earlier libertine one.

One obvious contradiction about Wilkes is that in an age of huge constitutional turmoil, he appeared largely opportunistic. Although he became a figurehead for many Americans involved in the War of Independence and was on familiar terms with enlightenment figures in France who would become involved in the revolution there, his own political philosophy was more flexible. His early associations were with the politicians gathered around Earl Temple at Stowe. These were the successors to the so-called 'Boy Patriots', chief among them William Pitt the Elder. Patriotism in these terms equated to opposing the kind of corruption in government associated with Sir Robert Walpole, and it was a similar line that Wilkes took in inveighing against George III's ministries in the 1760s. His fulminations in print charted a familiar line, warning of the dangers of readmitting the Tories to government. He was similarly hostile to the number of Scots perceived to be involved in George III's administrations: 'I am certain, that reason could never believe that a Scot was fit to have the management of English affairs.'[18] And, while he spoke of reform, he was openly disdainful of the uneducated and boorish followers who flocked to him. In the end, it seems not to have troubled him that he progressed from being a follower of an aristocratic patron, to an independent politician calling for reform, only to settle eventually as a supporter of the Younger Pitt. It is difficult to avoid the conclusion that Wilkes was principally concerned in securing his own advancement. At the beginning of his career, he was more than happy to stretch the rules of the electoral system to their limit, openly bribing his prospective constituents for their votes. Later, once he had attained his objective of a comfortable office in the City of London, he swiftly eschewed his earlier radicalism and became increasingly quiescent.

If Wilkes was no great political thinker, where his genius lay was in seeing how his own experience could be transposed onto that of others. When he was arrested for libel and his house was ransacked, as Sainsbury suggested, he equated this with any number of Englishmen who had experienced the depredations of bailiffs and court officers carrying off their possessions.[19] He made the same case when arguing against the introduction of the unpopular Cider Tax, as the legislation allowed government agents to invade property to check whether illegal cider-making was being carried on.[20]

One quality, often overlooked in Wilkes, was his eye for detail. One recent study has underscored his 'neatness', which was undoubtedly reflected in his exceptional organizational abilities.[21] He was an inveterate maker of lists and during his election campaigns was famous for keeping comprehensive notes of who had voted for him, as well as keeping tabs on who had not. Modern psephologists would have found much that was familiar about Wilkes. He studied his territory closely and entered elections with a clear grasp of where support was to be had.

There were many sides to Wilkes, which has been reflected in the number of studies of him, told from a variety of perspectives. He is in many ways a difficult character to grasp satisfactorily as there are many contradictions. He spoke of freedom and made well-documented gestures in favour of abolition of slavery, while members of his family and close friends were actively engaged in trade with the plantations. His brother-in-law, George Hayley, for example, was involved with insuring slave ships.[22] His most important relationship was with his daughter Polly, yet his behaviour towards other women was often highly questionable. He campaigned for election to Parliament claiming to be an enemy of corruption, but he was happy to outbribe his competitors. Such features may not make him so very different from any number of prominent figures from the period, but they are ones that require careful consideration in someone who professed himself so fiercely a 'Friend to Liberty'.

Few people made such a mark on a period as Wilkes did on the later eighteenth century. His image, whether the grotesque caricature by William Hogarth or the more sympathetic likeness made by Robert Edge Pine, was reproduced internationally in prints, on ceramics and even handkerchiefs. Having begun life as the son of a tradesman, he became a gentleman MP, a rabble-rousing journalist and ultimately a respectable courtier. In his final iteration as a retired figure living out a quiet existence on the Isle of Wight, he became a tourist attraction.

Never one to hide his light under a bushel, Wilkes was certain his was a story worth the retelling:

> In my time a private person has stood forth, who by the fond voice of his countrymen and the panegyrick of their poets, has been equalled to the patriots of former ages... This person is Mr Wilkes.[23]

1

Matthew, Mark, Luke and Joan

I prefer Plutarch to Suetonius. He brings me better and more intimately acquainted with his characters, and never descends to the trifling minutiae of the Roman biographer.[1]

When John Wilkes was born, George I was on the throne and Sir Robert Walpole getting settled in as Britain's first prime minister. By the time of his death, the world order had undergone a series of shocks. America had achieved independence and Napoleon Bonaparte had just completed his successful Italian campaign. Wilkes knew prominent figures both in America and France and his example influenced some of those involved in both revolutions.

When selecting the opening quotation for his autobiography, Wilkes settled on a brief line from the Roman author, Terence: '*Sic vita erat*', thus was life.[2] Ironically, by then Wilkes may well have forgotten key details about his birth and family. He had long given out his date of birth as 17 October 1727, after George I's demise, amended to 28 October following the calendar change of 1752.[3] It is much more likely, though, that he was born in 1725.[4] One reason for Wilkes insisting on the later date may have been so that he could emphasize that when he had married, he had been underage (see chapter 2). He was very keen to insist that his was a marriage entered into to fulfil parental expectations rather than because of personal choice. It also made it much easier for him to justify the marriage's breakdown. Altering his date of birth may, thus, have been a convenient sleight of hand of the sort he was often to employ. By 1797, though, when his end was drawing near he may well have believed the information he gave was correct. He would certainly have appreciated the neat symmetry of it: 1727-1797, meaning that he had been accorded his three score years and ten precisely. It all made for a tidy span for a man who had been brought up in a committed Christian household.

For a man so famed for irreligiousness as Wilkes, religion formed an important strand in his life. He had been born into a pious merchant family. His father may have been technically a member of the Church of England but seems to have been content to attend non-conformist services as well. His mother was, in Wilkes's own words, 'a zealous favourer' of presbyterianism.[5] She was sufficiently influential to ensure that her children were well educated at dissenting institutions. Thus, Wilkes and his brothers were ultimately entrusted to a well-known dissenting minister, who owed his preferment to the Mead family of Aylesbury. There, Wilkes probably first came into contact with his future wife, and possibly just as important, his future constituents.

Wilkes's Family

At the root of all of this, though, is uncertainty – and it is an important feature of Wilkes's life that needs to be grasped from the outset. Image and reality were very different things to Wilkes. It might be going too far to suggest that he was a stranger to the truth, but he certainly learned from an early age to present one front to the world and quite a different one to his intimates. Even his nearest and dearest, notably his daughter Polly, were only offered a glimpse of what was really happening in Wilkes's life for much of the time. Whether this was because he wished to save them from some of the grittier details, or because he was keen to present a more likeable front to those who mattered to him, is perhaps something that will never quite be settled. But what is very clear is that Wilkes possessed many lives and getting to the bottom of the real John Wilkes is as difficult now as it was to those who knew him.

The Wilkes family's origins are as uncertain as John Wilkes's date of birth. Wilkes ensured that there was an 'official version', but it was likely inaccurate.[6] According to Wilkes, the family descended from a respectable family of minor gentry hailing from Leighton Buzzard. The founder of the family fortune was said to have been Edward Wilkes, a curiously pious individual who wished to name his children after the evangelists, Matthew, Mark, Luke and John. Unfortunately for him, his fourth child was a daughter. So, he had to make do with Matthew, Mark, Luke and Joan.[7] Luke Wilkes had risen to minor court office at the court of Charles II as yeoman of the withdrawing wardrobe, and other members of the family had found similar success at the middle level of the gentry and professions.[8]

It was a pleasant story and an eminently suitable origin myth for a gentleman in 18th-century London, but very likely these were not Wilkes's forebears. Contrary to the family legend, Luke Wilkes appears not to have had offspring, his will making mention of his brothers, Matthew and Mark. He also mentioned a nephew Matthew Disney, then a scholar at Westminster School, but no children of his own. It is a shame, as his example would have fitted Wilkes's ambitions for a prosperous forebear well. Luke Wilkes was able to make substantial bequests of £1,000 apiece to Matthew Disney and to a niece, Frances Disney, as well as bequeathing £100 in addition to money he had already settled on a trust for the benefit of the poor of Leighton Buzzard.[9]

If this was not Wilkes's family, where did he come from? An alternative source was a Shropshire yeoman from Albrighton,[10] whose children appear to have made their way to London in search of better things. These may well have been Wilkes's immediate progenitors. They may not have fared particularly well in the heaving metropolis. According to one contemporary newspaper, within living memory John Wilkes's great-grandfather had been well known in London plying his trade driving a brewer's dray.[11] Certainly, one of Wilkes's more recent biographers stated that Wilkes's grandfather had 'climbed from lowly origins'.[12] It seems that the newspaper may have muddled the chronology and confused Wilkes's great-grandfather for his grandfather, who seems to have come to London, found work with a brewer and from there been taken on as an apprentice distiller. This might well explain Wilkes's eagerness to hide his arriviste family origins. It seems not to have stopped the family from claiming a right to a coat of arms, and in later life Wilkes was observed driving in London in a chariot with his arms emblazoned on the coachwork along with his motto: *Arcui meo non confido* (I trust not to my bow).[13]

If Wilkes's antecedents are a matter of some confusion, and may well have been less gentrified than he cared to suggest, what is certain is that Wilkes was the son of Israel Wilkes, a prosperous London distiller and Sarah Heaton (or Heston), whose family had run a successful tannery.[14] Israel was the son of another Israel (likely the man who had started out in life driving the dray), who had established a distillery in partnership with his brother. They were taking advantage of the recent growth in the distilling industry following the passage of the 1690 Act for encouraging the distilling of brandy and spirits from corn.[15] The Wilkes brothers (Israel the elder and Edward) appear to have begun their venture in Southwark, before moving the business across the river into the thriving area of Clerkenwell,[16] and in February 1699 Israel was one of over 50 distillers to put their names to a petition in response to the Spirits (Distillation of Corn) Act.[17] He was later elected master of the Worshipful Company of Distillers.[18]

As a City of London company, the distillers were relatively new, only having been in existence since 1638.[19] The company was formally enrolled within the City of London two years later, but remained without its own livery hall, possibly more interested in business than ceremonial.[20] Certainly, it was a burgeoning industry much liked by the government, and Israel Wilkes was able to exploit its potential to the limit.[21] It seems to have been around the time of the distillers' petition that he set about erecting a house in St John's Square on land previously occupied by one of the earl of Ailesbury's townhouses, Ailesbury having moved to the more fashionable Leicester Square. Wilkes's new house was one of only two substantial buildings in the square – most of which was made up of terraced housing – and comprised 'a squarish, three-storey brick building, with wainscotted rooms and marble chimneypieces, built up against the north wall of the church.' The adjoining distillery represented the gradual industrialization of the area as well as, ironically, bringing down the tone of a neighbourhood previously inhabited by members of the aristocracy.[22] The Wilkes family's substantial new house may have represented their arrival in Clerkenwell society, but it also made them potential targets. In December 1730, one John Smith was convicted of stealing 400 lb of lead from the Wilkes house – one of a number of people convicted in the course of the year for carrying away lead from the houses of the wealthy.[23] Not far from St John Street was the site of Clerkenwell's New Prison. In the summer of 1758, the press reported a breakout by six prisoners and how the escaping convicts had made their way into the Wilkes family garden. One was retaken, but the other five remained at large.[24]

The elder Israel Wilkes did not confine himself to the distilling industry. He also speculated in property in Spitalfields, a development that is still remembered in present day Wilkes Street. As a sign of his own growing prosperity, in 1728 one of his daughters, Deborah, described in the press as 'a lady of a considerable fortune', was married to a well-known physician, Robert Nesbitt.[25] By the time of his death in 1745, Israel the elder was noted in the press as having been 'a very great malt-distiller'.[26]

Like his father, Israel Wilkes (the younger) was a successful businessman, combining his running of the distillery with further property investments.[27] One of Wilkes's most recent biographers, Arthur Cash, has observed: 'It seems unlikely that anyone will ever trace the ins and outs of Israel Wilkes's fortune, but it is certain it was large.'[28] As another biographer, Charles Chevenix Trench, observed, bar one or two well-worn anecdotes that show that he did have a softer side to him, Israel comes across as a rather remote figure in the young Wilkes's life. He was 'too busy making money'.[29]

Eager to embellish his fortune he may have been, but Israel the younger also seems to have been aware of some of the negative connotations of running a distillery in a period when moral reformers were driving for the greater regulation of spirits. Many attributed the shocking mortality rates in London in the second quarter of the 18th century to the proliferation of cheap gin.[30] In the spring of 1743, the House of Lords debated the issue, with the bishops fully behind the idea of curbing gin production. The administration, however, spotted the advantages of taxing the stuff instead. Thomas Benson, bishop of Gloucester, expressed his frustrations in a letter to his friend, George Berkeley, bishop of Cloyne: 'There was, I thought, an absolute necessity of doing something to prevent the drinking of that poison which is called gin, but unhappily, the increasing of the vice was found to be a way to increase the revenue.'[31]

The Wilkeses' operation was far larger than the kind of back-room stills that produced the most noxious and dangerous tipples. Nevertheless, Israel was clearly sufficiently conscious of the problem that he seems occasionally to have styled himself a brewer (much more respectable) than a mere distiller.[32] He was also sufficiently wealthy to be the proud owner of a coach and six, which helped mark him out as one of the successful entrepreneurial merchants in the city.[33]

By the late 1730s Israel Wilkes was firmly established within the life of the City as a successful distiller, knitted into the community of others plying the same trade but also, increasingly, in the life of the corporation of London. Israel's politics appear to have been those of a thoroughly solid ministry Whig (the prevailing party of the day, headed by Prime Minister Sir Robert Walpole).[34] In the general election of 1727, for example, Israel's name was to be found among the members of the distillers company voting for what appeared to be a joint ticket of Sir John Eyles and Sir John Thompson standing for the city of London.[35] Eyles came top of the poll, but Thompson was beaten into fifth place behind John Barnard, Micajah Perry and Humphrey Parsons. Eyles and Perry were both 'government Whigs', Barnard an independent Whig while Parsons was 'an extreme Tory'.[36] Perry was mentioned, in no very flattering terms, by the artist and letter-writer Mary Delany in a letter of March 1728. She noted having danced with him but dismissed him as 'a married man and as blind as a beetle, so I was in no danger or being liked or disliked.'[37]

In the summer of 1739, Israel was named as the contact in a series of advertisements carried in the press for a property to let, formerly owned by another distiller, Thomas Trott. The place seems to have proved rather difficult to offload as advertisements continued to be placed in the press at intervals over the course of several months.[38] The year before that, it had been reported that Israel was one of nine individuals nominated by the Lord Mayor to be considered for the onerous but prestigious role of sheriff, and he was warmly hailed as 'a Gentleman every way qualified for so great a trust'.³⁹ In the event, at the election Israel disqualified himself by declaring that he was not worth £15,000, leaving it to his fellow nominees, John Wightman, a brewer, and James Brooke, a stationer, to fight it out among themselves.⁴⁰ Israel may have decided not to accept the burden of civic office, but it was to be a post his more famous son would occupy some years later under rather different circumstances. Israel would not live to see it, but Wilkes's mother Sarah would.

Wilkes's mother's family, the Heatons, also seem to have inhabited the middling area of society, though once again, Wilkes seems to have sought to embroider the reality. One account recorded Wilkes's grandfather as being John Heaton, Esq., 'a gentleman of considerable fortune'. The reality seems to have been slightly different. The Heatons were undoubtedly affluent, but they were below the level of gentry as Wilkes's maternal grandfather, John Heaton, was a tanner from Bermondsey. Tanning was not a pleasant trade, and as one recent historian of the senses has observed: 'All citizens drank beer, used candles and wore shoes, but few wanted to live near a brewer, a chandler or a tanner.'⁴¹ A John Heaton, tanner of St Mary Magdalen, Bermondsey, made his will on Christmas Eve 1679, conveying to his son John and other children a variety of legacies.⁴² It seems plausible that this was Wilkes's great-grandfather, the son John very likely father of Wilkes's mother, Sarah. We may perhaps have a further glimpse of Sarah's father in 1689 when a John Heaton was one of six tanners to put their names to a petition in response to the Leather (Explanatory) Act.⁴³ If nothing else, it indicates that this was a family that had prospered in the tanning industry since at least the second half of the 17th century and was eager to ensure their voice was heard in defence of their trade. It also suggests that if this was Sarah Wilkes's family, not only were they not from the gentry, neither were they 'old dissenters', and it may only have been Sarah's father who aligned with the presbyterianism for which his daughter was well-known. Another John Heaton, also noted a tanner of St Mary Magdalen, Bermondsey, whose will was dated 14 August 1753, and who was presumably a nephew of Sarah's, requested burial in his local parish church, so he certainly appears to have conformed to the Church of England by the time of his death.⁴⁴ It is a helpful indication of the fluidity with which some treated their religious identity. Wilkes himself would in time desert his mother's dissenting example and conform to the Church of England, even purchasing a pew, first at St Margaret's Westminster and latterly in the Grosvenor Chapel close to his final London residence.

It was into this affluent and aspirational middling sort family that John Wilkes was born, most likely at the family house in St John's Square, Clerkenwell. This was the area where the young John would first come to know the citizens of London who were to become so central to his various careers.⁴⁵ St John's Square was in many ways a microcosm of the world Wilkes was to go on to inhabit, and it is striking how many of the characters he would become close to seem at some point to have spent time in its vicinity. Here was the family's distillery, the source of their wealth, but across the square was St John's Gate, home to the printing press of Edward Cave, publisher of the *Gentleman's Magazine*. It was also the location of a coffee shop owned by Richard Hogarth, father of the artist and caricaturist William. Hogarth's father had come to London from Westmorland hoping to make his mark as an author but had ended up attempting to make his coffee shop, at least, a place where literary types might feel comfortable. An advertisement for it noted its pretensions:

> At Hogarth's Coffee House in St John's Gate … there will meet daily some learned gentlemen, who speak Latin readily, where any Gentleman that is either skilled in that Language, or desirous to perfect himself in speaking thereof will be welcome. The Master of the House, in the absence of others, being always ready to entertain Gentlemen in the Latin Tongue.⁴⁶

Cave's printing establishment also happened to be the venue for a temporary theatre where some of the great actors of the day, David Garrick among them, occasionally staged plays. Slightly later in the century, at least by 1753, Arthur Collins, bookseller and author of the multi-volume *Peerage*, was also resident in the square, though by April 1754 when he composed a begging letter to the duke of Newcastle he was in poor health with only another half dozen years to live.⁴⁷ This, then, was a spectacularly rich environment and it was a world in which the Wilkes family played a full part. In many ways this mix of industry and literary endeavour reflected Israel Wilkes's own interests and he often played host to artists, writers and thinkers: very likely he spent time in Hogarth's and attended plays at Cave's. It is impossible that the young John Wilkes would not early on have been exposed to these parties and this no doubt was a significant part of his formation.

Wilkes was the middle of three brothers. The eldest, another Israel, lacked his younger sibling's drive and was to prove an unsuccessful businessman.⁴⁸ We get a flavour of the young man (not yet twenty) in a letter sent to his father in April 1741, asking to quit his current employment and to try his hand at the law instead: 'I have tried trade but cannot I am afraid fix my mind to it … Universal Experience, as well as Reason, testifies the little prospect there is of advantage from engaging in a Business that is disliked, & unsuitable to the natural turn of the mind.'⁴⁹ The youngest, Heaton, ultimately took over the distillery but was as unlucky as Israel and proceeded to run the business into the ground. Alongside his two brothers, Wilkes also had three sisters, Sarah, Mary and Ann, the last of whom, who seems to have been known in the family as Nancy, died young.[50] Sarah was said to have been Charles Dickens' inspiration for Miss Havisham in *Great Expectations*.[51] Mary (born in 1728) grew to be quite as forceful a character as Wilkes. A first marriage to an older merchant left her a wealthy widow and she later married one of her brother's colleagues, George Hayley, who was elected one of the MPs for London in 1774, the same year Wilkes became lord mayor. After Hayley's death in 1781 she relocated to America, where she married for a third time and ran a successful whaling business. She eventually returned to England (sans third husband, whom she was said to have paid to keep out of her way) and lived out her days as a noted eccentric in Bath.[52]

Wilkes was by far the brightest of the siblings and was certainly the apple of his parents' eye. This was in spite of him suffering from fairly striking facial deformities. He had a severe strabismus that meant that he had practically to balance text on the end of his nose to read it, and a prominent jaw, which may have contributed to a pronounced lisp. Sir Joshua Reynolds, a long-term friend of Wilkes and his family, would later describe him: 'His forehead low and short, his nose shorter and lower, his upper lip long and projecting, his eyes sunken and horribly squinting.'[53] In spite of all of this, he had charm, presence and a ready wit that meant it took him 'only half an hour to talk away his face'.[54] He would go on to become adept at French, competent in Italian, proficient in the classics and a very decent Latinist, where his interests tended to some of the filthier examples of Roman verse. He also acquired a love of art and books, amassing two substantial libraries in the course of his career. His houses were crammed full of prints and ceramics, an interest he had probably inherited from his mother.

London in the Eighteenth Century

The world in which Wilkes grew up and made his career is in many ways familiar to us thanks to the striking images produced by the likes of Hogarth. One can get a feel for the bustle, the filth, the noises and the temptations created by one of the great cities of the period. Wilkes would have been all too familiar with the reality of Hogarth's *Gin Lane* and *Beer Street*, and the world depicted in the *Rake's Progress* and *Industry and Idleness*. During his formative years, London was seized with 'moral panics' as a result of the proliferation of cheap and noxious alcohol. Indeed, 1725 was the beginning of one such period of existential concern, and there was another covering 1735-6 when Wilkes was a schoolboy.[55] It was a world of contrasts, where a minor dispute could easily escalate into a riot and where crime and accidents were commonplaces. Even those living in the more fashionable parts of London expected to be subject to casual crime such as street robberies. This was an environment that called on all classes to be street-wise. A collection of poems by John Gay published in 1737 included a series entitled 'Trivia; or the Art of Walking the Streets of LONDON' advising on the best way to navigate the city at different times of the day. As a general guide, though, Gay advised sternly:

> If drawn by bus'ness to a street unknown,
> Let the sworn porter point thee through the town;
> Be sure observe the signs, for signs remain,
> Like faithful Land-marks to the walking train.
> Seek not from prentices to learn the way,
> Those fabling boys will turn thy steps astray;
> Ask the grave tradesman to direct thee right,
> He ne'er deceives, but when he profits by't.[56]

It was not just mischievous apprentices and more malign cut-purses of whom one needed to be wary. As well as a busy metropolis crammed with all manner of people, London was also one filled with livestock. Many of the wealthy, of course, maintained their own horses and carriages – and the animals had to be housed somewhere. There were famous horse markets too, where one could purchase a more or less well-vouched for steed either as a carriage or saddle horse. Clerkenwell, where Wilkes was brought up, was one area where substantial space was given over to raising herds of cattle, ready to be driven to the slaughtermen in Smithfield, not to mention several places given over to pig-rearing.[57] It was not just Smithfield where animals for consumption were processed. In December 1750, the press reported a new slaughterhouse being readied in Westminster, 'so that oxen may be killed in it against Christmas.'[58] Even when Wilkes established himself later in life in Grosvenor Square, he was never far from semi-rural areas: London was a burgeoning city, but one where people lived cheek by jowl with animals.

Edgy it may have been, but London was also, of course, a lively melting pot. As Robert Bucholz and Joseph Ward have emphasized, London 'offered something for every taste – even for those who did not like the place.'[59] By the time Wilkes was born the London 'season', closely mirroring the movements of the Court and Parliament, was well established.[60] There were also any number of theatres offering the latest in music and drama, as well as earthier pleasures, such as cock-fighting, and gambling covering all manner of different low- or high-stakes games. Interestingly, for a man who liked to live on the edge, Wilkes was never much attracted to risking his shirt at the card tables, though plenty of others were.

During his life, the London Wilkes knew changed markedly. At a very basic level there was a radical transformation of the infrastructure of both the City and other parts of London, including Westminster. In 1736 the City was improved with street-lighting, funded through taxation, and in 1760 the pavements were widened. Two years later, Westminster followed suit with the Westminster Paving Act and by the end of Wilkes's life Westminster also had improved street lighting.[61] Other areas underwent similar improvements. In February 1750, one newspaper reported that the inhabitants of St John, Southwark, had agreed to raise funds for erecting street lamps and to 'establish a regular watch' for the area between London Bridge and Rotherhithe, where 'the new road to Deptford begins'. It is a reminder that private initiatives remained important and that there was still no centralized police force.[62]

Wilkes was born on a Sunday, so there were no papers published that day. The newspapers that came out over the next few days, though, offer a flavour of the environment into which he was born. For example, on Monday the 18th it was announced that on that day there would be a performance at Drury Lane of George Farquhar's *Beaux' Strategem*. By a strange coincidence, one of the most celebrated actors of the day, Robert Wilks (or Wilkes) was in the company and playing one of the leads. The even more famous Colley Cibber was in the cast as well. Other examples of entertainment available for the people of London at the time included the opportunity to view a model of the temple of Solomon. It was on view in the long room of the Opera House in the Haymarket each day from eleven in the morning until five in the evening, for anyone willing to stump up the entrance fee of 5 shillings: enough to restrict access to all but the relatively wealthy.[63] The same paper advertised a newly imported supply of 'Right GORGONA Anchovies' available to view in a cellar under the Wharfinger's counting house on Wool-Quay next to the customs house, priced at 21 shillings a barrel.[64] Two days later, another paper reported on tensions in the city among those plying their trades as peruke-makers. A 'considerable number' of barbers and perruquiers were said to be 'asham'd of the wicked practice' of some of their number in working on Sundays and intended to bring the weight of the law to bear to rein them in.[65] For all the grime, the criminality and the stark contrasts of rich and poor in Georgian London, this was a society in which religious practice remained strong.

As well as being a varied centre, featuring areas of cramped and unhealthy garrets alongside far more genteel neighbourhoods and the town palaces of the social elite, London was the political heart of Britain. In the City of London itself there was the powerful corporation, headed by the lord mayor and the court of aldermen, manned by leading members of the various livery companies representing the city's trades as well as the people of the City in general. Much more so than now, the lord mayor and aldermen had a very real impact on the people of London, overseeing courts and making decisions about such basic issues as the price of a loaf of bread.[66] In adjoining Westminster, there was Parliament, home to the House of Commons and House of Lords. The old palace of Westminster was a confusing complex comprising older structures such as Westminster Hall and the chapel of St Stephens (home of the Commons), along with newer additions, many of them fairly ad hoc and badly built. Much of this would be lost in the great fire of 1834. Along with the Commons' chamber itself, the palace's coffee houses and taverns would become key locations for Wilkes in his later career. So, too, the law courts, at that point still located in Westminster Hall: the venue for some of his greatest triumphs.

At various other locations there was the Court, where the monarch, still a vital player in the politics of the day, resided. At the time of Wilkes's birth the king was still the Hanoverian-born George I, who had succeeded to the throne according to the terms of the Act of Settlement on the death of Queen Anne in 1714. While the British may have remained lukewarm to George himself, there was considerable support for what he represented: the continuation of a Protestant monarchy, rather than the return of the exiled Catholic Stuarts.[67] Indeed, Wilkes's family had largely benefited from George's accession as, although it was not universally the case, many dissenters recognized the benefits of a Lutheran king over a Catholic one.[68] Unlike some of his predecessors, George I had followed a fairly frugal path after arriving in England. He ignored calls for the construction of a splendid new London palace and instead made do with Kensington Palace and Hampton Court, both of which had been remodelled by William III in the Franco-Dutch style.[69] In addition to these, there was St James's Palace, the official central London residence, but much disliked for being old-fashioned and inconvenient. Outside of London, but within reasonable striking distance, was the favoured royal residence of Windsor Castle. George inherited some ongoing embellishments at Hampton Court and made some minor modifications to Kensington, but overall tended to opt for cost-effective options.[70]

George II, who succeeded in 1727, continued his father's parsimonious habits, in part because he suffered from a relatively precarious financial situation.[71] For significant periods of his reign, alternative courts were established during the lengthy periods when his heir, Frederick, Prince of Wales, was out of favour and busy establishing his own rival household.

Thus, in addition to the formal palaces, there were also royal residences at Leicester House in present day Leicester Square, Norfolk House and Carlton House. There were also royal retreats at Kew and Richmond-on-Thames, and Frederick established another retreat for himself at Cliveden, not far from the seat of Sir Francis Dashwood at West Wycombe, which Wilkes would also come to know much better as he was developing his political career. It was only during George III's reign that Kensington and Hampton Court came to be neglected in favour of Kew and Windsor, while Buckingham House was acquired as a dower house for Queen Charlotte.[72]

Above all, London was a lively place. It was full of sights and sounds that were no doubt entrancing and inspirational for a bright and ambitious youth like Wilkes.

Education

In 1734, at the age of around nine, Wilkes's formal education began when he was dispatched to a boarding school in Hertford run by the eminent dissenting scholar, John Worsley.[73] Among other things, Worsley produced a translation of the New Testament, which was published shortly after his death. The school, which Worsley ran for fifty years, was housed in the tower house of the old castle.[74] Worsley's son, also John, subsequently took over the establishment but was considerably less successful. Despite that, the place remained closely identified with educational establishments, and part of the castle was later the first home of the East India College (subsequently reborn as the public school, Haileybury). Worsley's grandson, born the year after Worsley's death, was perhaps significantly named Israel and became a prominent Unitarian minister.[75]

Wilkes was not alone there. All of the Wilkes boys spent time at Worsley's school, but it is clear that Wilkes in particular made an impression on his teacher, who was characterized by one of Wilkes's biographers as 'a classical scholar and a birch-wielding, Presbyterian schoolmaster of some renown'.[76] After Wilkes left in 1739, his former master wrote emotionally: 'Go on, dear youth and prosper in your noble pursuits: and I pray that the giver of every good and perfect gift may not only succeed [sic] your endeavors after human knowledge and sound learning, but also enrich your mind with that heavenly wisdom which is still more excellent and valuable'.[77] Worsley may have had a tough reputation, but he taught Wilkes Latin and Greek well and instilled in his pupil a lifelong love of classics.[78] A glimpse of the young student Wilkes, writing to his brother Israel, in March 1741 confirms some of his traits. He had already acquired a love of writing and the letter suggests his relationship with his older brother was, at that point, strong. He was keen to announce his current reading, Homer – while dropping in that he was aware his brother had only read Pope's translations.[79] If the letter suggested a certain amount of hero-worship, there was also what was to become a characteristic sense of superiority. Wilkes was more than aware that he had already surpassed his brother.

Wilkes left Hertford aged around fourteen to continue his studies with the reverend Matthew Leeson, another dissenting minister, who ran a school at Thame in Oxfordshire along with presiding over a presbyterian chapel there. Leeson had been in post since at least 1715 and was said to have had a congregation of between 100 and 200. It was principally made up of local tradesmen and farmers, but also eight drawn from the local gentry.[80] The relationship was to prove an important one in a number of regards, not least because it was through the Wilkes family that Leeson was introduced to Mary Mead, the wealthy widow of a London grocer. Mead attended the same chapel as Wilkes's mother and was able to provide Leeson with a living in Aylesbury after he was turned out of his post at Thame for his unorthodox, Arian, beliefs. In a letter to Wilkes's mother of April 1741, Leeson had detailed his increasingly difficult circumstances in Thame and how he had even contemplated setting up 'a small shop in the Linnen way' as an alternative means of subsistence, before he was handed an escape route thanks to the Mead family.[81] Mary Mead's daughter, also Mary, was heir to a substantial residence Aylesbury called Prebendal House and was ultimately to become Wilkes's (rather unfortunate) wife.

Wilkes's time with Leeson commenced in 1739 and he remained with him when Leeson relocated to Aylesbury in 1741, even though Leeson was succeeded in post by another nonconformist educator, Thomas Dixon. There was a brief hiatus while the move to Aylesbury was completed. Leeson was at pains to underline that their new base was 'very commodious' and that he had picked out a 'very convenient' apartment for Wilkes, with a fireplace and 'a closet adjoining to it, very proper for his study'. They were also to be allowed access to the Meads' gardens 'at proper times'.[82] Why the Wilkes family was willing to allow their precious son to remain in the hands of a noted deist is unclear, but perhaps speaks for both Israel and Mary Wilkes's charitable willingness to offer Leeson a second chance.

Whatever the motivation, until 1744 Wilkes's principal schooling took place at Aylesbury, and during his time there he lodged in the Mead house.[83] From there he had plenty of opportunity to get to know the town well, and to become acquainted with some of its more prominent inhabitants, not least his future in-laws. On 17 November 1742, he was also enrolled at Lincoln's Inn. This was a natural entry point for someone seeking to embark on a legal career, but it was also a traditional stopping off point for many of the sons of the gentry and nobility wishing to enhance their classical educations with at least some knowledge of law. The admissions entry notes merely 'John Wilkes, gen., 2nd son of Israel W., the younger, of Parish of St James, Clerkenwell, Middx., malt distiller'.[84] Wilkes may well never have spent any time at Lincoln's Inn (entirely normal for the time) but his enrolment there was a clear marker that his parents intended something better for him than helping to run the family business. This was all the more striking as their eldest had made it plain that trade was not for him.[85]

After five years of Leeson's instruction, in 1744 Wilkes was sent to complete his studies at the university of Leiden. As a dissenter, Oxford and Cambridge were closed to him, but many aspiring gentlemen, conformist and nonconformist alike, spent time at universities on the continent. The education at Leiden was, besides, generally thought far superior to what was on offer in the English universities.[86] It was especially popular for medicine. Jonathan Swift's hero Lemuel Gulliver had spent 'two years and seven months' studying 'physic' at Leiden following a period at Emmanuel Cambridge, and after being apprenticed to a surgeon.[87] It was also very popular with the Scots.[88] Gulliver supposedly maintained himself there on £30 a year but by the time Wilkes arrived it was by no means a cheap option. Only a few years before Wilkes took up residence, the Jacobite Ezeckiel Hamilton had advised the Earl Marischal that Leiden was 'a much dearer place than it was twenty years ago: few students, though they keep no servants, can live under a hundred pounds a year.'[89] Nevertheless, Wilkes's family evidently considered him well worth the investment. His brother Israel hoped that Leiden would prove useful 'for fixing such generous and virtuous and heroic principles, as will render you useful in the world, and an honour to your friends at least, perhaps to your country & the age you live in.'[90]

At nineteen, Wilkes was relatively old for university (many gentlemen attended Oxford and Cambridge at far younger ages) and it transpired that he was not quite free of Leeson either, as Leeson was to accompany him there as his tutor. Accompanying them was the younger son of a wealthy northern baronet, Hungerford Bland. Why Bland found himself in this company is not clear. Certainly, his background was rather different to Wilkes's and his family's politics was quite the opposite. Indeed, his father had been one of a clutch of Tory Members of Parliament arrested in 1715 on suspicion of Jacobite plotting.[91]

What Wilkes thought of his travelling companion is uncertain, but they must have made a particularly odd group: the elderly, no longer sharp, nonconformist minister, the witty son of a London tradesman on the rise, and the younger son of one of the north's wealthiest landed families. Leeson was certainly aware that he may not have been Wilkes's first choice as tutor. His response to the family's offer was a pleased acceptance, but he was at pains to ensure that 'master' was happy to have him. Might not someone who had actually been abroad before be better suited? Clearly, he was reassured, and he must certainly have been delighted with the 'generous' terms they were offering him.[92]

The journey to Leiden was a well-trodden path, and we can get a sense of the expedition from the experiences of other students around the same time. A Scots medical student, arriving in the United Provinces in the mid-1730s, was able to find lodgings for his first night on Dutch soil at the *Royal English* coffeehouse at Den Biel, a few hours away from his landing place of Hellevetsluis, while for those travelling via Rotterdam there were similarly familiar surroundings, such as *The English Parliament*, an establishment run by one Mr Moor. For Wilkes, Leiden itself would have appeared very compact after his experiences of London. There were around 55,000 inhabitants, of whom fewer than 1,000 were registered at the university, and of these less than half came from outside of the United Provinces, though within this number there was considerable variety, with students hailing from as far afield as Russia. Nevertheless, the surroundings were pleasant, and it was described by Hamilton as 'the quietest and the cleanest town I ever lived in.'[93]

Wilkes was enrolled at Leiden formally on 8 September 1744 and was to remain there for the best part of three years. He liked to claim that he spent his time indulging in 'incessant whoring and drinking', but it seems clear that he made rather more of the opportunity than that suggests.[94] He was one of around twenty-two British students, of whom at least of five of his immediate contemporaries went on to become MPs, though one of them, 'Willie Gordon', a future diplomat and MP for Portsmouth, was 'too young and too dissipated' to take part in the serious debates in which Wilkes and some of the others engaged.[95] Gordon aside, it was certainly a remarkable year-group. Leiden had a fine reputation, but Almon later observed that Wilkes 'owed more to his own application, and to study, than the assistance of the university'.[96] The problem may have been less Leiden itself than Leeson, who was rapidly showing his age. Certainly, Wilkes was showing every sign of having outgrown his tutor.

Among the other British students who were among Wilkes's cohort were Charles Townshend, a future chancellor of the exchequer, noted by Sir Lewis Namier for his 'brilliancy and fickleness' as well as for dying 'without positive achievement to his credit'. Just two months older than Wilkes, Townshend had the benefit of rather more elevated connections. He was a younger son of the 3rd Viscount Townshend. His grandfather, the 2nd Viscount, had been Walpole's brother-in-law and effectively co-premier for much of the 1720s before he retired to the country to cultivate turnips. For Townshend, Leiden represented the final stage in an educational round that had included three years at Clare College, Cambridge, though like Wilkes he had been entered at Lincoln's Inn in 1742, so it is just possible they had happened upon each other there, too. Even though they were contemporaries, he would go on to be elected for Parliament a decade before Wilkes, returned for Great Yarmouth thanks to his father's interest in the town. He would later support Wilkes over the general warrants affair, but is best remembered for the 'Townshend duties', which played a signal role in the breakdown of relations between Britain and the American colonies.[97] One of Townshend's close friends was another member of the group, and another future MP, William Dowdeswell. If less aristocratic than Townshend, Dowdeswell also came from a more solid gentry background than Wilkes, as the son of an established family in Worcestershire and a former student of Westminster school and Christ Church, Oxford. Like Townshend, he would be returned for Parliament in the 1747 general election thanks to his family's influence, in his case at Tewkesbury, and would coincidentally go on to be Chancellor of the Exchequer immediately before Townshend.[98]

Along with his compatriots, Wilkes took up with another of the new intake, Paul-Henri Thiry d'Holbach, who would become one of the most celebrated philosophes of the Enlightenment. Of German heritage but raised in France, d'Holbach was another member of Wilkes's circle from a considerably more affluent, landed background, but the two got on remarkably well and forged a bond that would last the rest of their lives.[99] Observing this remarkable crew was Alexander 'Jupiter' Carlyle, and it is to Carlyle that we are indebted for the clearest descriptions of Wilkes, his associates and Leiden in the mid-1740s. Three years older than Wilkes and Townshend, Carlyle was already a graduate of Glasgow and Edinburgh.[100]

Wilkes was one of the first British students Carlyle met, coming across him on his first Sunday in town, while taking a walk with another student, John Gregory. Carlyle was so struck by Wilkes's unusual features that he immediately asked who he was. Gregory's response, while correct on one level, proved to be as strikingly far off the mark as Wilkes's appearance. He said that he was 'the son of a London distiller or brewer, who wanted to be a fine gentleman and man of taste, which he could never be, for God and nature had been against him.'[101] During their time at Leiden, Wilkes and Carlyle came to know each other fairly well, and Carlyle was able to develop a more astute appraisal than Gregory. He recognized Wilkes's ambition to be 'thought something extraordinary' as well as his weakness for 'daring profligacy'. He also noted that Leeson, whom he dubbed 'an old ignorant pedant', was not up to the task of instructing someone of Wilkes's talents. According to Carlyle, Leeson was determined to convert his charge to Arianism and this provoked a quarrel between them that resulted in Wilkes quitting Leiden and seeking more congenial company in Utrecht, just over 30 miles inland. There Wilkes took up with the noted philosopher, Andrew 'Immateriality' Baxter, whom he had met shortly before on a visit to Spa, and who was to prove a formative influence on him.[102]

By the time Baxter and Wilkes met, Baxter was in his late 50s and had only five more years to live. Like Carlyle, he was a Scotsman, though in his case a graduate of Aberdeen. He had spent his career working as personal tutor for a number of aristocratic families but had achieved distinction as a severe critic of the philosophy of George Berkeley. Ironically, given Wilkes's later personal campaign against him, Bishop William Warburton was a prominent supporter of Baxter, whom he thought 'a great genius'.[103] It was probably one of the very few things on which Warburton and Wilkes might have agreed. Far more in tune with Wilkes's own personality, Baxter was a considerable intellect but also, as Carlyle put it, 'a man of the world, and of such pleasing conversation as attracted the young'. Carlyle went further, insisting that not only were the two well-balanced in terms of character but Wilkes was at this point naturally inclined towards Scots company, and that it was only much later as a result of his political campaign against the administration of the earl of Bute that he was to prove such a fierce critic of all things Scottish. Certainly, another of his associates during his time away was the Scots peer, Walter Stuart, 8th Lord Blantyre. Blantyre was a student at Utrecht and noted 'free from all manner of vice', though this was never fully tested as he died aged just 24 at Paris in 1751.[104]

One of Wilkes's later, snide criticisms of the Scots was that it was 'the ostentation of a Scotsman ... to let the world know he has a handkerchief.'[105] He could also never quite resist teasing the place for being so far away. An entry in his address books for Thomas Mitchell Esq of Perth noted, utterly unnecessarily, that it was '440 miles from London'.[106] Carlyle probably made too much of it, but it is certainly noticeable that in his later years Wilkes counted a number of Scots among his regular acquaintance, so perhaps he found them more congenial than his regular teasing of the dire state of the country suggested.[107]

Wilkes made quite an impression on Baxter, whom he knitted into what was to prove to be his final philosophical dialogue. Baxter wrote to his young friend, 'You are the Hero of my Dialogue. I would do Justice to your character: If I succeed in that, I am not so diffident of the rest.'[108] It was to be an intense but brief friendship, and in 1747 Baxter returned to Scotland, never to see Wilkes again. He died in 1750, not long after addressing a final letter to the young man who had inspired him, and his final posthumous work was dedicated to Wilkes.[109] Shortly after, Wilkes received a missive from Blantyre from the family seat of Lennoxlove, certain that 'you are as sensible to his loss as I am, and that is saying a great deal.' Blantyre pointed out that Baxter had left behind him 'his wife, a son and three daughters'. The son was employed in the French army, but the daughters were all 'unprovided for'. Blantyre hoped Wilkes might be able to find 'Business for any one of them at London', which would be 'a great relief to the poor mother'.[110] Evidently, Blantyre did not feel he could do anything for them and, in any case, within a year he, too, was dead.

Given such adulation, coming on top of a cosseted childhood as the favourite of both his parents, it is perhaps not surprising that Wilkes frequently exhibited a sense of entitlement. He enjoyed company and loved being at the heart of it, but he also expected to be admired, to be looked after financially, and his every bon mot greeted with delight. No doubt it was also why he grew so adept at presenting a particular public persona, while relishing his private moments. He had been bred to perform – and perform he did. He also craved privacy and the intimate friendship of those truly close to him, though as his later relationship with his daughter would suggest, even then he maintained something of a front. Less cynically, we can also conclude that Wilkes's formative years, first under Leeson but later, and much more importantly, at Leiden and in Utrecht, proved of enduring importance for him. He may have had his head turned by Baxter's praise, but he was also able to indulge in discourse with men like d'Holbach, debating the nature of society and the reality of religion. As ever with Wilkes, it is difficult to pin down precisely what he thought, though his beliefs more likely tended to the deistical. What is clear is that he was captivated by ideas and relished the opportunity to debate all and everything freely and openly.

2
Aylesbury
(1747–1757)

...a sacrifice to Plutus, not to Venus...[1]

Wilkes left Leiden in the summer of 1746, without troubling to take a degree. This was by no means unusual – many gentlemen spent time at universities without bothering with formal qualifications. Neither did it hint at a lack of application while he was there. Nevertheless, along with a smattering of law and acquaintance with a number of future luminaries, he had also 'well begun his education in profligacy': another common trait of the students of the day.[2] Wilkes himself was later to boast of a fairly constant round of whoring during his time abroad.[3] It was a habit – again a perfectly fashionable one for the time – which he would maintain for much of the rest of his life as part of his libertine identity. When his wife sued him for lack of maintenance, part of her complaint was that her husband 'and his Whores were rioting in Plenty'.[4] It has been suggested that his period of student experimentation may also have included sexual encounters with men, but this has broadly been discounted.[5] From all the evidence, Wilkes seems to have been fairly clearly heterosexual throughout.

Wilkes may have taken a brief break from his studies the year before his final return home in order to enrol in the City trained bands (the militia) at the time of the Jacobite rebellion. There is certainly evidence to suggest that he was not overseas for the whole time he was a student. On 23 June 1745, Baxter wrote to him from Utrecht, 'Let me hear from you when you get to London.' Another letter to him from Dowdeswell in February 1746 was addressed to him at St John's Street.[6] Wilkes was back in Leiden in the early months of 1746.[7] It would have been characteristic of him to demonstrate his willingness to defend the Protestant succession against the invading army of Charles Edward Stuart. It would also have offered an early opportunity of donning military uniform – something of which Wilkes was to become rather fond. Many of the later portraits of him show him wearing the coat of an officer in the Buckinghamshire militia, which he continued to sport long after he had ceased to hold a commission.[8]

If Wilkes did return home to do his bit, it was an early instance of his undoubted bravery. One should not overlook the genuine sense of emergency in London and southern England as the Jacobite army made its way south in the winter of 1745, reaching Derby in early December.[9] On 1 December, the duke of Newcastle, in a flap as usual, confided to the duke of Richmond: 'We shall assemble soon our Army about London, in expectation of them.'[10] Plans were put in place for a final stand of government forces on Finchley Common. Both the king and Prince of Wales were prepared to join their troops there and the moment was captured most famously by Hogarth in his painting *The March of the Troops to Finchley*.[11] In the event, there was no need for these emergency preparations as Charles Edward fell back from Derby after only a few days.[12] Having missed this opportunity, the Jacobites wound their way back to Scotland and to ultimate defeat at Culloden in April 1746. Even so, the government remained on high alert for some time, Newcastle alerting Richmond at one point, 'We are under the greatest Alarms of an immediate Invasion from France.'[13]

By the time the Jacobites had been defeated and Charles Edward was undertaking his famous flight in the heather, Wilkes's time as a student was coming to an end. After the conclusion of his studies, he appears to have taken the opportunity to travel in the Low Countries and Germany before finally returning to England for good.[14] A tour of the continent was de rigueur for a fashionable young man seeking to improve his deportment and conversation. The most popular destinations were normally in France and Italy. The latter may have been thought beyond his means at this point, and the former was difficult while Britain and France were at war (not that this necessarily prevented some well-connected people from doing so).[15] Wilkes's choice of destination (if it was his own) was 'the third most important' selected by British tourists in the period and offered him a further chance to develop the requisite polish expected of a gentleman.[16]

On his return to England, his family set about arranging a marriage for him. This appears to have been long in the making, and the family with which he was to be yoked was well known to him. His bride-to-be was Mary Mead, daughter of the wealthy widow who had previously been so serviceable to Leeson. Wilkes was later to make much of the fact that he had entered into the marriage underage, not knowing what he was doing, and only to please his parents. As we have seen, he was probably not technically underage: likely in his twenty-second year rather than his twentieth, as he claimed. Certainly, the marriage licence he applied for asserted that both he and his bride were twenty-one or over.[17] That said, there was a disparity in the ages of the young couple, Mary Mead being nearer thirty. It was also far from being an alliance in which he was totally ignorant of his bride's character. In all probability, he had known her quite well when a student in Aylesbury and he also made a visit to the Meads at some point in the summer of 1746. In August, d'Holbach had written to him letting Wilkes know that he was expecting 'with impatience' a promised letter 'from Alesbury'.[18] The visit was a success and Wilkes reported back to his mother his obligations 'to this excellent family for their exceeding kind treatment'. He added that he was to leave them 'with great regret'.[19] No doubt this was mere politesse, but it suggests his own family had no particular reason not to pursue the arrangement; also, that Wilkes himself was happy enough with his in-laws at this point. As for his prospective bride, he was no doubt aware that she was his polar opposite. Mary was staid, almost a recluse, and more than slightly neurotic, though one later description of her as 'dull, fat and thirty-two' was inaccurate on all counts.[20] As John Sainsbury has pointed out regarding her later reputation, Mary Wilkes was at a disadvantage 'because she was eclipsed by a husband who was a colourful self-publicist and who took a dislike to her.' After the collapse of the marriage, Wilkes certainly went to considerable lengths to emphasize his wife's disagreeableness. He also exaggerated the age difference between them, on at least one occasion stating she was twenty years older than he was.[21] What Mary made of the arrangement is not clear, but it seems likely that she was happy enough with her mother's choice at first and, like so many other women in Wilkes's life, may well have been won over by his charm, at least for a time.

The Meads

The family into which Wilkes was marrying, while from a similar milieu, was rather more distinguished than his own. His wife's father, John Mead, had been a successful London grocer who had left his widow (another Mary) a sizeable fortune to add to his daughter's expectations via her uncle.[22] John Mead may have come from a merchant background but was related to a number of eminent people, among them Sir Nathaniel Mead of Goosehays, a former MP for Aylesbury, and himself son of a prominent London merchant and early Quaker. Another relation was the famous medical man, Dr Richard Mead, who was later to be one of Wilkes's sponsors for fellowship of the Royal Society. It seems likely that

Robert Mead, who had been one of the lawyers involved in the high-profile legal case *Ashby v. White*, which had been fought out between the Lords and Commons over disputed elections in Aylesbury, was another relative.[23] This was rather appropriate, given Wilkes's own later career both as MP for Aylesbury and his subsequent efforts to be recognized as MP for Middlesex.

The connection with the Buckinghamshire town of Aylesbury was reinforced by John Mead's brother, William, a London draper who had acquired property there and built Prebendal House next to the town church. William Mead had died without direct heirs of his own, so had directed the inheritance to his unmarried sisters and thence to his niece. Mary Mead's maternal family, the Sherbrookes, hailed from a similar background, a London merchant family who had acquired land outside of the city. When Wilkes came on the scene, the elder Mary Mead had established a household with her brother, Richard Sherbrooke and daughter Mary, spending the winter months in London at their house in Red Lyon Court and the summer in Aylesbury.

Wilkes's family were no doubt aware of the enhanced social cachet of the family into which he was to marry. Indeed, that was the point. Having educated him as a gentleman, they now sought to establish him as a leisured man about town. To help him on his way, Israel Wilkes settled lands on his son accruing an annual sum of £330 'or thereabouts'.[24] While this was hardly a fortune, and far short of the sort of sums commanded by some of the people with whom Wilkes aspired to rub shoulders, it was a comfortable enough sum for a member of the lower gentry. Part of Wilkes's future money troubles stemmed from his insistence on being so much more than this. As John Sainsbury has put it, the income was not sufficient 'to support his inclination to cut a dash both as a Buckinghamshire squire and as a man-about-town in London and Bath.' And it certainly fell short of the kinds of sums needed to support his later political ambitions.[25] Meanwhile, by the terms of the marriage settlement Wilkes was to live with his in-laws between their London house in Red Lyon Court and their 'country estate' in Aylesbury. It was not to prove an especially happy arrangement. Although Wilkes grew to appreciate his residence in Buckinghamshire, he smarted at the restrictions imposed on him in London. He found his wife's family and their associates irksome, and consequently did all in his power to upset his staid in-laws and their overly serious, pious friends.

This, though, was in the future. For the time being, Wilkes assured his own friends that he was delighted with the arrangement and genuinely taken with his bride-to-be. On 23 May 1747, Wilkes and Mary were married at St John of the Cross in Clerkenwell, close to both the families' London residences, and to begin with all parties seemed happy enough.

In August, presumably in response to a suitably enthusiastic report from his old companion, Baxter wrote to Wilkes expressing his delight that 'your marriage has crown'd all your wishes.' He also passed on good wishes from other friends from his student days, Blantyre and Mr Hay.[26]

John Sainsbury has suggested that Wilkes was 'at heart an urban personality ... he never embraced the life of the bucolic squire in all its traditional aspects.'[27] In some senses this is correct. Not unlike the 17th-century rake, John Wilmot, 2nd earl of Rochester, who blamed many of his excesses on how London made him behave, Wilkes appears to have been particularly drawn to the fleshpots of London, which he dubbed 'this charming, warm, wicked town'.[28] Wilkes's greatest triumphs occurred in the hustle and bustle of London and it is noteworthy that his second political career, both as MP for Middlesex and a City dignitary, was concentrated in London, where he had had his upbringing. Even so, it perhaps misses a very important aspect of Wilkes's own conception of himself and his genuine enjoyment of some extremely rural pursuits, not least gardening and, possibly less predictably, bird watching. In his later years, these came to predominate as he sought to distance himself from his life as a City alderman. However, it is certainly true that Wilkes's London life was always of importance to him, and it was perhaps in London that he first ran up against the restrictions of his new domestic arrangements.

Wilkes never liked Red Lyon Court. According to Almon, 'Though the house was good, yet the situation and neighbourhood were disagreeable.'[29] The house may have been 'good', but it was elderly and far removed from the more fashionable areas of London developing westwards. In terms of location, it was not so very far from where Wilkes's own family resided, but the atmosphere was a world away from St John's Square. Wilkes clearly found the routine turgid and he could not resist attempting to liven things up. He offended his wife and her family by imposing on them some of his wilder acquaintances.[30] There were also episodes where he went out of his way to insult pious family friends, or complained about the way certain dishes had been prepared.[31] It seems, then, not to have been long before Wilkes and Mary were effectively living separate lives as he found his feet in London libertine circles, as well as cultivating a role for himself as squire of Aylesbury.

Although it was not long before Wilkes and Mary's marriage unravelled, it did endure long enough for them to have one child together. The daughter, born in August 1750, was also baptised Mary, but she was known from the beginning as Polly, and was to become the most significant relationship in Wilkes's life. Cynical and manipulative in almost every other arena of his personal affairs, Wilkes doted on her and spent the remainder of his life doing his utmost to cater to her every whim. However tight money was, Wilkes was never able to refuse her. Polly Wilkes was bright and engaging. Not all images of her suggest she inherited her father's looks, but she undoubtedly had not a little of his spirit.

Aylesbury

If Wilkes was eager to distance himself from his wife's London residence, he had no such qualms about exploiting to the full his role as a country squire in Aylesbury. It was one that he took to naturally, enjoying his distinction within the borough and spending his leisured time developing the house and gardens, as well as becoming acquainted with his more distinguished neighbours. These included a number of literary men, but it is clear that he also gradually found his way into the circles of some of the greater families in the area. He engaged in the natural pursuits of a man of his class and seems to have been a courageous (possibly even foolhardy) horseman. A letter from Baxter at the end of January 1750 alluded to his enjoyment of lively mounts:

> Your letter of December 12, 1749, alarmed me, by hearing you had had such a dangerous fall from your horse. Moderate exercise is good: but dangerous exercise, such as riding a fiery horse, is not commendable... We had a terrible instance in the newspapers lately, of a man who got his death by such a fall.[32]

As to the place itself, Aylesbury was a market town with pretensions. It was a close rival to the county town of Buckingham and had long vied with it as the home of the assizes (county courts). Around the time of Wilkes's marriage, a bill to settle the question of where the assizes should be held, Aylesbury or Buckingham, was being fought out in Parliament. Politically, Aylesbury was interesting, if expensive for prospective parliamentary candidates, being accounted 'squalid and venal'.[33] There was no particular resident patron and it was consequently left to moneyed carpet-baggers to try their luck in what was one of the more expensive seats in England.

In the pre-Reform era[34] there was no single franchise in the English boroughs. This meant that some seats were more 'democratic' than others, and the qualification to vote varied from place to place. A quick foray through Buckinghamshire offers some insight into how varied this might be. In Buckingham, for example, the franchise was 'in the corporation', meaning the members of the town council, of which there were just thirteen. No one else had a vote. At Amersham, on the other hand, the franchise was open to those inhabitants paying 'scot and lot' and there were about seventy of these. Although Wendover appeared more 'democratic', with around 150 householder voters, in reality the local patron, Lord Verney, expected them to vote for the person he nominated. Like Wendover, at Aylesbury the franchise was open to inhabitant householders, of which there were about 500, but with no particular patron the voters expected to be treated in return for the favour of their votes. This introduces another peculiarity of the pre-Reform system. While it was illegal to offer money for votes, many candidates did precisely this, but many others offered a variety of 'treats' to their prospective constituents, which included funding large entertainments where the beer flowed freely.

It was into this rather bumptious locale that Wilkes was to establish himself and first dip his toe into electoral politics, though it was to take him some time before he was ready to offer himself for election. A month after Wilkes's marriage, the country went to the polls in a snap election engineered by the governing Whigs, headed by the Pelham brothers, Prime Minister Henry Pelham and his brother Thomas, duke of Newcastle. According to the terms of the Septennial Act (1716), the election should have been put off until the following year, but the administration was concerned by the opposition alliance co-ordinated by the Prince of Wales from his alternative court of Leicester House and sought to move quickly before they were quite ready. At Aylesbury, in spite of the Pelhams' efforts, two opposition candidates associated with Prince Frederick, were returned without contest, so it is impossible to know what Wilkes might have done had anyone attempted to stand against them. One was Edward Willes, whose brother John was a friend of Wilkes's;[35] the other was William O'Brien, earl of Inchiquin.[36] One thing is for sure. There may not have been a poll, but there would have been plenty of treating and negotiating behind the scenes, and Wilkes no doubt took note of all of this for future reference.

Four years into the 1747 Parliament, Wilkes seems to have made his own first hesitant efforts towards securing election for himself. This was no doubt in part inspired by his developing relationship with Thomas Potter, at that point MP for St Germans in Cornwall. It is not clear where they first met, some have suggested in London, others in Bath.[37] There was, however, also a connection with Bedfordshire. Potter had an estate at Ridgmont, while Wilkes had acquired through his marriage to Mary two manors at Totternhoe. By virtue of these, Wilkes was nominated a Bedfordshire JP in 1749 and had the right to vote in the county election, though it seems he never did, concentrating his efforts on bolstering his interest in Aylesbury instead.[38]

Potter was slightly older than Wilkes, having been born around 1718, and came from a considerably more elevated background as the younger son of the recently deceased archbishop of Canterbury.[39] Politically, too, he was in a different league, holding office in the household of the Princess of Wales. Like Wilkes, though, he was a favoured younger son, who had inherited the vast bulk of his father's fortune after his older brother was disinherited for the unforgiveable crime of marrying beneath him. Also like Wilkes, he had submitted to a marriage arranged for him by his father, though this first wife had died in 1744, freeing Potter to marry once again according to his own choice.[40] Unlike Wilkes, he was reputed to have been strikingly good-looking.[41] Wealth and a distinct lack of morals had left him one of the most outrageous libertines of the period.

Potter and Wilkes quickly formed a bond that straddled both politics and an increasingly hedonistic lifestyle. Potter was more than happy to lampoon Wilkes's domestic surroundings. On one occasion he sent to Wilkes to join him on a jaunt to Bath, 'if you prefer young women and whores to old women and wives, if you prefer the toying away hours with little satin-back to the evening conferences of your mother-in-law.'[42] There was often a nagging tone to Potter's letters to Wilkes, that of a bored and slightly discontented member of the elite seeking distraction. There was something perhaps of the Lord Sebastian-Flyte/Charles Ryder relationship between Potter and Wilkes: 'I shall never forgive your unfriendly contrivance of passing three months at Bath when I had expected you there for three months in vain. What life do you lead? Are you a Wit among Wits or what I suspect a Wit among fools?'[43]

On another occasion, Potter, once again clearly in need of stimulation, flattered Wilkes: 'I have kept your letter in my pocket till it is wore out. Not so my Remembrance of the Writer. That is fresher than the Day, & more blooming than the Spring.'[44] Sometimes, the relationship became strained and Potter turned on his protégé, determined to show that he was in no way dependent on him for his entertainment. There were signs of such annoyance in one such letter from Bath in the winter of 1752: 'For Goodness sake what do you take me to be or where do you suppose that I am? Do you think that wherever I am I will not find out Amusements, or do you suppose this is a Place peculiarly deficient in them?'[45]

The following year, Potter was struck down with ill health and sought relief on the continent at Spa. From there, he sent Wilkes a sketch of himself, with gouty leg raised up on a chair. Wilkes apparently did not comment on it, as in November, by which time Potter was back in London, he complained:

> If you had any Gratitude or any Politeness you would have thanked me for the Picture which you received from Spa. Or did you receive it? &

did not the Scoundrel Postmaster of some German or Dutch Territory lay violent Hands on it & vainly exhibit it as the Effigies of one of his own Ancestors.[46]

According to Almon, it was Potter who was responsible more than anyone else for debauching Wilkes. Of all the men of fashion Wilkes had introduced to the otherwise extremely restrained table of Red Lyon Court, Potter 'was the worst; and was indeed the ruin of Mr Wilkes, who was not a bad man early, or naturally.'[47] It seems quite plain, though, that Wilkes was already well on the way after his experiences as a student. Ultimately, the handsome demigod with all before him would come off the rails, while the man from the more prosaic background would endure and achieve greater things.

In 1751 the next election was still some years off, but Wilkes was clearly already testing the water for his own potential candidacy. On 11 December, Wilkes wrote to John Dell, a substantial local farmer who happened to be one of his tenants, regretting that the weather was preventing him from quitting London ('this charming, warm, wicked town') and returning to Aylesbury.[48] Dell was to become one of his most important election agents, and was later praised by Potter as 'a Prince of Managers'.[49] Wilkes was keen to know about a visit to the town by John and Edward Willes, to discover whether Edward was intending to stand down at the next election and if John Willes was after the vacant seat. Wilkes was pondering throwing his hat into the ring on a joint ticket with Potter and failed to disguise his ambition in enquiring, 'If you all comforted them [the Willes brothers] under the rigour of the season, or whether you gave them a reception as cold as that.'[50] The enquiry was clearly met with an unsatisfactory response, and at the 1754 general election Potter and John Willes were unopposed. That did not mean, of course, that there was not a great deal to do to ensure their election passed off without trouble; and Wilkes was at the centre of assisting Potter in his campaign.

Potter was under no illusions about the need to spend freely to secure the seat: 'in a Town where so great a majority of the Voters are venal, whoever will come with a long Purse will be sure to find a great many who will engage to support him.' This chimed with an earlier assessment made by Lord Egmont, who expected one of the seats to go to 'a moneyed man'. Potter hoped, though, that it would not just be his 'long purse' that would do the job for him. He also had the advantage of the support of Wilkes and his family, who had 'the principal Inhabitants for their friends'. One potential rival, Lord Inchiquin, on the other hand, he was sure had no friends in the town.[51]

If Wilkes was disappointed in having to wait for an opportunity to stand for Parliament, in 1752 he was at least granted more independence when his in-laws decided to amend the terms of the marriage settlement. They ceded to Wilkes what might have been thought of as a husband's expected rights to the property in Aylesbury, making over to him the lease of Prebendal House along with some other estates elsewhere in the country. As the undisputed owner of the principal residence in the town, he became in reality squire of Aylesbury. With this came certain local distinctions, capped by his appointment to the bench as a justice of the peace. As such he presided over the local magistrates' court, located in the County Hall, a modern building designed by Vanbrugh which had been constructed in around 1727.[52]

Wilkes's correspondence with Dell may have had politics at its core, but there was often a seam of horticulture that passed through it as well. Wilkes's diaries, running from 1770, include pastings from newspapers advertising nursery specialists, seed-merchants, and the latest garden improvements. His address books also reveal his interest in all things horticultural. For example, accidentally listed under 'P' was William Ryles, 'Gardener at Hoxton, lives with Mr Jones, sent me gold fish & myrtles.'[53] Gardening was a genuine passion for him, perhaps the more so because of his early upbringing in the relatively restricted conditions of Clerkenwell. Just how important it was to him is indicated by the death of his head gardener, Thorpe, in 1751. Wilkes had a memorial erected in his honour, embellished with a quotation from the Eclogues: 'The laurel and myrtle wept for him.'[54] In January 1755, when he was otherwise busily engaged with issues of both local and national politics, Wilkes found time to write to Dell enquiring after the state of his gardens.

In the same letter, he referred to the recent death of another character from his past, Matthew Leeson: 'Poor Mr Leeson! I paid him the tribute of a few tears from the recollection of past scenes tho' I take it his death was a great deliverance to himself, as well as every one about him.' Never one to miss an opportunity, Wilkes asked if Dell might make enquiries about certain medals in Leeson's collection, which he thought had been bequeathed to him in the will. He was also keen to know what had become of Leeson's library. He wanted his name kept out of it, though.[55] As it happens, Leeson had not remembered his former student. The books, along with a five-guinea bequest, had been left to Jeremiah Dyson, a clerk in the House of Commons.[56] Leeson's final request was to be buried with his wife in Aylesbury, so no doubt Wilkes would have had an opportunity to bid his final adieus.[57]

Wilkes may not have featured in Leeson's will, but he retained throughout his life a keen interest in the classics. This had been inculcated by his tutors at Hertford, Thame and Aylesbury. Over the years he corresponded with a variety of the chief literary figures of the day, continuing what he had started in his interactions with Baxter.

Early trips to Bath seem to have brought him into the circle of Thomas Brewster, a physician, antiquarian and noted rake. In May 1754, Brewster responded to an invitation to join Wilkes in Buckinghamshire, referring to: 'the wonderful verdure of the rich vale of Aylesbury, and the fragrance of your bean-fields in full blossom.' At the end of June Brewster wrote again, insisting 'There is nothing I beg for so much, as to be reading a chapter with you at Aylesbury.' Early the following year, Brewster commended the Royal Society's decision to admit Wilkes. He hoped it was a sign that the society 'may happily once again favour us with a little common sense'.[58] In securing membership, Wilkes had been able to rely on some influential sponsors. Along with his wife's relation, Dr Mead, he was recommended by a former acquaintance from Leiden, Dr Richard Brocklesby, and the noted antiquarian Thomas Birch, secretary to the Society. Wilkes and Brewster's relationship was not only based on a love of literature, though. Brewster's letters also alluded to Wilkes's escapades in Bath: another common interest that they shared.[59]

As a sign that Wilkes had not yet given way to his later anti-Scots polemic, another such author-cum-doctor to make his way into his circle was John Armstrong. Armstrong in turn then introduced Wilkes to the novelist Tobias Smollett, who was a friend of Wilkes's cousin, John Nesbitt. Wilkes may have been behind securing Armstrong appointment as an army physician in 1760, and the same year Armstrong returned the favour by sending Wilkes a poem, *A Day: An Epistle to John Wilkes of Aylesbury, Esquire*. Wilkes then annoyed Armstrong enormously by publishing a bowdlerized version, printed by Andrew Millar (another mutual acquaintance), which seems to have precipitated a fracturing of their relations.[60] Another thing on which Wilkes and Armstrong did not agree were the writings of Laurence Sterne. The publication of *The Life and Opinions of Tristram Shandy* in 1759 had made a celebrity of the previously little-known Yorkshire parson. Armstrong disliked the book, but Wilkes loved it and was keen to make Sterne's acquaintance.[61] In May 1760, he put his money where his mouth was by subscribing to the publication of the initial two volumes of Sterne's *The Sermons of Mr Yorick*.[62]

If there was a Panglossian side to Wilkes, happy when cultivating his garden and mixing with writers and artists, he also remained inherently restless and ambitious. Two years after getting his hands on the lease of Prebendal House, he was offered the chance of seriously developing his profile as a politician. In January 1754 he was offered appointment as high sheriff of Buckinghamshire, by way of compensation for standing aside in Aylesbury. Being 'pricked' for sheriff (the official term) was something many people sought to avoid, as it was an onerous and costly role. Potter was thoroughly apologetic that Wilkes was being burdened with it.⁶³ Wilkes, though, clearly viewed it as a step on the ladder. Agreeing to serve as sheriff now, he calculated, would improve his chances of finding a parliamentary seat in due course. On 15 January 1754 he wrote to Dell, expressing his resolution to accept the post:

> I have consented to the persuasion of two or three particular friends, for some important services, and that I am to serve this year as High Sheriff. Be as silent as the grave ... you see I declare myself throughout a friend to liberty, and will act up to it.⁶⁴

This may have been his first self-conscious use of the phrase that was ultimately to become his epitaph. His appointment was duly gazetted at the end of the month, with John Wilkes of Aylesbury Esq. joining the ranks of the other county dignitaries who had been willing to take on the burden.⁶⁵

Four days after his letter to Dell, and perhaps even more significantly, Wilkes was elected to the Sublime Society of Beefsteaks.⁶⁶ Membership of the club was limited to twenty-four, so this election underscored the rapidity of his ascent into a particularly select cadre of eighteenth-century libertine society. At the time of Wilkes's election, the Beefsteaks were relatively new, having been founded in 1735 by John Rich, though the idea was not an original one and there had been similar societies before. The founding twenty-four members were a mixed bunch, but among them was the artist William Hogarth (who was re-elected in 1742) and the satirist Paul Whitehead. As the society's name implied, the eating of beef was at the heart of the club's activities with rule number four of the society's code stipulating that:

> Beefsteaks shall be the only meat for dinner, and the broiling begin at two of the clock on each day of meeting, and the table-cloth be removed at half-an-hour after three.⁶⁷

The society's motto was 'Beef and Liberty', not a million miles from the slogan that was later to accompany Wilkes throughout many of his campaigns. Another distinction of the society was its ability to bring together men of differing political outlooks. Wilkes was later to have spectacular fallings out with fellow 'brothers' Hogarth and the earl of Sandwich (elected a few years after Wilkes in December 1761) but such political ructions did not prevent them from settling contentedly around the table to consume steaks off the gridiron, tell bawdy jokes and sing patriotic songs. Wilkes remained a member throughout his career's ups and downs and his importance to the society was indicated by the fact that when it was finally wound up in the 1860s and its effects auctioned off, among them was a painting of Wilkes by Sibelius, based on the well-known portrait by Robert Edge Pine, which went for a very reasonable

£2 2s. There was also a marble bust by Roubiliac, which commanded a rather more significant £23 2s.[68]

Berwick-upon-Tweed

1754 witnessed a dissolution of Parliament and a general election was held through the late spring of that year.[69] If Wilkes was disappointed at not being able to stand for Aylesbury, he did not let it get in the way of undertaking to do all in his power to enable Potter's election there. Potter had previously sat for St Germans on the Prince of Wales's interest, but when the Prince died in 1751, he transferred his allegiance to the Pelhams. Potter now needed a new seat. Aylesbury required a fair amount of bribery, but Potter was a very wealthy man, having inherited £100,000 from his father.[70] Wilkes undertook to offer his support and on 2 April 1754 wrote to Dell from London, informing him of having written a public letter 'in case of an opposition' making plain his support for Potter. He was concerned that his absence from Aylesbury at the time of the poll might make people think he was 'cool towards Mr Potter, or to have drop'd him'. He instructed Dell to ensure that Potter was named 'first in the return. It is a point of honour.'[71] There was kudos in being the 'senior' member in a two-member constituency. His attitude to Potter's partner, John Willes, was more guarded. Back in March 1753 Willes had written to Wilkes from his London residence in Bloomsbury Square, lamenting his inability to visit. He had a turnpike bill to steer through the Commons and after that, he was required to oppose an enclosure bill. 'These two silly things,' he explained, 'keep me in hot water, & prevent my going out of town.' Willes meanwhile was clearly not convinced by Potter: 'I am not sure that Mr P is not a friend of ours.'[72] Wilkes, though, was quite clear as to his loyalties and when the election was upon them he insisted his friends should 'consult Mr Potter and follow his opinion'.[73]

The reason for Wilkes's inability to attend Potter's election at Aylesbury in person was because he had, at late notice, been offered a chance of being returned to Parliament himself. As he put it to Dell, 'Nothing but an election of my own (entre nous) cou'd have kept me from you.'[74] While he may have been prevented from standing for Parliament on his home patch of Aylesbury, Wilkes's steady cultivation of key figures meant that by 1754 his name had come to the attention of some of the more powerful political brokers. As ever, Potter seems to have been a noisy advocate for Wilkes joining him in the House of Commons. It was, he insisted, 'the only place ... in which a young man of Mr Wilkes's talents could commence the world with *éclat*.'[75] Potter looked into the possibility of

Wilkes standing in Bristol, but this was overtaken by a recommendation from more powerful backers for him to contest Berwick-upon-Tweed.[76]

There were around 600 freemen electors at Berwick, making it only slightly more populous than Aylesbury. It was also a place where the government was able to bring a considerable amount of influence to bear.[77] At the previous election in 1747 there had been no contest, enabling the two candidates, Viscount Barrington and Thomas Watson, who had been the town's MP since 1740, to carry their elections without the trouble of going to a poll.[78] Watson was a government supporter and stood again at the 1754 election, but this time the other local candidate was John Delaval, whose family had been influential in the area for generations and would go on to dominate at least one seat during much of the second half of the century.[79] Although Delaval was also a Whig, he was aligned with a faction headed by the duke of Bedford, which was in opposition to the Pelhams. In addition, he had brought his interest to bear in the borough of Newark – a Pelham stronghold – in favour of his brother, Edward. Furious at being challenged in their own backyard, the Pelhams decided to give John Delaval some of his own medicine and set about finding a candidate to challenge him at Berwick.

By this time, Wilkes had come to the notice of Richard Grenville, 2nd Earl Temple, having been introduced to him by Potter at some point in 1753.[80] Temple was one of the great political patrons in Buckinghamshire, whose seat at Stowe had long been an active political centre. Like so many others in Wilkes's social round at this point, Temple was also a noted libertine, and it was probably within his circle that Wilkes and Potter came to collaborate on a pornographic parody of Alexander Pope's *Essay on Man*, the *Essay on Woman*. Quite who wrote the original piece remains unclear, but it seems most probable that both had a hand in it. It would later come to bite Wilkes and contribute to his spectacular fall from grace.

Not everything about Temple and his grouping was so lewd. Stowe was to be the model for Wilkes's more modest acres in Aylesbury and, latterly, his garden on the Isle of Wight.[81] Temple's predecessor, his uncle, Richard Temple, Viscount Cobham, had established the place as a centre of opposition to Walpole in the 1730s, surrounding himself with a group of up-and-coming young politicians known collectively as 'the Boy Patriots', or 'Cobham's Cubs'. The core of them were friends and relations of the Grenville family, one of whom, William Pitt the Elder, was set to become one of the most celebrated politicians of the period, a Prime Minister and father to another.[82]

The whole place was a statement of political philosophy, the landscaping aiming to describe the story of English liberty. As George B. Clark put it, 'the ideals of the "Patriot" opposition spilled over into Cobham's gardening, so that his construction programme took on the character of a political manifesto.'[83] There were temples to friendship and English liberty, and statues of great figures from classical times, but also from English history. The most famous manifestation was probably the Temple of British Worthies, a structure containing busts of the 'greats' of English history, a truly eclectic assemblage ranging from Alfred the Great to Shakespeare, Elizabeth I and John Locke. Following Cobham's death, Temple continued his work developing the estate, though by the 1750s he was aligned with the ruling Pelhamite Whigs. By this point, it appears some visitors no longer recognized the political messages scored through the landscape, and only observed the place as a reflection of good (or bad) taste in garden design. Jemima, Marchioness Grey, who visited twice in the summer of 1748, commented that the 'only Aim of the Place is <u>Shew</u>' and she was fiercely critical of its practicalities.[84] However, if Grey was unimpressed, there seems no doubt at all that Wilkes was, and the way in which he replicated certain features in his own later more modest gardening suggests that the iconography was not lost on him. Besides, the connection with Temple was to be crucial for him in the first phase of his career. It seems to have been Temple who proposed Wilkes to the duke of Newcastle as a likely candidate to take on Delaval in Berwick. Temple's brother, George Grenville, also supported Wilkes's campaign warmly, writing on 2 April that it was 'with the greatest pleasure that I received your letter informing me of your resolution to offer yourself a candidate at Berwick.'[85]

No doubt flattered by being noticed by Temple and Newcastle, Wilkes 'resolved to go to Berwick'. He did so against the advice of his father, wife and mother-in-law, whose concerns about the debts he was likely to run up in the attempt proved to be only too prophetic.[86] Wilkes arrived in Berwick at some point in the first half of April and set about seeking the support of the local voters, none of whom could have had much idea who he was. Reputedly, he took with him a letter of recommendation from Temple's younger brother, George Grenville.[87] The poll took place over the course of eight days, on the first of which, 16 April, Wilkes mounted the hustings to address his would-be constituents. He opened that he had come to them 'with the utmost pleasure, to make you a tender of my services, from the assurances I had received of your steady attachment to the cause of liberty.'[88]

Wilkes had arrived in Berwick insisting that he was there as the anti-corruption candidate, standing in opposition to Delaval, whom he accused of being precisely the opposite. He returned to this theme in his address:

I come here uncorrupting, and I promise you I shall ever be uncorrupted. As I never will take a bribe, so I will never offer one. I should think myself totally unworthy of the great and important trust I am now soliciting, if I sought to obtain it by the violation of the laws of my country.[89]

Wilkes's protestations were, of course, a sham. Like many other candidates in the period, he made free with his money in an effort to buy support. Remote Berwick relied on bringing in some of its voters by sea and Wilkes even went to the trouble of trying to bribe one ship's master to land passengers in Norway 'by accident' so they would miss the election. A newspaper reported the arrival of another vessel in Rouen, loaded with gin and several voters bound for Berwick, which had lost its way.[90] His efforts, though, proved in vain. According to one account of the election, the sitting Member, Watson, and Wilkes initially appeared to have the majority of votes, but when the final tally was made on the 23rd, Wilkes had slipped back into third place. Watson topped the poll with 374 votes; behind him was Delaval, taking the second seat with 307 votes. Wilkes managed to secure 192 votes.[91] Ironically, it may have been problems with conveying his own voters by sea that had hampered Wilkes's efforts. On 24 April, the day after the poll closed, Newcastle had advised the king that Wilkes had 'a very good chance at Berwick, if the voters who went by sea can arrive.' He was later forced to revise that assessment, regretting 'the Berwick election is lost, the ship with a great many voters was not arrived when the poll was closed.'[92] Perhaps some of these were the ones who had found themselves becalmed in Rouen.

Potter expressed himself utterly furious for Wilkes. He lambasted Temple and the 'raggamuffin' crew at Berwick for wasting Wilkes's time and insisted that if only he had been approached, he could have got Wilkes elected at Bristol instead.[93] Nothing dismayed, Wilkes resolved to lodge a petition with Parliament to appeal the result, accusing Delaval of 'bribery and corruption'.[94] During this period it was common for election results to be challenged and many seats might not be finally settled for some months into a new Parliament. For any administration, it was thus crucial that they maintained a close hold on the House of Commons' committee for privileges and elections. Indeed, it was precisely the loss of this body that had cost Sir Robert Walpole the premiership in 1742. In bringing his case Wilkes was able to rely on the support of Pitt the Elder, who gave a characteristically tempestuous speech to the Commons on the question of bribery and corruption in the election. Indeed, so heated was Pitt's invective that for a while Wilkes seems to have believed that Pitt was laying into him! However, if he could expect support from heavyweights like Pitt, for Wilkes, the decision to appeal committed him to further trouble and expense, having already invested between £3,000 and £4,000 on the contest.[95] A year after the election, the case was still not settled, though by then Newcastle appears to have been eager for Wilkes to give it up. Watson, too, was bothered that having failed to dislodge Delaval, Wilkes might focus his attentions on his campaign instead. It was not until December 1755 that the petition was finally laid to rest. As his family had feared, Wilkes had gained little from the adventure but a mountain of debt. One small possibly apocryphal episode, though, pointed to Wilkes's development of his persona as a fearless man of honour. Shortly before his case was to be heard by the Commons, one of his lawyers, Alexander Campbell, decided to withdraw his services, but attempted to retain a fifty-guinea fee he had already received. He challenged Wilkes to sue him for its return, only for Wilkes to respond, 'I have brought my Advocate with me,' indicating his sword. Campbell promptly handed the money over.[96]

Wilkes's losses associated with the Berwick election and his continuing efforts to enter Parliament were probably the final straw for his marriage. Mary and his own family were heavily critical of the money he had wasted during the campaign and subsequent petitions. Added to their earlier obvious incompatibility and effectively separate existences, it is unsurprising that in October 1756 Mary finally decided to sue for formal separation. This was not divorce, which would have required an act of Parliament, but a formal separation recognized by the London consistory court. She sued on the grounds of 'cruelty' and after some initial resistance from Wilkes, both parties rapidly came to a mutually beneficial agreement. Mary was to receive a £200 annuity, while Wilkes maintained control of the property that had come to him by the marriage, including Prebendal House, along with custody of Polly. Both were likely content enough. Mary returned to her quiet existence in Red Lyon Court, untroubled by the excesses of her husband. Wilkes remained squire of Aylesbury but now assumed full control over Polly's upbringing and moved her out of Red Lyon Court and into accommodation in St James's Place in Westminster.[97] The stage was set for his political fortunes to be revived.

3

Parliament and Hellfire

(1757–61)

Squalid and Venal

On 6 July 1757 John Wilkes was elected Member of Parliament for Aylesbury.[1] There was no contest, but even securing the seat and, perhaps more importantly, holding onto it, set him back around £7,000.[2] Wilkes himself referred to the 'palmistry' needed in persuading the voters to back him. Considering his later identification as a friend of political reform, it is perhaps ironic that Wilkes first entered Parliament thanks to one of the frequent behind-the-scenes deals that was a feature of the electoral system. It is also worth noting that he was elected the same year that a young Edmund Burke composed his *First Essay on Party*. There was something prescient in it, as one of the themes touched on by Burke was his fear of the consequences of Pitt the Elder's reliance on popular support in sustaining his position.[3] They would continue to shadow one another and would die in the same year.

Potter's tenure as MP for Aylesbury had proved in the end to be just three years, during which time he was faced with the unwelcome prospect of two by-elections. At this time, MPs appointed to government offices were expected to resign their seats and fight by-elections to ensure that their constituents were willing to allow them to serve in both places. In the autumn of 1756, Potter was appointed joint-paymaster general, requiring him to contest Aylesbury again. Wilkes willingly rallied around to support him and in November wrote to the ever-obliging Dell to 'get handbills printed for my gates and chains', promoting Potter's re-election. He recommended that they could be procured most cheaply at Northampton and insisted that his name was not to feature on them.[4] On this occasion, Potter's election was challenged by a certain Frederick Halsey. No one seems to know quite who Halsey was, but at the poll in

December he actually secured more votes than Potter. However, Potter's side were highly suspicious of exactly who some of these voters were and demanded a scrutiny. On investigation, it transpired that over 100 had no right to vote in Aylesbury. Halsey then did the sensible thing and withdrew, leaving Potter once more in place as the town's MP.

If Potter hoped he might now be left in peace, he was rudely disabused. In January 1757, Wilkes predicted that Parliament was not likely to last much longer. This would, of course, offer the prospect of new elections and a fresh opportunity at securing election as an MP.

Of course, one obvious question is why Wilkes was so eager to seek election? He had been groomed by his parents for greater things than running the distillery and his new life as squire of Aylesbury allowed him to rub shoulders with the cream of county society. Many of his new acquaintances were themselves parliament men, so why not him? Besides, Potter quite clearly encouraged him to aspire to join him in the Commons. Wilkes was certainly eminently well qualified when compared with other men there. As Paul Langford has argued, MPs were made up of three types: 'landowners born and bred, men of commercial or other background who had purchased land, and adventurers.'[5] Wilkes inhabited the second category, though there was not a little of the adventurer about him too. It is intriguing that Wilkes's own family appear to have been so concerned about this latest move, given their determination to see him rise in society, but for Wilkes himself this must now have appeared an obvious step to which he was entitled. As Lewis Namier put it: 'Social advancement, more easily realized than political ambitions, was, and remains to those who need and desire it, an obvious incentive for entering Parliament.'[6]

Wilkes's opportunity came thanks to yet another alteration in Potter's fortunes. In the spring, he had followed Pitt the Elder into opposition, laying down his office as paymaster general, but in July Potter was offered a new position as joint vice treasurer of Ireland, triggering yet another by-election. This time he was anxious not to have to waste his funds on Aylesbury again, which had already proved such a thoroughly troublesome place. That is not to say that he was likely to be free of expenditure elsewhere. Most constituencies required careful treating. John Dickinson, an American visiting England at this point, observed that 'Bribery is so common that it is thot [sic] there is not a borough in England where it is not practisd.'[7] Not all were quite as venal as Aylesbury, though, and Potter was eager to find somewhere cheaper. Happily for him, a deal was on the horizon.

In December 1756, Pitt had been elected for the borough of Okehampton, where his cousin, Thomas Pitt of Boconnoc, had a long-standing interest recently 'pawned' to the government. Just as restless as

Potter, Pitt had since been courted by the city of Bath. This was largely thanks to the combined efforts of Potter and Ralph Allen, who dominated the corporation as the city's postmaster. Allen and Potter were close, with Potter a regular visitor to Prior Park, Allen's palatial seat on the outskirts of the city. It was there that Potter met Allen's niece, Gertrude Tucker, wife of the soon-to-be bishop of Gloucester, William Warburton. It was also there that Potter supposedly seduced Gertrude and fathered Warburton's only child (Ralph Allen Warburton). This would later be raised in parliament when Warburton and Wilkes locked horns over the *Essay on Woman*.

Aside from his ongoing career as a lothario, Potter had been plotting the exchange of seats for some time. In April 1757, he had written to Allen commending him for the role he had played 'in the Honours lately done to Mr Pitt by the Corporation of Bath.'[8] This was all part of a concerted charm offensive, and before the summer, Potter was able to report that he had 'With Difficulty' persuaded Pitt to accept the nomination at Bath. Pitt was already resident in the city, seeking a cure for his various maladies.[9] In turn, Pitt resigned his seat at Okehampton to Potter, thereby leaving a place vacant at Aylesbury, where Wilkes was encouraged to present himself as a candidate. He did so, but with it took on the worst of the bargain. It was a decision that left him ever more deeply in debt and brought him to the attention of money lenders, who would continue to plague him (and he them) for the next decade or so.[10] The financier with whom Wilkes was most closely involved was Isaac Fernandes Silva and it is quite plain by Wilkes's dealings that he regarded Silva's advances to him as debts he was at perfect liberty to ignore when it suited him. Besides, for as long as he remained a Member of Parliament, his privilege protected him from arrest for debt.[11]

A Year of Victories

The background to Potter and Pitt seeking new seats was the general political instability of the later 1750s. In May 1756 Britain had gone to war again, just eight years after the conclusion of the War of the Austrian Succession.[12] The new conflict, which would be dubbed the Seven Years War, would see Britain at first humbled and then transported into the premier league following the 1759 'Year of Victories', crowned by General Wolfe's victory at Quebec.

One year into the conflict, the year of Wilkes's election, things were not going so well. The country was troubled by rioting over the cost of food as well as popular agitation against the Militia Act.[13] There was tension at the very top of government. In March, Admiral Byng was executed for his failure to relieve a British garrison on Minorca. Indeed, even though Wilkes was for his entire career identified with the Whigs, in 1756 he had been involved with the Tories of Buckinghamshire and Bedfordshire in drawing up an address to be presented to the king on the subject of Minorca.[14] For the opposition, the Byng affair was an opportunity to mount a wider enquiry into the government's failings. They were unsuccessful and Byng became a scapegoat. He went to his death, then, as Voltaire put it, *'pour encourager les autres'*.[15]

The king had proved unwilling to intervene over Byng. George II was by now in his 70s but remained active in shaping administrations – 'still the source of all authority'.[16] Often portrayed as a rather stolid individual, according to one of his closest courtiers, the 2nd Earl Waldegrave, George had 'a good understanding tho not of the first Class; and has a clear Insight into Men, & Things within a certain Compass.'[17] He had lost his wife Queen Caroline two decades before, and his heir, Prince Frederick, with whom he was on almost permanently terrible terms, in 1751. Relations with his younger son, the duke of Cumberland, were normally good but Cumberland blotted his copybook in 1757 by agreeing to the Convention of Kloster Zeven, which left Hanover exposed to the French.[18]

As far as governments went, the king had strong views about many of the ministers with whom he had to work. At the beginning of his reign, he had been reluctant to continue Sir Robert Walpole in office but quickly changed his mind, not a little owing to Queen Caroline. Following Walpole's fall in 1742 there had been a couple of years of uncertainty until Henry Pelham, younger brother of the duke of Newcastle, emerged as Prime Minister. Between them, Newcastle and Pelham headed 'the Old Corps' Whigs, who viewed themselves first and foremost as the upholders of the 1688 Revolution settlement. After a decade of relative stability, Pelham's death in 1754 was the catalyst for renewed jostling for position before Newcastle, famous for his indecisiveness, emerged as his brother's successor. He went on to hold the office of Prime Minister twice (1754 to 1756 and 1757 to 1762). By the later 1750s, though, everyone was agreed that it was almost impossible to manage affairs without the involvement of William Pitt the Elder. Pitt, who had emerged from the ranks of the Stowe 'Patriots' and was closely allied with Earl Temple, dominated the House of Commons, famous for his fiery oratory and his rare ability to command the chamber.

Pitt had initially been reluctant to accept government office. In 1746, however, he accepted a job as joint-vice-treasurer of Ireland, before moving up to paymaster general, where he made his reputation. Put out in 1755, Pitt returned to government in December the following year. He was now in coalition with another of the great Whig leaders, the duke of Devonshire, as one half of the leadership of the 'Pitt-Devonshire' ministry.[19] In spite of his towering reputation in the Commons, Pitt was no favourite of George's and in January 1757 the king warned Pitt that he would need to work hard to gain his trust, reminding him that the same had been true of Walpole at the beginning of the reign.[20] By February, George was already examining alternative options and in the spring he took the decision to turn out Pitt and Temple. Following a period during which George and his proxies struggled to form a new administration, including a few days in the summer of 1757 when there was effectively no government, the king was forced to accept Pitt back in a new coalition with the duke of Newcastle as Prime Minister.[21]

While this was in many ways good news for Pitt and other members associated with him, it meant by-elections for those Members taking places in the new government, including Pitt himself. It was this that led Pitt to give way to the Potter-Allen plan for him to relocate to Bath, for Potter to succeed Pitt at Okehampton, and for Wilkes to stand for Aylesbury.

By the end of May it was clear that the tripartite arrangement was in place and in a letter of 28 May Wilkes advised Dell from his London residence in Great George Street that he expected to be back in Aylesbury in a week. There he intended 'to give you a grand supper ... and a rout for the Town, in the usual manner'. A 'rout' in this context was the kind of boozy entertainment candidates frequently threw for locals – voters and non-voters alike – to help persuade the former to cast their votes in their favour. He was delighted to note 'my worthy constituents approve me' and that in London, he was also 'caress'd in a manner, which does me the truest honour'.[22]

At this stage, Wilkes could not be certain of being unopposed, but even if his way had been entirely clear, elections still required careful diplomacy. He would still have been expected to treat and court his constituents. The duke of Newcastle, probably the greatest of the borough-mongers, dominated in Lewes, but that did not mean the place did not cause him trouble. The deaths of both MPs there in 1743 resulted in a ticklish double by-election and while neither of his candidates ended up being challenged, selecting them and ensuring the town accept the choice was by no means straightforward.[23]

It is no surprise then, that Wilkes determined not to take any chances, as Edward Willes was at this point expected to contest the seat as well.[24] On 31 May, he instructed Dell, by now firmly ensconced in the role of one of Wilkes's election agents, to 'invite all the independents (pointedly excluding Jack Bass) to sup with Mr Wilkes on Saturday evening at seven or eight, as they like best.' He also exhorted Dell to desire the landlord, Mr Hill, 'to let us have a good supper'.[25] Perhaps more importantly, he made preparations to outbid Willes, informing Dell that he intended to 'sink Willes by the weight of metal'.[26]

That things were still not settled with Potter until well into the following month is indicated by a letter from Wilkes to Dell again on 22 June, declaring triumphantly that Potter had at last relinquished 'to me your good borough of Aylesbury'.[27] There was even a suggestion that Potter himself might stage a mock opposition to Wilkes just to make it look as if there was a proper contest. The drawn-out uncertainty about Wilkes's candidacy was in part because Potter himself was not entirely sure until late June that Pitt would be willing to fall in with his scheme and quit Okehampton. It was not until the 28th that Pitt himself wrote to Edward Bushell Collibee, the mayor of Bath, thanking the corporation for his selection and assuring them: 'I have long ambition'd the honour of a Seat there, derived from a Body so independent, and so truly respectable as the City of Bath.'[28]

Besides, amid the uncertainties of the times, there was also reason to be doubtful until the very last minute whether the new ministry would hold, and whether Potter's post as vice-treasurer of Ireland would actually materialize. There were always competing interests to be considered. However, Wilkes now seemed confident that there were no more obstacles in his way. The very next day he announced to Dell that he would be in Aylesbury in two or three days when he would 'open the campaign'. Having previously undertaken to offer two guineas per man, Wilkes had now been advised to increase this to three guineas a man. He sought Dell's opinion on this: 'If you are of the same opinion, I will not hesitate.' This was, of course, bribery, entirely contrary to the rules of the day, but Wilkes, always able to view things in the most flexible of terms, defined it more loosely: 'It is a kind of retainer, or fee at entrance.' He saw no conflict whatsoever in doling out such sums while at the same time proclaiming as he had done in a previous letter that he was 'following the true interest of this kingdom'.[29] Anthony Bacon, who succeeded Wilkes at Aylesbury after his expulsion, would later pay five guineas a man to ensure his election.[30]

At some point in late June, Wilkes's only likely rival, Edward Willes, concluded that a contest was not worth his while and took the decision to withdraw.[31] He may have been suffering from poor health and reluctant to face the fatigue of a contested election. He may also have been unwilling, or unable, to stump up the sums Wilkes was willing to put into the contest. As Wilkes put it, 'W at last has gone out in a stink – I always despis'd such an opponent.' It was one of Wilkes's less attractive qualities that, while loyal to close friends, towards many of his more general acquaintance he was two-faced. He had, after all, supposedly been on decent terms with the Willes brothers.

Meanwhile, on 28 June (the same day as Pitt's letter to the mayor of Bath) Potter wrote to Wilkes 'to resign the Borough of Aylesbury into your hands'. He also wished him 'a safe and cheap election', saying that he would 'with great pleasure contribute towards it if I had any interest to contribute'.[32] The only remaining concern was that the duke of Newcastle might attempt to send a carpetbagger to contest the seat. Potter assured Wilkes that Pitt had done what he could to prevent the duke from doing this. Potter also insisted that he had played a signal role in saving Wilkes from further difficulties. He said he had happened upon Admiral Knowles at Newcastle's London residence, with his bags packed and ready to head out for Aylesbury to challenge for the seat. This was Charles Knowles, a reputed illegitimate son of the titular 4th earl of Banbury, who had previously been MP for the Surrey pocket borough of Gatton. He had also held various colonial posts, including as governor of Bocca Chica castle.[33] Potter had managed to persuade him not to make the effort.[34] Wilkes would come across Knowles again just two years later over a libel case brought by Knowles against Tobias Smollett. Smollett appealed to Wilkes for his assistance in persuading Knowles to drop the action, but to no avail.[35]

Potter's communications revealed starkly the extent to which Wilkes, in his eagerness to secure a place in Parliament, had been played. Although he would face no opponent and thus was able to avoid a poll, this was not to be a 'cheap election' for him. Besides, the fact that Potter was willing to do so little to assist in securing Wilkes's return for what had been his seat for the past three years says a good deal about the late archbishop's scapegrace son. Almost exactly two years later, Potter would be dead, and Wilkes was probably better off without him.

The result of several months of bargaining, negotiating and expenditure was ultimately entirely as the trio had hoped. On 6 July Wilkes was elected at Aylesbury and three days later, Pitt was returned for Bath. It took him until 20 July to bother to congratulate Wilkes.[36] In the meantime, Potter had secured his seat at Okehampton. Although Wilkes had not faced a challenge in Aylesbury, there is evidence of the election being lively and Wilkes wrote to Dell afterwards letting him know that he had 'written to young Burnham to get up evidence against the persons who broke Spur's windows, and I intend to move the King's Bench against them.'[37]

Wilkes's election cemented his place in Aylesbury and in wider Buckinghamshire society. He remained closely associated with the Temple group, and in Parliament a supporter of the Pitt-Newcastle administration. He also increasingly liked to see himself as an inheritor of the mantle of another great Buckinghamshire MP, the Civil War figure John Hampden. However, for the time being Wilkes was very much a junior partner of his Grenville companions. Pitt, Temple and Potter were all officeholders in the administration, as were Temple's younger brothers, James and George Grenville. Despite this, Wilkes put it, ever so modestly, to George Grenville, that he, too, was now 'one of the most powerful princes of your country', i.e. Buckinghamshire.[38]

A month after Wilkes's election, the press reported that a notorious highwayman, William (alias Beau) Page, had been committed to Newgate by Sir John Fielding. According to the report, Wilkes was one of numerous people targeted by Page who had been relieved of their possessions at Uxbridge.[39] It is not clear precisely when the crime had been committed, but presumably this was when Wilkes was on one of his frequent journeys around the environs of London. The victims were requested to present themselves at Bow Street to offer evidence about their respective cases.[40] The episode is a salutary reminder of the still fairly lawless state of many of the roads on the outskirts of London. Wilkes and many more like him would have risked encounters with such characters during their excursions to and from the capital.

Westminster in the 18th century

The Westminster that was now open to him was a very different environment from that of the present Houses of Parliament, constructed following the devastating fire of 1834. Westminster Bridge was still relatively new, while the Prime Minister's formal residence in Downing Street, granted to Walpole in 1735, was not yet a clear fixture. After Walpole's fall from office in 1742, his successor, Spencer Compton, earl of Wilmington, had chosen not to reside there as he had a much nicer house of his own in St James's. Number 10 had been taken over by the chancellor of the exchequer and until Lord North became Prime Minister later in the century, it was often the chancellor who was based there.

At some point prior to his election, Wilkes had quit his apartments in St James's Place and moved to new premises at Number 13 Great George Street, closer to the parliamentary estate.[41] When Wilkes arrived the street was in the process of being developed, but during the time he lived there he rubbed shoulders with a pleasing mix of politicians and literary men. From 1758, his next-door neighbour at Number 12 was the earl of Cork and Orrery. At Number 5 was Thomas Tyrwhitt, editor of the *Canterbury Tales* and at Number 15 James Beauclerk, bishop of Hereford, a younger son of the duke of St Albans. Over the next two to three years, other houses were completed and occupied. Wilkes's house, along with others on the street, was demolished in 1900, but some of the interior fittings survived and were reinstated in the buildings that replaced them. Number 29 would later be the original home of the National Portrait Gallery.[42]

As for the Palace of Westminster, it was a hotch-potch of buildings, or as Paul Seaward has put it, 'a higgledy-piggledy slum'.[43] Some of the structures were mediaeval, some relatively modern, and many of them only ever jerry-built as temporary additions. The finest of the surviving old structures was Westminster Hall, resplendent with the battle standards captured at Blenheim[44] and housing the courts of chancery, exchequer, king's bench and common pleas, along with a variety of stalls and book shops. The Painted Chamber was where both Houses convened for conferences. There was a variety of coffee shops and eateries, including 'Heaven' and 'Hell', with others jumbled in and around Old and New Palace yards. A number of officials and private individuals also claimed space within the complex.

The Lords sat in what had originally been part of the queen's apartments, while the Commons were housed in the former chapel, known universally as St Stephen's. According to William Kent, who drew up plans for rebuilding the palace in the 1730s, the Commons' chamber measured a fairly pinched 60 feet 8 inches by 32 feet 4 inches, with a height of 26 feet 8 inches.[45] It did, though, benefit from elegant galleries installed by Christopher Wren in the 1690s, whereas the Lords proved much less willing to put up with the inconvenience of such additions. In spite of its reputation as cramped, the place where Wilkes hoped to make his name was described by Edward Hatton in 1708 as 'a commodious Building accommodated with several Ranks of Seats covered with green and matted under Foot for 513 Gentlemen'.[46] That was not quite enough space to house all of the Members (558) but, as was frequently pointed out, it was rare that anything like all of the MPs were present. The chamber may have been elegant, but it was also notoriously difficult to make oneself heard in as the acoustics were extremely variable. Those listening from the galleries benefited from the vaulted ceiling and were able to hear quite well; sound around the Speaker's chair was also pretty good. In other parts of the chamber, though, it was the opposite.[47] Depending on where Wilkes sat, this would have been a major challenge for him, incommoded by what seems to have been a kind of whistling lisp. Engaging in private conversation, where he was able to let his natural wit shine, he was to find public speaking much more challenging.

While it was true that Wilkes was now one of the most prominent figures in his locality, his claim to be one of Buckinghamshire's most powerful 'princes' was largely bluster. He may have been a significant figure in Aylesbury and Buckinghamshire more generally, but in Westminster he was a minnow in a very large and competitive pond. It must have grated on Wilkes to find himself in Parliament at last, but a long way off from the friends and neighbours who had encouraged him to be there. In the Commons he seems to have struggled to make himself noticed. He clearly tried, and struggled, to employ his 'interest' (i.e. his influence). In July 1759 the duke of Newcastle responded to him in neutral terms about a request for an Aylesbury man to be appointed surveyor of the window lights.[48] Not long after, Wilkes attempted to secure a plum job for one of his brothers (likely Heaton) at 'Chelsea College' but was rebuffed by Pitt. Pitt did, though, insist that he 'should be extremely glad to promote your desires', adding as an afterthought, 'always meaning your virtuous ones'.[49]

Nevertheless, Wilkes was not totally anonymous in those early years in the Commons. He took his seat for the first time at the opening of the new session on 1 December 1757 along with several other new Members. Several MPs had died during the year, while the MP for Maidstone, Lord Guernsey, had succeeded to his father's peerage over the summer and thus been elevated to the House of Lords.[50] Many of the vacancies were still to be settled at the time Parliament met.[51]

On 14 December, the House received a bill sent down from the Lords, where it had originated, enabling Potter, the earl of Sandwich and Welbore Ellis to take the necessary oaths as joint vice-treasurers of Ireland in England.[52] On the 19th, the Commons referred the bill to a committee, headed by Wilkes, which was ordered to convene the same day at five in the Speaker's chamber.[53] Wilkes reported the bill back on the 20th, having made no amendments, and on the 21st he was noted in the Lords Journal returning the bill to the upper chamber.[54] Allowing ministers with overseas responsibilities to manage their commitments from England was common practice as it relieved them of the tiresome burden of a visit to their province. Not infrequently, they never visited their posts at all, deputing most of the work to local officials while they happily pocketed the fees. It was, perhaps, a small thank you to Potter for facilitating his election. Sandwich, 'a big man ... with a reputation for breaking china',[55] best known, of course, as the inventor of the sandwich, was also known to Wilkes from the Beefsteaks and the unruly group that met in the ruins of Medmenham Abbey, known familiarly as the 'Hellfire Club'.[56] Sandwich would later play a key role in bringing Wilkes down, thanks largely to inside knowledge he possessed of their goings-on at Medmenham. He had been one of the joint vice-treasurers since 1755, so for him this was merely a routine reappointment. Ellis, a fellow libertine who was later to become Wilkes's partner at Aylesbury, was an ally of Henry Fox.[57] He had better claims on office in Ireland than the other two, having been born there. His father was an Irish bishop and Ellis owned property in Dublin.

Parliament paused for the Christmas recess between 23 December and 16 January 1758 when they reconvened. On the 18th, Wilkes was named to another committee considering a petition submitted by the inhabitants of Hay, who were seeking a bill for improving the road between their town and Stockley Hill in Herefordshire.[58] Next day he found himself on a similar committee, this time a petition from Gloucester and Bristol for improving their road network.[59] Wilkes's nomination to these two committees tells us little about his own interests. It was routine work and there were to be plenty more examples, but it does underscore the fact that he was present in the chamber on those days and willing to play his part.[60] Rather more importantly, on 21 January Wilkes reported back to Dell on what seems to have been his first experience of significant political business. He had been involved in the Commons' committee the previous day voting in favour of granting £100,000 to maintain the Hanoverian army 'for the present'.[61] On 24 April he spoke, for what was perhaps the first time, in the debate on the third reading of the Habeas Corpus bill, joining Pitt and the attorney general, Charles Pratt, in favour of it. It was passed without a division.[62]

Wilkes chaired two more committees a couple of years later, on 28 February and 11 March 1760. On the first occasion he was returning the unamended bill enabling the singularly named Mark Goodflesh to divorce his wife, Elizabeth and to remarry.[63] On the second he was part of a delegation from the Commons returning a bill naturalizing Elizabeth, wife of Richard Spencer. It was clearly uncontentious, and the Commons returned it without making any amendments.[64] The following month, on 14 April, he was to be found before the Lords once more returning a private bill concerning the estate of a Northamptonshire gentleman, John Freeman.[65] He did so again on 13 May, this time returning a bill allowing the dean and chapter of Westminster Abbey to lease land to one James Mallors.[66] On 4 February 1762 he undertook the role once more, this time presenting a bill from the Commons for the Lords' agreement, naturalizing four men. None of them appear to have been known to Wilkes especially.[67]

Besides such relatively humdrum contributions to the House's business, Wilkes seems not to have made much impact in the Commons during his first term. It was still contrary to parliamentary privilege for the press to report debates, so any speeches he may have made were probably of little moment. Some of the more famous orators were reported in the press and in handwritten newsletters, in spite of the restrictions, but there is little reason to believe that Wilkes was among them.[68] Usually, it is assumed that he faltered in his early efforts as an orator. He failed to live up to the maxim laid down by Lord Chesterfield to his godson, that he must 'take pains to distinguish yourself as a speaker. The task is not very hard if you have common sense.' Wilkes would go on to prove that there were other ways of making himself noticed, though it might be said that he also emulated Chesterfield's subsequent advice to his godson: 'If on your first, second or third attempt to speak, you should fail, or even stop short ... do not be discouraged, but persevere; it will do at last.'[69] Wilkes was nothing if not persistent.

In September 1758, Wilkes took advantage of the period in between the session that had closed in June and the opening of the new session in November to travel to Scotland. It was not his first visit. He had made the most of his time in Berwick between 1754 and 1755 to cross the border and visit Edinburgh. There he had met David Hume, before carrying on to see some of the areas further west. The two had apparently got on well and after missing Wilkes on his return trip from Glasgow, Hume had sent him a copy of his newly published *History of Great Britain*, in a special large paper format,[70] so that Wilkes could 'read it with as little disadvantage as possible'.[71] If the two had got on well, Hume was not so obtuse as to have missed the indications that Wilkes was a man committed to a libertine manner of existence. He regretted Wilkes had not had time to visit the Highlands, where he would have found

> ... Human Nature in the golden Age, or rather, indeed, in the Silver: for the Highlands have degenerated somewhat from the primitive Simplicity of Mankind. But perhaps you have so corrupted a Taste as to prefer your Iron Age, to be met with in London & the south of England; where Luxury & Vice of every kind so much abound.[72]

During his 1758 visit, Wilkes did make further inroads into the country, making it as far as the Western Isles. He visited the duke of Argyll at Inverary and managed, as was so often the case, to charm his hosts. In spite of the hospitality received and his own professed affection for the place, Wilkes was unable to stop himself from mocking certain aspects of Scots society, in particular local standards of hygiene.[73] It was a kind of smutty trope about the backwardness of Scots society that was common in England. This was exemplified by a much-reproduced 1745 caricature by Charles Mosley, 'Sawney in the bog-house', depicting a lost highlander bewildered by the prospect of an English lavatory. Rather than evacuate into the void, he is shown with his feet placed in adjoining WCs while urine flows over the floor. Thus, writing to Dell from Edinburgh on 26 September 1758 Wilkes hoped that he had taken 'the necessary precaution of airing [the letter], drying it by the fire etc., and washing your own hands in vinegar, for fear of a propagations of some Scotch animals in our good County town.'[74] This kind of casual disdain for the Scots and Scotland resurfaced on occasion throughout Wilkes's life, aside from the concentrated campaign that was to be a feature in his newspaper, the *North Briton*.

If Wilkes struggled to make a mark at Westminster he was nevertheless enormously busy. No one could ever accuse Wilkes of slouching. In the year after his election, he was commissioned into the Buckinghamshire militia, first as a captain and latterly as a lieutenant colonel. It was a role he found rewarding and for years afterwards, long after he was no longer entitled to it, he would continue to sport his regimental coat. The Buckinghamshire militia was a relatively well-organized outfit. In the summer of 1759, the papers reported on the general state of the county regiments, noting which had managed to recruit and mobilize the requisite number of troops. Buckinghamshire was one of those to have raised the expected 560 men. Its preparations were nearly complete, if not quite as advanced as the Devonshires, under the duke of Bedford, whose full complement was already on duty. Others, among them Cornwall, Glamorgan and Rutland, were shamed for having failed to recruit or field the numbers expected of them.[75]

In April 1759, Wilkes attended a Militia Meeting held in Dean Street, Soho, along with a number of other peers and MPs, where it was decided to form themselves into a society and to hold an annual dinner 'some day in the last week of February'. Several of his regular circle were also there, including Temple, James Grenville and Sir Francis Dashwood. One of the stewards nominated to arrange the next year's annual feast was Sambrooke Freeman. In spite of being a Berkshire man (he had a seat near Henley-on-Thames) and sitting for Pontefract in Yorkshire, he was, like Wilkes, an officer in the Buckinghamshire militia.[76] In July there was another similar meeting in Aylesbury, featuring the deputy lieutenants and officers of the county militia. Once again, Temple was there along with Wilkes, noted among the local gentry holding commissions.[77] Wilkes was nothing if not clubbable.

Along with taking on a role as one of the many gentleman amateur soldiers bolstering the standing army, Wilkes became involved in a prominent local charity. In the same year as his election to Parliament, Wilkes was elected a governor of the London Foundling Hospital and in 1759 he became a governor of a new branch to be established in Aylesbury. He played a key role in seeing the necessary legislation through Parliament for establishing the Aylesbury branch. The original institution, founded thanks to the efforts of the philanthropist former sea captain, Thomas Coram, was based in Bloomsbury, and had attracted support from large numbers of the great and the good. Aristocratic women were at the forefront of raising funds for the charity, and members of the royal family were prominent supporters. Consequently, many of the orphans left at the hospital were baptized with names reflecting their wealthy patrons, meaning numerous Georges, Augustas and Augustuses, Fredericks and Williams. This and other charitable organizations founded around the same time also depended on backing from members of the middling orders, so Wilkes was far from out of place as the son of a distiller and representative of relatively new wealth.[78]

In March 1759, Wilkes was busy overseeing negotiations for the purchase of land in the town for the new charity. Typically, there were teething problems to be overcome and in May he was reporting to Dell how 'our wings are clipp'd as to the first reception of children in the different counties, but my scheme for Aylesbury goes on just the same as I first propos'd it.'[79] Later that month, Dell, too, was elected to the board of the Aylesbury branch and Wilkes announced his return to the town early in June in time for a committee meeting of the charity on the 9th. He also announced, 'We mean strictly to have no children under our care,' by which he no doubt meant very young children. It was at the meeting on the 9th that Wilkes was appointed treasurer of the Aylesbury Foundling Hospital, a decision that the other trustees were ultimately to regret.[80]

Through the remainder of 1759 and into the following year, Wilkes remained periodically engaged with his work for the charity. He attended another committee meeting on 5 October and on the 11th was pressing Dell to take a more prominent role, as basic matters such as paying workmen's bills continued to feature in his correspondence. At the end of October 1759, he was contemplating a trip to Bristol with his father. This may well have been for Israel's health, as he died in January 1761. 'Nothing however absolutely fix'd', the projected visit did not come off as in early November Wilkes was actively engaged with what was in effect a spin-off from his activities with the Foundling Hospital. That month he was (along with Hogarth, also a governor of the Foundling Hospital) one of the leading figures behind the establishment of the Society of Artists of Great Britain, a breakaway group from the Society of Arts.[81] Another artist involved was Robert Edge Pine, who was responsible for one of the finest and much copied depictions of Wilkes, now in the Parliamentary Art collection. On 5 November Wilkes presided over a meeting outlining the need for establishing such a group, which led to an inaugural exhibition the following year. The Society aimed not to 'dictate taste, but help *artists*.'[82] It was an early instance of Wilkes's interest in patronising art and artists, which was to remain a passion throughout his life. Nevertheless, there were tensions within the new Society and Hogarth was later to distance himself from it. He and Wilkes were also to become keen enemies in Hogarth's final years with one using his art to underpin the ministry while the other battled to destabilize it.[83]

By early 1760, the Aylesbury Foundling Hospital was up and running with three boys and eleven girls enrolled. There were ambitious plans to expand the offering, with a former barn to become accommodation for an additional 100 orphans. This scheme, promoted by Wilkes, was never realized, but it points to his active involvement in establishing the Hospital.

Throughout all this, Wilkes proved pretty reliable in turning out for committee meetings, attending sessions in 1760 on 19 January, 18 July and 10 October, only skipping one, on 19 April. In 1761 the pattern continued, but in the course of that year Wilkes appears to have begun to make use of the funds in his care to service his own debts. Strictly speaking, what he was doing was probably not embezzlement. At the time it was considered acceptable for people in such offices to employ funds with which they were entrusted for their own use, provided they were able to pay them back. The problem was that as Wilkes found himself further and further in debt, he was not able to do so. Arthur Cash thought Wilkes, 'not dishonest', rather 'irresponsible'. Lloyd Hart, who studied the Aylesbury Foundling Hospital, was less forgiving and concluded that 'Wilkes had been fiddling the Hospital Funds from July 1761.'[84] From that month, the Hospital bills stopped being paid, though Wilkes continued to claim for them.

Perhaps the most extraordinary feature of the Foundling Hospital episode was the willingness of the other trustees to cover for Wilkes. By 1763, a series of meetings were held, several of which he attended, at which the issue of the increasingly messy accounts was discussed. At a meeting on 7 October 1763 the committee formally approved Wilkes's accounts (in his absence), declaring that the trust owed him £218 6s. 6d. It was yet another instance of Wilkes's ability to recover from a situation that might have floored most people. He had been a key figure in establishing the charity. He had proposed a significant expansion, overseen the accounts, embezzled the funds (by accident perhaps) and yet still emerged with a claim for reimbursement agreed by the rest of the committee. By the summer of 1763, though, Wilkes had other, rather more pressing matters on his mind than a modest sum like £218.

Hellfire

Along with his efforts to make a mark as a conscientious militia officer, as a somewhat corrupt, or at least sticky-fingered, local worthy, and an occasional parliamentary committee chairman, Wilkes also continued to cultivate relations with the local grandees in Buckinghamshire and develop his libertine persona. Throughout his career Wilkes would be elected to numerous clubs and societies, some august and worthy, others little more than drinking societies. But the most notorious of them all was that of the 'Knights of St Francis of Medmenham', also known as the Order of St Francis, and widely known (spuriously) as the Hellfire Club. Exactly what went on at Medmenham Abbey will probably never be known for sure. Many of the lurid tales, though, were peddled by Wilkes himself to discredit the order's leader, Sir Francis Dashwood, after the two had fallen out.[85] Undoubtedly, it was a gathering place for men of a certain libertine mindset, but many of the more extreme details associated with the place, the quasi-satanic rituals and most abandoned orgiastic parties, are likely fanciful.

The venue was a ruined abbey on the banks of the Thames, which Dashwood had acquired and remodelled. The entrance sported a quotation from Rabelais' Abbey de Thélème: 'Fay ce que voudras' (do as you will).[86] It might as well have been Wilkes's personal motto. Dashwood was an MP, later a peer, Wilkes's commanding officer as colonel of the Buckinghamshire militia, founder of the Dilettanti Society and the Divan Club, and later a famously inept chancellor of the exchequer. That was Dashwood's own assessment. In keeping with the quasi-monastic organization of the society, each of its members was known simply by their first names with a locational 'surname'. Dashwood himself, thus, was Francis of Wycombe, while Wilkes was, obviously enough, John of Aylesbury. The earl of Sandwich was almost certainly a member, hidden under the guise of John of Hinchingbrooke. Potter was one, but his Medmenham identity is unknown.[87]

Quite when Wilkes became associated with the fraternity is not clear, but as was so often the case, Potter was probably his entrée into the society.[88] Whether Wilkes was ever a 'full' member is also contested, though he seems to have taken a lively interest. According to John Sainsbury, he visited Medmenham at least twenty times, acted as the club librarian and was responsible for buying in certain items. These included breast-shaped cups and, rather characteristically, he seems never to have paid for them.[89] He was also responsible for introducing new members to the group. The most important of these (for Wilkes) was Charles Churchill. Churchill was perhaps best described as a renegade clergyman turned schoolmaster turned journalist, and he and Wilkes were to enjoy one of the closest friendships of Wilkes's life. It was with Churchill that Wilkes would launch the *North Briton* in 1762 and Churchill's early death in 1764 affected Wilkes more than any other loss ever did. Churchill then in turn brought Robert Lloyd, another struggling author, along to Medmenham.[90]

While some have attempted to characterize the club as a secret society that indulged in faintly satanic rituals, the reality was likely much more prosaic. Wilkes's morals were loose enough to permit him to engage in many things, but even he would probably have drawn the line at some of the more occult activities sometimes attributed to the Hellfire club. As Paul Langford has suggested, Wilkes's views 'might kindly be described as deistic'.[91] However, he was mischievous and came to delight in undermining what went on there. Most famously, he was said to have released a baboon, dressed as the devil, in the middle of one of the 'secret rituals', terrifying Sandwich and thereby bringing to a sudden end the meetings of the society.[92] Wilkes later published an outrageous account of the goings on of what was probably little more than a frat society. What also seems wide of the mark is the suggestion that Medmenham ever had any systematic political influence. True, those associated with it included several prominent politicians, some of them at one time or another government ministers. There seems little reason to believe, though, that the club itself was a place where anything very serious was ever hammered out. Rather, the members seem to have enjoyed relaxed days boating on the river, wandering the grounds, sharing filthy jokes, fine dining and sex with courtesans shipped in for the occasion.

What seems most important about all of this, for Wilkes, was that it highlights a number of themes of his career. He both craved and scorned, in equal measure, acceptance by his social and political superiors. He regarded involvement in libertine groupings, such as Medmenham, as an important part of his identity. Maybe it was also for him a badge of honour to be able to bed attractive women. But he was also very quickly bored and disillusioned. Naturally quick-witted, he found some of the more absurd features of Medmenham tedious and ripe for satire. His willingness to turn on those who had sheltered him also pointed to a running leitmotif. Never content with what he had, Wilkes could not resist pushing matters to extremes. It was a feature that would result in some of his greatest triumphs, but also bring him more often close to disaster.

The death of George II in October 1760 transformed national politics. George had reigned for 33 years, been in the country for over 45, but never been able to shake off the impression of being 'foreign'. His English was fluent, but he continued to speak French or German within the family. As his elder son, Prince Frederick, had died in 1751, it was George's grandson who now succeeded to the throne as George III. Just 22, the new king was a youthful contrast to his grandfather and, most importantly, had been born in England. Beyond his natural, unquestioning loyalty to George II as king, Wilkes had not had much to do with the former monarch. He would be much more closely involved with the new one.

What was most immediately important for Wilkes was the question of re-election. As George II had died so close to the opening of a new session, it was resolved not to dissolve Parliament as might have been expected on his demise, but to allow the full seven-year term to run its course.[93] It was thus not until 20 March 1761 that Parliament was finally dissolved, triggering a general election.

By the time of the election, Wilkes had long been busy shoring up his position in Aylesbury. His role as commander of the county militia gave him particularly strong standing, and in a letter of 17 March to Dell he undertook to 'grant furlongs [furloughs] for ten days to every Aylesbury man in my Company'.[94] Besides this, he had been busy entertaining the town at every opportunity. According to Almon, he held fortnightly parties for his supporters as well as ensuring that the 'usual *gratifications*' were administered to those 'accustomed to expect it'. Wilkes would later advise that no one should attempt to stand for a seat where they lived, because of the tendency of their constituents to eat them out of house and home.[95] There was also the rather less subtle question of how much money to distribute. Wilkes wrote quite openly to Dell of the need to 'batter' the town 'with 5 pounders' – alluding to an artillery barrage, but clearly indicating how high he was willing to go to ensure his voters turned out for him.[96]

If he was plagued by needing once more to treat the town, Wilkes was assisted by the fact that his former partner, John Willes, had decided not to contest Aylesbury again.[97] Willes and his brother Edward appear to have approached Lord Temple to see if he would support their joint candidacy, but Temple stood firm for Wilkes. Wilkes also made it clear that he was willing to pay more than the Willes brothers to keep his seat.[98] Instead, the second candidate was Welbore Ellis, son-in-law of Sir William Stanhope, one of the Grenvilles' rivals in the county. Ellis, who had previously represented two other seats, was also a junior minister. In the event of there being a contest, Wilkes was clearly concerned about Ellis taking supporters from him. In February 1761 Wilkes and Dell estimated Ellis having 322 votes in the bag. Of these, he was ready to challenge twenty-six of them.[99] In the end, as so often happened in eighteenth-century elections, a compromise was hammered out between the county patrons. The Grenvilles agreed not to challenge Stanhope standing for the county, if he agreed not to upset matters in Aylesbury.[100] Consequently, on 25 March 1761 Wilkes once again had the satisfaction of being returned one of the Members for Aylesbury alongside his new partner, Ellis. He was back in Parliament, protected from arrest for debt and more ambitious than ever to be noticed.

4

The *North Briton*

I will not be the dupe of the mob.[1]

Wilkes returned to Parliament in 1761 determined to secure what he considered his due recognition. This was in part because he wanted to be recompensed for his financial outlay in holding Aylesbury; also, because he clearly thought it was time for his patrons to do something for him. Undoubtedly, his finances had taken a battering over the last few years, though he was typically blasé about how much notice he should take of his predicament. As he had written to Dell back in February 1758 about his level of indebtedness: 'These things hurt Merchants, not Gentlemen.'[2] Wilkes was prepared to work hard for his reward. Indeed, what emerges from his experience of the next few years is his sheer energy and ability to divide his attention across multiple areas. One moment he would be in Parliament, the next with his beloved troops or cavorting at Medmenham, and all the while developing his profile as a feared pamphleteer.

While 1761 had begun well for Wilkes with his re-election for Parliament, he was arguably more exposed than ever before. He had lost Potter, his partner in crime, back in 1759. One of Potter's close acquaintances had commented on his early death, 'I see the vanity of all worldly pursuits. I have seen a man sacrificing his quiet, his health, and his fortune, to his ambition, who in the forty-first year of his age died unpossessed of every comfort of a rational being.'[3] Shortly before Wilkes's re-election, he lost his father, too. On 2 February one newspaper announced the death of Israel Wilkes the previous Saturday, while another paper reported that he had died on the Sunday.[4] Such minor disagreements were commonplace in the eighteenth-century press. He may have died late at night or early in the morning, hence the discrepancy. A few days later a third paper reported that Israel was 'reputed to have died worth £100,000'.[5] If the figure was right, Wilkes saw only a small part of it. In his will, Israel recorded the details of settlements already made on his older sons and one of his daughters. The younger Israel had received property and a lump sum of £5,000. Wilkes had also already been given estates. Neither were to expect anything more and Israel left it to his widow to decide what was fit to be given to his other children.[6] On 16 February, a notice was placed in the press by Sarah Wilkes calling on her late husband's creditors to put in their bills so the accounts could be settled.[7]

Israel had always been a slightly ambiguous figure for Wilkes, who had supposedly been his father's 'favourite'. The much-retold anecdote regaled by Wilkes to his daughter, Polly, about Israel teasing the young Wilkes over a gift of cash if only Wilkes had a purse to put it in reveals both his affection for his younger son but also his remoteness. Possibly, there was something of the old Mr Bennet about him. It was also telling that it was, according to Wilkes, 'to please an indulgent father' that he had agreed to marry Mary Mead.[8] Wilkes was determined to make his father proud but clearly felt there was still a lot of winning to do.[9] So, he can only have been disappointed by this final apparent snub, the ultimate conclusion to that early mischievous interaction.

There was to be another death in the family a few months later. In late April Robert Nesbitt, noted in one newspaper as 'a famous man-midwife' died at his house in Pater-Noster Row.[10] He had been husband of Wilkes's aunt, Deborah and it was through their son John that Wilkes had been introduced to Tobias Smollett, with whom he was soon to lock horns in the press.[11]

Wilkes might have liked to assume a front about such things, but the extent to which he was concerned at how stretched he was by the beginning of the 1760s is revealed in a letter to Dell a month after the 1761 election. In it he fretted about the opposition he had faced in Aylesbury. He was clearly frustrated by some elements of this and confessed himself: 'tir'd when I was last in the country, with the stories I was told, some of which I found to be true, of the insolence of some of the inn-keepers etc.'[12] Another reason for Wilkes's irritation at this time was his failure to convince his patrons, Pitt and the Grenvilles, to help him to a post that might alleviate his situation. Around the time of George III's accession, Wilkes put out feelers for appointment as ambassador to Constantinople, understanding that the incumbent, James Porter, who had been in post for the last 16 years, was intending to stand down.[13] Wilkes was not an obvious candidate for the post, which normally went to someone with rather more direct trading associations with the Orient. By the time he had been appointed in 1746, Porter had undertaken a number of secret commercial negotiations on the continent as well as assisting with diplomatic missions in the Empire. Wilkes had none of this kind of experience. Wilkes also approached Pitt directly for appointment to the Board of Trade. In both cases he was unsuccessful.[14]

If re-election had stretched Wilkes's resources to the limit and his inability to secure a job was beginning to jar, it was clear that he was still revelling in his life at Westminster. He was able to exploit his influence as an MP to secure Dell a ticket to the coronation of George III and Queen Charlotte on 22 September. On the 12th he wrote to Dell from Great George Street: 'Your ticket and apartment are ready, and I hope in civility you will come some time before to see Miss Wilkes and me, not merely for the show.' As ever with Wilkes, reference to the ceremony in London was mixed with domestic concerns, one subject flowing without pause into the next. Why, he wondered, had he not received any game from Aylesbury recently? 'I never saw anything like the greatness of the preparations going on. I kissed the Queen's fair hand on Thursday. I hope my gamekeeper does not forget me as scarcely feather or lever have yet reached me.'[15]

Wilkes's gift to Dell was no mean present for a Buckinghamshire farmer. The area around Westminster Abbey was filled with seating on raised scaffolding, with prices for the best places costing substantial sums. After all, there was always money to be made from such grand public spectacles. Seats in the galleries within the abbey went for 10 guineas, but one house with a particularly good view of the formal procession route was let out for 1,000 guineas: more than most workers would see in a lifetime.[16] Chairmen operating in the vicinity expected to make handsome sums from the event. They were in such high demand that it was reported they were charging between five and eight guineas a turn.[17] The event brought normal life to a standstill. The day after, one newspaper reported that there had been 'an entire stagnation of all sorts of business', all the shops were shut, and the city felt like a Sunday. Horace Walpole described the party atmosphere in a letter to George Montagu in Dublin: 'All the vines of Bourdeaux [sic], and all the fumes of Irish brains cannot make a town so drunk as a regal wedding and coronation... Oh! The buzz, the prattle, the crowds, the noise, the hurry!... If I was to entitle ages, I would call this the *century of crowds*.'[18] He could also not resist describing one of the more ludicrous episodes when Earl Talbot, in his role as steward of the royal household, made a fool of himself attempting to ride into Westminster Hall on horseback. Trying to keep to the convention of never turning one's back on the monarch, Talbot had schooled his horse, said to have been the one ridden by George II at the battle of Dettingen, to enter the hall and then reverse out. Unfortunately for him, it did the opposite and entered rump-first: 'At his retreat the spectators clapped, a terrible indecorum.'[19] It was a farcical moment that

Wilkes would in due course not be able to resist making the most of in the pages of his newspaper.

A Conflict over War, 1761-1762

The accession of George III might, on the face of it, have seemed beneficial for the old Patriots, formerly associated with the new king's father. It was, after all, out of the Stowe group headed first by Cobham and latterly by Wilkes's political mentor, Earl Temple, that much of the programme of government espoused first by Prince Frederick and then by George III himself had emanated. Certainly, George III's accession was greeted with huge optimism. He made much of the fact that he was the first monarch since Queen Anne to have been born in England. 'The omens seemed unreservedly propitious.'[20] By the time George III came to the throne, however, there were serious fissures between Leicester House, where the Dowager Princess of Wales resided, and a number of prominent Whig grandees previously associated with Stowe. Pitt the Elder, for so long resented by George II, had become the architect of British successes in the Seven Years War. He believed the conflict should be continued and that greater gains were there to be had. George III, influenced by his former tutor and now political prop, John Stuart, earl of Bute, saw things differently. He ascended the throne convinced of the need for Britain to withdraw from the conflict and made it very clear from the outset of his reign that Pitt and Pitt's somewhat unwilling partner, Newcastle, were to take their orders from Bute.[21]

By October 1761, matters had reached a head and that month Pitt and Temple handed in their resignations, largely over the king and Bute's refusal to extend the conflict to Spain. As one of Temple's followers, Wilkes thus also found himself at odds with the new regime's direction of travel, even though Temple advised against falling out with Bute.[22] Wilkes would not be told. Opposition to ending the war and deep suspicion of Bute's true motivation were to be the watchwords of Wilkes's increasingly strident criticism of the new ministry.

Wilkes lost no time in making clear his attitude to the new regime, following the opening of Parliament on 3 November 1761. In the debate on the Commons' address in reply to the king, Wilkes made a clear allusion to Bute in passing 'some censures on the King's speech, which, in the language of Parliament, he said he was authorized to call the speech of the minister; though of what minister he could not tell.'[23] Among the points he made in criticism was the failure to respond to Spanish provocations but the Commons ultimately passed a loyal address without division. The following month, Wilkes was again to the fore, this time speaking over George Cooke's motion for the Commons to have sight of important Spanish papers. According to the account compiled by the duke of Devonshire, Wilkes was second on his feet, following Lord Strange, who had concluded by stating he had 'confidence in the King not in ministers, whoever they are, [who] are split and distracted.'[24] Wilkes's contribution, as recorded by Devonshire, was relatively brief, though as usual it was unreservedly pro-Pitt in tone. He asserted himself in favour of the motion 'not to gratify idle curiosity, but to satisfy the alarms of the people'.[25] Devonshire noted this amounted to 'a panegyric on Mr Pitt'. Cooke's motion was defeated, but by the beginning of the following year, Britain had declared war on Spain.

On 9 March, Wilkes made his debut as a political pamphleteer with the publication of the not very snappily titled, *Observations on the Papers relative to the Rupture with Spain, laid before both Houses of Parliament on Friday the Twenty-ninth Day of January, 1762, by His Majesty's Command*.[26] The pamphlet, released anonymously as 'a letter from a Member of Parliament to a Friend in the Country', was written as an unwavering defence of Pitt in response to George Grenville's production of material laid before Parliament explaining the background to the declaration of war. Unlike his brother Temple and brother-in-law Pitt, Grenville had chosen to remain with the ministry. He retained his place as treasurer of the Navy until May when he was promoted secretary of state.

In the *Observations* Wilkes demonstrated many of the features that were to become associated with his style in the *North Briton*. Pitt was lauded as a far-seeing statesman, while Bute's new ministry was dismissed out of hand.[27] Wilkes concluded with hoping that the new ministry would not suffer from 'feeble, procrastinating, and undecided Counsels, founded in Weakness and Duplicity'.[28] He was also unable to resist winding up a rather pompous cleric, Dr John Douglas, by attributing authorship of the pamphlet to him.[29] This was particularly characteristic of Wilkes and was to be something he would do again and again. Wilkes's attack did not go unanswered. The same year at least two anonymous ripostes appeared, countering Wilkes's arguments.[30]

A month after the brouhaha occasioned by his first foray into political journalism, Wilkes was in Winchester with his militia regiment as part of a larger deployment under the command of the earl of Effingham. The majority of the regiment's duties involved guarding prisoners of war. Probably the most action Wilkes saw as a soldier was when some of his troops were involved in chasing and recapturing a handful of French prisoners who had attempted an escape. He reported the incident to his commanding officer, Sir Francis Dashwood, noting that twenty-four of the French had managed to make their way into a large drain late one night. They were safely rounded up, though two of them were shot in the process.[31]

In April he found himself in Reading, attending as one of the board overseeing the court martial of Lieutenant-Colonel John Dodd.[32] One of the other board members noted in the press was 'Captain Gibbons', a minor press error for the historian Edward Gibbon, then serving in the Hampshire militia.[33] He renewed his acquaintance with Wilkes in September, when Gibbon and other officers from his regiment entertained Wilkes at a dinner in Southampton. Gibbon confided to his diary: 'I scarce ever met with a better companion,' in spite of, or rather because of, Wilkes's by then well-known libertine character. Wilkes informed his hosts that 'in this time of public dissension, he was resolved to make his fortune.' He had spotted an opportunity and meant to make the most of it. The evening descended into predictable drunkenness, with Gibbon's colonel and other officers (though Gibbon insisted, not himself) breaking into Wilkes's room and forcing him to down another bottle of claret in bed.[34] The tale has the ring of truth about it. Wilkes enjoyed an evening with the bottle, but even he was probably not quite up to imbibing the quantities downed by army officers.

Winchester was close enough to London to mean that Wilkes was able to divide his time between his duties with the militia and attendance in the Commons. He was back in the House on 12 May when he spoke in a debate on the war, triggered by Lord Barrington urging support for Portugal. Barrington spoke first and was then followed by Richard Glover, a former member of 'Cobham's Cubs' who had been elected for Weymouth and Melcombe Regis on the interest of Prince Frederick's man of business, George Bubb Dodington.[35] After Glover had concluded, Wilkes got to his feet. He insisted that he did not do so to oppose Barrington,

> ...being willing to strengthen Administration even in the weak hands it was in at present, But desired to know from these Gentlemen whether the German War was to go on, for he observed a Noble Lord [Granby] who led his Countrymen always to Victory, [had] not yet taken the Field.

He complained that reports seemed contradictory, saying one day that troops were to be brought home and the next that the war was to be pressed on. He concluded by insisting 'the House had to know with Certainty what was so variously talked off [sic].'[36]

It may not have been a particularly noteworthy intervention, but it indicated Wilkes's political thinking at the time. The following month, there was another routine appointment, when he was nominated one of the commissioners for the act for better paving, cleaning and lighting the streets of Westminster.[37] Wilkes may not have represented a London seat, but his house in Great George Street was just a stone's throw from Parliament, so he would have been more than familiar with the area's shortcomings.

Around the time of the composition of the *Observations* Wilkes became acquainted with the larger than life clergyman, schoolmaster and poet, Charles Churchill.[38] Like that of Wilkes himself, Churchill's appearance was captured most memorably by Hogarth, though in Churchill's case Hogarth abandoned all pretence of depicting him as a man and instead represented him as 'The Bruiser', a bear wearing clerical preaching bands holding an overflowing flagon of ale.[39] After years struggling as a not very successful parson and teacher, Churchill had made a name for himself by publishing an epic satire on the state of the London stage.

Wilkes and Churchill struck up what for Wilkes was probably the most important friendship of his life.[40] He had always known himself superior to his brothers, as he had made so obvious to his brother Israel, while Baxter had been more a mentor than friend on equal terms. Potter had been Wilkes's social superior and early guide in libertinism rather than someone with whom he was truly on an equal footing. Now Wilkes was the senior partner in the relationship, and he clearly revelled in the new experience. Closing off one letter he signed himself Churchill's 'heart, head, soul and body – except prick' – they were two of a kind and enjoyed comparing notes on (and sharing) their various amours.[41]

If Wilkes was Churchill's social superior, it was not a wholly uneven relationship. Churchill arguably came from a more establishment background than Wilkes. The son of another clergyman, he had been educated at Westminster School and St John's College, Cambridge. At the former he had made a lifelong friend in another poet and satirist, Robert Lloyd, who was along with William Hogarth a member of the 'Nonsense Club', founded in the 1750s.[42] They in turn introduced Wilkes to other members of London's literary set, who encouraged Wilkes in his early efforts at political journalism.[43]

On 22 May, ten days after his latest major parliamentary intervention, Wilkes published an essay on the subject of royal favourites in *The Monitor*, a pro-Pitt weekly newspaper founded by Richard Beckford.[44] It was the first in a concerted campaign Wilkes was to wage against Bute, who was on the verge of appointment as Prime Minister. A fortnight later, Wilkes's essay was answered in a new government paper, edited by Smollett. The paper was called *The Briton* and had been established as a way for the Bute administration to counter the attacks of the opposition in print. Unfortunately for Bute, while Smollett was a talented writer, he found quickly that defending an administration was infinitely harder than attacking one. Probably his heart was not really in it either, as Smollett admired Pitt, having previously dedicated a work to him.[45]

The *North Briton*

On the same day that the *Briton* made its first appearance, the public were greeted with another new weekly paper. The *North Briton*, a canting term for Scotland, entitled so deliberately to mock its rival, was owned, edited and part-authored by Wilkes. He would continue to pen contributions to *The Monitor* until the end of October.[46] But the *North Briton* increasingly took over Wilkes's attention and it would go on to change his life. At its height, the paper had a circulation of 2,000 copies, far outstripping its ministerial rival.

The opening sentence of issue number one neatly summarized one of the major causes that would continue to dominate Wilkes's career:

> The liberty of the press is the birth-right of a BRITON, and is justly esteemed the firmest bulwark of the liberties of this country. It has been the terror of all bad ministers; for their dark and dangerous designs, or their weakness, inability, and duplicity, have thus been detected and shewn to the public, generally in too strong and just colours for them long to bear up against the odium of mankind.[47]

The article then continued to highlight the dangers of government by a Stuart, highlighting none-too-subtly one of Bute's major political weak points (his full name being John Stuart, 3rd earl of Bute). While Bute's identity as a Stuart was a gift to Wilkes, the assault on Bute came from various directions. Principally, there was 'familiar language of xenophobic patriotism', inveighing against Bute because of his Scottishness. In doing so, Wilkes was tapping into a vigorous suspicion of all things Scots and the long tradition in England of complaining about impoverished adventurers from north of the border displacing Englishmen.[48] The duke of Bolton, a friend of Lord Temple's, who was also to become one of Wilkes's aristocratic supporters, betrayed his own anti-Scottishness over a competition for the post of steward to the dean and chapter of Winchester. The candidates for the job were a Mr Yalden, sponsored by Bolton, and a Mr Duthy, whom Bolton decried partly for his Scottishness but also because, as he recounted 'I remember him a footman and a Roman Catholick.'[49] Anti-Scottishness was not the only rich vein mined by Wilkes. There was also a line of attack developed against Bute as the supposed lover of the Dowager Princess of Wales. Here, Bute was equated to earlier favourites. Isabella and Mortimer were called to mind, as was Charles I's intimate, the 1st duke of Buckingham.[50] It would prove a particularly successful mode of assault and helped inspire protests in the streets with people parading jackboots (for Bute) and petticoats (for the princess). The fact that there was almost certainly nothing in the story did not trouble Wilkes in the slightest. He simply insisted, 'It will make excellent North Briton!'[51]

Time and again Wilkes would return to his suspicion of the inimical designs of the Scots on the government of Britain, but he also revisited old arguments from the previous century, so familiar in Whig circles, of the dangers apparent to the Revolution Settlement. Indeed, one of Wilkes's earliest publications had been on John Hampden, one of the great parliamentarian leaders of the early 17th century. Hampden had stood out against Charles I over ship money and gone on to serve in the army of parliament in the Civil War, before being cut down in a skirmish in 1643. Wilkes considered Hampden a personal hero – the more so as Hampden had been MP for Buckinghamshire, and Wilkes also represented a constituency within the county.[52] However, if Wilkes was genuinely attached to the memory of Hampden, and to the defence of the Revolution, he was also more than willing to bend the truth, or rather to embroider the truth with falsehood, in order to get his message across. A saying attributed to him was: 'Give me a grain of truth and I will mix it up with a great mass of falsehood so that no chemist will ever be able to separate them.'[53]

One thing that it is easy to forget is that the launching of the *North Briton* all happened while Wilkes continued to be torn between his duties in London and his role as colonel of militia down in Hampshire. Wilkes was frequently on the road, travelling between Winchester, his house in Aylesbury and back to his residence in Westminster. It spoke to his nervous energy but also his astonishing organisational abilities. Throughout his life, Wilkes compiled detailed address books, noting the people he met and occasionally jotting down additional small details about them. Such aides-mémoire must have been invaluable for someone who spent so much time on his way to somewhere else.

Issue one of the *North Briton* was released on Saturday 5 June 1762. The following Saturday, issue two was published, opening in a similarly provocative vein:

> I cannot conceal the joy I feel as a North Briton, and I heartily congratulate my dear countrymen on our having at length accomplished the great, long sought, and universally natural object of our wishes, the planting of a Scotsman at the head of the English Treasury.[54]

The paper's conceit was that the author was a fellow Scotsman with Bute, by which Wilkes was able to poke fun at his victim while apparently lauding his advancement. A few issues later he dropped the mask and simply gave vent to his opinions openly. Three days after the release of issue two, Wilkes was in Winchester, corresponding with his partner Churchill on the next edition. The letter revealed much of the hecticness of Wilkes's life at the time and he apologised to Churchill that 'no contrivance of mine wou'd answer till now to send you' the draft manuscript. He asked him to 'add, subtract, multiply and divide it, as you like.' Wilkes meanwhile had sent a copy to William Johnston (he spelled the name Johnson), a bookseller in Ludgate Street, who would then send Churchill proofs. Johnston also fulfilled the important role of advising the two on whether what they were proposing to publish was libellous.[55] Issue four of 26 June continued the theme of attacking the Scots, pretending to delight in Bute's advancement as it would mean many more of his countrymen would benefit from his patronage.

If Wilkes was absurdly busy, charging between his troops, Aylesbury and London along with occasional forays to Medmenham for drinking and sex, Churchill was beginning to reveal his tendency to leave things to the last minute. On 13 July, with issue seven due in four days, he wrote to Wilkes to alert him to the fact that he had not 'wrote a Letter of it, according to my usual maxim of putting everything off till the last'. He assured Wilkes, though, 'of its being done in time; I have the cause too much at heart to let it be out of my head.' Wilkes, meanwhile, continued to produce his own copy for the paper, writing on 27 July from Winchester that he had 'sent a strong North Briton for next Saturday' and asking Churchill to undertake any necessary corrections.[56]

In the midst of hammering out a weekly opposition newspaper, Wilkes and Churchill's friendship continued to develop. Wilkes had by now firmly taken on Potter's mantle. There was the same impatience when Churchill would not drop everything and join him at Aylesbury whenever he felt the need for company. If Churchill was damnably unreliable, he clearly enjoyed the times they spent together. At some point around the turn of August into September, Churchill was crammed into a stagecoach on his way back to London from a few days at Aylesbury and clearly not relishing the experience. He was squeezed between 'One Old Woman, who having [never se]en London, expects me to give her an account of the plea[sur]es of it, and another full as old who never designing to see it entertains me with the superior pleasures of the Country.' As if this was not annoying enough, they were then joined by a Frenchman, who annoyed Churchill so much that he insisted he would pay for his dinner 'if he will hold his tongue'. He concluded, 'to leave you was Hell – but to leave you for such Company is a Hell which none but a Scotchman can deserve...'[57]

Not long after this visit, Churchill was struck down with a bout of ill health, which turned out to be the result of his sexual activities. Wilkes demonstrated perhaps surprising dedication in seeking out news of his friend and collaborator. In a letter of 9 September, he mentioned to Churchill that he had written him three letters as well as calling at his house in London, but was still anxious to know how he was faring. His anxiety may have been the more pronounced because he also informed Churchill that Hogarth had 'begun the attack today'. Not content with attempting to get its message across through the *Briton*, the Bute ministry had also turned to Britain's most famous artist and satirist. On 7 September, so two days before Wilkes's letter, Hogarth had published a satirical print called *The Times*. It depicted Bute as a heroic lone firefighter fending off a blaze in the heart of London, while Pitt was lampooned for his role in feeding the flames.[58] Wilkes had got wind of what Hogarth was planning a few weeks before. On 29 August he was aware of at least some of the details of Hogarth's composition, knowing for example that he was not featured himself.[59] However, as Hogarth had 'abus'd my dear friends Pitt and Lord Temple' he intended to return the favour in print. Via a couple of friends he also let Hogarth know 'that such a proceeding would not only be unfriendly in the highest degree, but extremely injudicious'. Hogarth ignored the warning and pressed ahead, only pausing to respond that neither Wilkes nor Churchill were depicted in the piece. This did not satisfy Wilkes, who let him know 'if his friends were attacked, he should then think that he was wounded in the most sensible part' and would feel obliged to weigh in in their defence.[60]

This was not the only time when Wilkes made a point of responding even when he was not the subject of attack. On another occasion he remarked to Kearsley how the government paper, *The Auditor*, had been printing material relating to a trial for criminal conversation involving Lord Temple. He reckoned the paper was becoming 'foolishly civil' and resolved to 'trim him, and his old Master Fox' (Henry Fox, later Lord Holland).[61]

Hogarth was by now in his mid-sixties with just two years left. His intervention attracted a full counter-attack by Wilkes and Churchill, the latter delighted at the prospect of having a true heavyweight to joust with, even if he thought *The Times* far short of Hogarth's best works. One mutual friend, the actor David Garrick, begged Churchill to reconsider but was ignored.[62] The response, which seems to have been a joint effort between Wilkes and Churchill, came accordingly on 25 September in *North Briton* issue seventeen.[63] The paper was devoted to a vicious attack on the elderly Hogarth and was then followed by further assaults as others joined in. Wilkes lamented that Hogarth had chosen to abandon his proper calling as a moral satirist, for which he praised him, and had instead wandered into party politics, where he now appeared ridiculous.[64]

The assault on Hogarth was sustained, personal and very effective. The following month, thoroughly unprepared for the barbs he had attracted, Hogarth collapsed and it was thought was unlikely to survive for long.[65] To his credit, Wilkes expressed heart-felt regret. Hogarth lived just long enough to have a final revenge on Wilkes by devising one of the most famous satires of the entire period.[66]

A month before Wilkes launched his assault on Hogarth, he had taken aim at a rather more elevated figure at court. Earl Talbot, son of a Walpolean lord chancellor, hailed from a cadet branch of the old noble family, representatives of which had included one of the heroes of the Hundred Years' War and, more recently, Charles Talbot, duke of Shrewsbury.[67] The latter had been one of the 'Immortal Seven' who signed the letter of invitation to William of Orange, helping to trigger the Glorious Revolution and, latterly, was the final holder of the office of lord high treasurer of England.[68] Talbot was rather less impressive than either of these distant forebears. Nevertheless, he held a significant court office as lord steward: the officer in charge of the royal household below the stairs. Talbot had come to prominence during the coronation when his horse refused to behave itself, and this offered Wilkes an irresistible opportunity to poke fun in issue twelve, published on 21 August 1762.[69] The issue was dedicated to criticising all of those in receipt of 'pensions' from the court, the heading stating boldly: 'Pensions, which reason to the worthy gave,/Add fresh dishonour to the fool and knave.'[70]

Talbot was far from being the only person attacked by Wilkes in the issue. Samuel Johnson was subjected to the *North Briton*'s by now well-known style of attack. The earl of Lichfield, a former Jacobite turned court supporter, prominent in Oxfordshire politics, was another to be singled out. After Lichfield, the paper moved onto the 'sixteen': the clutch of Scots nobles elected every parliament from among the body of the Scots peerage to serve as 'representative peers', according to the terms of the 1707 Treaty of Union. Then Wilkes turned to Talbot or, more properly, to Talbot's horse. Goading Talbot for the embarrassment of the coronation mix-up, Wilkes's jibed: 'Caligula's horse had not half the merit. We remember how nobly he was provided for.' The Roman emperor, Gaius Caligula had reputedly planned to appoint his favourite horse a senator. After further jokes at Talbot's expense regarding his horsemanship, Wilkes then proceeded to criticise recent reforms of the royal household, before concluding the section: 'I sincerely venerate his lordship's great abilities, and deeply regret that they are not employed by government in a way more confidential, more suited to his manly character.'

Just when Talbot read the paper is uncertain, but it took him over a fortnight to respond. On 10 September he wrote seeking out the author of the offending passage. Wilkes responded in characteristic fashion, asking first by what right Talbot claimed 'to catechise me about an anonymous paper' but also offering him 'any other satisfaction becoming me as a gentleman'. A series of letters then passed between the two; Talbot insisting Wilkes confess to being the author and Wilkes refusing to give him that satisfaction. Efforts at mediation by Lord Temple failed to calm matters down, with the result that Wilkes found himself waited on by Norborne Berkeley, a fellow MP, acting as Talbot's second. On 30 September Wilkes wrote to Berkeley from Winchester offering to make himself available on Tuesday 5 October, at the Red Lion at Bagshot, though Wilkes expected them not to exchange shots until early on the morning of the 6th.[71]

On the afternoon of Wednesday the 6th, Wilkes dashed off a brief letter to Churchill: 'I have seen and fought Lord Talbot. I long to give you the particulars. I shall continue in great George Street till to-morrow morning.'[72]

The affair had not quite come off as Wilkes had expected. At three in the afternoon of the previous day, he had arrived at Bagshot with his own second, named Harris, his adjutant in the Buckinghamshire militia. At five they were told that Talbot and Berkeley had arrived. Berkeley made it plain that Talbot wanted the matter dealt with at once, while Wilkes had anticipated the foursome sitting down to a civilised supper and then fighting early next morning. It was a way of averting suspicion, if the others in the inn assumed the party to be there for a friendly meeting. Duelling was, after all, illegal. Wilkes certainly seems to have been wrong-footed by Talbot's approach. He objected that he had not expected fighting until the next day and had some business to attend to first. Moreover, he claimed to have come straight from Medmenham, where he had been up carousing until four in the morning. If word got out that Talbot had fought him while still drunk, he pointed out, it would not look good for Talbot. Berkeley likewise stuck to his guns, telling Wilkes that he had merely been requested to bring Wilkes and Talbot together and suggested that the two of them sort it out.

When Wilkes was shown into Talbot's room, he found his opponent, as he put it in a letter describing the affair to Temple, 'in an agony of passion'. Talbot began at once harping on in the same mode as in his letters to Wilkes. Did he write issue twelve? Wilkes repeated his line. Why did Talbot keep accusing him of being the author of an anonymous piece? Talbot proposed fighting that evening; Wilkes preferred the following morning. When Wilkes suggested they fight in the room, Talbot accused Wilkes of trying to murder him. Wilkes would be hanged if he killed him, Talbot insisted. Wilkes surmised that Talbot was evidently already in possession of a royal pardon and that he was clearly in danger whichever way the bout worked out.[73] In the end, a compromise was arrived at. Talbot allowed Wilkes time to write the letters he needed to, including one to Temple arranging for Polly's upbringing should he not survive. They then left the inn just before seven in the evening and found a place on Bagshot Heath where they would not be interrupted. Wilkes noted that 'the moon shone brightly' – possibly a piece of poetic licence as the sun can only have gone down half an hour before. With the seconds refereeing, the two stood eight yards apart and on Harris's command each fired their pistols. Both missed. With honour satisfied, Wilkes walked up to Talbot and admitted authorship of the paper. Talbot, calm at last, was said to have admitted Wilkes to be 'the noblest fellow God had ever made' and suggested they all return to the inn and share a bottle of claret. After they had done so, Berkeley and Harris set out back for Winchester and Talbot to Windsor. Wilkes stayed behind, waiting for his manservant, and filled the time by writing an account to Temple. Berkeley, he claimed, had apologised for Talbot's behaviour and commended him for his 'coolness and courage'.[74]

While the account of the duel was Wilkes's own, and thus no doubt carefully couched to his own advantage, there can be no doubt that his first foray into the world of duelling did him little harm. Quite the reverse, it established him as a man of genuine courage who had more than held his own on the field of honour. Indeed, in contrast to the less than dignified earl who was said to have spouted 'a Torrent of Billingsgate' before the affair was over, he came across as far the more gentlemanly of the two.[75] This was important, as it formed a significant stage in Wilkes's continuing development from distiller's son to gentleman. While every effort had been made to keep the argument secret before the combatants met, now it was over – and no one harmed – the duel was gossiped about widely.

If Wilkes emerged from the affair with some credit, his activities were beginning to test the patience of his patron, Temple. On 10 October Temple wrote to his sister, Lady Chatham (wife of Pitt the Elder) complaining about the cleft stick in which he found himself: 'Because Wilkes professes himself a friend of mine, I am for ever represented infamously as a patron of what I disapprove, and wish I could have put an end to.'[76] Despite Temple's private misgivings, Wilkes was welcomed back at Stowe in the aftermath of the duel before heading back to his duties in Winchester. From there he wrote to Churchill boasting of how his prowess was beginning to have some very welcome unlooked-for advantages. Berkeley, he explained, had spread the news of the duel 'so much that I am surfeited with caresses.' Better still, a 'sweet girl' he had his eye on for months 'now tells me she will trust her *honour* to a man who takes so much care of his own.'[77] It has been speculated that this 'sweet girl' might have been the future wife of the wealthy city merchant, John Barnard.[78] While the timing is suggestive, though, the geography is not. Wilkes and Jane Barnard (as she became) began their liaison 'at Blackheath at Grace Ozier's', which seems too far off from Winchester to be very likely. More plausibly, then, this was one of any number of conquests Wilkes was to chalk up in the course of his career.[79] Meanwhile, Wilkes continued to be lauded in polite society for his conduct in the duel with Talbot. In a letter of 23 October, Churchill reported that Viscount Weymouth 'gives you the greatest Encomiums', while the members of the Beef Steak asked after him 'with the greatest zeal'.[80]

That said, not everyone viewed the duel in quite that way. At some point soon after the duel at least two satires were published relating to the event. One, a caricature dubbed The Bagshot Frolick, or the Pot-lid and the Ink horn, depicted Wilkes and Talbot facing each other across a screen, Wilkes backed by Churchill and Talbot by Smollett.[81] In another, an anonymous broadside producer printed a new song – B[AGSHOT] H[EATH] OR, THE MODERN DUEL, which was to be sung to the popular tune of Chevy Chase.[82] It portrayed both men, Wilkes under the guise of Squire Witful and Talbot as Lord Edifice, as comic figures, eager to fight at first but then transfixed with fear through the interposition of the goddess Pallas (Athena). The song made much of the fact that they had chosen not to fight with swords, preferring pistols which they were then able to discharge into the air. It may not have presented Wilkes as he would have liked, as a brave gentleman, happy to take the field of honour, but the sketch at the top of the sheet must have been one of the earliest representations of someone who was soon to be one of the most famous people in the country. Given the ructions Wilkes was to cause subsequently with his pen, it concluded presciently:

> God prosper long our King and Queen,
> Our Commoners and Peers;
> And let all Scribblers cease to set
> The Nation by the Ears.

Against the Government

While Wilkes continued to live off his new-found fame as a duellist, the *North Briton* persisted in its attacks on the government. It pressed on with assailing the ministry as well as individuals at Court that Wilkes and Churchill deemed most in need of humbling. Lord Lichfield came in for further abuse. This was in spite of (or perhaps because of) an apparent effort on his part to make peace with his tormentor. Wilkes noted in a letter of 23 November how Lichfield had come to him at court 'and entered into a good deal of chat in his usual easy manner'.[83] Temple professed himself unsurprised at Lichfield's conduct, observing 'I thought it impossible he could take that matter up in our house' (the Lords).[84] Lichfield was later dissuaded from launching legal action when Wilkes suggested to him that he was more than willing to settle the matter as he had with Talbot.[85] This then freed Wilkes to poke fun at him twice more, in issues thirty-two and thirty-seven.

Besides attacking the likes of Lichfield, the paper also mounted a strident defence of prominent opposition politicians, in particular Pitt. On 21 November, Temple wrote to Wilkes addressing the letter to my dear Marcus Cato (on another occasion he was 'my dear Senator'). He praised the latest issue, twenty-five, a strident defence of Pitt, which he reckoned 'unanswerable, as it is founded in stubborn facts, which cannot be controverted.' This came only a week after Temple had written to him far more cautiously, advising him: '…weigh your own conduct very maturely. You have to deal with a very strange world.'[86] His concern was not without foundation. If Lichfield was unwilling to risk annoying Wilkes unduly, members of the administration were increasingly eager to close down some of the more egregious assaults in the press. On 18 November, a general warrant had been issued on the orders of Lord Halifax, one of the secretaries of state, with the aim of closing down the *North Briton*. He had recently taken similar action against *The Monitor*. While his actions did not scare Wilkes or Churchill, it was more than enough to put the frighteners on William Richardson, who had printed issues one to twenty-five. On 24 November, the day before the new session of Parliament was to commence, Wilkes wrote to Churchill telling him of Richardson's decision to quit the work while also drawing up plans for the next issue, 'for fear our new printer shou'd not be ready at so short a warning.' Issue twenty-six was overseen by a stopgap printer, but one of his employees was then also threatened by the government, prompting the unfortunate man to plead ill health 'to avoid printing the paper'.[87] Wilkes and Churchill then managed to recruit a new printer, Richard Balfe, who was willing to take the risk and would go on to produce the remaining issues.[88]

The same day that Wilkes was telling Churchill about Richardson's unwillingness to continue, he attended the pre-sessional meeting, where MPs were offered an opportunity to deliberate on the king's speech in advance of parliament meeting. One of those present was Edmund Burke, who found himself sitting next to Wilkes, 'a capital enemy'.[89] Parliament gathered the next day with one clear item on the agenda: peace. Over the summer negotiations had been undertaken by the principal parties in the war that had begun back in 1756 and seen Britain achieve some of its most spectacular victories – notably the fall of Quebec in 1759, the so-called 'Year of Victories'. The peace terms proposed were, unsurprisingly, not to everyone's taste and Britain was asked to relinquish a number of claims in return for a speedier cessation of hostilities. For the king and Bute, this was a sacrifice worth making. For others, Pitt at the head of them, this was a betrayal. Bute, moreover, was increasingly panicky, uncomfortable in his role as prime minister, and insisted that the peace terms should be agreed to by parliament. Writing to Wilkes on the 25th, Temple queried the relative strengths in both Houses. He reckoned fifty in the Lords and 150 in the Commons supported the opposition.[90]

Until the peace was completed formally, hostilities continued. In mid-October, with the new session still a month off, one pro-Bute MP, John Campbell, reported back to his wife from London:

> I entirely agree with you that it is a shocking thing for British and French to be knocking one another on the head in Germany if Peace is so nigh as reported. How right it is I cannot say, but am satisfied Lord Bute will make Peace very soon, if he is allow'd to do so, and is not hinder'd by the Malice of some, the Madness & folly of Many and the Cowardice, & selfish fears of others.[91]

The degree of tension present at Court over the peace terms was indicated when the duke of Devonshire, a pre-eminent Whig grandee and former Prime Minister, refused to attend a cabinet meeting to discuss the administration's plans.[92] The king took it as a personal slight and ejected Devonshire from the privy council.[93] A contemporary (likely George Bussy Villiers, Viscount Villiers) recorded the event emphasizing the extent to which Devonshire had been blanked. On 8 November, Devonshire was said to have gone 'up the back stairs' at St James's seeking an audience with the king, but George 'would not see him'. Instead, Devonshire went to the house of Lord Egremont, one of the secretaries of state, where he handed over his insignia of office. Four days later at a meeting of the privy council, the king 'called for the list of Privy Counsellors & scratched his [Devonshire's] name out'.[94]

Alienating Devonshire was not a sensible move. As Paul Langford has emphasized, the duke was 'imbued with good sense and judgement; he was no pawn of the Pelhams, nor was he overly impressed with Pitt.' Crucially, also, he had 'had no animus against either the King or Bute initially'. Between them, both George and Bute managed to infuriate

Devonshire, the one with his ignorant naïveté, the other with his tendency to offer dressings down to people much more elevated than himself. George's decision to cut Devonshire out had not come out of the blue, but it was ill-advised for all of that.[95] Devonshire's removal gave Newcastle and others the excuse they had been looking for to seek new alliances and patch up old ones. While neither Newcastle nor the 'great commoner', Pitt, were particularly fond of each other, the prospect of a Newcastle-Pitt alliance threatened serious consequences for the king and Bute. Devonshire had noted in his diary that together they could 'easily get the better of a Favourite'.[96]

All of this was, of course, grist to the *North Briton*'s mill, and while Wilkes and Churchill negotiated the difficulties coming their way from an increasingly belligerent administration, Wilkes took soundings from his political patrons. On 2 December 1762 he reported to Churchill that he had 'pass'd three hours to-day in Pitt's bed-chamber at Hays [*sic*] – He talks as you write – as no other man ever did or cou'd'.[97] It was to be a significant few days. Even though Henry Fox was confident of getting the government's business through the Commons, Bute's nerve failed him and he asked the king to accept his resignation. He had been jostled by the crowd on his way to the opening of Parliament on 25 November and was convinced that he was about to be assassinated. For the king, their work was only half complete. They were on the point of achieving peace, but there was still the not inconsiderable challenge of 'purging out corruption'. So, although the preliminaries were eventually agreed in mid-December by a majority of 164, there were storm clouds on the horizon. Soon after the vote, office-holders who had not toed the party line were turned out in what came to be known as 'the Massacre of the Pelhamite Innocents', as so many of them were close associates of the duke of Newcastle. None of this was disposed to make a pusillanimous man like Bute feel much safer. For the time being he limped on (he would remain in office until the next April) but his heart was no longer in it. In January 1763 he was to declare 'The angel Gabriel could not at present govern this country but by means too long practised and such as my soul abhors.'[98]

While the great officers of state jostled for position, Wilkes and Churchill continued to hammer out a *North Briton* each week. Wilkes also pressed on with his hectic schedule. There were plans to be at a meeting of the Shakespeare Club on 6 December, a somewhat mysterious grouping that may have also included the earl of Sandwich among its members.[99] Wilkes and Churchill's correspondence also continued to reveal their friendly, jesting relationship. A letter from Wilkes on 12 December asking when he was next to see him was answered by Churchill on the same day, responding 'not so soon as I could wish.'

Poor health – caused by another bout of venereal disease – seems to have been the reason as he explained, 'My teeth begin to loosen but yet I think they could bite the proud Scot,' referring to the ongoing campaign against Bute. Wilkes followed up with a letter next day, sympathising that 'the Lord has visited you in David's way, or if you are more classical than divinical, in Dido's way,' before going on to quote a section of the *Aeneid*. He explained that he was to be at Reading in a few days to 'give the Militia a farewell drink'.[100]

The early months of 1763 found Wilkes and Churchill maintaining their campaign against the Bute administration, chalking up ever more attacks on prominent politicians and their associations. Bute's identification both as a Scot and a Tory continued to be targeted without mercy. In issue number thirty-three of 15 January the paper proclaimed clearly: 'Shew me a TORY, and I will shew you a JACOBITE.'[101] The increasingly vituperative tone may in part have been prompted by a degree of desperation in those opposed to the peace treaty. According to one of the duke of Bedford's correspondents, who had found the House of Commons remarkably quiescent on the subject, Wilkes had confessed to him the challenge it was posing. According to this source, Wilkes said, 'If what he had heard of it was true, it was the damn'dest peace for the Opposition that ever was made.'[102] In this atmosphere, *North Briton* number thirty-nine of 26 February zeroed in on William Beckford, the Jamaican-born London politician. Previously an opponent of Bute, Beckford was thought to be changing tack which had attracted the *North Briton*'s attention.[103]

How often Wilkes and Churchill were able to see one another at this point is unclear. Wilkes certainly demonstrated his familiar impatience when they were much apart, writing on 8 March how he was 'impatient' to see Churchill 'and to submit to you my feeble productions'.[104] Perhaps more importantly for him, Wilkes wanted Churchill back on form as he was planning a trip to France at the end of the month. It was one of the happy circumstances of the recent peace, which Wilkes opposed of course, that travel between Britain and France had become much more straightforward. On 14 March he wrote assuring Churchill that he was dealing with his partner's financial problems – as well as sorting out his own – 'that we may neither of us want money in the other kingdom.'[105]

Meanwhile, the *North Briton* continued to goad Bute and his supporters. Through March there was a spirited attack on the unpopular Cider Bill and Wilkes also poked fun at the favourite by reviving tales that Bute was having an affair with the king's mother. The latter was by means of a dedication appended to an old play of Ben Jonson's, *The Fall of Mortimer*, detailing the relationship between Edward III's queen and

Roger Mortimer. Issue forty-two attacked members of the administration who had gained through stock-jobbing.[106]

Wilkes was also attempting to maintain his profile in the Commons. It was not just through his journalistic enterprise that he aimed to hold the administration's boots to the fire. On 18 March the duke of Newcastle wrote to Lord Hardwicke to discuss a scheme Wilkes had come up with. His aim was to 'move the House, that the names of the subscribers, upon the last loan, might be laid before the House, in order to observe upon the Immense Profit of it.' Newcastle explained that Temple had already called on him to discuss Wilkes's motion, Temple appearing to have adopted it 'as a Thought of his own'. Newcastle's view was that the matter needed to be considered carefully, but tellingly, both he and Temple agreed that Wilkes was 'the last Man in the House, who should make such a Motion.' They favoured instead someone of 'great Weight and Credit' like Sir George Savile.[107] Useful as a disruptor Wilkes may have been, but more cautious (irresolute some might have said) political figures like the duke were wary of unleashing him on such sensitive topics within Parliament.

Wilkes's preparations for his French trip were dealt a blow just days before departure when Churchill wrote to say that he could not join him. Typically, Churchill was unable to give an absolute undertaking: 'If I can, you may expect me to morrow with a Paper in my hand; if I cannot, depend on my care of the N.B. till your return.' Wilkes did not hide his annoyance. 'Your letter has vex'd me more than I can tell you: for I had built on the happiness of passing 3 weeks with you.' He bequeathed to Churchill in his absence the sole management of the *North Briton*, but cautioned him not to attack his old comrade from his Leiden days, Charles Townshend, recently appointed head of the Board of Trade, 'for reasons too long to give you'. Instead, he wanted Churchill to concentrate on 'the East India business, & Lord Clive'. As usual, the angle was to be an assault on Bute for interfering in the Company's affairs. He referred Churchill to the Worcester MP John Walsh, Clive's secretary and consequently a staunch supporter of Clive and the East India Company.[108] Walsh would later return the favour by voting with the opposition for Wilkes over expelling him from the Commons.

Wilkes may have emphasized the pleasure he had been anticipating of a few weeks on the continent with Churchill, but the ostensible purpose of the trip was to settle his thirteen-year-old daughter Polly in Paris, where she was being sent to continue her education under a tutor named Madame Carpentier. He had mentioned the scheme to Dell back in February, noting that Polly was 'much delighted with the future idea of Paris'.[109] Wilkes would continue to indulge her with regular seasons on the continent for the rest of his life.

It is not possible to underestimate the extent to which Wilkes was attached to Polly. Throughout his struggles with the administration, king and legal system, he always had time for her. Her needs were foremost in his mind and whenever she was involved in a falling out or a misunderstanding, he always took her side.[110] Immediately before his duel with Lord Talbot, he had insisted on taking time to write letters arranging for Polly's care should he not survive. Later in life he would redecorate the house they shared with bewildering frequency to ensure that it was pleasing to her. They maintained a steady correspondence throughout his life and if he elided carefully certain details of his goings on, it was for the most part an honest one. Thus, from Dover on 27 March, he wrote to Churchill, letting him know that he was 'recovering my good humour, which I had lost at the disappointment of your not being with us on this tour – The heavens, and my little girl ... both smile upon me.' He then went on to remind Churchill to speak to Walsh, before instructing him to write to him while he was away '*in French*, that you may get on a little in the Language.' He had lost none of the patronising superiority he had formerly directed at his older brother.[111]

Without Churchill to distract him, Wilkes seems to have concluded that he no longer needed the full three weeks he had originally intended to spend in France, though he was in Paris long enough to dine three times with the British ambassador, the duke of Bedford.[112] By 9 April he was back at Calais awaiting a boat home. From there, he wrote to Polly underscoring what he expected of her while she was in Paris. He insisted that, health-permitting, she should always be sure to attend the ambassador's chapel on Sundays. He also wanted her to find out from Richard Neville Aldworth, Bedford's secretary, 'about the dancing-master belonging to the court. He mentioned him to me, and he is the only man for you to learn of.' Commending her for her 'excellent genius given you from heaven' her enjoined her to cultivate it and, above all, to read Boileau, Racine, Molière, Shakespeare, Pope and Swift. 'You cannot read them ... too often.'[113]

It was while he was waiting for his passage home that news reached Wilkes of Bute's resignation. Lord Villiers noted 'His ill health is pleaded as the excuse,' but no one would have believed that.[114] Bute had been begging the king for permission to quit for some time, though when he applied to step down in March and recommended Henry Fox to replace him, the king was still taken aback. He refused to countenance Fox's promotion, explaining to Bute "Tis not prejudice but aversion to his whole mode of government.'[115] Nevertheless, against all his instincts the king allowed Bute to offer Fox the Treasury. He was heartily relieved when Fox turned the job down, recommending instead George Grenville. For the king, this was not much better. He had complained to Bute in mid-March that 'Grenville has thrown away the game he had two years ago.'[116] Unlike Fox, Grenville was, though, willing to take on the burden. So, after a hiatus of around a week following Bute's resignation on 8 April, Wilkes's old Buckinghamshire companion succeeded as prime minister, inheriting a host of problems left to him by Bute.[117]

Where did this leave Wilkes and the *North Briton*? Wilkes had set out for France entrusting management of the paper to Churchill, who had dutifully continued to publish issues each Saturday, grinding away at the regime. The next issue, Number forty-five, was due to be published on 9 April, but Bute's resignation interrupted it. Although there was a paper all ready to go, it was decided not to run with it and on 13 April Wilkes published an open letter explaining that the *North Briton* would pause production while they assessed the new administration. 'The Scottish minister' as he dubbed Bute may have retired but, 'Is his influence at an end?'[118] That there were already signs that Wilkes was beginning to have influence at a national political level was also indicated by reports coming out of Essex, where a by-election was due in the borough of Maldon. One observer believed that much of the opposition fomented there sprang from 'that ingenious gentleman Mr Wilkes and his crew'.[119] As to what Bute's fall would mean, for Wilkes the answer came all too soon when the king delivered his speech bringing the parliamentary session to a close on 19 April.

In fact, Wilkes had already seen a draft of the address before the king gave it. Grenville had delivered a copy to his brother, Earl Temple, as part of their discussions about his re-election to Buckingham after accepting office. Temple then cheerfully shared it with Wilkes, who was thus able to make a head-start on the next issue of the *North Briton*.[120] Four days after the session closed, on Saturday 23 April, North *Briton* number forty-five was published. Only the day before, a prosecution against the paper had been launched in the court of king's bench by Peregrine Cust, MP for Bishop's Castle and brother to the Speaker of the Commons, 'for some words concerning him' in a previous issue.[121] Cust later withdrew his suit and was quickly forgotten. Number forty-five, on the other hand, created an instant sensation. Never exactly restrained, here Wilkes made no effort to hold back, assuring his readers meanwhile that 'All his reasonings have been built on the strong foundation of *facts*.' He blasted the king personally, querying how he had allowed himself 'to give the sanction of his sacred name to the most odious measures, and to the most unjustifiable public declarations'. There was a foreshadowing of what he was soon to argue over his own arrest and the invasion of his property, when he asked: 'Is it to be expected between an insolent Exciseman, and a peer, gentleman, freeholder, or farmer, whose private houses are now made liable to be entered and searched at pleasure?' Most provocatively, though, he appeared to call on his fellow Englishmen to rise up: 'A nation as sensible as the English, will see that a spirit of concord, when they are oppressed, means a tame submission to injury, and that a spirit of liberty ought then to arise ... in proportion to the weight of the grievance they feel.'

The mismanagement (as Wilkes saw it) of the peace treaties, most of all the abandonment of Prussia, was criticized without restraint and he revisited his abiding leitmotif of the danger of Stuart-style absolutism:

> The Stuart line has ever been intoxicated with the slavish doctrines of the absolute, independent, unlimited power of the crown. Some of that line were so weakly advised as to endeavour to reduce them into practice: but the English nation was too spirited to suffer the least encroachment on the antient liberties of this kingdom.

He concluded by reminding the king that he was only 'the first magistrate of this country'. Wilkes was careful to express the country's satisfaction in the 'amiable' character of their monarch, before noting again the 'general odium' prompted by Bute's example.[122]

It took the administration just three days to respond. The ministers were no doubt heartened by the uncompromising attitude of those like the earl of March, who reckoned Wilkes ought to be put in the pillory for his behaviour.[123] In any case, George Grenville was a very different sort of character to the excitable Bute and was 'sensitive to criticism of his newly installed ministry'.[124] He decided a show of force was appropriate. Following consideration of the legal ramifications of moving against Wilkes, protected as he was by parliamentary privilege, it was decided to round up everyone involved in producing the *North Briton* by means of a general warrant. This would enable the government's agents to seek out and arrest all those they considered responsible for producing the paper. To ensure that Wilkes could not wriggle free, the term 'treasonable' was included, as treason was not covered by privilege. To begin with, the officers targeted the smaller fry: the printers and publishers engaged in producing the paper. By the end of the month, though, they were confident they had enough information to arrest Wilkes too.

On Friday 29 April, ten days after the king had delivered his speech, and six after *North Briton* Number forty-five had first seen the light of day, messengers lay in wait for Wilkes outside his house in Great George Street. A battle royal between Wilkes and the power of the state was about to take place.[125]

5

Wilkes and Liberty

I have never lost sight of the great object of the liberty of the subject at large.

On 10 May 1763 Wilkes wrote from his house in Great George Street to his daughter, Polly, still in Paris. He thanked her for a recent letter, 'which came to my hands in the Tower, and was infinitely the best thing I saw there.' He looked forward to the following month, when he would be able to join her in France for several weeks.[1] In the past few days Wilkes's life had been turned upside down. Through the early 1760s he had steadily built a career for himself in Parliament and without, not least through the fame (or infamy) he achieved through the *North Briton*. But what was to follow through 1763 and thereafter would transform him into a national celebrity.

By the end of the year, few in London can have been ignorant of his appearance or can have failed to have an opinion about him. To the king he was to be 'that devil Wilkes' but for plenty more he was to become a folk hero, goading the establishment with his antics. Wealthy and privileged he may have been, but he became the darling of the crowd and, above all, a self-proclaimed friend of liberty. How truly committed he was to the interests of the masses is highly questionable. Wilkes was, after all, always interested principally in Wilkes. Yet, as one historian has insisted: 'such charges should not obscure the fact that his contribution to the development of British radicalism was considerable. Wilkes showed great skill in bringing fundamental issues before a mass audience and in opening up political debate to the people at large.'[2]

Arrest

One constant in the story of Wilkes and his struggle with the establishment was the number of unforced errors made by the authorities. Their first happened shortly after the nominated king's messengers were despatched to start rounding up suspects just a few days after Number forty-five had been published. They got the wrong men.[3] The foul-up is the more interesting when one considers that all of the men assigned to the task were experienced. Nathan Carrington, the senior messenger, was noted as 'very conversant in affairs of that sort'.[4] He was also quite long in the tooth, having been a messenger since 1728. The three others were James Money, James Watson and Robert Blackmore. Even Blackmore, the most junior of the bunch, had been in post for over a decade. Despite this, they seized Dryden Leach and a number of his employees as a result of misleading information that Wilkes had been seen with him on numerous occasions, even though Leach had only had a hand in printing one earlier issue. Leach subsequently sued Money, Watson and Blackmore for assault and false imprisonment.[5] Under examination, Leach admitted to printing Number twenty-six and even said that he had been offered the chance of printing all of the subsequent numbers 'but declined it'.[6]

At the same time that Leach was taken up, George Kearsley was also arrested. In this case the ministry did get it right. Kearsley was the paper's principal publisher via his bookshop on Ludgate Hill. Three witnesses described him as 'an Elderly Gent', who they believed to be the proprietor of the shop from which they acquired copies of the *North Briton*.[7] Under examination, he quickly offered up Richard Balfe's name as the most recent printer and offered further information that Wilkes had written most of the issues. Kearsley was subsequently offered bail and provided the names of two men willing to act as his sureties for £500.[8] Balfe was in consequence the next to be seized and was actually caught in the act of printing issue forty-six.[9] He in turn dropped Churchill in it, naming him as the other main author.[10]

Balfe was clearly dismayed to have been arrested, having been assured by Wilkes that 'they would not trouble themselves with him'. It must have been unnerving for a city printer to find himself dragged in front of secretaries of state Egremont and Halifax. Under examination, Balfe outlined the intricate process by which Wilkes had set up the paper's production. Both the original manuscript, in Wilkes's hand, and the proofs were returned to Wilkes via 'a poor man' named Leserfe (appropriately enough). He also detailed how Wilkes had convinced him that he had nothing to fear from printing the paper. Wilkes had undertaken to 'stand between him & danger' but also informed him that three lawyers perused each issue before going to press.[11] It certainly chimes with Wilkes's earlier correspondence with Churchill and Kearsley. Writing to the latter, Wilkes had insisted that the copy he was submitting for the press was 'safe, but very teazing'.[12] All of this underscores how aware Wilkes was that he was always treading a fine line.

Balfe's intelligence emboldened Halifax and Egremont to press for Wilkes's arrest. Including Wilkes, a total of forty-nine suspects were taken up during the swoop, showing just how wide a net the government was willing to spread.[13] The ministers received poor advice, though, from the Treasury Solicitor, Philip Carteret Webb, who thought it unnecessary to issue a new warrant in Wilkes's own name. Webb had been instrumental in drawing up the original warrant, something he was probably later to regret. In February 1764, he was brought before Parliament and examined on the issue. When Prime Minister Grenville invited the Commons to decide whether or not to adjourn the session, an irate Pitt rose and insisted he would 'neither live nor sleep till he knew, whether we had a Constitution or not.' And so, the Commons was forced to continue hearing evidence.[14] But all this was for the future. As a result of Webb's decision, it was under the terms of the same general warrant that had been employed to take up the printers that messengers were now despatched to take in Wilkes as well.[15] They were also instructed to seize any papers they found in his house. As the duke of Newcastle reported it to Lord Hardwicke, 'Your old friend Carrington has found a way to beat up Mr Wilkes's headquarters.'[16]

It was thus on the morning of Saturday 30 April that the messengers arrested Wilkes at his house in Great George Street. He was expecting them. Indeed, two of them had posted themselves outside his house the day before, but he had evaded them. He returned home thoroughly plastered after spending the evening roistering with Leach at Blackmore's house. It was normal for suspects to be attached in this way rather than packed off to a formal prison. The party, in fact, was not just Wilkes and Leach but Blackmore himself, who invited his prisoner and guest to join him upstairs for refreshment. He was the more eager that they should do so away from prying eyes as Leach was supposed to be under close confinement.[17] Somehow, Wilkes always had a way of getting people to settle down sociably and make an evening of it, even those supposedly set against him. Of course, by doing so he also laid Blackmore open nicely to a spot of blackmail, should that happen to come in handy.

Wilkes coasted his way home from Blackmore's in the small hours of the 30th. As a sign of just how closely he was following the story, the king reported to Bute that it was 'near 4' when Wilkes returned to his house.[18] Perhaps wary of taking on a man known to be willing to defend his honour, or just reluctant to argue with a drunkard, the waiting messengers decided it was best to let him sleep it off.[19] According to one contemporary diarist, they had been instructed to 'come into his house' at two in the morning 'but would not do it'.[20] Their conduct rather confirmed Egremont's assessment (as reported by the king) that they had 'not been so diligent as they ought to have been'.[21] Wilkes's own later recollection, penned for the benefit of his constituents, claimed 'The most cruel orders were given ... to drag me out of my bed at midnight.' It was only 'a good deal of humanity, and some share of timidity' on the part of the messengers that 'prevented the execution of such ruffian-like commands'.[22] A few hours later, Wilkes continued with his performance. First, in typical Wilkite style, he teased the waiting officers by getting up bright and early, greeted Blackmore cheerfully, who was probably nursing a hangover, and then made off again, claiming that he needed to see his lawyer. In fact, he was seeking out Balfe and what he hoped was a new edition of the *North Briton* (number forty-six). Finding that Balfe had also been arrested, he made an effort to get hold of the proofs and printing frames. He may also have made a point of destroying evidence relating to number forty-five, before returning to his house to deliver himself up.[23] As a result, there was no *North Briton* published on 30 April, as would have otherwise been expected. Another newspaper, reporting the events of 30 April to 3 May noted the omission. It criticized Wilkes, saying that 'Envy, Malice, and Presumption, alone guided his pen.' Of Churchill it merely noted 'he writes for bread.'[24]

Even at this point, Wilkes refused to make things easy for the unfortunate messengers. Watson informed him of their orders to arrest him under the terms of the general warrant, which Wilkes pooh-poohed, reminding him that he was armed and willing to resist. He then invited Watson and the others inside, where he lectured them on the illegality of the warrant. Wilkes was always at his best under pressure. While the messengers were attempting to convince him to accompany them into custody, Churchill stumbled into the room. Without batting an eyelid, Wilkes greeted his collaborator as 'Mr Thompson'. Churchill took the hint and beat a retreat before anyone found out who he really was. Wilkes no doubt meant well towards Churchill, but there may also have been an element of not wishing to share the limelight. He would later demonstrate a similar attitude in France when comparisons were made with the Chevalier d'Eon. Wilkes would insist grumpily that there was no similarity between them.[25]

Meanwhile, the debate with the messengers became a stand-off of about two hours. As more of Wilkes's friends arrived, so too did more officials as the messengers sought further assistance. In the end they informed Wilkes that their orders were to take him by force if necessary. Wilkes claimed to be outraged but probably enjoyed the performance. In any case, there was an important point to him dragging his heels. The tactic gave his friends time to find out what was happening and flock to the house, among them his brother Heaton and Lord Temple. He only agreed to quit the house after he had made sure that his allies knew to go at once to the Court of Common Pleas to demand a writ of *habeas corpus* to secure his immediate release.[26] In his later account, Wilkes insisted that he had been carried before the secretaries 'by violence'.[27] This matched the account provided by the king himself, who said that it had taken nine messengers to get him into a coach to be taken to Lord Halifax's house.[28] A later biographer suggested that it had all been rather more calm and that a sedan chair conveyed Wilkes to the secretaries.[29] No doubt the truth was somewhere in between: Wilkes certainly did not need to take a coach to travel the few yards to Halifax's residence.

Once Wilkes was out of the door, the remaining officers set about breaking open his desks to take whatever papers they could find, much to Temple's disgust. Meanwhile, Wilkes was subjected to a 'good cop, bad cop' routine by Halifax and Egremont. The former tried to show him at least some courtesy and expressed concern that Wilkes had got himself into the predicament. The latter 'was brutal'.[30] Charles Wyndham, 2nd earl of Egremont, had inherited the peerage from his uncle, Charles Seymour, 6th duke of Somerset, known as 'the proud duke'. According to Horace Walpole, he had also inherited his grandfather's self-conceit. By the early summer of 1763 he was not a well man, described some time before that by one contemporary as 'in a confirmed lethargy'.[31] Indeed, this was to be one of his last prominent actions as secretary, as he died of apoplexy at his Piccadilly mansion three months later, just a few days after his fifty-third birthday.[32]

During the interview, Wilkes insisted on his absolute loyalty to the king and emphasized that his beef was with the ministry. He then repeated the tactic he had employed previously with Talbot, by carefully avoiding admitting to authorship of *North Briton* number forty-five. All issues were, after all, published anonymously. Declining to answer questions, he declared that the papers on the table in front of them would remain 'as milk-white' as at the outset of the interview. Less coolly, he threatened to impeach both Halifax and Egremont on the first day of the next parliamentary session. There proceeded a notably unprofitable exchange, mostly between Halifax and Wilkes, with Wilkes sticking to his guns and refusing to loosen his tongue. Realizing that they were getting nowhere, Halifax asked Wilkes whether he would prefer being imprisoned in Newgate or the Tower. Wilkes remained unhelpful, responding, 'The odious idea of restraint is the same odious idea anywhere. I will go where you please.' He could not, though, stop himself from teasing Egremont and asked if he might have the same cell Egremont's father had occupied when he had been sent to the Tower as a suspected Jacobite. If that were not available, he asked only that he should not have a cell previously inhabited by a Scot: 'I have no wish to catch the itch.'[33]

There was, in fact, more to it in the selection of Wilkes's place of restraint than mere verbal jousting between Wilkes and the secretaries.

George Grenville had expressed a desire for Wilkes to be sent to Newgate, but the king informed Bute that he had been advised that MPs were normally sent to the Tower as 'a civility'.[34] In any case, the secretaries' decision to pack Wilkes off breached his first line of defence. This was because a new warrant was issued committing him to prison, invalidating the writ of *habeas corpus*, which his friends had just secured from lord chief justice Pratt, a 'sound, penetrating, and lucid judge' who was allied to Pitt.[35]

News of Wilkes's arrest spread quickly. His friends may have been busily engaged in trying to secure his speedy release, but for those he had offended this was justice at last. Writing on the same day from his London residence in Burlington Street to Lord Milton in Scotland, Bute's brother, James Stuart Mackenzie, took evident pleasure in relating the fall of someone who had been so abusive to their nation and his family. He recorded, mistakenly, that it was Newgate to which Wilkes had been committed but went on to wish fondly, 'May He never come out of that dungeon, but in Procession to the Gibbet! where, in my Conscience, I believe, no man has suffer'd for this twelvemonth past, who was not a more virtuous man, than this same Wilkes.'[36]

Long famed as a prison, the Tower was also, of course, a royal palace and an important part of the defence of London. At one point it was a repository for important state archives as well as being the home to the crown jewels. As a place of incarceration, however, the place was undoubtedly ominous. This was in part because of the long history of executions that had taken place there, along with the mysterious disappearance of the 'princes in the Tower'. But it was also because rooms in the Tower, however well equipped, were notoriously damp and unhealthy. Sir Robert Walpole had been incarcerated there during the reign of Anne and under George I, Robert Harley, earl of Oxford, had spent two years awaiting an impeachment trial. Ultimately acquitted, Oxford's health never recovered from his time there. Two years after Wilkes's incarceration, the same room was used to house Lord Byron while awaiting trial for killing his cousin, William Chaworth, in a duel. He, too, seems to have fallen foul of the noxious environment and having been there a month was being treated by the family doctor for a fever and sore throat.[37]

In spite of its evil reputation, in many ways Wilkes was fortunate to go to the Tower. Wilkes's imprisonment occurred before the first hints of gaol reform began to emerge, and in 1763 things remained exceedingly unregulated and unpleasant in most of the capital's prisons. Newgate was particularly grim. When the printer William Woodfall was imprisoned there in 1771, he petitioned the House of Lords outlining the dire conditions. On arrival, he found himself faced either with incarceration among the most hardened criminals or crammed in with the debtors. There were so many of these that he was terrified of 'the noxious effluvia occasioned by a number of bodies (many of them very uncleanly) confined in a prison uncommonly close'.[38] Things were worse for the convicts awaiting execution, though some might find ways of avoiding death if they were willing to risk their lives in the furtherance of science. On the same day that Wilkes was arrested, a convicted highwayman, George Chippendale, was visited by two 'eminent surgeons' and offered a chance to avoid the noose. All he had to do in return was allow them to saw off one of his legs, so they could experiment with a new styptic. Chippendale was said to have taken the offer and submitted a petition for his sentence to be altered. In the event, he avoided both the gallows and the loss of his limb. He was, instead, sentenced to be transported and the styptic reserved for use on a hospital patient.[39] In spite of these rather macabre features, there could be a sociable aspect to places like Newgate. Debtors were allowed to hold meetings in their rooms, where drink might be purchased, making it appear a slightly more convivial place.[40]

In any case, Wilkes was not to be imprisoned for long on this occasion. Temple and the duke of Bolton offered to stand bail (possibly for as much as £100,000 each), but this was refused and they were initially not even permitted to visit him.[41] There were other repercussions for Temple showing such open support for Wilkes. He was stripped of his office of lord lieutenant of Buckinghamshire; Wilkes was also deprived of his colonelcy in the militia.[42] The king had 'intimated' his intention of having Wilkes stripped of his commission soon after his arrest. Egremont had persuaded him to wait until he had had a chance to examine the seized papers as he hoped there would be grounds for removing Temple as well.[43] Wilkes's displacement prompted a letter to the *London Chronicle* complaining about his removal, which the author (or authors) insisted would be much resented in Buckinghamshire, where Wilkes was 'respected almost to adoration'. The letter was signed ominously 'Five Millions'.[44] Temple was also at pains to emphasize his disappointment at Wilkes losing the command, later writing to him as 'My dear discarded Colonel'.[45]

On 3 May, at about 10.30 in the morning Wilkes left the Tower in a coach accompanied by the deputy constable. They trundled over London Bridge and through St George's Fields in Southwark and onto Westminster Hall, where Wilkes was brought before the Court of Common Pleas in answer to a new writ of *habeas corpus*, arranged by Temple.[46] His incarceration had made him a talking point. James Boswell recorded that he had made his way to the Tower to see Wilkes emerge but was too late. Plenty more were not disappointed and by the time Wilkes arrived in Westminster Hall a substantial crowd had gathered to find out what was going on.[47]

Wilkes had one major difficulty: identifying a lawyer who would be willing to represent him. In the end he settled on John Glynn, a radical Cornishman who had hitherto enjoyed a not particularly spectacular legal career.[48] Gynn was slightly older than Wilkes, but he may have been at Leiden at the same time as his new client. He had been called to the bar in 1748 and for fifteen years had laboured away without much acclaim. All that was about to change. When Pitt the Elder finally met Glynn in 1770 he assessed him as 'A most ingenious, solid, pleasing man'.[49] Solid certainly chimes with the surviving images of a robust-looking type, who was to become a key partner for Wilkes over the next decade.

Proceedings opened around eleven with Wilkes making an address (one newspaper noted drily that he 'spoke much on the occasion'), touching on a number of points that were to become a familiar part of his repertoire.[50] He said he was delighted to be 'brought before judges whose characteristic is the love of Liberty'. He hoped that his wrongs would be righted and thus 'teach the Ministers of Scotch and arbitrary principles that the liberty of an English subject is not to be sported away.'[51] Labouring the Scots point, he also complained that he had been treated worse than one of the Scots rebels from the '45.[52] The point was picked up by Stuart Mackenzie, once again reporting to Lord Milton. 'I suppose,' he observed, 'he thought that a fortunate allusion.'[53] Once Wilkes had said his piece, it was over to the lawyers to argue out the case in detail, with proceedings continuing past two.[54]

Glynn's defence was based on three points: Wilkes had not been named in the warrant; the *North Briton* had not been described correctly; and most importantly, Wilkes could not be subject to arrest because of his privilege as an MP. On the other side, the government lawyers argued that the libels contained within number forty-five were so heinous that they risked a breach of the peace, which would trump an MP's privilege, though one (anti-Wilkes) commentator thought they made their case 'very poorly'. Lord chief justice Pratt, on the other hand, was commended for behaving 'with proper spirit and Dignity'. He would not be hurried and 'animadverted very strongly upon the Noise and Bustle in the Court, and, there being some shouting & clapping & Hissing upon Wilkes's speech, threaten'd He would commit who ever dared to behave so.'[55] Pratt ordered Wilkes remanded to the Tower and adjourned the court until the 6th, when he would offer his judgment.[56] He ordered that Wilkes's friends should be allowed to visit him, a not insignificant reversal of the government's heavy-handed effort to keep him isolated. As Wilkes was led out, a report circulated through the crowd that he had been released, prompting them to begin chanting 'Wilkes and Liberty',[57] the slogan that would resonate from London throughout the country in the months and years ahead.

Wilkes and Liberty

Whether by accident or design, Wilkes had now become a symbol of something much bigger. Members of fashionable society were suddenly eager to be seen with him and it was reported that a greater number had flocked to wait on him 'than was ever known on the like occasion'.[58] Unsurprisingly, over the coming days his case was reported extensively in the press, many newspapermen having a vested interest in seeing how far the question of press freedom was to be pushed. There were also a series of letters to the various editors commenting on Wilkes's case. On the 5th, a letter appeared from 'A freeborn Englishman' placing Wilkes's predicament firmly in a much broader context stretching back into the previous century. Their message to the ministry was clear:

> The sending of Mr Wilkes to the Tower has occasioned an universal alarm. Ministers should weigh matters well before they take such steps as can only serve to irritate a whole nation. The flame of discontent is now very high and general throughout the kingdom. We know when it began, and who were the authors; but there is now no knowing where it will end.[59]

The same day, under the heading MAGNA CHARTA, the *Public Advertiser* offered to its readers a blow-by-blow account of the actions against Wilkes from 30 April through to the eve of his appearance in court. This, the paper suggested modestly, could not be 'unseasonable' and 'perhaps absolutely necessary to be laid before the public'.[60] Another paper pointed out the 'unlucky or remarkable' fact that the proceedings against Wilkes coincided with the public thanksgiving for the peace. As a result, these were much more restrained than might have been the case otherwise. Some government offices were illuminated in celebration, but on the 5th only a few of the City churches troubled to ring their bells. Those that did, the paper speculated, probably only did so because the ringers wanted the exercise.[61]

Wilkes duly returned to court on the 6th. As word of the case spread, a festive atmosphere suffused Westminster and he was now accompanied not just by his political mentors but also by a huge crowd of all sorts of people eager to see what would happen next. Previously a poor speaker, Wilkes now found his voice. More to the point, he had found his audience. He had proved in his previous campaigns in Aylesbury that he could master the detail of an election, but now more than ever he showed how he could adapt to a new constituency. This was a world away from the small, venal borough he had treated and lorded it over for the past few years, but he was able nevertheless to hit exactly the right notes. Offered a chance to speak to the charges against him, he launched into a speech that would transform his profile. He identified his cause not just with that of peers and gentlemen, like him, but with 'that of all the middling and inferior set of people, who stand most in need of protection'. Today, he proclaimed, it would be decided 'whether English liberty be a reality or a shadow'.[62] They did not have long to wait for Pratt to deliver his opinion. Pratt dismissed the first two points raised by Glynn, either of which would have played neatly into the narrative Wilkes was trying to develop. He did, however, find for Wilkes on the question of parliamentary privilege. As a libel was no felony, an MP could not be arrested on the basis of one. Pratt declared Wilkes free to go.

Wilkes might have been disappointed to have been released on a technicality, but he made no demonstration of it now. Neither did the crowd worry about why their new hero had been liberated. They saw only that Wilkes had managed to put one over the authorities, and they loved it. Amidst the by-now familiar cries of 'Wilkes and Liberty' he was escorted out of Westminster Hall by his new supporters. According to the press, perhaps as many as 10,000 accompanied him the short distance to his house in Great George Street.[63] The numbers are most unlikely to have been so great, but it was clearly a sizeable following that trailed him back home. Boswell noted the event, remarking that 'an immense mob' had accompanied Wilkes home, where 'he stood bowing from his window' as they hailed him with 'loud huzzas'.[64] Of course, just who all of these people were is impossible to determine, but what Wilkes had succeeded in doing was uniting a number of disparate groups with a range of grievances. There was ready-made symbolism in the number 45. Previously associated with Charles Edward Stuart's failed Jacobite rebellion, it was now adopted by Wilkes's supporters – dubbed thereafter Wilkites. They also appropriated Tory blue as their colour. In spite of the fact that the *North Briton* had been so noisily anti-Jacobite, Jacobites, disaffected Whigs, radicals and any number of other interest groups were all able to see in Wilkes a convenient figurehead and the cause of liberty as their own.[65]

Another way in which Wilkes had been able to transcend some party labels was by setting himself up as an example familiar to many who had found themselves hounded by the bailiffs. Making much of the way his house had been 'ransacked' by the government agents looking for evidence, Wilkes showed that he understood the plight of those whose homes had proved equally vulnerable to invasion.[66] This idea of being the victim of theft was also reflected in an anonymous satire published in response to Wilkes's release, entitled *The Three Conjurors, A Political Interlude, Stolen from Shakespeare*. The work, drawn from *Macbeth*, cast Grenville, Egremont and Halifax in the role of the witches, subtly altered to conjurors, while Bute was sketchily hidden behind the guise of MacBoote.[67] The play was dedicated to 'that distressed and unfortunate gentleman, John Wilkes, Esq', while the second edition included a letter to 'that great Guardian of our Liberties', Pratt.

Wilkesism may have become a handy shorthand for all manner of different political and social groupings and causes, but for Wilkes himself on that day in May 1763, it is easy to see how this adulation might have gone to his head. Of course, not everyone was so delighted. A few days after Wilkes's release, Boswell found himself in the presence of Samuel Johnson who held forth on how he would have dealt with the great disruptor. According to Johnson, Wilkes was now 'safe in the eye of the law. But he is an abusive scoundrel; and instead of sending my Lord Chief Justice to him, I would send a parcel of footmen and have him well ducked.' Boswell had a chance of meeting the man himself a few days after this at the house of Bonnell Thornton. He found Wilkes 'a lively, facetious man' and Churchill 'a rough, blunt fellow, very clever'. Both were 'high-spirited and boisterous' but the occasion clearly went off well, as it concluded with Wilkes extending an invitation to Boswell to call on him at Great George Street.[68]

Boswell may have found Wilkes good company, but Johnson was soon to have his wish to see Wilkes 'ducked' effected, albeit metaphorically. Staring down from the gallery as Wilkes addressed the crowd had been Wilkes's old friend, now dangerous foe, Hogarth. He produced a rough outline of Wilkes seated before a desk spread with papers, which was to be the basis for one of his most devastating caricatures. It remains the best-known image of Wilkes, an unshakeable impression of the demagogue as demonic trickster. Over his head, propped on a pole in place of the traditional liberty cap, the classical symbol of manumission, was a chamber pot inscribed 'liberty'. This was not freedom Wilkes was peddling, Hogarth contended, but filth. Advertising the print, Hogarth had one final trick up his sleeve noting that this new image was 'in direct Contrast to a print of SIMON Lord LOVAT'. It was a reminder that Wilkes, like Lovat, who had been executed as a Jacobite rebel in 1747, was rebellious and a deceiver.[69]

Hogarth's print became an instant best-seller. On 23 May the Rev. T.O. Young wrote to the Hon. George Townshend from Caius College, Cambridge, telling him that he had tried but failed to get hold of a copy of 'the Caricatura's of Wilks', which he explained 'are only at the Coffee houses'. He had, nevertheless, managed to persuade a print seller to secure him one, which he hoped to be able to pass on that weekend.[70] As well as becoming a totemic image in its own right, Hogarth's impression of Wilkes also became the basis for many copycat images that would be produced over the coming years. The German engraver Johann Friederich Bause, based in Halle, created one version, which was fairly close to Hogarth's original,[71] while another German engraver, Christian Benjamin Glassbach, was responsible for a rather more naive take on the image.[72] What all of these engravings did, though, was to make Wilkes's unmistakeable features familiar to people across Britain and Europe. This was a far cry from the state of affairs the previous year. Despite his role as a Member of Parliament and fast-growing notoriety as a journalist, Wilkes had not been much noticed by the print satirists. One rare attempt to capture him in 1762 was a stunningly unsuccessful sketch that might have been anybody. Appearing as one of five archers lining up to fire arrows at Bute and his associates, Wilkes's depiction in 'The Scotch Butt or the English Archers' offered the viewer few visual clues. The same, to be fair, was true of his companions. Only the duke of Cumberland, unmistakeable because of his girth, bore much resemblance to the original.[73]

Wilkes himself affected to dismiss Hogarth's attack, praising it as 'an excellent' caricature. Many of his friends recognized its potency, though, and responded with fury. Chief among them was Churchill, who published at the end of June a savage assault on Hogarth in the form of a satirical poem, *An Epistle to William Hogarth*.[74] Hogarth responded to that with another print, this time of Churchill 'The Bruiser' in the guise of a bear guzzling a tankard of ale. In a letter of 3 August, Churchill raised the matter of this print with Wilkes, saying 'I take it for granted You have seen Hogarth's Print – was ever any thing so contemptible – I think he is fairly Felo de se' (suicidal: 'a felon of himself').[75]

Churchill may have been enraged but the print war that had broken out is a helpful reminder of the commercial aspects of the case. There was, after all, money to be made from such a public spat. The Wilkes affair spawned a whole industry of commemorative wares, from engravings to bowls and teapots decorated with Wilkes's image or simply the number forty-five. It may have been around this time too that the up-and-coming artist Ozias Humphry attempted to secure permission to create a realistic portrait of Wilkes. He approached Glynn to attempt to secure an introduction but was rebuffed. As has been pointed out, it was not just the cachet of securing such a prominent sitter that mattered to Humphry but the prospect of rich takings from subsequent engravings.[76] He was later to paint Wilkes's daughter, Polly, in miniature: a strikingly pretty image of someone who is usually shown as having inherited her father's looks. He also seems to have gained access to Wilkes himself at last, as an entry in his accounts for 1771 noted receiving £12 12s. from 'Mr Wilkes for his portrait'.[77]

If Humphry was unable to secure access to Wilkes immediately, another artist was more fortunate. Robert Edge Pine likely already knew Wilkes, as both a governor of the Foundling Hospital and a fellow member of the Society of Artists of Great Britain, which Wilkes had been a key figure in establishing back in 1759. They also shared a critical approach to monarchy. In 1763 Pine had exhibited a painting of King Canute castigating his courtiers, and it was likely in the same year that he set about portraying the new political hero, though it was not until 1768 that the likeness was finally exhibited.[78] It shows Wilkes seated at a desk, quill in hand, and dressed in his familiar blue coat and red waistcoat. The strabismus is there, but handled much more generously than by Hogarth. He appears as a determined figure, brows knitted, apparently poised to add to the papers lying on his desk. On the left of the image is a nude goddess bearing a shield and mirror, while in the left-hand corner, a touch Wilkes would have appreciated, there is a plaque with an image of John Hampden. This was a painting with which Wilkes would have been more than comfortable.

While Wilkes undoubtedly was damaged by Hogarth's pictorial assault, in other ways the next few weeks saw him chalk up further successes in his campaign against the ministry. He had returned to his house in Great George Street, just a few hundred yards from Westminster Hall, to find the place had been turned upside down. Desks had been rifled and papers carried off. Eager to make sure that Egremont and Halifax suffered to the utmost, Wilkes and a companion presented themselves at Sir John Fielding's in Bow Street demanding the return of Wilkes's property. Wilkes also saw to it that a short letter outlining his grievances made its way into the press and was distributed as a handbill.[79] Fielding was not in residence and the sitting justice, John Spinnage, refused to issue a warrant.

Nothing deterred, over the course of the summer Wilkes and the ministry launched a series of legal actions against each other. In these Wilkes continued to be represented by Glynn, along with John Dunning. Like Glynn, Dunning was to make his name thanks to his work on Wilkes's cases and was later lauded by Pitt the Elder, 'Mr. Dunning is not a lawyer, at the same time that he is the law itself.'[80] On the other side, Webb was defended by, among others, the notable jurist William Blackstone. Formerly lauded by the *North Briton* as 'lawyer Keene', for uncovering a £20,000 black hole in Oxford University's accounts, he was now to become one of Wilkes's chief bugbears.[81]

Others caught up in the drama were also encouraged to bring their own actions. As the summer rolled on, Wilkes found himself constrained by needing to attend to the various suits being played out. On 9 June he wrote to Churchill letting him know that 'The plot thickens so fast, that Serjeant Glyn [sic] will not give me leave to go so far as Aylesbury the next ten days.' He forbore saying much more in the letter, as he had good reason to believe his post was opened by the authorities and did not wish 'to say it likewise to the Secretaries of State'. As the momentum remained with Wilkes and his associates, one of the printers received £300 in damages, while Leach and twelve more of his men were awarded £200 apiece plus costs.[82]

For the ministry, Pratt's judgment awarding Wilkes his privilege was a considerable problem. It was not just the fact that Wilkes had been let off the hook. It was also that he had given Wilkes a gold-plated defence for almost anything else they might try to bring against him. Despite this, there was a determination not to let Wilkes triumph over them. For as long as the judgment recognizing his privilege was in place, it would be difficult for them to move against him. The obvious solution was to deprive him of that. The question was, how?

While court cases rebounded as a result of the *North Briton* affair and the ministry plotted its next move, Wilkes persisted with his plan of decamping to France for the summer. He was anxious to see his daughter. He was equally eager to see whether he would be able to seduce her governess. On 14 June, with so much still up in the air, he wrote to Polly to tell her he was hurrying to settle his affairs to enable him to set out for Paris. He would not be able to be with her until the second or third week of July as he would be obliged to attend the county assizes on the 18th. However, once free of his obligations, he would remain with her in Paris until November. The whole tone of the letter was bullish, and he was still clearly revelling in his notoriety: 'Everything in England goes on as I wish it... I am a greater favourite here than I ought in modesty to say.'[83] Success in the legal cases in July prompted Temple to write to Wilkes alluding to the 'gilt ball' in which the Hellfire Club members had met and indulged in milk punch. They had no such thing at Stowe, but his celebrations were no less lively as a result.[84]

It was not until 26 July that Wilkes was finally able to start out for France.[85] He was hailed at Canterbury and Dover with the now familiar chant of 'Wilkes and Liberty' and arrived in Paris at the end of the month.[86] While he was *en route* a meeting of the gentlemen and freeholders of Surrey was convened at Croydon to thank their Members of Parliament. The sympathies of the assembled company were in little doubt and at a dinner following the meeting, numerous toasts were drunk. Among those honoured were Lord Temple, Wilkes himself and 'May all judges have the wisdom, spirit and integrity of Lord Chief Justice Pratt'.[87] In early August, Wilkes received a lengthy epistle from Churchill outlining the salient points of what was happening back home. Churchill was also eager to have his say about Hogarth's attack on him as 'the Bruiser', a description of which was reported in the press early in the month.[88] Wilkes penned a brief response with an enclosure on 23 August, declaring Churchill's letter 'the most agreeable thing I have seen at Paris – except Miss Wilkes.'[89] In saying so, Wilkes failed to mention that at one of the dinners he had attended at the duke of Bedford's, he had been informed by the duke of Richmond that when he (Richmond) had been at Versailles, Louis XV had shown a great deal of interest in all things Wilkes.[90]

He was not, though, able to avoid some of the ongoing ructions caused by his activities and while in Paris was challenged to a duel by a Scots soldier in the French service, named Forbes. Forbes had stopped Wilkes while he was out in the streets in company with Lord Palmerston. He demanded his name and whether he was the author of the *North Briton*. Wilkes had warned Forbes off from trying to pick a fight in such a public spot, but he gave him his address. They met again early the next day when Forbes insisted on a duel, accusing Wilkes of having 'written against my country'. Wilkes took out his diary and gave Forbes the disappointing news that he would have to wait his turn as there were another nineteen in the queue ahead of him.[91]

Wilkes's excuse for not dealing with Forbes then and there was based principally on his intention of fighting Lord Egremont first. This was dealt a blow when he heard of Egremont's death.[92] Writing from Paris on 29 August, he complained to Churchill (for once saluted as 'My dear Charles' rather than his more usual opening of 'My dear Churchill'): 'What a scoundrell trick has Lord Egremont play'd me? I had form'd a wish to send him to the Devil, but he is gone without my passport.' With Egremont out of the picture, Wilkes informed Forbes that he was now willing to meet him. He set off for Menin, just beyond the frontiers of France, to await his antagonist. From there he wrote to Churchill again, dismissing Forbes as 'a pitifull fellow' and declaring that if he heard nothing from him he would head for Lille, where he happened to have met 'one of the most charming of our country women'. Wilkes never let anything get in the way of an amour. A postscript confirmed that Forbes had disappeared, leaving him free to start making his way back to England.[93]

Following this rather Wilkite interlude, Wilkes returned to England, where his movements were closely tracked by the ministry. His post had already been subject to monitoring – something of which he was perfectly aware. Prior to heading overseas, he had written a typically jaunty letter to Churchill, which he signed off 'I have only time to tell you and the Secretaries of the Post Office, what kind of man you are to my *sartain nolledge.*'[94] Back from France, though, it was not just his post that was being examined; a close watch was being kept on his every movement. On 5 November, the earl of Sandwich reported to Prime Minister Grenville, 'You know that we have had Wilkes regularly watched ever since his return from France; I send you a note of his conduct upon the 2nd of November, where you will observe one very extraordinary visitor, who stayed with him half an hour.'[95]

The reports detailed the minutiae of Wilkes's existence each day in the run-up to the new session of Parliament. The government was clearly eager to find out what he might publish next. There were regular meetings with printers, including various cloak-and-dagger goings on involving Henry Woodfall. On 8 November, Wilkes was spotted visiting the critic, Bonnell Thornton, though it was observed that he did not spend long there. The length of his visit was immaterial. It was long enough for him to deposit a copy of *The Parliamentary or Constitutional History of England* (1751 edition) with a note asking Woodfall to publish an excerpt either the next day or on Thursday. He assured Woodfall 'the whole is innocent and safe.' Thornton then backed this up with a note asking Woodfall to ensure the piece made the press as soon as possible.[96]

Another regular contact noted by the government messengers was Arthur Beardmore. He was described by the reporters as an attorney but perhaps more importantly was the editor of *The Monitor*, the paper on which Wilkes had cut his teeth. These exchanges were significant. After all, Beardmore had been arrested and imprisoned in 1762 for publishing an article reflecting on Bute and the Dowager Princess of Wales. He would later successfully sue Halifax and others in Common Pleas, securing £2,500 in damages.[97] Wilkes would no doubt have been eager to learn from his example, but also to see where he could improve on Beardmore's experience.

As with Woodfall, Wilkes employed a degree of 'tradecraft' when they met. On 5 November Wilkes was observed crossing Westminster Bridge in a coach, getting out half-way across and engaging in a discussion with Beardmore at the midway point for about a quarter of an hour. His attempt to avoid being overheard was wise, as the government was keeping close tabs on him. Over the next few days detailed reports were submitted by government messengers describing Wilkes's meetings with several parliamentarians, Lord Mayor Beckford and an intriguing one with the French ambassador. That the messengers felt no need to show any subtlety about their task is perhaps indicated by the fact that on one day, one of them was noted talking at the door with one of Wilkes's footmen for ten minutes. All the while, the reports included frequent references to the printing presses that had been installed in Wilkes's home on his release from the Tower, the account for the 9th being ending with 'The printers are very busy at work.'[98]

Attacked by both Houses

While Wilkes had been away, the government had been making careful preparations to reverse their defeat of early May. The ministers were the more eager to make progress, as Wilkes's own case for false arrest was due to be heard before Common Pleas in December and there was every reason to think that he might be successful there.[99] The result was to be a two-pronged attack, with Wilkes assaulted in both houses of Parliament. The plan was that at the opening of the new session on 15 November, the Commons would be presented with two resolutions: first that *North Briton* forty-five was a seditious libel and second that this was not something comprehended by parliamentary privilege. The ministry hoped thereby to sidestep Pratt's judgment and open the way for Wilkes to be expelled from Parliament.

There were some difficulties to be overcome in persuading someone to lead on the case. Lord North, the future prime minister, was lined up for the role but as late as the end of October was evincing signs of reluctance to take it on. He expected a reward for raising his head above the parapet and took the opportunity of reminding Grenville and his colleagues of his family's disappointment when his father had been overlooked for promotion. Halifax conceded that this was only 'natural' but that it was 'not to be imputed to us', who had 'done our best to promote it'. He advised Grenville to persevere in trying 'fix him in the part he agreed to take in Wilkes's affair' and undertook to do the same.[100] The stakes could not be higher as Grenville made it clear that he regarded the issue as a matter of confidence. If the vote failed, he would resign and George III would need to find his fourth premier in as many years.[101] At least one well-placed observer thought that Grenville's position was safe enough. William Strahan, publisher and later MP, wrote to Ralph Allen on 25 October noting that 'The audacious Wilkes, it is thought, will be forthwith expelled.'[102]

The Lords were to take a different approach. Wilkes had set up presses in Great George Street after failing to persuade any printers to agree to produce the *North Briton*. If no one else would take it on, he would do it himself. This was a considerable undertaking, requiring parts of the house to be adapted, as well as calling on the expertise of professional printers to operate the machinery. Temple was, understandably, nervous about what Wilkes was up to and tried, unsuccessfully, to persuade him to change his mind. This did not stop Wilkes appealing to his patron for funds, or Temple from paying up. Temple had been wise to urge Wilkes to desist because along with the *North Briton*, Wilkes used the press to print a variety of political pamphlets and to prepare (for private circulation) an edition of the *Essay on Woman*. This was a pornographic skit on Pope's *Essay on Man*, first composed by Potter but since adapted and annotated by Wilkes himself. Papers seized by the government from Wilkes's house made it plain that it was his, if not proving that he intended to 'publish' it. In a letter to Kearsley he stated unambiguously: 'I am impatient for my Essay on Woman. Let it be on very good paper.'[103]

What followed was a tale as preposterous as the poem was filthy. First, one of the printers, Samuel Jennings, who was not in on the secret, found a proof page of the *Essay* lying on the floor at Great George Street and took it home to show his wife. She used it to wrap up some butter and as such it then passed into the hands of another printer, William Faden. No friend of Wilkes's, Faden in turn handed it on to the unsavoury cleric, John Kidgell, who surrendered it to his patron, the earl of March, by whose means it ultimately ended up in the hands of the government.[104]

Encouraged by the secretaries of state to secure more of the offending *Essay*, Webb in his role as joint-solicitor to the treasury, recognized that here at last was an opportunity to bring Wilkes down. Publishing this kind of libellous, blasphemous pornography was illegal, so he set about obtaining more evidence to be sure of a cast iron case. What had fallen into his hands was only a small part, so he set his spies to work to recover more of the text. After failing to persuade one of Wilkes's regular printers to hand over any material, Webb had more success with Michael Curry, a printer from Norwich, whom Wilkes had taken on.[105] Curry admitted that he was in possession of a full set of proofs but then proceeded to play hard to get, turning down the money offered him as insufficient. When Wilkes returned from his summer trip to France, Curry attempted to sell the proofs back to his employer, but Wilkes told him to go to hell. Rebuffed, Curry finally decided to do business with the authorities and handed the proofs over.[106] A new version of the *Essay* was then run off to be used in evidence, which contained additional material interpolated by Kidgell, who could not resist adding some touches of his own in the hopes of making the *Essay* just that bit more offensive.[107] The ultimate charge brought against Wilkes in 1764 over publication of the *Essay* accused him of

> ...Intending and endeavouring to vitiate and corrupt the minds and morals of his said majesties subjects and to introduce and diffuse amongst the people of this Realm a General Debauchery and Depravity of manners and total contempt of Religion Modesty and virtue and also most impiously and prophanely presuming and intending to blaspheme

Almighty God and to Ridicule our blessed Saviour and the Christian Religion.[108]

After all these shenanigans, a new player entered the scene, the earl of Sandwich, who had been appointed one of the secretaries of state following Egremont's death at the end of August. Wilkes's relationship with Sandwich is a matter of some speculation. They undoubtedly knew one another as both were members of the Beefsteaks, but it is doubtful they were ever close. The suggestion that they coincided at Medmenham has also been queried.[109] While it is possible that they resumed friendly relations later in life, the evidence, again, is slight. Only once does Sandwich appear in Wilkes's diaries. The occasion was a small dinner held in Oxford Street in April 1788, almost exactly four years before Sandwich's death.[110]

The evidence suggests, then, that while Wilkes and Sandwich doubtless knew one another they had never been especially good friends. Sandwich certainly had no qualms about leading the assault on Wilkes in the House of Lords. On 5 November, Sandwich reported to Grenville a conversation with Bishop Warburton, whom Wilkes had impugned in the *Essay* by attributing the lengthy annotations to him. Warburton was a notoriously prickly man, well-known for launching any number of angry put-downs in print against those he felt had questioned his learning. His wife, niece of Ralph Allen of Bath, was widely believed to have been Potter's mistress and his only son was generally thought to have been Potter's child. Although he and Wilkes had much in common – a pedantic interest in literature and close association with Pitt – they were very different personalities and loathed one another. He was only too willing to help bring Wilkes to book and swiftly acceded to Sandwich's plan for the case to be presented to the Lords as one of breach of privilege against Warburton as a member of the upper chamber.

A generation before, Wilkes might have been proceeded against for the archaic crime of *scandalum magnatum* (insulting a lord), but it had since fallen into disuse. Coincidentally, Sandwich would go on to be the last person successfully to sue for *scandalum magnatum* a decade later.[111] Breach of privilege was a more uncertain weapon, but the fact that the *Essay* had been printed enabled the ministry to argue that this constituted publication, even though it had only been intended for a select private audience, which left Wilkes open to charges of blasphemy and libel.

While the ministry was busy planning its attack on Wilkes, Wilkes had been no less preoccupied with planning his own next moves. On his return from France, he appears to have been offered a deal by the government. Whatever it was, either it was not enough, or he had resolved to stick to his guns and remain with the opposition.[112] This was the purport of a letter from George Onslow to the duke of Newcastle. Onslow reported meeting with Wilkes in late September when Wilkes had insisted he remained 'devoted to the service of the Opposition' while also being 'in great spirits'.[113] Wilkes's plan involved persisting with his legal actions to secure damages for his wrongful arrest and the damage to his property. He also wished to complain to the House of Commons formally about his privilege as a member being breached. On 9 November he called on the Speaker, Sir John Cust, to find out how best to ensure that his business was given priority. Cust had not sought to become Speaker and was viewed with disdain by Newcastle as nothing more than 'a sort of a plodding orderly man'.[114] He was certainly not particularly well equipped to deal with the passionate session that was about to overwhelm Parliament. If taciturn, though, Cust was well enough informed about parliamentary procedure and advised Wilkes that a message from the Crown would take precedence. If Wilkes was unprepared for what was to come, then he was at the very least forewarned that something might be presented which would forestall his efforts to be heard first.[115]

As well as calling on Cust, Wilkes also seems to have chosen to goad the ministry on its own turf. In advance of the opening of new sessions, it had become customary for MPs and Lords to attend meetings to hear what was on the government's agenda. Just such a meeting was convened at the Cockpit in Whitehall a day or two before the new session. It was attended by 254 or 255 MPs and reported to the king by Grenville as having been 'in all Respects a very good one, except that Mr Wilkes thought fit to make his appearance there, & was, as I am informed, universally Avoided.'[116] A similar assessment of the Crown's strength had been made by Stuart Mackenzie some days earlier. He reckoned the king had 'the ball at His foot, and the majority in Parl[iamen]t will be a very great one; especially as the faction [i.e. the opposition] seem now to lower greatly their Crests, and to perceive that the King is <u>somebody</u> in this Country.'[117]

The opening of Parliament on Tuesday 15 November 1763 found Wilkes thus assailed on two fronts. More to the point, in spite of his apparently careful preparations, he appears to have been taken entirely by surprise. Witnesses, such as his former employee, Curry, had been conveyed out of town in advance of Parliament opening so the possibility of any information leaking out was kept to a minimum.[118] That said, all appeared as usual as the session got underway, with the Commons gathered at the bar of the Lords to hear the king's speech. George opened with an address full of hope:

> The Re-establishment of the Publick Tranquillity, upon Terms of Honour and Advantage to My Kingdoms, was the First great Object of My Reign. That salutary Measure has received the Approbation of

My Parliament, and has since been happily compleated and carried into Execution by the Definitive Treaty. It has been, and shall be, My Endeavour to ensure the Continuance of the Peace, by a faithful and steady Adherence to the Conditions upon which it was concluded.[119]

After proceeding with details of the business he hoped to be covered in the session to come – and the finances the government needed – he concluded with a further hope for peace in the nation: 'I trust that My Subjects ... will be taught, by your Proceedings, to unite their utmost Endeavours to support such Measures as may equally tend to the Honour and Dignity of My Crown, and to their own Security and Happiness.'[120]

Of course, what followed immediately was far from the amicable state of affairs aspired to by the king. Back in the Commons, Wilkes and Grenville rose to their feet at the same time, the one to make his complaint about privilege, the other to inform the House of a message from the Crown. There followed some procedural jiggery-pokery, resulting in a clear victory for the ministry, before Grenville was permitted to proceed with his business ahead of Wilkes. Wilkes, he informed the House, had employed his privilege to obstruct justice and after evidence was presented, Lord North moved that

> ...the Paper, intituled, 'The *North Briton*, N° 45' is a false, scandalous, and seditious Libel, containing Expressions of the most unexampled Insolence and Contumely towards His Majesty, the grossest Aspersions upon both Houses of Parliament, and the most audacious Defiance of the Authority of the whole Legislature; and most manifestly tending to alienate the Affections of the People from His Majesty, to withdraw them from their Obedience to the Laws of the Realm, and to excite them to traitorous Insurrection against His Majesty's Government.

These were charges against which Wilkes's parliamentary privilege would not protect him. Despite the severity of the charges, Wilkes was not without his supporters in the House. An effort to have the phrase 'and to excite them to traitorous Insurrections against His Majesty's Government' removed from the main question was, however, rejected by 273 votes to 111.[121] Wilkes's own attempt to move an amendment removing the word 'false' from North's motion, was also unsuccessful. News of the 'publication' of the *Essay on Woman* had clearly left Pitt torn over his relations with Wilkes. While he was willing to defend Wilkes over the *North Briton*, he wanted the House in no doubt that he was disgusted by his conduct and berated his associate as 'a Blasphemer of his God, a Reviler of his King, and one who had endeavoured to subvert the Constitution of his Country'.[122]

After North's motion passed, it was resolved that the paper should be burned by the common hangman. The debate had been long and angry. William Strahan noted that 'the strenuous Opposition and Management of Mr Pitt' was responsible for drawing proceedings out until past two in the morning.[123] The Commons' own Journal recorded that it was 'till near One of the Clock'. Either way, it was not until late into the night that Wilkes was finally able to rise to present his own business, but further consideration was put off until Thursday morning.[124]

By then, he must have been aware that the tide was against him. Government motions had been carried by large majorities and although Pitt had been his usual fiery self, his support for Wilkes himself had been lukewarm.[125] Grenville was able to report to the king with some satisfaction: 'Upon the whole the Day was extremely successful tho' very tedious, & the majority was not only a great one, but seemd [sic] to be in very High Spirits.'[126]

In the Lords, matters went even worse for Wilkes. After the king had departed and some routine points of business had been dispensed with, Sandwich rose to denounce Wilkes for breach of privilege against Bishop Warburton for the publication of the *Essay* and another work, the *Veni Creator*. Sandwich was a well-known libertine himself, so no one was deceived by his assumed revulsion at the *Essay*'s contents. He was ever-after mocked as Jemmy Twitcher from *The Beggars' Opera*, for having turned evidence against his former 'comrade'.[127] Unabashed, Sandwich insisted on reading out sections of the *Essay* to his colleagues, who all adopted pretended shock at what they were hearing. Lord Lyttelton, generally thought 'totally ignorant of the world',[128] affected to be so offended that he appealed for Sandwich to desist, only for the other Lords to urge him to carry on. As this was the opening of the session, it was not just the Lords themselves who were present but numbers of other dignitaries as well, all crammed into the relatively small chamber. Indeed, once Sandwich had finished, and Warburton indicated that he wished to speak as well, Black Rod was required to clear away some of the ambassadors squatting on the woolsacks in front of the bishops' bench, so that Warburton could be seen and heard.

After Warburton had said his piece, denying authorship of the annotations and making various predictable damning references to the diabolical Wilkes, several more lords piled in. Temple found himself in the unenviable role of defending Wilkes, arguing that as the evidence had been acquired illegally it was inadmissible, only for Lord Mansfield to contradict him.[129] Having made that contribution, though, Mansfield then wrong-footed Sandwich by insisting that Wilkes should be given an opportunity to be heard before the Lords condemned him.[130]

The subject matter made it hard for some of those formerly associated with Wilkes to stretch their necks out on his behalf. The duke of Newcastle, for example, had made an attempt to rally some of the bishops in his group to attend but they proved wary of speaking up for someone as lewd as Wilkes.[131] Following these opening addresses, the Lords ordered nine witnesses to be brought before them, among them Curry and Jennings, who were the last to be heard before the Lords adjourned to the 17th to continue with their investigation.[132] Later in the session, Newcastle acknowledged that the opposition in the Lords was up against it: 'We have Weight, but not Numbers; & what is still worse, a great Superiority of Debaters against us.'[133]

Wilkes was clearly shaken by what had happened. The day had ended for him with fellow MP Samuel Martin launching a devastating personal attack in the Commons, dubbing the author of the *North Briton* 'a cowardly rascal' who had resorted to 'stabbing another in the dark'. Martin had been plotting this for some time, after being the butt of Wilkes's own invective in two issues of the *North Briton*. Criticizing the way in which Martin had secured his post in government, Wilkes had derided him for being a 'treacherous, base, selfish, mean, abject, low-lived and dirty fellow'.[134] Now it was Martin's turn to goad his tormentor and Wilkes took the bait. On his return home early in the morning of the 16th he wrote to Martin confessing that he was the paper's author.[135] A duel was hastily arranged in Hyde Park for later the same day. What Wilkes could not possibly have known was that 15 November 1763 would be his final appearance in Parliament as Member for Aylesbury, and his last in the chamber as a recognized MP for over a decade.

Wilkes's second duel was to be a very different affair to his first with Lord Talbot. For one, it was a hastily arranged affair and neither man troubled to bring a second with him. The mood was also thoroughly toxic. Where Talbot had been querulous and at the end reluctant to fight, Martin was determined to see the thing through. It was even said (possibly spuriously) that he had been practising for months.[136] There certainly seems little doubt that he truly meant to hurt Wilkes. Later, it was even speculated that this had been a kind of government-sponsored assassination attempt: a view popularized by Churchill. That would be going much too far, but there were plenty of people by the close of 1763 eager to see the troublesome demagogue silenced.

Wilkes's own demeanour was also very different. In his earlier scrape with Talbot he had been jocular, but now a very different mindset had taken over. He appeared confused by his handling in the Commons. William Strahan had reported to Ralph Allen the success of the ministry's parliamentary ambush: 'The affair was happily kept so secret, that neither he nor his Friends were apprised of, or prepared for, the Blow, which most effectually reduced the seditious and profligate fellow to that State of Insignificance and Contempt he so justly merits.'[137] Bishop Warburton thought there was something near suicidal about the way in which Wilkes approached the meeting with Martin. Writing an account of what had transpired, Warburton dubbed Wilkes's eagerness to rush into the duel an 'action of madness and despair'. In another he described Wilkes as being 'thunderstruck' at what had happened in Parliament, so much so as to become 'desperate'.[138]

Wilkes had undoubtedly been blindsided by the efficiency of the ministry's assault. His loss of confidence may have been short-lived, but for those few days around the opening of Parliament in November 1763 he presented a very different character to the one who had so recently lapped up the adulation of the crowd. There is every reason to think that he approached the duel expecting to die. He certainly had a lucky escape. He and Martin met in Hyde Park and tried several shots, all of which misfired, before Martin was finally able to get one off, using Wilkes's own pistols, that did the job. According to one report the bullet hit Wilkes's waistcoat button, saving his life, but driving the projectile into his groin.[139] Wilkes clearly thought the injury was mortal. Showing remarkable *sang froid*, considering the agony he must have been in, he advised Martin to make his escape. Martin, on his part, demonstrated equal gallantry by refusing to go before he had summoned a chair and a surgeon. Martin then withdrew to Paris waiting for the hullaballoo to subside, following a polite exchange of notes, in which he insisted that he would not take any further part in the proceedings against Wilkes in the Commons.[140]

At home, Wilkes underwent what can only have been a particularly ghastly procedure to remove the bullet, the surgeon eventually succeeding in extracting it from behind. Among the first on the scene to see to him were Temple, Pitt and the duke of Bolton, but it is an indication of how important all of this was for Wilkes's enemies as much as for his friends, that on the same day Halifax reported from Lord Sandwich's residence what he understood to be the facts to the king. One account doing the rounds was that Wilkes had been hit twice, which Halifax was able to discount, but he was at pains to emphasize that Wilkes had been caused much less hurt than was truly the case. The bullet, he reported,

> ...had enter'd the skin in the Middle of the Body, and without going deep into the Body had been lodged in the Side, that the Ball had been extracted, and that Mr Wilkes was not thought to be in any Danger. This Report Lord Halifax has the Stronger Reason to believe true, as he has been informed Mr Wilkes was seen walking from the Field of Battle with his Hand on his Side.[141]

Writing on the 17th to George Lucy at Charlecote in Warwickshire, William Dobson repeated the line that Wilkes was believed not to have been seriously hurt. He left no doubt, though, about where his own sympathies lay in describing the encounter 'fought yesterday between Martin of the Treasury and the famous wicked Wilkes'.[142] Halifax, Sandwich and some others were the more concerned to assure themselves that Wilkes was likely to survive his injury because they were already considering how they might prevent him from fleeing overseas 'to the Prevention of his Tryal [sic] for his most infamous Performance'.[143]

As it turned out, they had a month in hand to make preparations before Wilkes was in any condition to escape. He had certainly not strolled away. For several days his condition remained extremely serious, though he was eager to assure his friends and family that the wound was not mortal. On 18 November, he was well enough to write to his daughter with his own account of the affair. He noted that at 'the second fire I was wounded by a ball, which entered the lower part of my belly on the right side... The pains I have suffered are beyond what I can describe, but both physician and surgeon declare me out of all danger.' He assured her that she could depend on seeing him in Paris before Christmas. There was a final concluding section insisting that all was well on the most important point – his honour as a gentleman: 'It was an affair of honour, and my antagonist behaved very well. We are both perfectly satisfied with each other on this occasion.'[144]

The day after this letter was written, another correspondent related his thoughts on the affair to the earl of Moira. Wilkes, he assessed 'with the House of Lords and Commons on his back and a shot in his Belly, is in a fine pickle.' Like Dobson, he thought Wilkes not nearly so badly injured as was in fact the case, but pointed the finger squarely at the printers for betraying their former master.[145] Stuart Mackenzie, once again, had his own take on the case. He dismissed Wilkes's wound as 'fortunate to him in point of delay' as it would 'postpone further proceedings on that subject till He is in a condition to attend'.[146]

Wilkes had hoped to be on his way within a fortnight of penning the letter to Polly, but on 8 December he wrote again to explain that there had been a delay. He still planned to be with her for Christmas and asked her to contact the Hotel de Saxe to secure him his old rooms. Trying to remain upbeat, he reported to her news of the damages he had received against Robert Wood and how he hoped to win ten times that amount from Halifax in due course.[147] William Strahan also remarked on Wilkes's victory over Wood. Writing to Ralph Allen, he noted that the proceedings, heard before Pratt, had lasted from eight in the morning until eleven at night. After that, the jury had only needed a quarter of an hour before bringing in their verdict in Wilkes's favour.[148]

Wilkes finally made it off his sickbed towards the end of December and set out to join Polly in France. His recuperation had not been without incident and both his servant, Matthew Brown, and an engraver, Matthias Darly, deposed that there had been an assassination attempt on him while he was still bedbound. According to them, a Scots officer named Alexander Dun tried to force an entry and had only with difficulty been prevented from barging his way into Wilkes's bedchamber.[149] Wilkes was no doubt relieved to be away from all this as he wrote to Humphrey Cotes from Dover on the morning of Christmas Day. He noted that he had been greeted in the town by fourteen 'gentlemen of this place' who waited on him and drank his health in 'good claret'. He admitted that his wound had been 'a good deal fretted by the vile jolts through the rascally towns of Stroud, Rochester, Chatham, &c' and confided that the previous two days had been 'the two most unhappy days I have known.' Normally so good at hiding what was really going on beneath a mask of wit, banter and caustic rib-poking, Wilkes was clearly suffering severely from his injury and in no condition to disguise it. He was fortunate to manage a quick crossing to France, travelling in a packet boat named, appropriately enough, the *Hanover*.

On arrival at Calais, he settled down to write to Lord Temple, paying his compliments 'on leaving England even for so short a time'. He admitted having been 'chid not a little' by his medical men for undertaking the journey but assured Temple he would be back at Great George Street by 14 January, in good time to present himself before the Commons. He also tested Temple's patience by wishing him, and Lady Temple, 'all the compliments of this merry season'.[150] He reported to Cotes that the voyage had lasted just two and three-quarter hours. However, it had not been easy: 'The wind was so high that I was dreadfully sick, and most violently strained with it.' He was in no condition to continue his journey that day and resolved instead to retreat to an inn. He finally arrived in Paris three days later, informing Cotes he was now 'better than I had reason to imagine I should be' after the rigours of the sea crossing and the miserable coach journey through Kent.[151] But he was there. The question was, how long he would have to remain abroad – and what now for Wilkes and Liberty?

6

Exile

I believe, both parties will rejoice at my being here.

On 6 January 1764 Wilkes wrote to Humphrey Cotes, to whom he had delegated management of his affairs in his absence, detailing his recent activities in Paris. Never one to miss an opportunity of doing the right thing socially, while knowing full well it would put the host in an awkward position, he had been to call on the British ambassador, the earl of Hertford. Hertford had been warned in advance by the administration that Wilkes was on his way, though Grenville had doubted 'whether he will now attempt to pay his respects'.[1] Unsurprisingly, Hertford had not been at home to him. Hertford had deemed that diplomatically he could not possibly receive Wilkes, but it was his duty to call upon him as a British subject abroad. In a letter of 4 January, Hertford had reported his dilemma to Grenville. When Wilkes called, he had not thought it 'proper to admit him' but he then took advice on what his predecessors (Bedford and Mr Neville) had done when Wilkes had been in Paris previously. Bedford had visited Wilkes and invited him to dine at the embassy twice. Neville had confined his notice to having 'his name wrote at his door'. Hertford considered the latter course the best for him to pursue, so had sent one of his servants to leave his name at Wilkes's lodgings. That, he considered, was enough: 'I shall think it my duty, in the situation I am now placed here, not to shew this gentleman any further countenance,' unless the king instructed him otherwise. He concluded his report with the information that Wilkes's wound was still not healed but that he retained 'the spirits which usually attend him'. He understood Wilkes intended to return to London by the 16th.[2]

Something similar happened with David Hume, who was in Paris as Hertford's secretary, though in this case Wilkes was touched to have the call returned. The two men eventually met at the home of Baron d'Holbach, Wilkes's old friend from his days at Leiden. On the Sunday Wilkes had attended the ambassador's chapel. Hertford could not have refused that visit and Wilkes continued to make things uncomfortable for the ambassador by haunting the parts of the embassy open to him for the duration of his time in Paris. Hertford was, though, in a position to ensure that a few months later Wilkes was not invited to the celebration dinner attended by around 70 English notables marking the king's birthday: there were limits.[3] Wilkes in turn insisted that he was happy not to be invited, enjoying a much better evening than he should have done 'in a set of mixed or suspicious company; a fulsome, dull dinner; two hours of mighty grave conversation, to be purchased (in all civility) by six more of Pharaoh – which I detest, as well as every other kind of gaming.'[4] Wilkes closed his report to Cotes by announcing that he intended to set out for England on 13 January, so he could be back home on the 16th, in good time to present himself before the Commons on the 19th. He was looking forward to getting home, 'though I am to go through the fire ordeal of both Lords and Commons'. Even so, he felt he could be satisfied that he had

> ...never done anything unbecoming a man of honour, the glory of having obtained two such important decisions in favour of English liberty, and the friendship of Mr Cotes and a few like him, are noble distinctions for any man; and round life well, as our Shakespeare says.[5]

The quotation sums up Wilkes, and how he viewed himself, remarkably concisely. There is the lofty aim of furthering the cause of liberty. There is also the pleasure of attracting a small cadre of worthy friends, and the inevitable reference to a heroic author.

Wilkes's period abroad was to prove a formative experience. He undoubtedly enjoyed his celebrity status and proved jealous when anyone attempted to compare his situation with anyone else. He attracted a small group of what might best be described as fans: James Boswell was one and John Horne another. It was also important for his thinking. Prior to his time in France, Wilkes seems not to have shown much interest in America. If anything, he was rather dismissive of the colonies. Introduction to a number of Americans in Paris changed his outlook. He was certainly well known over there. The New York press reprinted materials relating to the *North Briton* case, helping to spread news of his struggle with the establishment across the colonies.[6] If there were positives, there were frustrations too. Wilkes liked France but he was at heart an Englishmen, suspicious of the effects too long a sojourn overseas might have on him. His cause was above all the cause of English liberty, and it was hard for him to make that case while he was out of the country.

France

Wilkes was to spend most of the next four years in self-imposed exile but he does appear, genuinely, to have intended originally to stage a return within weeks of arriving in France. This was certainly the purport of his letter to Temple from Dover, in which he referred to 'leaving England even for so short a time'.[7] Making preparations for his return trip, he even seems to have gone so far as to order a dinner to be ready for him in London when he got there.[8] He certainly had good reason not to want to be stuck in France permanently. There were still legal cases outstanding and he had the fight of his life on his hands to counter the charges being brought against him in both Lords and Commons.

Matters had continued to develop while he was on his sickbed. On 24 November, the Commons had resolved by 258 votes to 133 that parliamentary privilege did not extend 'to the Case of writing and publishing seditious Libels, nor ought to be allowed to obstruct the ordinary course of the Laws'. Despite that reversal there were early indications of who he might look to for support. George Onslow was proving a stalwart ally, being one of the tellers in a division in the House of Commons against the 24 November resolution, along with Richard Hussey, MP for St Mawes.[9] Wilkes would later commend 'Sir George Savile, Sir William Meredith, the Onslows &c for their noble endeavours' on his behalf.[10] There were potential supporters in the Lords, too, notably Temple, Shelburne and the dukes of Grafton and Newcastle. In return, Temple was told 'how very unbecoming it was for a Member of that House, who was indebted to the Crown for the most distinguishing Honours, to mix and associate with the Dregs of the People' and to 'abet a Man who ... had endeavoured to calumniate Majesty itself.'[11]

If Wilkes did indeed intend to be back in London within a short space, what prompted the change of heart? As far as the authorities were concerned, he had never meant to come back in the early months of 1764. Well-placed members of the royal Court were anxious to bring legal actions against him and had voiced concerns about him fleeing justice overseas. To them, this was precisely what he had managed to achieve, and they had no reason to expect him to return to face the music. This was not, however, the story Wilkes was keen to propagate.

There seems no reason to doubt that his duel on 16 November had left him seriously injured, nor that his recovery was slow. Wilkes's privilege case had been deferred on several occasions while he continued to recuperate. On 7 December the Commons had heard from a physician, Dr Brocklesby, and Mr Graves, a surgeon and, as a result of their report, agreed to allow Wilkes another week before appearing before them 'if his Health will then permit'.[12] The designated day, Friday the 16th, had come round with Wilkes still in no position to attend: his state of health again attested to by the doctors. With the recess fast approaching, the Commons granted him another delay until after the Christmas holidays.[13] Meanwhile, the House continued to prepare the ground for the proceedings in the new year, and on 19 December issued summons to a dozen people to present themselves to give evidence on 19 January.[14]

Wilkes's journey to France clearly worried the wound and left him weaker than he might have been otherwise.[15] It was not much of a surprise, then, when on 11 January he wrote again to Cotes to say that he was too sick to travel and that he had written to the Speaker of the Commons, Sir John Cust, to advise him that he would not be in his place on the 19th as required.[16] He had accompanied the letter with a certificate signed by two French physicians, Ninnin and Dufouart, to secure the House's formal permission for his continued absence.[17] Otherwise, there was nothing for it but to be patient: 'I am now confined to my room for some time longer, and I have nothing for it but don Quixote's remedy, patience and shrug my shoulders.' A few days later he was still complaining that he was so ill that he had been unable to leave the house: 'I have been confined to my room for several days, and I fear that the fever will not let me this week even pass the threshold.'[18] To his solicitor, Alexander Philipps, he insisted, 'I am really too ill to undertake such a journey, on a cursed pavement of 170 miles to Calais, and afterwards the violent agitation of the sea.' He assured his lawyer he shared his allies' frustration, but this was no help: 'The feelings I have of this do not assist my recovery.'[19]

Wilkes's letter was read out before the House of Commons on 19 January, but his excuse was rejected. His reliance on foreign medical professionals certainly did not go down well. It was emphasized that the paper bearing their names was 'in the *French* Language' and their credentials were clearly treated with suspicion. The Journal recorded it as 'purporting to be a Certificate of One of the *French* King's Physicians, and of a Surgeon' in the French army. The certificate had not been notarized and the House contended that there was no proof of signature. An attempt by Wilkes's friends to gain some time and adjourn the business to the next day was rejected by 102 votes to 239 and a subsequent motion made plain that the Commons had finally lost patience with him. It emphasized that he had been 'from Time to Time excused from his Attendance upon the Days appointed, on the Representations made to this House of his utter Inability to attend in respect of his Health'. He had refused to admit doctors Heberden and Caesar Hawkins, who had been sent to him by the Commons in December, and 'withdrawn himself into a foreign Country, without assigning a sufficient Cause'. Consequently, he was found in contempt of the House and by 275 votes to seventy the Commons decided to press on with the business.[20] The division does not adequately reflect how hard-fought this all was, one commentator reporting back that the House kept at it until four in the morning.[21]

When he heard about it, Wilkes was irritated, but not willing to let the matter drop. He sent again, this time with the letter authorized by two notaries and accompanied with a half-hearted note by Lord Hertford.[22] Hertford's note annoyed Wilkes considerably. It was just two lines long and even within those small confines contained, as Wilkes believed, 'three palpable blunders'.[23] Once again, the information was rejected by the Commons. In any case, by then he was too late as he was no longer a Member of Parliament. Late on the 19th, after several witnesses had been heard, Lord North proposed two motions to the House. First, that Wilkes should be condemned for being the author and publisher of *North Briton*, number forty-five; second, that he should be ejected from the Commons. Proceedings continued into the morning of the 20th, when the motions were finally carried against Wilkes. According to James Harris, 'a very loud affirmative' was voiced by the whole House, bar just one dissenting voice (Onslow).[24] When he eventually received the news of his expulsion, Wilkes exhibited his usual sardonic sang froid:

> I am neither surpriz'd nor mortified. I rather think it an honour to be expell'd by men, who have voted the Peace of Paris, honourable, advantageous and adequate to our successes, but their mode of proceeding I shall ever declare to be unjust and barbarous.[25]

If it was all over for Wilkes as an MP, however, many of the themes covered in the preceding days and weeks were far from settled. While the opposition continued to press a case arguing against the use of general warrants and criticizing his expulsion, though, they were likely relieved that he was not on the scene to complicate the issue.[26] Oddly, Wilkes himself was more than aware this would likely be the case. Writing from Paris, he observed, 'I believe, both parties will rejoice at my being here.'[27]

The same day that he ceased to be an MP, Wilkes wrote to Cotes again. He had been contacted by Philipps, who urged him to come back at once. Wilkes admitted he thought Philipps right 'from the partial view he takes of my affairs', though he believed that he and Cotes 'have more extended views'. He then went on to 'peep into futurity'. Although confirmation of his expulsion had not yet reached him, Wilkes was sure that it was not far off, and his sense of how things had gone in the Commons was strikingly accurate. As he put it to Cotes, in setting out his predicament and his options he was arguing 'upon the supposition that I was expelled this morning, at one or two o'clock, after a warm debate'. He was unable to prevent himself from indulging in some self-pity. To be fair, though, given the roller-coaster he had been riding since his arrest the previous spring, he might be forgiven for some sense of bewildered displacement: 'I have in my own case experienced the fickleness of the people. I was almost adored one week; the next, neglected, abused, and despised.'[28] There was also the concern about what he might expect were he to return: 'Persecution from my enemies; coldness and neglect from friends, except such noble ones as you and a few more.'[29]

Despite this, even at this late stage he seems to have thought the administration might be willing to make peace with him. He suggested that he would be prepared to let bygones be bygones in return for appointment as ambassador to Constantinople. He even thought 'the ministry would wish it' but that the sticking point was the king, by now an inveterate foe, who 'can never be brought to this'. As far as his atrocious financial situation went, he blamed Potter for tendering bad advice and getting him into the hands of the moneylenders.[30] Wilkes's apparent belief at this point that there could be a way back to a place within the establishment may appear extraordinary, even delusional. At the same time, it is clear that Wilkes felt abandoned by many of his former allies. He made an exception of Lord Temple, for whom he retained considerable affection and loyalty. He was determined, though, not to go quietly into the night. If he was to be left adrift, he would not be forgotten: 'I will feed the papers, from time, with gall and vinegar, against the administration.'[31]

What settled the thing for Wilkes and left him with no option but to plan for a lengthy sojourn abroad was that with his ejection from the Commons, he lost his privileges as an MP. One of the most crucial of these, for a man in his situation, was immunity from prosecution for debt. If he were to step foot in England, he would now be vulnerable to multiple suits against him by his creditors, almost certainly resulting in him being carted off to debtors' prison. So, it is quite possible to see that Wilkes may well have intended originally to recuperate in France and then return home to fight his case in Parliament. The Commons' refusal to accept his explanation for not being there in time and determination to settle the thing without waiting for him, pulled the rug from under his feet. As well as being expelled from the Commons, he was also convicted of having penned a seditious libel. The latter prompted him to write to Temple, conceding at last that establishing the printing press at Great George Street had been an error.[32] He ought to have anticipated it, but having taken the path he had, he now had no choice but to accept exile.

Exile

It is hard not to concur with John Brooke that Wilkes had made a serious tactical mistake in retreating to France when he did. Wilkes's own advisers said the same. The driving explanation for why he chose to quit the scene and risk his health with a winter Channel crossing is, however, perfectly clear. He had promised Polly that he would be with her for Christmas and it was a promise he was determined to keep. He admitted as much to Philipps in a letter penned hastily from Dover prior to making the crossing (the hurry is evident from the way the address was dashed off, 'Silver ~~Red~~ Lion, Dover'). There is a touch of the naughty child about its tone: 'I had not the courage on Friday to tell you of my little excursion to Paris,' but he had not been able to restrain himself: 'I am all impatience to see my dear girl, whose anxiety on my account has been beyond what I can describe.'[33] While the case now was more dramatic, given the state of his health and the acute political pressure he lay under, it is also worth bearing in mind that Wilkes had done the same thing earlier in the year. His visit to France during the summer had also been ill-advised – it should be remembered that Serjeant Glynn had instructed Wilkes against quitting London. If on that occasion Wilkes had mixed his paternal duty with libertine bravado and the quest to sleep with Polly's companion, there was a common factor. He had promised his daughter and did not want to disappoint her. He was no doubt eager to demonstrate to her (and maybe also to himself) that his wound was not all that serious. But once there, he found quickly that he had left himself in a predicament from which it would take him years to extricate himself. It spoke both to the sympathetic side of Wilkes – his quite undoubted devotion to Polly – and to his infuriating impishness. After all, the basic inconsistency in his behaviour here is obvious. He was happy to risk his health crossing the Channel in December when it suited him, but to plead the unreasonableness of expecting him to do the same again when it did not.

Forced to think now about a lengthier stay overseas, at first, Wilkes's gaze seems not to have carried much beyond the boundaries of France. Paris was familiar to him and it is also worth noting that as far back as his duel with Lord Talbot he had had half an eye on it as a possible retreat, should things not go to plan. As he had explained to Lord Temple then: 'if he [Talbot] fell, I should not tarry here a moment ... but would proceed to the next stage ... and from thence I would make the best of my way to France, for men of honour were sure of protection in that kingdom.'[34]

One thing Wilkes seemed clear about was that he had struck an important blow for liberty and his exile was a small price to pay for the glory of it. Writing to Cotes, reflecting on the coming libel trial over *North Briton* number forty-five, Wilkes insisted: 'The crime of having wrote No 45, in the eyes of men of sense, will ever be small and pardonable ... I regret it not. Glorious discussions in favour of liberty have grown out of it.' That said, he acknowledged that if he were to be convicted it would be 'impossible for me to return to England. No man can stand Mansfield's sentence against the author of a libel.' As he declared himself 'too proud ever to ask pardon', Wilkes concluded: 'To cut the matter therefore very short, I think myself an exile for life.' His only apparent regret was to have caused Lord Temple so much trouble.[35]

His was an assessment shared on the government side. Towards the end of February, following Wilkes's conviction in the courts, Lord Barrington gave it as his opinion that it was impossible Wilkes could ever return. He concluded with extraordinary inaccuracy, 'He and his cause are already forgotten by the only friends he had, the mob.'[36]

Wilkes did, though, now have to think about how he was to survive long-term. He liked France but had never expected it to be his permanent abode. He was an excessively social creature, who thrived in an environment charged with risqué, edgy, and often sexually charged conversation. But he also craved a deeper, more lasting kind of connexion and Wilkes was concerned that France may not be the best place for him: 'As to the French, though they are a very amiable and entertaining people, full of wit, and abounding with pleasing sallies of fancy, they are incapable of solid actions, or real friendship.' The last, in particular, seems to have weighed on his mind. His chief friend, Churchill, was now cut off from him. Who else might there be? Another issue with France, of course, was that it was still home to a number of Wilkes's natural enemies, members of the Jacobite diaspora. That this was not just a matter of mild distaste to him was hinted at in a letter to Almon, in which he complained of being 'frequently and grossly abused, because I am known to hate the [Stuarts]'.[37] Even when he was a more positive talking point, there were frustrations. Horace Walpole later commented on the decline of 'Anglomanie' in Paris and the number of mistakes the French made about English society. Worst of all, he observed, 'they take Wilkes and Lord Sandwich for the same person.'[38]

While he continued to daydream of the greater good his own difficulties had created, Wilkes could not ignore the question of how he and Polly were to live. His initial accommodation in the Hotel de Saxe was not cheap and by the middle of February he and Polly had moved into less expensive lodgings in the rue St Nicaise. In one of his letters to Cotes, he detailed the move to the new lodgings, and how he expected his more frugal lifestyle would make things more tolerable. In reality, he was still living far beyond his means. The apartments came at a cost of 2,400 livres a year and his and Polly's servants had 15 pence a day 'to find themselves everything'. Wilkes and Polly generally dined alone, paying half a crown for their food. Wilkes fretted about the cost of

Polly's education but insisted this was something on which he would not economize.

Longer term, he aimed for them both to travel to Rome. The plan was for them to spend a year there, and Wilkes would then continue to Constantinople on his own for six months. It is interesting how Constantinople continued to haunt his thoughts. Something about the place clearly fascinated him and now, at last, he saw an opportunity to see it for himself.[39] Along with planning for how he and Polly would subsist, Wilkes also entrusted Cotes with looking after his son. The boy, known as John Smith, was the result of an affair Wilkes had had with his former housekeeper in Aylesbury, Catherine Smith. Wilkes sometimes passed him off as a nephew.[40] He was by then, he thought, about two years old and was 'a lively little rogue'. Cotes could find more about him from a surgeon named Llewellyn, formerly attached to the Buckinghamshire militia and now working as an apothecary at the Westminster Hospital.[41] A few years later, Wilkes was to instruct his brother Heaton to give ten guineas 'to a certain person at Harlington' and to let him know 'how the young one is': very likely a reference to Smith and her son.[42]

Wilkes may have thought he was demonstrating admirable restraint in his planning, but the fact of the matter was that he was always irresponsible with money. As in the case of the Foundling Hospital (investigation of his management of the Aylesbury funds was still ongoing at this point) and the expenses for the Buckinghamshire militia, there seems little evidence that he was actually dishonest. It was more that he was supremely careless and had little ability to control his spending. He may have thought that he was tightening his belt significantly, but removal from the luxury of the Hotel de Saxe had not proved nearly enough of a retrenchment. Wilkes was left with no choice but to make some more drastic savings. To this end he proposed selling the manor of Aylesbury. It must have been a wrench, but from earlier discussions with Cotes it was clear that the place was mortgaged to the hilt and had been used as collateral against his other debts.[43] It was eventually taken on by Sir William Lee at some point in 1765,[44] who paid £4,000 for it. Losing Aylesbury cost Wilkes dear. It was not just the loss of his house and the social cachet of being lord of the manor. He also had to say farewell to his beloved gardens and, perhaps worst of all, his library.

The loss of property and social position undoubtedly smarted, but what was most troubling was that this drastic shedding of property did not go anywhere near settling his financial predicament. This was owing a great deal to him being badly served by Cotes, who has been described as 'a wine merchant with a drinking problem'.[45] Another, kinder, interpretation is that he was 'more willing than able to cope with such a task'. In either case, Cotes proved to be a staggeringly poor choice as his man of business. Thus, in spite of Aylesbury fetching £4,000 (more than they had expected) and the sale of his plate and library another £504, by mid-August Cotes was claiming that he was unable to send Wilkes any more funds. As Thomas notes, Wilkes had been led to believe his retrenchments would leave him comfortably off with £500 a year.[46] It is striking that, in spite of Cotes's poor service on his behalf, Wilkes remained remarkably loyal to him.

He had much less patience with Philipps, who he suspected was not labouring particularly hard on his behalf. At one point he let his frustration boil over: 'I believe there is not a man in France, who knows less of Mr Wilkes's proceedings in the Court of Law than I do.'[47] Philipps was clearly eager to disabuse him of this impression. On 11 May 1764 he wrote to Wilkes underscoring the successes that had been achieved in the legal actions against Webb, efforts which he hoped would 'screen me from the imputation either of perfidy or neglect'. He also wanted to emphasize that Wilkes's legal team were 'driving on lord Halifax's causes' and hoped 'to recover handsome damages for you'. Glynn was also still hoping to overturn the two judgments against him by writs of error. Wilkes was not persuaded. On the 24th he commented on Philipps' advice to Cotes, wondering whether he had been bribed: 'How cautious, how subtle, he is!' He admitted Cotes was 'on the spot' and so in a better position to judge, but there seems little doubt that Wilkes's mind was made up on the matter. Possibly, he was unable to let go of Philipps' unwelcome advice from earlier in the year, when he had told Wilkes bluntly, 'I will not give you a sixpence for the reversion of your popularity after the 19th, if you absent yourself ... you cannot be defended in your absence.'[48]

It was no doubt in part as a distraction from all these unwelcome matters that as Wilkes recovered from his injury, he steadily turned his attention to the pleasures of Parisian society. That spring he was able to renew his acquaintance with Laurence Sterne, who had been on an extended tour of France. On 25 March, Sterne preached in the ambassador's chapel, with Wilkes present among the congregation. He was probably grateful to have a change from James Trail (later bishop of Down), who had presided at the first services Wilkes had attended, dismissed by Wilkes as 'a dull preacher'.[49] Wilkes and Sterne spent time in each other's company over the coming weeks, sharing a decidedly unclerical holiday.[50] Sterne finally turned his head back for England on 24 May, leaving Wilkes once again on the lookout for a sympathetic partner in crime. Sterne's time in the country had softened his view of France and he concluded 'we ought not to abuse it – for we have lived (shag, rag and bobtail), all of us, a most jolly nonsensical life of it.'[51]

Divided by the Channel they may have been, but Wilkes also kept up his correspondence with Churchill. On 4 March he had written to him lauding the *Duellist* and *Gotham*, two of Churchill's most recent verses: the first being his account of the Wilkes-Martin duel. The way Wilkes was treated in them made up for at least some of his travails: 'I find ... my name recorded in such noble strains, as more than indemnify me for the injustice and ingratitude of my countrymen.' He reported that while he was 'much better' he was still not 'quite recover'd'. He hoped Churchill would find time to come out and visit: 'I believe you wou'd approve the plan of life I have chalk'd, or charcoal'd out, for Paris.'[52] Nothing, one suspects, would have given Wilkes greater pleasure than the prospect of roaming the streets with Churchill, identifying likely conquests and then sharing notes on how each had fared. Letters between them continued over the coming months, though Wilkes expressed his frustration at the irregularity of Churchill's replies – 'Am I to accuse the roguery of a Postmaster, the negligence of a private friend, or your own indolence, that I have not a line to comfort me here?' There seems to have been a plan for Churchill to visit him in France relatively soon. In the meantime, that he was far from lacking in entertainment was made clear by the 'odd party' he was looking forward to that night hosted by his landlord, Hope. The company was to include Hope himself and his mistress, along with 'two lively, young, handsome actresses'. He concluded 'Ah! poor Mrs Wilkes!'[53] Though whether he meant by that his outraged mother, or his estranged wife, is not obvious.

Churchill may have been the biggest gap in Wilkes's social circle, but there were other friends that he missed, too, among them William Fitzherbert. A fellow Beefsteak, Fitzherbert was one of the MPs for Derby and closely allied to the all-powerful Cavendishes. He had lost his place at Court as gentleman usher of the privy chamber for supporting Wilkes in the winter of 1763. His disloyalty had been noticed by the king himself, who recommended his dismissal.[54] He was thereafter a firm supporter of Wilkes and one of those to speak in Wilkes's favour in the 19 January debates. Fitzherbert's loyalty – and the wider connexion he represented – was alluded to in a letter Wilkes wrote to him on 10 September:

> I am not sour'd by the persecutions I have suffer'd and the treachery I have met with, but I regret exceedingly the losing your society and that of a very few more... I honour you for so virtuous a connection, and the very name of Cavendish is dear to me, and to every true son of liberty. I love the head and every branch of that illustrious family... My best compliments to our agreable friends of the Beef Stakes whom I think of oftner than Saturdays...[55]

Wilkes still saw himself as an ally of the Old Corps Whigs, the upholders of the 1688 Revolution, of which the Cavendishes were some of the original heroes.

Deprived of his familiar company, Wilkes steadily built up a new social round. In June he reported to Churchill that George Colman had been in Paris for 'some weeks, and has been so obliging as to favour me with his company almost every day.' Although Wilkes found him 'very engaging', his opinion was apparently not shared by the French, who complained that he was 'very cold'. But as Wilkes pointed out, 'Fellows in a fever feel every thing they touch cold.'[56] There was still Polly, of course, who remained a particular delight to Wilkes as doting father. Interestingly, his relationship with her also enabled him to maintain a distant one with his wife's family. At the end of April he had announced to Cotes that he was sending over one of Polly's drawings for his mother-in-law and another piece for his estranged wife.[57] He was also able to resume his old university friendship with d'Holbach, and was welcomed into his 'coterie', where he was delighted to be 'caressed'.[58] There, d'Holbach provided Wilkes with access to the fashionable society of the Parisian *philosophes* and he maintained correspondences with other members of the salon long after he had quit his French exile. Although their views by no means always coincided, chief among them was Jean-Baptiste-Antoine Suard, founder editor of the *Gazette Littéraire de l'Europe*.[59] There was also Suard's wife, Amélie, arguably the more talented of the two and a prominent salonnière in her own right. The German thinker, Friedrich-Melchior von Grimm, was another of d'Holbach's set to come into contact with Wilkes and became a particular supporter of his subsequent political campaigning. In 1768, at the height of the rejoicing over Wilkes's successes on his return from exile, Suard told Wilkes that all of d'Holbach's salon were toasting 'Wilkes and Liberty'. Grimm, most of all, viewed him as 'a hero of political atheism'.[60] Of course, it was not just notable European thinkers like the Encyclopaedists (Diderot, Morellet and others) with whom Wilkes was able to rub shoulders. D'Holbach welcomed a number of other British visitors as well, among them David Garrick, Adam Smith, Laurence Sterne, David Hume, Horace Walpole, Edward Gibbon and Lord Shelburne.[61]

As an indication that the wound to the groin had done no lasting damage, by the spring Wilkes had his sexual appetite back and was ready to indulge in, as he termed it, 'a carnival for Pego' (meaning his penis).[62] His activities were closely monitored by the French authorities, who were astonished he was able to bed so many beautiful women. In June he was involved with one named Dufort Cadette. She was noted to be among the prettiest girls in town, but also among the most wayward.[63] This promiscuous lifestyle was checked when he started an intense relationship with the nineteen-year-old Italian dancer, Gertrude Corradini, whom he had met at one of his landlord Hope's evening entertainments. A former mistress of the British consul to Venice, John Udny, Corradini had been born in Bologna, a fact that prompted Wilkes to refer to his visits to her as ones to 'the Bois de Boulogne'. After their relationship soured, he would characterize her as 'the Aurelia Orestilla of antiquity', comparing her with the mistress of Lucius Sergius Catilina (Catiline), who had led a conspiracy against the republic of Rome in 63 BC.[64] Corradini had come to Paris after Udny had been made bankrupt and, as soon as he saw her, Wilkes began his pursuit. She proved at first reluctant to entertain his overtures, rejecting the presents he offered. As he put it, she was no Danae, 'yielding to a shower of gold'. He tried another tack, softening her mother up with gifts of money. She proved more willing to accept 'in her lap a few louis in silver'. It was, though, a more personal gesture that finally convinced her to become his mistress. She had lost a silver crucifix while on the road between Milan and Turin. Wilkes scoured Paris looking for a replacement, a 'mark of attention' that won her over.[65] He was probably not faithful to her, nor she to him, but he does appear to have been sincerely attached to her, enjoying the contrast of his paternal days with Polly with their nights of vigorous lovemaking.[66] He was also, clearly, knocked sideways by her sexuality, referring to her 'flexibility of the limbs, worthy the wanton nymphs so celebrated of Ionia'.[67]

While it is easy to be cynical about this relationship, there seems to have been genuine sexual passion between the two. On occasion they seem not to have been able to keep their hands off each other. Later in their relationship when they were being shown round Rome by Johann Winckelmann, the noted art historian, Wilkes noted that Winckelmann politely turned the other way while he and Corradini absented themselves to have sex in a neighbouring apartment. Wilkes found Winckelmann's behaviour all the more commendable as he was stuck having to make polite conversation with Corradini's mother all the while.[68]

That said, they must have made an odd couple. Sexual attraction aside, they had little in common and Wilkes was contemptuous of her 'childish and weak' conversational abilities. Physically, too, they must have stood out: Wilkes with his strikingly ugly face; Corradini 'a perfect Grecian figure, cast in the mould of the Florentine Venus, excepting that she was rather taller, and 'more flat about the breasts'.[69] Of course, keeping a mistress did nothing to assist his supposed efforts at retrenchment. He established her with her mother, 'a ragged footboy' from Italy and 'a spruce Frenchman' in lodgings in the rue Neuve des bons-Enfants. The footboy had accompanied them from Italy; characteristically, the more fashionable French servant was provided by Wilkes.[70]

Wilkes and Corradini enjoyed a passionate summer together, but he was not able to blank out the ongoing proceedings back home. On 21 February he had been tried in his absence by Lord Mansfield in the court of King's Bench and convicted of republishing *North Briton* 45 and the *Essay on Woman*.[71] Due process meant that he needed to return home for sentencing, if he was not to forfeit his rights as a subject. On 5 August the undersheriff of Middlesex appeared at the door of St Margaret's Westminster, summoning Wilkes to appear in King's bench before a certain day that autumn. If he did not, he would be outlawed. Wilkes responded waggishly that the undersheriff should speak up, as he had been unable to hear him. Writing to Cotes on the 20th he was less flippant about his predicament. He acknowledged that his affairs were reaching a crisis: 'By the outlawry I shall be cut off from the body of English subjects.' He was concerned that while, as an outlaw, he could not be sued, being to all intents and purposes legally dead, neither could he sue others. This, obviously, had implications for his own action against Lord Halifax.[72] It was vital, then, for his personal affairs to be sorted out before the outlawry took effect.[73] He returned to the subject on 27 August, writing to Churchill for clarification. 'I take it for granted that the summons for the first day of next term means an outlawry.' Unlike in his correspondence with Cotes, with Churchill he pretended not to mind the turn of events:

> I am not the least frighten'd at the word. I may be cutt off from the body of English subjects, but I can never be depriv'd of that ardent filial love I will ever have for my country...

The only point on which he expressed mild concern was to confirm that were he to be outlawed, it would not affect Polly. Wilkes suggested that he might be willing to appear if his friends advised it, 'and submit to all the terrors of a sentence to be dictated by a provoked Scottish chief-justice of England'. There seems little reason to believe, though, that at this point he would have risked a return.[74] Wilkes always had it in his mind to stage a comeback, but only on his own terms.

By the beginning of September 1764, Wilkes was listless. He complained of the weather in Paris – 'The dog-days have been as cold as December' – but he at least now had the prospect of Churchill's much delayed visit to look forward to.[75] That autumn, Corradini left Paris to return to Italy. She had fallen sick – Wilkes thought their nightly acrobatics to blame – and set off seeking a cure in a better climate. Wilkes furnished her with a coach, sixty louis and a draft for a further 1,000 livres to be drawn on at Lyons, along with spare change in silver to cover the posts through France. The plan was that Wilkes would follow in due course with Churchill in tow.⁷⁶ Any dismay at her departure was quickly made up for with the arrival of Cotes and Churchill at Boulogne. Wilkes set out to meet them there, taking with him a copy of his *Letter to the Worthy Electors of the Borough of Aylesbury*, which he had had printed in Paris as a vindication of his activities in the run-up to his exile.

The document is interesting both because of the point-by-point refutation Wilkes employed of the charges against him, but also because of what the *Letter* revealed about his conception of his role as a Member of Parliament. It opened with an acknowledgment of the favour his electors had done him 'by committing to my trust your liberty, safety, property, and all those glorious privileges which are your birthright as Englishmen'. He then continued to insist that he was not merely anxious 'barely to justify myself' but also, quite as importantly, 'to obtain the sanction of your approbation'.⁷⁷ It sits in contrast to Edmund Burke's famous exposition of the role of an MP in the period. Wilkes seems to have accepted (or affected to accept) a more delegatory role, when he spoke of the voters' choice of him 'as your deputy to the great council of the nation'. He could not resist adding that his election had been achieved 'with an unanimity equally honourable and endearing'.⁷⁸

The Letter justified Wilkes's behaviour, but he was also contemplating a much grander work of political history going forward. It was an ambitious project that he would never complete, but the sheer scale of his Casaubon-like vision was outlined in a letter to John Almon in June 1764:

> My large work opens with the general idea of political liberty; then proceeds to examine the sentiments of the European nations on this head, as distinguished from the almost universal gross despotism of the rest of the world. The third part is a critique on the various governments of Europe. The fourth and last is entirely on the English constitution; the various changes it has undergone, the improvements made in it by the glorious revolution, and the no less happy than timely accession of the house of Brunswick... A large appendix contains, I hope, a full justification of Mr Wilkes, upon constitutional grounds.⁷⁹

At the end of October, Wilkes, Cotes and Churchill (the last accompanied by his fifteen-year-old mistress, Elizabeth Carr) finally met at Boulogne. While Wilkes and Churchill plotted a tour to Italy with their respective mistresses, Cotes presented Wilkes with bills and accounts that needed signing. All was going well until suddenly, on day three, Churchill fell seriously sick. His condition was diagnosed as a 'putrid fever' and by 3 November it was clear that he was reaching the end of his life. He composed a will and the next morning died 'in the arms of his friend'.⁸⁰

Churchill had been Wilkes's most important friend and one he was never able to replace. Throughout his life, Polly alone equalled Churchill as a companion. Their relationship was, of course, very different. As he had put it to Cotes back at the beginning of his stay in France: 'She is devoted to me, beyond what you can imagine; and is really all that a fond father can wish.' His genuine affection for her should not be doubted, though it is hard to ignore his aside that she also had great expectations from her Mead and Sherbrooke relations, from which he no doubt hoped to benefit.[81] In Churchill, though, Wilkes had found a kindred spirit, with an equal appetite for sexual escapades. They had also shared a delight in teasing the establishment through the *North Briton* and exchanging their other literary endeavours. Put simply, he was his best friend and they enjoyed an equality of standing which Wilkes had never achieved with Potter. Indeed, it is striking that Wilkes commented of Churchill's death, that he had 'never before suffer'd the loss of any friend, to whom he had been greatly attach'd'.[82] In time there would be other friendships, but no one would ever come close to Churchill. While we must always regard Wilkes's protestations with some caution, when he wrote on the death of Churchill that he had 'past the day and night alone in tears and agonies of despair', that he was unable to sleep, and had 'the idea of Churchill ... ever before my eyes', we can believe him.[83] Equally so, when he exclaimed: 'I begin to recover from the late cruel blow, but I believe I shall never get quite over it.'[84] A letter from James Boswell some months later, while Wilkes was in Naples, showed that Wilkes was still grieving for his friend. He replied, telling Boswell he had touched 'a string, which sounds most harsh and discordant to my ear'. He was trying 'by every way I can devise to divert my mind from the gloomy idea of so irreparable a loss'. What Boswell had written had undone this, and left Wilkes miserable for the rest of the day.[85]

A final sadness for Wilkes was that he was unable to follow Churchill's body back to England for his interment. He went as far as Calais but left it to Cotes and Elizabeth Carr to make the final journey. Churchill's death also broke another link with the old days, as their mutual friend, Robert Lloyd, had been highly dependent on Churchill's handouts to keep him alive in debtors' prison. Without Churchill to help him, Lloyd followed him to the grave on 15 December. Not long after, Churchill's sister, Lloyd's fiancée, also died.[86] Their losses must have made Wilkes feel more than ever, very alone.

Italy

Churchill's loss seems to have galvanized Wilkes into making some difficult decisions. On 11 November he wrote to Cotes saying that he had given notice to his French servants and would 'quit this expensive place as soon as possible'. Polly was to be sent back to lodge with his brother, Heaton. He wanted her to visit Lord Temple once she was settled, and rather hoped they might take her in.[87] She was to be free to visit her mother but was not, under any circumstances, to live with her. Polly set out from Calais on 4 December accompanied by her maid, and Wilkes received word of her safe arrival a few days later. His brother's report did not please him as Heaton had taken the opportunity of dismissing the maid. Denied her 'handy person', Polly was forced to dress herself, likely for the first time in her life. Worse was to follow. In spite of Wilkes's strictures that Polly was not to stay with her mother, Heaton quickly entered into talks with the Meads and agreed that she should visit them at Red Lyon Court. Polly was clearly taken by surprise that they expected her to remain with them and insisted on returning to St John's Square, only for the Meads to threaten Heaton with legal action. They argued that as her father was now an outlaw, Polly's upbringing reverted to her natural mother. Heaton conceded the point, and Polly was dispatched back to her maternal family.[88]

Wilkes was evidently annoyed by how Polly had been treated. He called his brother a 'barbarian' for his conduct and protested he had cried ever since receiving a letter from Polly informing him of what had happened. Wilkes, though, now had nothing to hinder him from setting off.[89] On Christmas Day 1764, he began his journey to Italy. He passed his lodgings over to the Garricks.[90] On New Year's Eve he was in Lyons. He complained to Polly it had taken him six days to reach it because the roads were so bad (a typical traveller's gripe). He spent three days in Turin admiring the royal art collection, then on to Milan and Parma, before reaching Bologna on 18 January 1765, where he was reunited with Corradini. From Parma he boasted to Polly that he was beginning 'to make myself understood in Italian' as well as being able to 'read tolerably well their best authors'.[91] His later 'autobiography' (composed in the third person) was dominated by this 'grand tour', in which he cast himself as a latter-day Odysseus or Aeneas, undertaking a form of heroic challenge on a par with his earlier patriotic labours.[92]

As was characteristic with him, he maintained a close correspondence with Polly, but was careful to sanitize the story. Corradini's role in his journeyings was airbrushed. Thus, he told her he was staying in lodgings in Bologna, when in fact he was living with the Corradini family.[93] The household comprised Corradini, her mother and brother. The father, 'a low, despicable fellow' and a former hairdresser, had vacated the place before Wilkes's arrival and Wilkes never met him.[94] One thing he certainly would not have shared with his daughter was that he was tickled by the fact that Corradini had a painting of the Madonna at the head of her bed, with a green silk curtain, which she drew across it so the Virgin would not be offended by their night-time antics.[95]

After ten days in Bologna, Wilkes made for Naples, where he aimed to live as cheaply as he could and busy himself with his literary endeavours. He had undertaken to produce an edition of Churchill's works as well as wishing to get started on the grand history he had laid out some weeks before. There had been some bargaining with Corradini about the terms on which she was to accompany him. They eventually compromised on a party including Corradini's mother and as many servants as she wished. He departed for Florence in advance, but the whole group made it to Rome in time for Valentine's Day. Wilkes was impressed by the elegance of the city, but disappointed by the people.[96] He was, though, delighted to make contact with Winckelmann, with whom he struck up an immediate rapport. Even though Winckelmann had been 'born a subject of the tyrant of Prussia' and submitted to work under 'the despotism of the Roman Pontiffs', Wilkes found he had 'a heart glowing with the love of liberty'. Under Winckelmann's attentive guidance, Wilkes was evidently delighted by the sights, praising in particular the unparalleled grandeur of St Peter's: 'There is nothing tawdry or glaring. The whole is plain, modest, and sublime, a taste which the French are yet to learn.'[97] It was also while he was in Rome that he first came across Willoughby Bertie, 4th earl of Abingdon. It was the beginning of a cordial friendship, underpinned by Wilkes's appreciation of Abingdon's 'easy wit' and 'gaiety of temper'.[98]

Wilkes's party reached Naples towards the end of February. Having initially set up shop in one of the city's most fashionable hotels, St Stephano's, Wilkes removed to a villa a mile outside the city.[99] There he reminded himself of Polly with two pictures she had undertaken in crayon: one of a woman's head, and another of a basket of fruit. He also had a likeness of his daughter by Fossier, 'which I always fill a glass to in the absence of the dear original'.[100] As had been the case in Paris, Wilkes's relations with the British diplomatic resident were awkward. Sir William Hamilton, who would later become much better known as the husband of Nelson's mistress, Emma, took a stricter line than Hertford had done and refused to receive or wait on Wilkes. He was, though, willing to interact with him on neutral ground, so the two met at Lady Orford's villa: a general social hub for all of the English élite visiting or living in Naples. Hamilton had good reason to be distant with Wilkes. He owed his place to Grenville as well as playing host to Bute's heir, Lord Mountstuart, who was also in the area undertaking his own grand tour.[101] Wilkes observed to Polly that he and Mountstuart had both been at Stephano's at the same time, 'but not a word passed between us'.[102]

Hamilton may have been keen to avoid Wilkes as far as possible, but others were only too eager to seek him out. Wilkes noted the presence of his old friend, Sir William Stanhope, who seems to have been a frequent companion.[103] Not long after his arrival Wilkes received a missive from James Boswell, who had been travelling in Italy and now wished to renew his acquaintance. There was much that divided them. Boswell was a Scot and a Tory, both of them red rags to Wilkes's patriot bull. However, they shared a love of classical learning as well as an interest in sex. In March they teamed up for an ascent of Mount Vesuvius.[104] Wilkes needed five porters to help him during the trek and described sinking 'up to the knees in ashes'.[105] Although they had chosen 'a clear but cold day', he noted the heat of the place, so extreme 'that all the skin of my face peeled off in two or three hours'.[106] During his stay, Wilkes also witnessed one of the twice-yearly celebrations that accompanied the ' pretended miracle' (as he put it) of the liquefaction of the blood of St Januarius. He displayed predictable, protestant scorn for the whole event, which he dubbed 'a very dextrous charlatannerie'.[107]

Wilkes's sojourn in Naples proved to be of much shorter duration than he had originally intended. After just a few months, he and Corradini had a rather predictable falling out. She had been pressing Wilkes for a cash settlement that he could not afford. Also, she was pregnant, and the child may well not have been his. Certainly, he never acknowledged it. She took the opportunity of Wilkes's absence on a trip to Ischia, where he was visiting a sick friend, to pack up her things – and some of his – and head for home.[108] The affair reflected poorly on Wilkes, which is no doubt why so much of his fragmentary autobiography was given over to his analysis of the relationship. He clearly believed that the way he had been in thrall to her had threatened his masculinity and he celebrated breaking the chain.[109] They likely never met again, though Corradini was in London the year that Wilkes returned from his exile. She appears subsequently to have travelled to Madrid, where she was observed by Frederick Robinson dancing a minuet in December 1771.[110]

The end of the affair with Corradini coincided with a potential change in Wilkes's political fortunes, which also helped him refocus after the failed relationship. Following several months of instability, George Grenville resigned as prime minister in July 1765 and was succeeded by Charles Watson Wentworth, 2nd marquess of Rockingham, someone much more sympathetic to Wilkes's cause. As Wilkes himself put it the 'enemies of liberty and Mr Wilkes' were out of office, and Rockingham in place 'with the general good will of the people'. Rockingham and his followers viewed themselves as the natural successors to the 'Old Corps Whigs'. They also shared with Wilkes a natural antipathy to Bute and the new ministry was quick to insist on the removal of a number of Bute's appointees.[111]

The change prompted calls from some of Wilkes's friends for him to leave Italy and make his way back, as they believed there was now a plausible chance of securing a pardon. Wilkes decided that the time was ripe and accepted a berth in a 'wretched French Tartan' sailing from Naples to Marseilles, so that he could avoid an unwanted stop off in Bologna. He set out on 27 June, six months after he had first set foot in Italy. Pausing in Marseilles, Wilkes attended to his bruised heart by resorting to the city's fleshpots, which kept him entertained for a few days. Guarding Polly from such details, as usual, Wilkes merely noted that he had not seen much of the place while waiting for his servant, Brown, to catch up with the luggage. He was on much safer ground in a subsequent letter, when he told her he was sending a print by Angelica Kauffman, 'the first painter in Europe'.[112] From Marseilles Wilkes pressed on to Grenoble, before taking in Savoy and Geneva, where he visited the tomb of John Calvin. The true object of his pilgrimage though, was Voltaire, 'who has done more to free mankind from the gloomy terrors of superstition and to persuade the practise of humanity and benevolence, than all the philosophers of antiquity'.[113] Wilkes had expressed his admiration for Voltaire some years before, dubbing his *La Pucelle* 'the wittiest poem I ever read'. Others had criticized it for its 'profaneness'.[114] Wilkes waited on the great man with Lord Abingdon, with whom he had once more fallen in. Although he professed himself highly entertained, he told Polly, 'after all, I had rather be with my dear girl than with the first wits or beauties in the world.'[115]

Wilkes remained with Voltaire at Ferney for some weeks, but by the end of September 1765 he was back in Paris, at the Hotel de Saxe. The altered state of affairs was reflected in the fact that he was able to wait on the new ambassador, the duke of Richmond, and even had his visit returned. While Richmond was cordial, though, Wilkes's hopes for something more were still a long way off. He resumed his application to be sent to Constantinople as ambassador. It would buy him time before the next election, due in 1768, which he also hoped would see a resumption of his parliamentary career.

Negotiating a return

Unsurprisingly, the ministry was not particularly eager to appoint Wilkes to so potentially sensitive an office as an embassy. Through the mediation of his old friends George Onslow and William Fitzherbert, an offer was made of an annuity of £1,000. The money was to come from the ministers' own private funds, and acceptance was conditional on him not pressing the point about staging a return. The question of his outlawry was yet to be settled, but it was clearly on the table. As his friends and political allies pointed out to him, his convictions were not easily done away with, as he had been convicted of extremely serious crimes. Wilkes huffed and puffed and suggested another solution: send him to Jamaica as governor. There were also barely veiled threats about what he might be able to spill in Parliament should the ministry not want to help him. Rockingham was unmoved. He responded via Lauchlin Macleane, a contemporary of Edmund Burke's at Trinity College, Dublin. Macleane insisted that what was being proposed was done 'from friendship, not from fear', and Wilkes might do what he liked.[116] In the end, Wilkes had little option but to accept the proffered annuity, which he did with a very bad grace. Discussions then persisted into 1766. These culminated in Wilkes risking a visit to England to try to force matters along, but not before he had had to deal with the unwelcome news of Pitt and Temple falling out and of Temple's reconciliation with Sandwich, Halifax and George Grenville.[117]

Rumours of his expected visit appeared in the press around a month before his arrival. In mid-April one newspaper had reported that 'As the present administration have not, nor will, do any thing for Mr. Wilkes, it is said that he begins to think seriously of returning home.' The report was followed, without apparent irony, with a notice that the king and queen had been to Drury Lane the night before to see *The Plain Dealer*, as part of a double bill with *The Deuce is in him*.[118] That the cause of Wilkes and Liberty had not been forgotten in his absence was also indicated by reports later in the month of a meeting held in Exeter to celebrate the repeal of the Cider Act. Among the toasts drunk were 'The liberty of the Press' and 'may Wilkes soon be recalled from his exile!'[119] Not long after, on news of general warrants being declared illegal, there were similar rejoicings in King's Lynn. A large piece of paper with the words 'General Warrants' written on it was taken to the market place and burnt. The evening saw celebrations rounded off with loyal toasts to the king and constitution, along with less loyal ones to 'Mr. Wilkes and Liberty'.[120]

It was amid this spirit of celebration, then, that Wilkes staged his quiet return to England, landing at Dover on the evening of Sunday 11 May 1766 and reaching the capital next day.[121] He reported his safe arrival to Suard, entertained that even as he wrote a hawker was positioned beneath his window advertising *An Elegy on the lamented Death of that much admir'd Patriot John Wilkes*.[122] During the trip there was time for a meeting between Wilkes and Burke, which Burke later alluded to in a letter directed to Wilkes back in Paris:

Whether your late excursion hither was within the frigid rules of sedate & measured prudence, I will not undertake to determine; but I know, I consider myself as served by that step; as it gave me the opportunity of your conversation, which supported the opinion I always entertained of your abilities, & improved that which I had conceived of your heart & Temper.[123]

Strikingly, it seems to have taken Wilkes four days to write to Temple.[124] The next day, a report appeared in the press suggesting that 'A Proposal has been made to obtain a Pardon for Mr. Wilkes, with a View of his pleading it, the first Day of next Term, in Bar of the Sentence of King's Bench.'[125]

Temple responded to Wilkes's letter on the 20th, addressing his letter to the 'Most celebrated Exile!' and congratulating Wilkes on the prospect of his pardon.[126] By the end of May, though, it was plain that he was getting nowhere. A report in the press for 31 May noted without elaboration that he had not appeared at King's Bench the day before to plead a pardon, as had been expected.[127] Indeed, by the time the newspaper appeared, he was already on his way back to France, worried that if he lingered much longer, he might find himself back in gaol. So, with little achieved, and his friends and family only too relieved to be free of the embarrassment of harbouring an outlaw, he flitted back across the Channel on 31 May, taking Polly with him.[128]

Just over a month after his return to France, news reached Wilkes of the fall of the Rockingham administration, and its replacement with a new one headed by the earl of Chatham (as Pitt had become) and the duke of Grafton. These were men with whom Wilkes hoped he would be able to do business, though the Rockinghams believed that Chatham had made some sort of accord with Bute. This was reflected in the perception that there was no effort to keep Bute's friends out of office.[129] Grafton's brother, Colonel Charles Fitzroy, was now sent to Paris to open talks with Wilkes.[130] Although little more than warm words appear to have been exchanged, Wilkes was buoyed by the development. That said, he regretted Chatham's decision to get into bed with the Court, referring to his old patron as 'the apostate patriot'. He also remained mindful that even with this more promising administration his post would still be subject to checks, so when requesting a list of publications he wanted sent to him, he offered two proxy addresses for his mail. One was that of L'Abbé Arnauld, publisher of the *Gazette de France*; the other was Suard's.[131]

In the autumn of 1766, Wilkes staged another visit to England, arriving at Dover on 28 October. The ever dependable Heaton had been busy trying to arrange accommodation for him in London, assuring Wilkes that he had maintained strict anonymity in making his enquiries.[132] In the event, Wilkes stayed with William Wildman, proprietor of an opposition club and, coincidentally, brother-in-law of the radical parson John Horne (later Horne Tooke), whom Wilkes had met on his return from Naples.[133] From there, Wilkes wrote to Grafton renewing his request for a pardon. One newspaper reported that 'every thing had been made easy in regard the reception of Mr. Wilkes in his own country,' while another informed its readers that Wilkes had been visited on 1 November by 'several persons of great distinction'. It also relayed the news that he was to be 'gratified in his former desire' of being appointed a governor in one of the American colonies.[134] Such optimism was far off the mark. Grafton showed Wilkes's letter to the king, who 'read it with attention' but made no comment. Chatham meanwhile 'remarked on the awkwardness of the business' and advised they do nothing about it. Grafton concurred and Wilkes was left to stew.

Having haunted London for just over a week, Wilkes was back on the road, arriving in Paris a few days later. His experience precipitated him into one of his familiar destructive modes and he responded in the only way he knew how, by resorting to print. Publishing the letter he had sent to Grafton, he attacked both Grafton and Chatham, as well as rehearsing once again the well-worn theme of the *North Briton*. It wrecked any chance of a reconciliation with Chatham, but at least it reminded the public of his existence.[135]

As well as burning his bridges with Chatham, over the coming months Wilkes and Temple also faced a parting of the ways. In spite of all that Wilkes had done, the two had thus far remained on cordial terms. Now Wilkes chose to publish the letter he had sent Temple in the aftermath of the duel with Talbot, severely damaging his standing with Temple at a time when he needed allies badly.[136] It was another example of Wilkes making a critical error of judgment. As well as political travails, Wilkes was also facing renewed financial headaches. In February 1767 the hapless Cotes was finally made bankrupt. Wilkes showed considerable kindness by expressing his sorrow on Cotes's account, but he must have realized that it meant an end to any hopes of recovering his own money.[137] By the summer Horace Walpole was writing to his friend Madame du Deffand in Paris noting how 'le pauvre diable' was desperately in need of funds.[138]

It was in this context that Wilkes decided to see what more he could do to rescue the situation through his pen. In July, he made an agreement with John Almon for the publication of his much-vaunted history, in return for a £300 advance and a final £300 on delivery of volume one.[139] The anticipated work was trailed in the press in September but when the due date fell, all that Wilkes had to show for it was a fragment.[140] It was all of a pattern with him: Wilkes rarely finished what he began, but this did not stop Almon from publishing what he had.[141]

Champion of English Freedom

In debt and isolated politically, Wilkes began to conceive a new scheme. Parliament was due to be dissolved in March and he resolved to stand at the general election. Being an MP again would grant him immunity from arrest for debt, and even if he was not elected, it would offer him a chance to raise the political temperature back home. He had not forgotten the adulation of the Wilkes and Liberty days and no doubt hoped that he would once again be able to enthuse the crowd. Aylesbury was lost to him, so he turned his attention instead to the City of London, approaching one of the aldermen, Sir William Baker, for his support.[142] Baker's response was not entirely dispiriting, so even though other friends cautioned him against, Wilkes resolved to throw the dice one more time. At the end of November, he and Polly quit Paris and arrived in London two days later. Concerned at the length of time he would need to remain incognito between then and the election, he left her with her mother and struck out again for the United Provinces. He would remain there, on and off, until February of the following year. His campaign to re-enter Parliament was under way.

7

London and Middlesex

(1768)

> In politics, as in war, great and bold actions succeed,
> when more cautious fail.

In February 1768 Wilkes returned from exile, under the alias Osborn.[1] For the past three months he had been living a peripatetic, celebrity existence in the Low Countries. Some of the time was spent at his alma mater, Leiden, where he was offered the opportunity of taking his degree. He turned it down. He complained from the Hague that 'the Dutch torment me with compliments' and how he was thronged with people armed with copies of Hogarth's caricature to see if he resembled it. During his travels he had met his old nemesis, John Kidgell, who tried to sell him evidence that the government copy of the *Essay on Woman* had been tampered with, but Wilkes sent him off with a flea in his ear.[2] By the beginning of 1768 he was clearly impatient for action, prompting him to make his move over a month before Parliament was due to be dissolved. Several of his friends had advised caution, but Wilkes was never one to take advice he did not want to hear. Besides, he was running out of options. As he pointed out: 'I owe money in France, am an outlaw in England, hated by the King, the Parliament, and the bench of bishops... I must raise a dust or starve in a gaol.'[3]

In London, Wilkes made first for the house of his sister, Mary Hayley, before taking lodgings with a Mr Thomson under his assumed name, where he was forced to wait out the next few weeks. On 4 March he broke cover to write to the king, renewing his application for a pardon but it was returned to him unread. He had ignored convention by sending it via a servant rather than having it presented by one of his patrons at a formal levée. It did not much matter. Wilkes expected the request to be turned down and it offered him an opportunity to publish news of the rebuttal to help gain him public sympathy. In the meantime, he began to barrage the press with notices about his case and his intention of standing in the coming election. Cotes had tried to persuade him to try his hand in Westminster, but Wilkes ignored the advice, aiming for one of the City of London seats instead.[4] This made good sense. Although Wilkes was a former resident of Westminster and the constituency was lively with a large population, he probably felt he had a better chance in London, where he had contacts. What was certain was that if Wilkes had ever been forgotten, he was back in the news now. One interested observer of events throughout the tumultuous year of 1768 was Benjamin Franklin, an acquaintance of Wilkes's brother, Israel. Israel had even invited Franklin to spend Christmas with them in 1766.[5]

The General Election of 1768

On 11 March Parliament was dissolved. The day before, Wilkes had been admitted to the freedom of the Worshipful Company of Joiners and Ceilers, paying a 'fine' (the technical term for the admission fee) of £20. His certificate was presented to him in a box carved from 'the Heart of true English Oak, *like his own*'.[6] Membership of one of the City livery companies was a prerequisite for someone wishing to contest the City of London. Why he selected the Joiners rather than one of the companies with whom he might have been able to claim ties of family or profession (the Distillers for example) is not immediately obvious. That said, it had long been the case that there was no requirement for members of most livery companies to practise the trade promoted by the company.[7] Many members pursued quite separate careers or, in the case of gentlemen, none. That there may have been some competition for securing Wilkes for their company is suggested by a report in one newspaper that he had been admitted to the Worshipful Company of Musicians.[8] As for the Joiners themselves, no doubt they hoped their famous new member would help boost their profile within the City.[9] They were a numerous body and Wilkes was also no doubt keen to secure as much support as he could for the contest ahead. One newspaper, reporting a few days after his admission, noted 'It is extremely remarkable, that the Motto of the Worshipful *Joiners* Company, in which Mr. Wilkes has lately taken up his Freedom, is JOIN LOYALTY and LIBERTY.'[10] As Young notes, some have assumed that the company adopted its motto to reflect its support for Wilkes, but this suggests that it was already current.[11]

That Wilkes was not just expecting support from the Joiners is indicated by reports in the press announcing that he could rely on backing from members of the Fishmongers' Company, and that he was courting the Grocers as well.[12] The same day that he was admitted a freeman of the Joiners, Wilkes also visited the Poulters' Company at their entertainment at Whitechapel. A newspaper reporting the developments shared the information that 'many hundred Liverymen have determined to give John Wilkes, Esq: their single votes, as the only effectual means of serving him.' This tactic, known as 'plumping', meant that the electors would withhold one of their two votes to ensure that their favoured candidate had the best possible chance of success. It was also reported that 'Many of the Nobility' were 'exerting themselves' on his behalf. The same edition reported confidently that Wilkes had secured a pardon, even though there was no impediment to an outlaw standing for election. One tale told that Wilkes had secured the pardon in return for a promise 'not to stand for the neighbour city of this great metropolis', meaning Westminster. Another, that Newcastle had presented his petition, which had been granted on the understanding that Wilkes would not appear at Court. A subsequent issue of the paper printed a correction explaining that reports of the pardon being given were not true.[13]

Four days after Wilkes was admitted to the Joiners, lengthy advertisements were published in the press, setting out his stall. Wilkes's case underlined the despotic tendencies of the administration and the importance of the election to come for the voters who wished to assert their desire for liberty:

> You have now gentlemen, an opportunity put into your hands, 'of making a grand and solemn determination in favour of Liberty,' you have it in your power to return a man to parliament, who, by appearing there as your representative, will give such strong proof of your detestation to every tyrannical and unconstitutional measure, as must necessarily confound every enemy to the Liberties and Privileges of free born Englishmen.[14]

If Wilkes's case appeared fairly desperate at the outset, in a short time he was able to dominate press coverage of the coming election and, remarkably, to turn his position around. His cause was bolstered by popular ballads, including one set to the popular tune of 'Gee Ho, Dobbin', which concluded:

> O! Seize this occasion your worth to approve,
> Let your votes shew the world that your country you love;
> Chuse Wilkes for your Member, none else can so fit ye, -
> Chuse the first greatest man for the first greatest city![15]

The 1768 election was to prove to be one of the most controversial of the period. There were widespread reports of 'nabobs', carpet-baggers who had enriched themselves in India, appearing in a number of seats, challenging more established interests.[16] There were also early reports of disturbances connected with electioneering far away from London, with some of the Scots seats said to have been subject to 'great disturbance'.[17] That Wilkes was able to capitalize on this threat to the natural order of things shows just how effective he was at getting his message across.

Even so, securing election in London was a tall order. Unlike most English seats, the City of London returned four MPs and all of the sitting members were presenting themselves for re-election. While the City was certainly open to the kind of radical politics Wilkes now represented, it required careful courting and only one of the sitting Members, Sir Richard Glyn, appeared at all vulnerable. The others, Sir Robert Ladbroke, Thomas Harley (the sitting Lord Mayor of London) and William Beckford, all seemed as safe as houses. And as was usual in the City, there were other challengers besides Wilkes. Barlow Trecothick, an American merchant attached to the Rockinghams, had the best chance. A sixth contender, John Paterson, was clerk to the Barber Surgeons' Company. He had chosen to give up his seat at Ludgershall in Buckinghamshire, which he had secured through the intervention of Bute and Henry Fox, to try for the City.

It was, thus, already a fairly crowded field that Wilkes had chosen to enter, and he was late putting his hat into the ring. Winning in the City depended enormously on careful cultivation of the corporation and Wilkes had had no time to do that. Even so, in the short space between him declaring his candidacy and the beginning of the election at Guildhall on 16 March, his prospects changed dramatically. Once dismissed as a long shot, by the time of the election he was believed bound to succeed.[18] One newspaper reported that a wager of 100 Guineas had been laid at one of the City coffee houses that Wilkes would be elected. The same sum was also wagered that he would secure twenty more votes than any of his rivals.[19]

On the eve of the poll, Wilkes played a characteristic game of cat and mouse with his supporters. He had been expected to appear at Guildhall on the 15th to take up his freedom formally. A 'prodigious number of people' gathered to witness the event, but he failed to show. It was reported that he would instead attend Guildhall on the morning of the 16th, in advance of appearing on the hustings with the other candidates.[20] The meeting at Guildhall commenced with those present voting via a show of hands. On this basis, Wilkes appeared to have done well and in his address to the assembled freemen he was delighted to announce being 'once more among the friends and patrons of liberty... I stand here, gentlemen, a private man, unconnected with the Great, and unsupported by any party: I have no support but you: I wish no other support: I can have none more certain; none more honourable.[21]

Not everyone was impressed with his oration. Wilkes always struggled as a speaker. He was much more comfortable on paper. The opinion of one correspondent, signing himself ' A Liveryman', was printed in the press soon afterwards, in which he concluded that Wilkes's speech 'was not equal to my Expectations from a Man who has *one* of the best Pens, if not the *best* of any modern Writer'.[22] Nevertheless, following the show of hands, the sheriffs declared that Ladbroke, Beckford and Wilkes were all in the majority. It was not clear, though, who had secured the final spot. On a second show of hands to settle the issue, Lord Mayor Harley was declared the winner, but this prompted demands for a poll from the three defeated candidates. Having started so strongly, Wilkes's campaign began to lose impetus. At the end of the first day's polling, he was trailing in last place with just twenty-nine votes, a poor showing next to Ladbroke's eighty-one, Harley's sixty-four and Trecothick's sixty.[23] He continued to trail his rivals for the remainder of the election. By the close at four in the afternoon on 23 March he was still in last place. With just 1,247 votes, he was around 500 votes adrift of the next candidate, Paterson. Trecothick, who secured the fourth seat, had 2,957 votes.[24]

If Wilkes was disappointed, he did not show it and promptly put Plan B into operation by announcing his candidacy for Middlesex instead. The county was not due to begin polling until 28 March, so he announced that he might yet 'have the honour of being useful to you in the British Senate'. He then quit the hall, in the hopes of averting a riot by his disappointed supporters. According to one paper, the crowd broke the Guildhall's gates to pieces and smashed the lamps. Some of the 'mob' (as the paper characterized it) mounted the hustings and called out that they would choose their own representatives.[25] Another commentator described how 'mischief' by the 'mob' was only prevented 'by the spirited conduct' of the Lord Mayor.

That Wilkes was far from being a spent force was indicated by the fact that Brentford, the county town of Middlesex, was 'full of blue cockades' that morning, a colour that had been adopted by his supporters. The writer noted seeing Wilkes and Churchill's brother 'in a chaise and four ... going to declare for Middlesex'.[26]

Middlesex

Middlesex was a very different prospect to the City of London. Although its electorate was half the size (3,500 voters to London's 7,000), it was a much more diverse and difficult group to control. The county embraced both urban and rural areas ranging from the borders of Essex and Kent to the east, Hertfordshire to the north, Buckinghamshire in the west and Surrey south of the Thames. The county town, Brentford, was the place of polling at the time of elections, but meetings prior to them took place in a variety of places including Hackney. The nature of the franchise meant that along with the local gentry and professional men, there were also large numbers of voters from the shopkeeping and skilled artisan classes. These were precisely the kind of people Wilkes hoped to enthuse. The irony of Wilkes's success at cultivating these people was not lost on contemporaries and has been commented on since by one of his most astute biographers. Men who would have thought twice about extending Wilkes credit were happy enough to trust their votes to him.[27] Certainly, there was something in the air of Middlesex that welcomed a disruptor and grandees found the county difficult to manage. In July 1759, in a memorandum to the king, the duke of Newcastle had characterized Middlesex as a place of 'Factious Representation against me'.[28]

Despite that, for the last two elections Middlesex had returned members without troubling with a contest. Wilkes's challenge may have upset several years of relative calm, but it is striking that the 1768 general election as a whole witnessed the most contested elections for twenty-seven years. One newspaper reported bets being laid 'at the West end of town' that the elections would result in the return of as many as 200 new MPs.[29] Wilkes may have been the most prominent, but he was far from the only challenger upsetting the applecart.[30] Just like the ministry had been with regard to the City poll, the two sitting candidates, Sir William Beauchamp Proctor and George Cooke, were taken entirely by surprise by Wilkes's decision to throw his hat into the ring.

Proctor was a wealthy country gentleman, with lands in the county as well as in Norfolk. He had been created a baronet when in his early 20s and might generally be characterized as an opposition Whig, though he had been thought a safe ministry vote in the 1750s. Cooke, on the other hand, was a Tory and had been at one point reckoned a Jacobite. Although the two were very different, Wilkes's decision to enter the fray prompted them to work together to oppose the challenge. Both of them had backed Wilkes in the debates in 1763 and 1764, so his decision to try to unseat one of them might seem at the very least ungrateful. Their efforts at maintaining their constituents' good will met with mixed results. One newspaper reported that Cooke and Proctor provided two butts of beer for the people of Brentford to enjoy. These were soon emptied, with the drinkers noisily toasting 'Wilkes and Liberty'.[31]

Wilkes's campaign for Middlesex may have been fermenting longer than his surprise announcement on 23 March implied, but it required, nevertheless, a quick change-around. Campaigning for a county seat also required a good deal more logistical sophistication than a relatively compact borough like Aylesbury. It demonstrated once again Wilkes's impressive organizational abilities and his attention to detail. Wilkes was always punctilious in sending a card of thanks to anyone who polled for him and kept careful notes of his likely supporters.[32]

Choosing to contest the large and diverse county of Middlesex demonstrated Wilkes's keen grasp of political reality. No other county would have welcomed him as Middlesex did, and he was able to tap into his Clerkenwell roots. Indeed, it is noteworthy that all bar one of the eighteen voters from Clerkenwell featuring in the pollbooks either 'plumped' for Wilkes or voted for him with one of the other candidates.[33] In managing the campaign he was assisted by the tireless work of a committee assembled to oversee his election. Their headquarters were the King's Arms (the place to which he had been carried during polling for the City) and the Mile End Assembly Rooms. The latter, located in East London, was the general meeting place for the diverse population of the area, though increasingly dominated by respectable families with maritime interests.[34] From these two bases, Wilkes's supporters arranged transportation for the voters spread out across Middlesex, who would need to present themselves at the county town of Brentford to lodge their votes. Announcements were made that carriages would be laid on at twelve locations, including the Assembly Rooms, the King of Sweden at Wapping Dock, the Three Tuns in Spitalfields and the Angel, Islington. For those preferring to travel by river, there were also barges provided. On the day of the election, each freeholder was to be given a cockade and a card bearing the slogan, 'Liberty and Wilkes'.[35] Similar arrangements were made for future contests.[36]

In Brentford itself, rooms were secured for Wilkes's backers. In this he was aided by John Horne, who was for a time to become one of Wilkes's key political allies. Horne was ideally located as perpetual curate of St Lawrence, Brentford, and used his local knowledge to maximum effect. The detail of Horne's guidance was made clear in a later letter, when Wilkes was gearing up for a new election, giving him details of several people eager to assist:

> Some very good friends of yours, freeholders of the County of Middlesex, have applied to me that they may have the honour of serving you in the Neighbourhood of Fulham. I know them very well and know how zealous and disinterested they were in your behalf.
> Mr Mackender, Butcher
> Mr Young – Baker
> Mr Barrow – Keeps Carriages at the King's Arms
> Mr Chapman – Brewer at Putney
> Mr Blake – Watchmaker at Fulham
> Mr Bestley – Shoemaker at Fulham[37]

The men recommended by Horne underscored the kind of skilled artisans on whom Wilkes was relying in Middlesex.[38]

As the day drew near for the poll at Brentford, some of the ephemera that would soon be so closely associated with the Wilkite cause began to appear on the scene. Along with '45' Wilkes's supporters had appropriated the colour blue from the Tories. As well as cockades, cards bearing familiar Wilkite slogans were distributed to encourage people to turn out, whether they had a vote or not.[39] There was even some indication that Wilkes's anti-Scots rhetoric had failed to put off a number of Scottish voters offering their votes for him.[40] Just as he had in the City, Wilkes made efforts to keep his supporters in good order, urging them 'to convince the world that Liberty is not joined to Licentiousness'. Despite this, voters attempting to make their way to Brentford in support of Cooke and Proctor were subjected to violence and abuse, with a number turning back rather than risking running the gauntlet. This was particularly true around Hyde Park Corner, a natural gathering point.[41] The zone around the polling booths at Brentford Butts was generally calm, however, and Wilkes himself intervened to ensure that it stayed that way.[42] It was, after all, in his interests to make sure that the poll proceeded peacefully so that there was no risk of it being challenged on the grounds of violence and intimidation. While many papers carried pro-Wilkite sentiments, it is notable that one letter, signed 'Jack Ketch' posed a series of critical questions, among them what had happened to the missing Foundling Hospital funds Wilkes had 'filched'?[43]

The poll was due to commence at ten in the morning of the 28th. Wilkes was conveyed to Brentford Butts, where the polling booth had been erected, in a carriage drawn by six 'long tail horses'. According to one paper, he was joined there by Proctor, but Cooke stayed away, pleading gout. In a later justification for his supporters' behaviour at the poll, Wilkes and his committee asserted that Proctor had not arrived until 1pm, causing some restlessness among the crowd. They also complained that their opponents had goaded them by erecting blue banners inscribed 'No Blasphemer, No French Renegado', at Piccadilly, which had been brought along to Brentford and set up near the hustings. In spite of the provocation, it was asserted in the press that Wilkes's supporters remained remarkably peaceable.[44] At 11.30 there was a show of hands, which suggested Wilkes to be far in the lead, Proctor second and very few votes for Cooke at all. Nonetheless, Cooke's supporters demanded a formal poll, which got underway at one in the afternoon.[45] In the course of the poll there were further examples of Wilkes's repartee. When one voter told him that he would rather vote for the devil than for him, Wilkes responded easily 'And if your friend is not standing?'

At the close of the poll (around eight that evening) it was clear that Wilkes had come first, though there was some uncertainty about the overall numbers. The poll was reopened the next morning so that any remaining votes could be tallied. The newspapers announced a variety of figures, all placing Wilkes at the top, but recording Proctor as the second placed candidate over Cooke. When the official numbers were finally released, though, it was found that Cooke had nudged ahead with 821 to Proctor's 809. Cooke's success owed something to Wilkes's intervention as, late in the day when it was clear that he could not be caught, he had urged his supporters to give their second votes to Cooke.[46] He presumably distrusted Proctor as a Rockinghamite working with the Grenville faction. What was in no doubt, though, was Wilkes's victory, with 1,268 votes.[47]

Wilkes's success has been attributed to 'a cocktail of superb organization and popular enthusiasm'.[48] The former was something that had been apparent in his earlier contests in Aylesbury. The degree of popular support that he had been able to harness off the back of the *North Briton*, his imprisonment and remarkable return from exile was new, but something he was to prove adept at exploiting to the full. Once the results had been announced, he mounted the hustings once more to offer a victory speech, closing with what would prove to be only slight hyperbole; 'The eyes of the whole kingdom, of the whole world, are upon you, as the first and foremost defenders of public liberty.'[49]

Unsurprisingly, in the aftermath of the Middlesex poll, there was considerable discussion about Wilkes, his followers and what the new movement meant. For many they were a worrying threat. There was even a story in the press that one man, Alexander McCloed, had been so shocked to hear of Wilkes's election that he dropped dead on the spot.[50] While dismissing Wilkes as 'a trouble-maker and a sort of firebrand to light the flames of sedition', though, Sir William Jones could not avoid admitting that Wilkes was a man 'of energy and intelligence'.[51] It was not just in England that Wilkes's progress was being watched carefully. His former French hosts were particularly intrigued and when congratulating Wilkes on his election Diderot insisted 'the love of liberty fired every breast, and procured you the suffrage of the independent electors.'[52]

As to the underpinning causes of the Wilkite movement, it was clear that Wilkes had not come out of nowhere, and the protesting crowds were a complex and dynamic force. For some 'Wilkes and Liberty' was little more than a flag of convenience and Wilkes himself a lord of misrule, allowing them to express a broad range of grievances.[53] One historian has gone so far as to state that even without Wilkes, the country would have been rocked by disturbances. There had been poor harvests and the country was in the midst of an economic downturn.[54] One MP, Henry

Seymour, seemed to concur. In May he complained in the Commons about having to fight his way past a 'mob' of tailors, trying to present a petition. He went on to observe 'You have mobs of different kinds springing up every day.'[55] One correspondent wondered how Wilkes had ever been permitted back into the country and foresaw perceptively that the result would be the overthrow of the ministry.[56] What is clear is that Wilkes was supremely talented at catching the national mood and exploiting the zeitgeist to the full. This was reflected in Colonel Bate's assessment that 'Wilkes and Le Diable have possessed the populous [sic].'[57] It was not just 'Le Diable', of course. Supporters like Matthew Christian, a gentleman of some means, helped fuel the crowd with quantities of ale to celebrate Wilkes's victory.[58]

While many papers commented on the surprising good order with which the Middlesex poll had been conducted, it rapidly became apparent that Wilkes had unleashed a force that he would struggle to rein in. Thus, in spite of his efforts to ensure his supporters restrained themselves, there was widespread disorder. Carriages carrying his opponents' supporters had their windows smashed and pro-Wilkite slogans daubed on them.[59] From Brentford all the way to the City, windows were illuminated and the number forty-five was chalked and scratched on walls, window shutters and doors. Those not agreeing to place lights in their windows or drink toasts to Wilkes risked being roughed up. Days after, and even once the chalked-on messages had been rubbed off, evidence of the damage to property was still to be seen. Walls and columns bore the marks of 'stones, brick-bats & lumps of dry mortar with which they were batter'd plentifully'. So great had been the rioting that the king and queen had opted to avoid attending the opera or playhouses for a time.[60] Of course, not everything was necessarily riotous. One report from Witney in Oxfordshire relayed that news of Wilkes's success was greeted by the local college youths by ringing forty-five peals of Bob Major. There was also money to be made. One ballad singer was said to have been able to earn between eighteen shillings and as much as a guinea a day during the election, singing pro-Wilkite songs.[61]

For many, there was general bemusement about those who had chosen to underwrite Wilkes's campaign. The costs of the election had been taken on by the Committee operating out of the King's Arms and Mile End and there were also moves afoot for Wilkes's debts to be paid off. What were otherwise respectable men doing consorting with this brand of popular politics? 'Men whose circumstances in life ought to render them friends to good order instead of rendering them fomenters of Riot & confusion.'[62] The assumption, though, that it had only been the lower orders who had voted for Wilkes was challenged in the press a few days after the poll. Signed simply 'An Independent Yeoman', the correspondent insisted that over 200 of Wilkes's voters were gentlemen with incomes in excess of £400 a year.[63] Locality was also important. One voter named John Preston, whose address was given as Aylesbury but clearly also qualified in Middlesex, unsurprisingly voted for Wilkes (along with Proctor).[64] Despite this, it is clear that the bulk of Wilkes's supporter base did indeed come from the shopkeepers and artisans of Middlesex. One such was later highlighted by Sir John Fielding in a report concerning demonstrations in London in October 1769. He drew attention to a certain carpenter living near St Clement's Church, who had 'always distinguish'd himself on these Occasions' as a particular supporter of Wilkes.[65]

As well as trying to comprehend the motivations of those who had backed Wilkes, there was also a desire to understand what he wanted. After all, he was still in receipt of a pension, privately fed to him by some of the Rockinghams. One observer thought it remarkable that Wilkes's 'venom seems more darted at what is usually call'd Mr Grenvill's Administration than at the present'. He also pointed out the prominent role of non-Anglicans among Wilkes's supporters and that they comprised a significant part of the organizing committee, 'And these people voted for Trecothick & him [Wilkes] in the City and for Wilkes in the Country.' He also pointed out that Wilkes now transcended London metropolitan politics and that 'in Yorkshire the same language of Wilkes and liberty prevails.'[66] Other places followed suit, including Berwick and Morpeth in the far north-east.[67]

Perhaps unsurprisingly, one of the towns to celebrate Wilkes's success was his former manor of Aylesbury, where the bells rang without ceasing for well over a day.[68] In fact, 'Wilkes and Liberty' was already chiming far beyond Aylesbury or Yorkshire. During his exile Wilkes had met a number of Americans, many of whom came to see his cause as inherently bound up with their own. By 1768, Wilkes's name was as familiar across the Atlantic as it was in Britain and regularly toasted.[69] Not everyone was a supporter of course. In April 1769, one correspondent in Dublin reported to the British attorney general, William de Grey, that there had been 'an attempt to celebrate Wilkes here, but without success'.[70]

Wilkes's triumph in Middlesex took everyone by surprise, but none more so than the administration. Grafton's handling of the 1768 election has been criticized as 'incompetent'. He lacked the application of his predecessors and was, at the time, more focused on an extra-marital affair than he was with managing the government's electoral campaign.[71] The same neglectfulness could be seen in the government response to Wilkes's success. Horace Walpole thought him best left alone. Had he been permitted to take his seat in the Commons, Walpole reckoned he would soon have disappeared, 'for he is a wretched speaker, and will sink into contempt.'⁷² Nevertheless, the administration was clear that Wilkes's victory required an official response. Had he not won, they would much rather have preferred to leave him alone. As Grafton noted in his later reminiscences: 'So little indeed was there a desire of molesting Mr Wilkes ... that I firmly believe, had he not stepped forward as the chieftain of riot and disturbance, he might have remained unnoticed.'⁷³

Immediately after the election, Wilkes retreated to Bath for a few days, accompanied by Polly.⁷⁴ One observer reported that he had 'made no great éclat' there but also noted the various musings on what would happen next. Wilkes had undertaken, once elected, to present himself before the courts so that the question of his outlawry and convictions could be settled. Some thought King's Bench would 'pass a slight sentence upon him, and so end his affair at once'. Others thought the matter would be postponed until after Parliament had met, when a general act of grace would be passed, which would take care of the whole matter in one fell swoop.⁷⁵ What all of these assessments agreed on was that the legal position was murky. In spite of that, Wilkes's victory lap continued with him being admitted to membership of the Honourable and Laudable Society of Anti-Gallicans on 14 April.⁷⁶ Admission to other more or less distinguished clubs would continue throughout the year.

Surrender

True to his word, on 20 April, just under a month after his election, Wilkes presented himself before the Court of King's Bench to settle his legal status. The month after the Commons had resolved to expel him in January 1764, Wilkes had been tried in his absence before Lord Mansfield and convicted of libel for *North Briton 45* and the *Essay on Woman*. His failure to appear for sentencing had resulted in him being outlawed. Four years later, Mansfield was still presiding over the court, mottled with extensive bruising following a recent fall from his horse.⁷⁷ Wilkes made a brief speech complaining of his convictions, rehearsing old arguments in defence of the *North Briton* and asserting that the *Essay on Woman* had not been published, but only intended for private circulation. It was, he said, a 'mere ludicrous production'.⁷⁸

Buoyed by his election, Wilkes appears to have particularly enjoyed goading the court with one of his more conceited performances. To the consternation of the Attorney General, present in court as the government's chief law officer, Mansfield refused to let the case continue, announcing that the correct writ had not been issued against Wilkes, so he was to all intents and purposes a non-person. The technicality was corrected the next day and on the 27th Wilkes appeared again.

In the meantime, his case had, unsurprisingly, remained a hot topic of conversation. At least one contemporary thought Wilkes had little chance of having the outlawry set aside, thinking his main aim to 'lengthen out the business and gain time, which I believe is what he now chiefly aims at.'[79] In front of Mansfield once more, Wilkes applied for bail but was turned down and instead remanded to King's Bench prison while the court considered his sentencing. As he had not been sworn in as an MP, he was not able to claim privilege to secure his release.[80]

En route to prison there were further farcical shenanigans. While Wilkes was being conveyed over Westminster Bridge accompanied by John Horne, the marshal of King's Bench prison and several court officers, their carriage was halted by a crowd. In spite of Wilkes's protestations, the horses were unhitched and the coach, newly emblazoned with '45', turned about and dragged along into the City. Wilkes's rescuers ignored his request to be let down at the Devil Tavern at Temple Bar, and insisted on taking him to a tavern in Spitalfields for a celebration. It was not until evening that Wilkes was able to give his rescuers the slip and make his way back to prison in disguise to hand himself in.[81] The episode clearly went to his head and, when writing to Suard shortly after, he not only credited himself with saving the lives of the court officers but also of being 'king of this great people'.[82]

While Wilkes found himself caught up in the legal system, the ministry continued to deliberate on how best to deal with him. On 22 April, Grafton had advised the king that the cabinet thought it best that Wilkes should be prevented from taking his seat in Parliament, if it might be achieved legally and constitutionally.[83] The Wilkes affair, unsurprisingly, proved a central topic of discussion when Parliament gathered for a brief session commencing on 10 May and running to 21 June. Any control the ministry had was, though, quickly overtaken by events.

Ever since Wilkes had been imprisoned, large numbers of people had gathered in the open space in front of the gaol. That it was far from being a bad tempered 'mob' is suggested by a report by one of the prison's turnkeys. For some of the time the apparently perfectly good-humoured crowd enjoying a holiday atmosphere was entertained by 'mountebank performances' and by 'diversions and amusements'.[84] Such groups of people, after all, were complex and dynamic entities. Some may have been there to cause trouble, others merely taking advantage of the carnival that followed Wilkes wherever he went. It is also worth remembering that in May 1768, many of those engaged in London trades were on strike, seeking better pay and conditions.[85] Matters had almost got out of hand on 8 May, though on that occasion Wilkes himself was able to persuade his supporters to disperse. On the 10th, the opening day of the parliamentary session, there was to be no such peaceful resolution. Amid reports of Wilkes's likely release, anything between 15,000 and 40,000 were said to have assembled outside the gaol and become sufficiently unruly for the magistrates on duty to call for back-up. Unfortunately, the troops were from the 3rd Regiment of Foot, a Scots outfit, and tensions rose as members of the crowd began throwing missiles at the soldiers and magistrates. One of the latter, Daniel Ponton, proved the catalyst for more ill feeling, after he removed a pro-Wilkes paper from the prison wall. His colleague, Samuel Guillam, eventually had recourse to reading the Riot Act after being felled by a brickbat. When the crowd failed to disperse, the troops opened fire.

Accounts differed about who gave the order. One witness, Bamber Gascoyne, believed that the troops had done so of their own volition and exonerated the magistrates of ordering the soldiers to fire on the crowd. Whoever was to blame, six or seven people were killed, in what was to become known as the Massacre of St George's Fields. What does seem clear is that by no means all had been involved in the rioting. As Thomas notes, one victim had been selling oranges, another happened to be driving past in their cart at the time. The most notorious victim was an innocent bystander, William Allen, son of a local innkeeper, who happened to be wearing a red waistcoat matching that of one of the rioters who had particularly annoyed the troops. A party of soldiers was despatched to find the rioter. They found Allen instead and shot him dead. The killings sparked further rioting across London.[86] For Wilkes, the event would later prompt him to launch a spirited attack on Viscount Weymouth, the secretary of state who had authorized troops to be deployed.

The massacre sparked fury, but some of those involved were lampooned in contemporary print satires. Alexander Murray, the commander of the detachment from the 3rd Foot, may have been the target of one of Matthias Darly's caricatures: 'The Tiger Macaroni, or Twenty More, Kill'em'.[87] Guillam meanwhile was derided for being an illiterate in a cartoon which depicted him as 'Midas', complete with ass's ears, requesting a copy of the Act of Parliament relating to JPs. Wilkes stands behind him, lamenting 'Not satisfied with the Murder of the English he must also Murder the English Language.'[88] Rather more seriously, Guillam was tried for murder as a result of his involvement in the affair. Although he was acquitted, he clearly believed that he was being thrown to the wolves and passed out twice in court.[89] Two of the soldiers involved in the murder of Allen were also tried in August at the Surrey assizes. They were both acquitted. A third had absconded. Many assumed the authorities had connived at his escape.[90] At the same assizes that saw the soldiers exonerated, members of the crowd were tried for their role in the rioting. Wilkes himself had been summoned as a witness, conveyed from prison to Guildford, where he arrived early in the morning and spent the whole day there before being carted back again late in the evening. There was a striking contrast between the way he was greeted by local supporters, with bells ringing, and his rather shoddy government-authorized accommodation while in the town.[91]

The massacre cast a pall over the opening of Parliament, though the soldiers' brutality seems to have resulted in fewer people gathering to protest in the days ahead. Meanwhile, things remained tense both within Parliament and among supporters of the government. On the 12th, Lord North hosted a meeting at which most of those speaking out advocated expelling Wilkes from Parliament at once. The followers of Chatham present at the event were noticeable by their unwillingness to fall into line. Supporters of the ministry, meanwhile, found Grafton's half-hearted approach to the Wilkes problem difficult to understand. On 18 May the firebrand member for Bossiney in Cornwall, Henry Lawes Luttrell, moved that the House should be informed why nothing had been done about Wilkes. He had tried to broach the subject two days before, in a rather eccentric oration rounded off with a quotation from *Henry IV*: 'I should think myself criminal, if I did not mention [Wilkes's name], though there be enchantment in the sound; though a starling in the gallery should catch the sound, and convey it to him.'[92] North offered him support, but an adjournment saved the ministry from having to put Luttrell's ill-timed intervention to a vote.[93]

All the while, Parliament was thronged with a growing crowd of discontented Wilkes supporters, chanting the familiar cry of 'Wilkes and Liberty'. Elsewhere, there were more demonstrations. Following a pro-Wilkite riot in Southwark, two soldiers who had joined the crowd were punished by being subjected to forty-five lashes and then given forty-five days of drill on short rations.[94] The authorities were not shy of reappropriating the Wilkite symbols to make a point.

On 8 June Mansfield was finally ready to deliver his judgment on the question of the outlawry. He commenced with a lengthy harangue against Wilkes, making it clear that he had only himself to blame for his predicament after fleeing the country. Despite this, he concluded that the outlawry should be reversed on the grounds of a technical mistake made by the sheriff at the time. The writ ought to have stated where it had been executed (Middlesex), but the sheriff had omitted this vital phrase. Consequently, it was of no force and the outlawry needed to be set aside. As had happened before over Wilkes's release from the Tower by Pratt, he had been saved by the most minor of errors. The crowd, packed into Westminster Hall to witness the result, gave way to by now familiar jubilation. They even offered to pull Mansfield's carriage home for him, but he chose not to indulge them.[95]

The regularization of Wilkes's legal status allowed his legal team to revive his dormant case against Halifax, though it was noted they would have to give the courts a term's notice as the suit had been allowed to lapse for four terms.[96] Despite the delay, as general warrants had been declared illegal four years before, there was every reason to expect that Wilkes's case would succeed. In November he was finally awarded damages of £4,000 in the court of Common Pleas, but it is an indication of the strength of the Wilkite crowd by then that this was thought a disappointing result. Wilkes had demanded £10,000.[97]

Wilkes may no longer have been an outlaw, but he was still a convicted felon. On 14 June he made a final bid to overturn his convictions but was unsuccessful. The febrile atmosphere in London at the time was captured by one contemporary, writing the same day from his house in Lincoln's Inn Fields. Although he explained that he could not find out precisely what had happened in Westminster Hall that day, he reported just seeing a number of coal-heavers passing beneath his windows. They had been sent from Sir John Fielding's in Bow Street to Newgate under guard 'for riots & murders committed on the riverside'. He concluded, 'These are times full of strange events.'[98] He was presumably referring to the notorious rioting by the Shadwell and Wapping coal-heavers, which culminated in the murder of one of the coal undertakers named John Green.[99]

Having failed in his legal bid, on 18 June Wilkes was in court again to hear his sentence. It fell to Justice Joseph Yates to inform him of his fate. He was fined £500 for each of the publications, along with ten months in gaol for the *North Briton* and another year for the *Essay on Woman*. Wilkes was, though, spared the pillory. No doubt the judges wisely concluded that attempting to impose what was otherwise a normal element of a sentence for seditious libel would be likely to rebound against them.[100]

8
Parliament and Prison
(1768–1770)

...our sovereign lords, the mob.

From April 1768 when he first surrendered himself to the court until April 1770, Wilkes was incarcerated in the King's Bench prison, over the Thames in Southwark. Wilkes's fellow prisoners were mostly debtors, though there were others, like him, who had been imprisoned for various felonies. Wilkes was himself, of course, massively in debt as well. In the first year of his imprisonment his debts were said to have increased from about £6,000 to £14,000, not including the £1,000 fine.[1] Quite how many people were in the prison at any one time is difficult to assess, as many debtors were there with their families as well. In 1776, it was estimated that in addition to the 395 prisoners there were 279 wives and 725 children. A quarter of a century later there were 570 prisoners, of whom about 340 had wives and children with them.[2]

Wilkes's conditions there were far from bad. The site had been selected just under twenty years before Wilkes arrived there on the basis of its relatively healthy location. There was a high wall surmounted with spikes, but otherwise the prison regime was pretty lax. The gates were locked at night but remained open during the day. Prisoners had keys to their rooms and while there were some prohibited items such as spirits and weapons, little was done to enforce the restrictions. Wilkes would probably have kept hold of his sword as a standard item of his attire as a gentleman. It was not unheard of for inmates to possess duelling pistols.[3] Wilkes was regularly entertained with gifts of food, drink and clothing. The Chevalier d'Eon, the notorious trans French soldier-diplomat, sent him a gift of larks' tongues. Someone else sent him a turtle, which became the centrepiece of a feast thrown for his supporters.[4] Well-wishers in Covent Garden sent him twenty guineas and a hamper of booze, while the duchess of Queensberry sent £100.[5] Much of this largesse was offered up in symbolic quantities. 'An honest chandler' sent him a box containing forty-five dozen candles.[6] There was a salmon said to weigh forty-five pounds, forty-five pounds of tea from Norfolk, and a forty-five pound Cheshire cheese. There were smaller, humbler gifts too, from starstruck individuals. Some gifts came from the other side of the Atlantic, where the cry of Wilkes and Liberty was adopted by a number of those beginning their campaign for greater independence. The 'Sons of Liberty' from Boston sent turtles. Some Maryland planters sent forty-five hogsheads of tobacco, undoubtedly the product of slave labour.[7]

As well as receiving lavish gifts, Wilkes was free to entertain visitors, who no doubt all added to these charitable donations. One of those to pay him a visit was John Barnard, son of Lord Mayor Sir John Barnard, and a long-standing supporter. Barnard made the error of bringing his wife, Jane, with him, with whom Wilkes managed to rekindle an affair. Being locked up proved no problem for him on this score. They had been involved with each other years before she married Barnard, as his second wife. She was bored and frustrated by her spouse, whom she dubbed 'King Log' for his sexual inadequacy as well as his tightfistedness. Wilkes, on the other hand, she praised as a lively and satisfying lover. Horne helped engineer her visits, gaining himself the soubriquet of Wilke's 'pimp-general' from Barnard after he found out about the liaison. It would persist for several months, only concluding after Wilkes's release from prison.[8]

Prison did not stop Wilkes remaining in touch with his European contacts and developing new ones. One of those eager to make his acquaintance was Mozart's patron, Gottfried, Baron van Swieten.[9] There was a lively correspondence with his Parisian circle. Suard remained a particularly close friend and Wilkes expressed his obligations to him for looking out for his 'nephew', John Smith. He was worried Smith had been 'much neglected' and had contracted an ague from 'the cold marshy ground of Calais' but hoped that he might improve under Suard's guidance.[10] He also discussed with Suard the founding of the new Royal Academy of Arts under the king's patronage. Writing in June 1768, some months before the academy's official foundation, Wilkes commented dismissively that the new body could 'never thrive under the inelegant, and banefull shade of the Northern (i.e. Scottish) heresy, which has been fatal to the eye in painting, to the ear in music, to the smell in incense.'[11] Wilkes would later be depicted in Richard Earlom's mezzotint *The Exhibition of the Royal Academy of Painting in the Year 1771*, showing him among an array of strange-looking spectators viewing that year's exhibition in Pall Mall.[12]

As ever with Wilkes, family remained extremely important. Both Polly and Wilkes's mother paid him frequent visits, and it was from his lodgings in the prison that Wilkes penned one of several poems in honour of Polly's birthday on 16 August:

How shall the Muse in prison sing,
How prune her drooping ruffled wing?
Maria is the potent spell,
E'en in these walls all grief to quell...[13]

Besides all of these, there were also more obviously political contacts. The American Arthur Lee, soon to be a member of the Society of Supporters of the Bill of Rights, was one such, who would be instrumental in developing Wilkes's views on the American question.[14] Wilkes gushed about the younger man that he was 'one of the *greatest* this Country ever saw ... his *first* and *best* friend'.[15] Wilkes's attitude to the colonies had hitherto been somewhat ambiguous, but he would happily tap into the influential American community within the City of London. Increasingly, the cause of Wilkes and Liberty and that of the American radicals were seen as one and the same.[16] As a result, Wilkes began increasingly to receive missives from over the Atlantic.[17] This correspondence reveals his changing political stance. Having entered politics as a fairly typical scion of a major faction, circumstances had pushed him into ever more radical territory. He was now both a celebrity and a hero of the 'mob'. By the time he left prison, there was significant distance between him and his old noble patrons as he increasingly identified the world of London radical politics as his natural home.

Imprisonment, after all, in no way settled Wilkes's political position. Through the autumn of 1768 there was talk of a possible deal between Wilkes and the ministry. By now Grafton had taken over as Prime Minister, following Chatham's resignation in October 1768. Ostensibly, this was on the grounds of poor health, but quite as important was the infighting within the administration. Chatham was furious about his protégé Lord Shelburne being side-lined.[18] It fell to Grafton, then, to respond to the unhelpful incarcerated Middlesex MP. Wilkes clearly did not expect any favours, so on 3 November he pressed on with publishing an Address to his constituents, undertaking to submit a petition for redress of grievances as soon as Parliament resumed later that month.[19] Grafton was in no mood for having Wilkite grievances swamping business, so opened negotiations via William Fitzherbert and John Almon. The actor, David Garrick, whom Wilkes had met during his exile in France, attended some of the discussions as a witness to ensure that Wilkes did not try to misrepresent what was being offered. Like with so many others, Wilkes's relationship with Garrick was ambiguous. Although part of the same artistic and literary circles, Wilkes was capable of being quite dismissive.[20]

What was on the table was the prospect of release from prison in return for a private submission to the king and an undertaking that Wilkes would not present his petition to the Commons. Wilkes would then be able to resume his privileges as an MP, saving him from his creditors, and the disagreeable prospect of another seventeen months behind bars. Wilkes refused.[21] Why? Was this out of a high-minded sense of duty to the people he now represented? Perhaps that was true, in part. But the reality was probably more complex. Wilkes had every reason to distrust Grafton and must have found the prospect of being in his debt distasteful. Also, he had tasted fame and the adulation of the crowd. If he were to accept the government's offer, he might be able to resume his libertine existence in peace and quiet, but he would be nobody and derided for deserting the cause of Liberty. So, if not high-minded exactly, and shot through with a conceited sense of his own importance, it was not out of character for him to refuse the olive branch. As he had when standing up to Lord Talbot and ignoring Lord Temple's advice over the *North Briton*, Wilkes rarely took the easy route. The result was the continuation of the cause of 'Wilkes and Liberty', which might otherwise have been smothered within months of being born.

The first Wilkites

Consequently, on 14 November 1768 Sir Joseph Mawbey rose in the Commons to present Wilkes's petition. It rehearsed a number of well-worn themes. It complained of his arrest under the general warrant and of Mansfield's supposed alteration of the wording of the indictment against him. It also repeated the claims that Webb had bribed Michael Curry to hand over papers to incriminate Wilkes over the *Essay on Woman*. According to James Harris, the House was not particularly well attended for the occasion. In spite of the hullaballoo everywhere else, and later hot-tempered debates over the issue, on this day the matter was treated fairly soberly. Another contemporary also observed that there was not much of a crowd to witness the proceedings: just 'a few second rate Gentry in the lobby'.[22] Mawbey himself was a slightly absurd figure. He was five years younger than Wilkes but came from a similar background. The family money came from distilling and they also shared an interest in pigs. Mawbey had received a baronetcy from the Rockingham administration in 1765 but otherwise had spent most of his political career in opposition. After presenting the petition, he moved that it lie on the table of the Commons, a motion that was received with surprise by Lord Strange, one of the MPs for Lancashire. Concerned for the privileges of all Members represented by the case, Strange moved for papers relating to the case in King's Bench to be laid before the House as well. Mawbey then excused himself for having confined himself to presenting the petition before the debate was taken over by others.[23] The next to speak was William Beckford. Beckford had been abused in the *North Briton* and was clearly less committed to Wilkes's cause than some others: he even professed himself 'tired of Wilkes and Liberty'. However, he also considered Wilkes to have been badly treated and argued in favour of the petition being considered.[24] After him, John Sawbridge rose to his feet. He was a new Member, who had been elected for the first time at the general election as MP for Hythe, a seat close to the family seat of Olantigh. Although a landed gentleman, there was another distilling connexion, as his father-in-law, Sir William Stephenson, was a hop-merchant and distiller. In spite of his landed background, Sawbridge was also developing a significant profile in the City and would go on to become Lord Mayor immediately after Wilkes. His sister, Catharine Macaulay, would come to know Wilkes well, too.

During the debate, some prominent figures in the City, previously sympathetic to Wilkes, changed their position. It resumed on 23 November, when Mawbey was again prominent in Wilkes's behalf. Lord Barrington had spoken critically of those who had elected Wilkes but Mawbey replied, insisting: 'it was not the refuse of the people, it was not the mob, who elected Mr Wilkes. The characters of those who supported him were as good as that of the noble lord, at least'.[25] Proceedings then continued until 10 December when the ministry was finally able to kick it into the long grass by adjourning further discussion until 27 January 1769. Wilkes then turned up the heat by submitting to the press evidence that Viscount Weymouth had written to Daniel Ponton well in advance of the 10 May riot, reminding him that troops could be made available. Wilkes's accusation was that the 'massacre' had been planned in advance. It was this final provocation, as much as anything else, that persuaded Grafton at last that Wilkes had to be expelled from Parliament. On 15 December the Lords passed a motion that Wilkes's latest outpourings constituted 'an insolent, scandalous and seditious libel', which aimed to stir up the king's subjects to 'sedition'. The resolution was then sent to the Commons, where there were angry scenes prompting an adjournment of further deliberation for four days. Witnesses were heard on the 19th confirming Wilkes as the author, but the business was then adjourned once more, to be taken up at the same time as Wilkes's deferred petition on 27 January.[26]

In the meantime, Wilkes had scored a signal victory over the government. Just a few months after being elected, George Cooke died, triggering a by-election in Middlesex. The new election offered to Wilkes and his followers an opportunity of extending the cause of Liberty beyond his own narrow focus. Beauchamp Proctor chose to stand again, but he was not permitted an uncontested election. Against him, the Wilkites put up none other than Serjeant Glynn, Wilkes's lawyer. From the summer through to the close of polling on 14 December both sides fought vigorously for votes. As the by-election was set to overlap with the ongoing debates in Parliament on Wilkes's petition, one observer noted 'here is a fair Preparation for Mobbs & Riot, that rise as naturally in free Countrys, as Cucumbers in a Hot bed'.[27] He was right, and the election was characterized by violent clashes, many involving heavies hired by Proctor. During the scuffles, some of the poll books were purloined prompting Parliament to intervene to ensure that duplicate books managed by the candidates were made safe so the votes could be tallied accurately.[28] Although Proctor was able to improve on his previous performance, securing 1,267 votes, his tactics were not enough to gain him the seat and he was defeated by Glynn, polling 1,538 votes.[29] Two of Proctor's toughs, Lawrence Balf (or Balfe) and Edward MacQuirk, were subsequently convicted for murder after one victim died from injuries sustained during the scrum. Both were sentenced to death.[30] George Clarke's death makes plain that it was not just Wilkes's followers who were prepared to intimidate their opponents. Most of all, though, Glynn's election gave the cause of Wilkes and Liberty a fillip just as Parliament was about to turn its attention to Wilkes's petition.

In spite of the provocation caused by Glynn's success, with just days to go before Parliament was set to consider what to do about Wilkes, it was believed the ministry had still not settled the question of expelling him. A meeting in late January 1769, however, seems to have resolved any lingering doubts.[31] This prompted the banker, Joseph Martin, MP for Gatton (Surrey), to rise in the Commons and propose that Wilkes was entitled to privilege as MP for Middlesex. Martin was at pains to underline that he had no particular connexion with Wilkes himself. Indeed, he had voted against him in the City election. It was, he insisted, 'the cause that animates me'.[32] After interventions from Lord North and George Grenville, Martin's motion was rejected. When Parliament met on the 27th to consider the adjourned business about Wilkes's petition, the atmosphere was bad-tempered. The same day the king himself made his own views apparent. He insisted on the necessity for Wilkes's expulsion, as a matter 'whereon almost my Crown depends'.[33]

Of course, it was not just the question of Wilkes's expulsion that was at issue. As one observer reporting to Lord Townshend pointed

1. View of Old Palace Yard, oil painting by unknown artist.
(© UK Parliament, WOA 6263, heritagecollections.parliament.uk)

2. 'Het stadhuis van Leiden' (Leiden Town Hall), Jan de Beijer, 1751.
(Rijksmuseum)

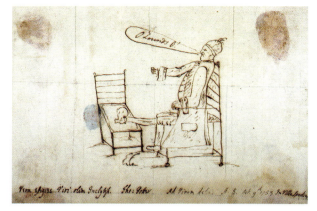

3. Thomas Potter, self-portrait in ink. (© British Library Board. All rights reserved/Bridgeman Images)

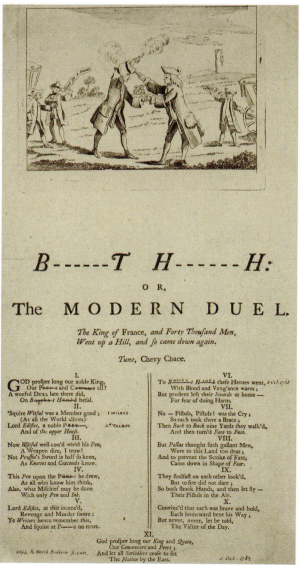

4. 'Bagshot Heath, or the Modern Duel.' (© Trustees of the British Museum)

5. 'Westminster Hall: the first day of term.' (Rijksmuseum)

6. 'The Colossus', depicting the Earl of Bute. (Wellcome Collection)

7. John Wilkes by William Hogarth. (Metropolitan Museum of Art)

8. Charles Churchill, 'the Bruiser', by William Hogarth. (Metropolitan Museum of Art)

9. Mary (Polly) Wilkes by Ozias Humphry. (© National Gallery of Victoria)

10. John Glynn, John Wilkes and John Horne Tooke, monochrome mezzotint by Mr Richard Houston and Robert Sayer. (© UK Parliament, WOA 272 heritagecollections.parliament.uk)

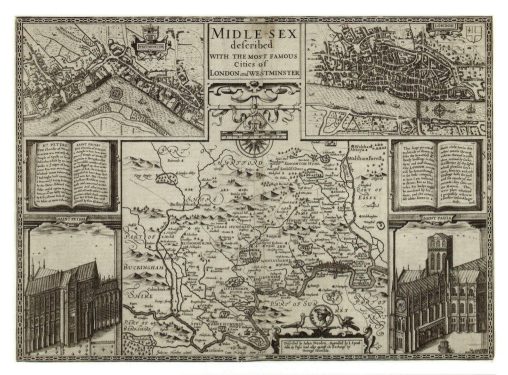

Above: 11. Map of Middlesex by Jodocus Hondius. (Rijksmuseum)

Right: 12. 'Arms of Liberty' Punchbowl. (© Art Institute of Chicago)

Below right: 13. Egyptian Hall dinner, Mansion House, coloured etching by Thomas Rowlandson, Auguste Charles Pugin, John Bluck and Rudolph Ackerman. (Metropolitan Museum of Art)

14. Gordon Riots, 1780, monochrome line engraving by James Heath and Francis Wheatley. (© UK Parliament, WOA 1474 heritagecollections.parliament.uk)

15. John and Polly Wilkes (with Roma) by Johann Zoffany. (© National Portrait Gallery, London)

16. 'Westminster Election' by Robert Dighton. (© Museum of London)

17. 'Master Billy's Procession to Grocers' Hall.' (Metropolitan Museum of Art)

18. The Grand Coalition Medal. (© Trustees of the British Museum)

19. Grosvenor Square. (Rijksmuseum)

20. Fetter Lane statue of John Wilkes.

out, he doubted the Commons would see the thing through and insist on Wilkes being incapable of being re-elected. Without that, he concluded, 'expelling him will be a foolish measure.'[34] For the time being, the government was able to maintain control of the agenda by securing acceptance of a resolution that the Commons would limit their consideration to the points relating to Mansfield altering the wording of the indictment, and the bribery charge against Webb. Wilkes was, though, able to secure a small victory for himself at the end of January when John Hatsell, the Commons' Clerk, wrote to apologise for a mistake whereby papers submitted to the House had been amended to imply that Wilkes had been convicted for blasphemy. It is interesting that Wilkes seems to have been so stung by the inference, but honour was an important thing for him.[35]

By 1 February the points relating to Mansfield and Webb had been settled in the ministry's favour. Proceedings then opened on the 2nd with Wilkes's publication of Lord Weymouth's letter to the magistrates outside King's Bench prison, and his accusation that this had amounted to a state-sponsored plan to kill members of the crowd. Wilkes himself was released from gaol for the day so that he could be heard. He made no effort to deny printing what he referred to as Weymouth's 'bloody scroll'. The ministry then moved that Wilkes's publication amounted to 'an insolent, scandalous and seditious libel'. Following a lengthy debate, only concluded in the small hours of the next morning, the motion was passed in the ministry's favour, with a majority of just over one hundred.[36] With Wilkes once again condemned for seditious libel, the way was now clear for a new motion expelling Wilkes from Parliament.

On 3 February, just over five years after first expelling Wilkes from the House, the Commons debated once again ejecting Wilkes from his seat. The issue raised the key question of the rights of electors to choose the member they wanted. One MP, Sir Grey Cooper, jotted down the arguments that appear to have been raised at this point. One was that, once the electors had cast their ballots, they 'divested themselves, & absolutely transferred all their power to their representatives collectively'. Another emphasized the Commons' right to select its own members: 'The meanest court in England has by operation of law the implicit powers necessary to enforce its jurisdiction'.[37] One unexpected voice in Wilkes's favour was George Grenville. He was far from uncritical of Wilkes and later that year Wilkes showed his disapproval by publishing a pamphlet attacking Grenville, whom he thought 'an odious fellow'. This had the unintended result of further damaging his relations with Lord Temple.[38] Once, Temple might have greeted Wilkes's latest antics with the aside, 'Wilkes in a new scrape! The foolish ministry in a greater', but those days were long gone.[39]

Certainly, there was never much doubt that the government would get its way. After Lord North rounded up the debate, the motion to expel Wilkes was carried early in the morning of the 4th by 219 votes to 137.[40]

The government may have been relieved, but Wilkes's unseating played into his hands. It kept his name in the papers and he did not regard his confinement as any sort of impediment to standing at the ensuing Middlesex by-election, thereby keeping the story rolling. Besides, as one observer queried, 'What will be the end of this if the military does not interfere?' Wilkes, this writer suggested, had wanted to be expelled and already distributed handbills referring to the fates of Charles I and James II when the 'rights of the subjects' had previously been infringed.[41]

Wilkes may have been confident of being able to stand again, but there were concerns among some of his supporters that the government intended to have him disqualified on the eve of the new poll. The diarist Sylas Neville, visited Wilkes to pass on the information but Wilkes purported to be untroubled. He thanked Neville for the intelligence but displayed characteristic high-handedness by not bothering to ask him to sit.[42] In the event, there was no proactive attempt to disqualify Wilkes and at the 16 February by-election Wilkes was returned once again. Two days before, he had been adopted at a meeting held at the Mile End Assembly Rooms, proposed by the radical City figure James Townsend and seconded by John Sawbridge. Both were to be appointed sheriffs for the City of London in the course of the year.[43] In spite of rumours to the contrary, no one was willing to set up against him. Writing late in the evening of the 16th, Lord Temple reported the news to Lady Chatham: 'W was rechosen this morning, with great Triumph, & is to be declared to morrow, with great Rancour, incapable of being elected during the present Parl[iamen]t.'[44] As Temple had predicted, on the 17th Wilkes was expelled once again and a new writ ordered. Writing from Madrid, James Harris celebrated news of Wilkes's expulsion while also demonstrating the growing international reputation of Wilkes, 'who people that did not know our manners & ways, took for a second Oliver Cromwell, whereas those that knew him, regarded him, (as he really is) as a wild, ill judging debauch'd fellow: who in all probability will from this moment sink into oblivion'.[45]

As to the last observation, Harris could not have been further from the truth. With yet another by-election triggered, once again, Wilkes was adopted at the Mile End Assembly Rooms, though this time it seemed as if there would be a challenger. Charles Dingley, a sawmill owner, who had had his property destroyed in earlier rioting, agreed to stand on the ministry's ticket. However, although he appeared on the hustings on 16 March he suddenly changed his mind and withdrew his candidacy. He had been promised several votes but mounting the hustings he was 'hissed' by the crowd: 'A panic scared him & away he flew.'[46] With Dingley no longer in the picture, Wilkes was elected once more. On the 17th, the Commons voided the return and ordered a new poll. There was some ribbing of the ministry about the new fashion for monthly elections in Middlesex, but otherwise little opposition to Wilkes being expelled once again.[47] Outside of Parliament, disorders continued as some people made the most of Wilkes thumbing his nose at the establishment. On 22 March an address was supposed to be presented to the king from the City of London, but one of those involved in the presentation, Edmund Boehm, found his carriage beset by rioters and he was forced to seek refuge in Nando's Coffee House. From there he wrote to one of the secretaries of state explaining that he could make no further progress towards St James's because of 'the rage of the Mob'. Even were he able to escape, he was now 'quite covered with dirt' and so felt himself unable to appear before the king in such a pickle.[48]

Middlesex's third election of 1769 was due to take place on 13 April. This time, the ministry was prepared and a contest guaranteed with the entrance of three challengers. One was the 'swashbuckling Irishman', Daniel Roache.[49] Although he turned up for the poll, however, Roache withdrew before voting began. The second, was a Rockinghamite lawyer named William Whitaker. He may as well have followed Roache as he was only to poll five votes on election day, in absentia. The serious contender was Henry Lawes Luttrell, a combative MP who had spoken against Wilkes on several occasions. Now, he resolved to put his money where his mouth was and stand against him. Indeed, by the beginning of April it was said that 'The conversation of the political world is quite reduced to Col[onel] Luttrell and Mr Wilkes.'[50] In the event, Luttrell fared poorly in spite of emulating the Wilkites' preparations by ferrying voters to Brentford from central London. Polling day at Brentford passed off fairly quietly, though Luttrell was assaulted en route 'by a large party of the Black Guard'. He lost his hat in the fracas, and seems to have ridden over one of the men trying to bar his way.[51] At the close of the poll, Wilkes had secured 1,135 votes: around 150 fewer than he had managed the previous year, but still a commanding majority. Luttrell mustered just 294. However, as the government had indicated that they would accept any candidate securing a majority of legal votes, it was determined ultimately that he was, in fact, the victor. Following debates in the Commons on the 14th and 15th, Wilkes's votes were all deemed invalid and Luttrell was seated accordingly as the new MP for Middlesex.[52]

If polling day had been peaceful enough, the days surrounding it were accompanied by now familiar running riots in London and elsewhere. One correspondent, writing a few days before the poll, complained:

> Such tumult, anarchy, & uproar have not been heard in our streets since the days of Wat Tyler, & Jack Straw. The allusion may be carried further, as the Lord Mayor of London was at both Era's [sic], the only magistrate who had spirit enough to withstand the insolence, of our sovereign Lords, the Mob.[53]

That Wilkes's supporters were unwilling to let the matter rest was made clear a few days after Luttrell's controversial victory. Another meeting at the Mile End Assembly Rooms, chaired by Sawbridge and attended by 'many hundreds' resolved to compose an address to be presented to the king, communicating to him their 'grievances and apprehensions'.[54] Petitions were subsequently submitted in May and July, complaining both about the Middlesex result and other political concerns. Lord Holland (the former Henry Fox) for one, believed that rioting in May had been fomented and paid for by d'Eon.[55] Petitions from other areas also flooded in over the summer, with disagreements over the election rumbling on into the following year. Indeed, in 1769, petitions over the election were submitted by eighteen counties and twenty boroughs.[56] Getting people to sign the petitions was not always straightforward, though, and at least one person admitted, 'Wilkes's character, of which Men are inclined to think much worse than it really deserves' put some people off signing.[57] However, the movement helped unite the opposition factions and eventually proved the undoing of Grafton's administration.[58]

Even before contesting Middlesex, Wilkes had been a well-known figure, especially in London. The *North Briton* affair, his imprisonment in the Tower and release by Chief Justice Pratt had all contrived to make him a household name. Middlesex transformed him still further into a celebrity politician, the like of which the country had not seen before. This was aided by the commercialization of his image. There was, of course, nothing new about popular figures and politicians appearing in a variety of media, but the sheer scale of the Wilkes industry eclipsed what had come before. Prints of Wilkes derived from Hogarth's satire and Edge Pine's far more flattering depiction were widely produced. One publication, *English Liberty*, was serialized to make it affordable, with the added draw of offering a free engraving of Wilkes with the final issue.[59] There were various types of chinaware bearing his likeness and medals with Wilkes in relief on one side and an appropriate message on the reverse. There was even a country dance, apparently appropriated from an earlier Jacobite jig, called 'Wilkes's Wriggle'.[60] Not all of these productions were necessarily owned, or commissioned, by supporters. It may be that some examples like a Chinese porcelain bowl decorated with a fine reproduction of Hogarth's caricature were intended for opponents.[61] However, Wilkes's biographer Rough did not exaggerate very much when he stated: 'Every wall bore his name, and every window his portrait. In china, in bronze, or in marble, he stood upon the chimney-piece of half the houses of the metropolis.'[62] In Wilkes the people believed they had found a folk hero they might reshape according to their own personal concerns.

The Bill of Rights Society

While all of this was going on, Wilkes remained in prison. His term was due to expire on 18 April 1770, but a problem loomed on the horizon. For the time being he was out of reach of his creditors, but fighting elections and entertaining royally had done nothing to alleviate his woeful financial situation: quite the reverse. As usual, Wilkes was simply incapable of reining in his expenses. One contemporary satire depicted him as the Byzantine general, Count Belisarius, entreating a motley group of followers to give him cash: '*Date Obolum Belisario*'.[63] In response to this, a new society was established following a meeting at the London Tavern on 20 February 1769. On that day, John Glynn was in the chair and the initial meeting secured subscriptions for over £3,000 to go towards settling Wilkes's debts. On 25 February, the new group was formally christened as the Society of Gentlemen Supporters of the Bill of Rights (SSBR). Its aims were twofold. First, to raise funds to save Wilkes from the prospect of being released from one gaol only to be plunged straight into another. Wilkes had long attracted ad hoc support. When the bookseller, John Williams, was sentenced to stand in the pillory in New Palace Yard on Valentine's Day 1765 for republishing the *North Briton*, not only were the crowd sympathetic to him (staging an angry protest against the 'Jackboot'), they also raised 200 guineas.[64] The SSBR sought to tap into this sentiment in a far more systematic way. Quite as importantly, though, it also set out to provide a campaigning platform for the wider Wilkite movement. It was not, after all, only in London and Middlesex that Wilkes was beginning to strike a chord. Wilkite clubs were founded in towns and cities nationwide, including in Bristol, Durham, Newcastle and Norwich.[65] Around ten per cent of the membership of the new society came from the legal profession, which helped make it particularly effective in prosecuting Wilkite causes.[66] In the course of 1769 alone, the SSBR contributed 30 petitions on a range of issues of interest to the Wilkites.[67] In all, petitions bearing perhaps as many as 60,000 signatures were presented through the SSBR's operations. In part, these represented alliances of convenience struck with other groups, such as the Rockinghamites, Chathamites and Temple's group, but petitions from the west country bore the imprint of John Glynn, who was influential in Devon as well as in the City.[68]

The central organization of the SSBR was controlled by several key players in London politics, many of them already familiar to Wilkes. The founding members included six MPs, three former MPs and several up-and-coming figures in the City, who would go on to become MPs. Significantly, Wilkes's brother Heaton and his brother-in-law George Hayley were also among the founder members, as was Churchill's brother, John. Wilkes himself was elected a member on 8 May 1770, shortly after his release from prison. The Society quickly settled upon a system of fortnightly meetings, with breaks during parliamentary recesses. Various sub-committees were established and over the next few months detailed efforts were made to establish the scale of Wilkes's debts and arrange for them to be paid or compounded. Sums were also granted to Wilkes for his day-to-day requirements. By the autumn, tensions were in evidence within the Society, in particular between Wilkes and John Horne. Indeed, as early as May 1769 Lord Holland reported that Wilkes had quarrelled with his friends, worrying that they were diverting attention from him.[69] Certainly, Horne believed that the Society should be about more than just Wilkes. They would eventually fall out in spectacular fashion in 1771, triggering a split in the Society.

From its foundation in February 1769 until Wilkes's release date in April 1770, the SSBR laboured to ensure that he would be able to stride out of King's Bench a free man. Unsurprisingly, after the initial rush, the levels of donations tapered off and on 14 April, just four days before he was due to leave prison, there were still substantial sums outstanding. Last-minute talks with creditors and a final heave secured enough to keep trouble at bay and on the evening of 17 April Wilkes departed King's Bench. His emancipation was marked by prisoners in Newgate lighting candles in their windows.[70] Wilkes's period of incarceration was over. The SSBR had set him back on his feet and provided him with an organization on which he could base the next stage of his campaign. His sights were now set on the City of London.

9

An Alderman of London

> Wilkes single ... easier to manage than a whole pandemonium.

Towards the end of February 1770, the *Independent Chronicle* announced that the young Welsh aristocrat Sir Watkin Williams Wynn was planning a very particular celebration for his coming of age two months later:

> We hear there is a cask made at Millbank ... which will contain 45 barrels, & is to be sent down to his seat in Wales: it is also to be tapped with 45 brass cocks, and the liquor to be given away to his tenants on the day of his coming of age, which is the 18th of April next, the same day that Mr Wilkes will be released from his confinement in the King's Bench prison.[1]

Williams Wynn was not alone in making plans to celebrate Wilkes's release. Robert Morris, secretary of the SSBR, was also able to use his attendance at the Welsh spring assizes to arrange entertainments marking their hero's freedom.[2]

Wilkes's release from imprisonment in the spring of 1770 could hardly have been more symbolic, as he was now in his forty-fifth year. His birthday the previous October had been celebrated with a number of clubs singing 'A New Song' set to music by 'H.B.' It may have been new, but it rehearsed very familiar themes, notably the belief in the existence of some malign, secret influence about the king:

> Health to our King, Let's rejoice, drink and sing,
> And may he grow wiser and wiser;
> And may he grow wiser and wiser;

And wise he'd now be, Were it not for a she,
And a damnable Scottish adviser...

After wishing damnation on Bute and lamenting the fate of men ruled by petticoats, the song returned to the usual praise of its hero:

'Tis for WILKES we are met, in a FORTY FIVE sett,
And his Foes may the Devil take all:
This Day gave him Birth, and we free Sons of Mirth,
As blithe as the Birds are in May,
Will Join Heart and Hand for LIBERTY stand,
So for WILKES and fair FREEDOM HUZZA![3]

Wilkes had been due to leave King's Bench on 18 April. In the event, he snuck out a day early, quitting the quarters which he had called home for the last two years at six in the evening. On the eve of his release there was an entertainment and ball at the Mansion House, attended by the cream of Whig society. Temple was there, as were Shelburne, Camden and the duke of Portland. Perhaps just as significantly, the papers reported crowds gathered around the tomb of Allen, the young man killed during the St George's Fields massacre, like devotees at the shrine of a 'tutelar saint'.[4]

Avoiding all of this, Wilkes was whisked away in a coach and four accompanied by John Churchill along with the lawyers John Reynolds (another member of the SSBR) and John Trevanion. During his imprisonment Wilkes had paid Reynolds the somewhat backhanded compliment of being 'a fair, candid, and true-hearted private gentleman' noting he had 'rarely seen these qualities in a sound lawyer'.[5] They were taken to Reynolds' house at South Barrow in Kent, where Wilkes spent the night.[6] According to one account, he managed to evade the crowd gathered outside the prison in anticipation of his release by sending Polly off in another coach as a decoy.[7] A convenient downpour may also have helped deter them from marking the event with a riot.[8] Wilkes may have been eager to avoid creating a rumpus, but all over the country his release was celebrated. The papers noted rejoicing in, among other places, Derby, Witney and York. At East Grinstead there was a lively celebration, part funded by Lord Abergavenny, an associate of the Pelhams and Rockinghams, who had taken Wilkes's part in several of the proceedings in the Lords.[9]

Safely out of London, Wilkes settled in for a few days respite at South Barrow. There he was introduced to the rest of the household, including Reynolds' wife and her sister, Miss West. He also met the young Frederick Reynolds, future playwright and amateur cricketer, who later claimed his first words, taught him by his nurse, had been 'Wilkes and Liberty!' Frederick's recollections offer a description of Wilkes's appearance, which was suitably disturbing for a young lad of not quite six. Wilkes was no doubt used to his visage prompting alarm and tried to disarm the situation with a little speech. Reynolds no doubt embroidered it slightly in the retelling, but it offers a glimpse both of Wilkes's consciousness of his looks and his innate self-belief in his ability to win through come what may: 'Ugly as you think me, little gentleman… there are people who are rash enough to assert that in affairs of gallantry, my victories are not ten minutes behind those of the handsomest men in England. So henceforth, be not seduced by first impressions.'[10]

The next day he was joined there by his sister and brother-in-law, Mary and George Hayley, and their daughter. On the 19th, a Mr Edridge joined the party, and Cotes the day after. On the 21st the group was swelled with the addition of several more members of the SSBR, including Horne, Sawbridge, Wilkes's brother Heaton, and James Townsend, a stalwart supporter and notable as a mixed-ethnicity politician, who would go on to become Lord Mayor of London.[11]

We know all of this, because from the time that he was released until just a few days before his death, Wilkes maintained a series of diaries, which detailed the people with whom he dined and where, rather than offering a space for reflection. If frustrating for anyone hoping to find insights into Wilkes's views on certain key events, the diaries have the merit of placing him on almost every day of his final twenty-seven years and describing many of the people he met. They emphasize the importance of his family, in particular the irrepressible Polly, who remained her father's constant companion. There are, however, some notable omissions. The diaries, for example, make no reference to a visit to Lord Chatham at Hayes the day after his release, where he also met Temple.[12] As well as Wilkes, Reynolds also counted Chatham among his clients. Relations between Wilkes, Chatham and Temple were still fraught and there is little indication that this brief rendezvous did much to heal the rift. Neither man features in the diaries, clear evidence that Wilkes had moved on. After spending five nights in relative seclusion in Kent, Wilkes returned to London on 22 April and took up residence in new temporary lodgings in Prince's Court, around the corner from his old house in Great George Street, while he set about searching for a longer-term solution. In the end, he was to take on another house in the same street at a rent of fifty guineas a year. This would be his principal abode for the next few years, before his final move to a considerably smarter address in Grosvenor Square.[13]

The City

By the time he had left prison, Wilkes had set his sights very clearly on the City of London for the next stage of his campaign. As ever, he was not being wholly innovative here. He had seen, previously, how the likes of Pitt had been bolstered by their reputations in the City.[14] Long the home of radical, reforming political initiatives, the City was to bring out both the very best and very worst of Wilkes. As an imaginative campaigner, unafraid of making use of 'the mob', Wilkes enlivened London's politics. When given the opportunity, he was also instrumental in implementing reforms that made a genuine difference to London's citizens. However, he was also divisive. Lord Shelburne, who was ultimately to inherit Chatham's mantle and was busily building his own reforming interest in London, was fearful of what Wilkes represented.[15] Shelburne's lieutenant, Isaac Barré, dubbed Wilkes tellingly as nothing more than 'a wretched scribbler'.[16] Even had the Wilkites and followers of Shelburne seen eye to eye, Wilkes himself was not good with competition. When he did not get his own way, he could be petulant. He was always the star of his own show.

Not long after Wilkes's release, news reached England of the Boston Massacre, highlighting the increasingly tense relations between colonists and mother country.[17] An account of what had happened was contained in a pamphlet, *A Short Narrative of the Most Horrid Massacre in Boston*, which Catharine Macaulay ensured was reprinted in London.[18] A number of prominent figures in the City were closely involved with trade in America, several of them American by birth, and it increasingly seemed the right place for Wilkes to be making his centre of operations. By doing so he was emulating a number of people before him, among them several high-profile figures from the previous century.

In January 1769, while still behind bars, Wilkes had been elected alderman for the ward of Farringdon Without.[19] The election had not been uncontested, or uncontentious, but Wilkes easily outpolled his rival Thomas Bromwich, by 255 votes to just sixty-nine. The Court of Aldermen then rejected the return citing a technical breach. Just as in Middlesex, at the new election a few days later Wilkes was again successful and in spite of a last-ditch effort by his opponents to query the result on legal grounds, he was eventually recognized as the winning candidate.[20] Such, remarked Edward Gibbon to his father, 'is the spirit of the times'.[21] Wilkes wrote to the inhabitants of his new ward on 2 January expressing his gratitude for the honour they had done him in electing him to their 'large, opulent, and respectable ward'. He assured them that 'Every power I derive from that high Office shall be employed in the Preservation of the Rights of the Livery of London, and of all the Freemen of this great Metropolis.' He also urged them to advise him of any matters of importance to the ward, insisting he would 'always take a public-spirited, decided, and disinterested Part' in representing them.[22]

As one of the City's aldermen, Wilkes was able to officiate as a magistrate, a task he undertook with reasonable regularity. Indeed, Horace Walpole found the newly released Wilkes surprisingly staid. He marvelled in particular at his apparent happiness to spend long hours hearing cases and then dining with his fellow justices. Wilkes may not always have enjoyed the frequently tedious duties as much as Walpole assumed. In one letter to Polly he complained of one long sitting, 'dulness reigned triumphant the whole day.'[23] Besides, Walpole's analysis rather missed the point. By demonstrating his commitment to his role, Wilkes was making a powerful statement. One of the key issues highlighted by Wilkes and now by his associates in the SSBR was abuse of the legal system. For Wilkes, this may have started with the case of general warrants, but it had much broader applications. As John Brewer has argued, by serving 'as exemplary justices', Wilkes and his colleagues 'attempted legal reform through example'.[24] And there were other ways in which Wilkes was at pains to demonstrate how his brand of patriotism reached beyond his own milieu. On occasion he was known to roll up his sleeves and help out extinguishing fires in the City.[25]

In the days following his release Wilkes began a concerted campaign of wooing key figures in the City and dining with a number of the clubs to which he had been elected. A melting pot of ideas, London was torn between differing visions of how change might be effected. There was a division between the followers of rival political heavyweights: Rockingham and Chatham. There was also a steady interest strong for the Crown. Even among the more radical members of the Corporation, for many City grandees Wilkes was little more than a demagogue happy to set the mob to work. It was up to him to demonstrate that there was more to him than simply the politics of disorder. Thus, on 23 April he was at the Mile End Assembly Rooms, where he was elected president of the Antigallicans, and on the 25th with the Beefsteaks, at Appleby's in Parliament Street. His diary noted wryly that there were '44 in company' that day: just short of the magic figure.

Wilkes's proximity to Parliament that day may have been behind a rumour 'strongly reported' that he was going to attempt to claim his seat in the Commons. He had never accepted his expulsion and enjoyed teasing the clerks by presenting himself at calls of the House. Richard Rigby related Wilkes's failure to appear on this occasion to the duke of Bedford, concluding, with some relief no doubt: 'The town is as quiet as if Wilkes was in the King's Bench again.'[26] The rumours continued to circulate, though one correspondent could not believe that he would 'venture at such a daring stepp'.[27]

In between these two social events, he had attended at the Mansion House and from there made the short way to Guildhall to be sworn in as an alderman in front of Lord Mayor William Beckford, before returning to the Mansion House for a celebratory dinner.[28] He recorded being taken by the hand and wished joy by the eighteen aldermen present and was astute enough to note this all happened with 'great *apparent* cordiality'.[29] By this point, Wilkes's and Beckford's relations were complicated. Like many in London, Beckford was suspicious of Wilkes's willingness to resort to the mob while also recognizing that he was too important to be neglected. He felt clearly that it was important he be seen to offer his support whatever his misgivings. Thus, soon after Wilkes's release from prison, Beckford's house in Soho Square had been decorated with a banner stating simply 'Liberty' in letters three feet high.[30] Wilkes for his part was happy to wait out the older man, whose health was failing.[31] Beckford had been a leading light in opposing the government's policies towards America and a month before Wilkes's release had presented the king with an address from the City calling for ministers to be sacked and Parliament to be dissolved. To the delegation's considerable discomfort, George and his courtiers responded by bursting out into laughter.[32]

The end of April and early May saw more of this wining and dining, both with family and his City colleagues. He also made his first appearance as a justice at the Old Bailey on 26 April: just nine days after he had quit prison himself.[33] 4 May saw him attending a Court of Aldermen and Common Council, after which he entertained several of the councilmen to dinner.[34]

If his main focus was on his new life as an alderman, almost as soon as he had quit prison Wilkes had been plunged straight back into parliamentary electioneering. On 21 April, Edwin Sandys, one of the sitting MPs for Westminster, had succeeded to a seat in the Lords following the death of his father. Many hoped that Wilkes might take the opportunity of throwing his hat into the ring, but he declined the offer. He was, he insisted (and whatever Parliament thought) already MP for Middlesex and was unwilling to resign that seat in an effort to secure another. Indeed, the conviction that Wilkes was the true MP and therefore Middlesex was not properly represented would shortly be the prompt for some freeholders to stage a tax strike, so his case could be tried before the courts.[35]

Wilkes was probably right to maintain the position he did on Middlesex. In spite of his expulsion, there remained great uneasiness in Parliament about how the case had been handled. On 1 May, Chatham moved in the House of Lords for Wilkes's expulsion to be overturned. He argued Luttrell was 'no representative of the people: he is a mere nominee.'[36] Chatham's motion failed, but debates on the issue persisted right up until the dissolution in 1774. Although the government always won, its majorities were slimmer than it achieved on other issues.[37]

Unwilling to serve himself, Wilkes offered his public backing to Sir Robert Bernard. Bernard was a member of the SSBR and had previously been MP for Huntingdonshire, before a falling out with two of the county's great patrons, the duke of Manchester and Wilkes's old bête noire, Sandwich. For once, the Court was unwilling to risk further disturbances by sponsoring a challenge, so Bernard was elected unopposed.

In the midst of his campaign to develop his ties with the City, Wilkes allowed himself some time for leisure. On 10 May his diary recorded a visit to an exhibition. This was likely the one hosted by the Royal Incorporated Society of Artists of Great Britain at Spring Garden, which had opened at the end of April. Four days later, he was at a masquerade at Teresa Cornelys' in Soho Square. At least two of his fellow guests were there in Wilkes costumes, one wearing a visor with a squint and bearing 'a cap of liberty on a pole'.[38] This made a nice contrast with a later occasion when Wilkes's rival, Luttrell, was noted appearing at a masked ball as Death.[39] He also found time to reacquaint himself with some of his more edgy associates. He was hosted by d'Eon in Petty France at the beginning of June, with the party including another French family, the Vignoles. Later that month, Wilkes returned the favour for the same group.[40]

For all this, Wilkes was always at heart a domestic creature, and he seems early on to have begun to resent the endless dinners and calls on his time from his devotees.[41] To Polly, he noted that he was 'visited by all the town' but only allowed entrance to a select few, among them Churchill and Reynolds.[42] It was always to be one of the contradictions of Wilkes's personality. On the one hand he was unable to bear not being centre of attention; on the other he always craved peace and quiet and found the din of his supporters a nuisance. In need of a place of retreat from his hectic life in London while his new house in Prince's Court was being renovated, Wilkes rented a small abode in Elyzium Row in Fulham, at an annual rent of sixty guineas.[43] It was about an hour's walk away from Westminster and Wilkes chose sometimes to trudge back and forth rather than use a chair or carriage. One diary entry noted 'Walked to Fulham, eat no dinner'.[44] There, he was at home to no one and, as he insisted, lived 'very economically'. He installed a small menagerie, including his daughter's cat and several pet birds.[45] These were mostly of the exotic variety, though his daughter Harriet (his child with his mistress Maria Arnold) would later have an owl named Peter.[46]

Wilkes had a couple of days in Fulham recharging his batteries before returning to London early on the morning of 22 May so that he could attend a dinner at the London Tavern, where he had an opportunity of thanking the members of the SSBR. Wilkes's diaries made no mention of the electric meeting between a delegation from the City headed by

Beckford to the king with a new address on 23 May, when Lord Mayor Beckford had the temerity to answer George's response to yet another request for a dissolution and ministers to be removed from office. However, he was among those backing an address of thanks to the Lord Mayor on 25 May. Beckford's boldness had turned him into a popular hero, for a while eclipsing Wilkes himself. He was even depicted on tankards and other commercial ware, much like his younger rival.[47]

On 21 June, Wilkes was pulled again towards the prospect of a spirited parliamentary election. His diary entry for the day noted merely dining with some of his familiar associates in the SSBR at the London Tavern, making no mention of Beckford's unexpected death at five o'clock that morning.[48] A letter to Polly the next day made up for the omission. While the two had been uncomfortable allies, Beckford had offered Wilkes useful support in the weeks following his release, which Wilkes now acknowledged: 'He had, of late, behaved with spirit and honour in the cause of liberty.'[49] Now Beckford's removal from the scene offered Wilkes a further opportunity to make his mark on the City. It also left another seat vacant, as Beckford had been one of the four MPs for the City. Beckford's loss highlighted the divisions within City politics. By no means all of the Corporation were pro-Wilkes and the man selected to succeed Beckford as Lord Mayor for the remainder of the year, Barlow Trecothick, was firmly in the opposition camp. No one quite knew where Trecothick was born. His early years had been spent across the Atlantic, in Boston, and then on the island of Jamaica.[50] He had settled in London by about 1750, but his business interests remained closely focused on trans-Atlantic trade. He had been one of Wilkes's rivals in the 1768 City election, when Trecothick had mopped up the last of the four seats. There seems to have been little love lost between them, so Wilkes would certainly not have viewed Trecothick's election to the mayoralty as helpful to his interests. This did not prevent him from fulfilling his duties as an alderman, though, attending the new Lord Mayor on 29 June.[51]

Beckford's vacant seat in the Commons was another matter. Like Trecothick, Richard Oliver, the man who was to succeed to the place in Parliament, hailed from across the Atlantic. He was the son of an Antiguan judge who had come to London to work in his uncle's counting house. As a founder member of the SSBR, Oliver made an obvious Wilkite choice to contest the vacant City seat. In fact, he was second choice, but when his brother-in-law withdrew through ill-health, Oliver was selected instead. Wilkes made a point of visiting Oliver that day, no doubt eager to keep tabs on the new candidate.[52] Like Bernard, he secured the seat without a contest at the poll held in July. The same month, Wilkes secured another distinction for himself with his election as Master of the Joiners' Company, a victory secured over eleven rival candidates.[53] His diary entry for the day (the 25th) was spare but proud: 'at Joiners Hall, Thames Street, elected Master unanimously'.[54]

Intriguingly, while making a name for himself as a reliable, even fastidious, Justice of the Peace, Wilkes seems to have been much less bothered about fulfilling his duties with the livery. He failed to turn up to be sworn in formally in August or September and only finally bothered to attend at a formal quarter court on 2 October. He then reverted to form and deputies were named to officiate for him on days when he was absent.[55] One rather suspects that the Joiners had served their purpose for Wilkes and he was too busy elsewhere to do more than pay lip service to his duties with them.

The remainder of the summer of 1770 saw Wilkes maintaining the fierce pace he had set since his release. In late July, he headed off for a few days with the Reynolds family at South Barrow before making a brief tour of stately homes and, one suspects quite as importantly, gardens. These included the duke of Newcastle's at Oatlands. From there, he proceeded to Guildford to attend the trial between Horne and George Onslow, who had sued Horne for damages. The case had first been heard before Blackstone shortly before Wilkes's release. Although Blackstone threw Onslow's suit out, he left the way open for a new trial, which Onslow happily took up. It came on before Mansfield, who made short work of Glynn's arguments on Horne's behalf and Onslow was awarded damages of £400. A year later, Horne would finally be successful in having the second verdict laid aside on appeal.[56]

From Guildford, Wilkes headed to Dover so he could greet Polly off the boat. She was newly returned from one of her regular visits to Paris, where she had witnessed the marriage of the Dauphin to Marie Antoinette.[57] She had also taken the opportunity of visiting Jack Smith, whom she knew as a cousin, and was otherwise kept busy by Wilkes's demands for various fashionable items. Among the shopping list was a set of knife handles in Sèvres porcelain and scarlet cloth to be made into a new coat.[58] Wilkes always had a weakness for French design.

In between the high-profile political campaigns, the periods in prison and goading the authorities, it is easy to forget the more commonplace aspects of Wilkes. He had his likes and dislikes, weaknesses for nice clothes and could never say no to Polly. He delighted in gardens and nature: he was a keen birdwatcher. He enjoyed a holiday. The second half of August 1770, then, found him on the south coast at Ramsgate and Margate, and then on to Tunbridge Wells. There was more 'great house tourism', taking in Lord Le Despenser's seat at Mereworth and the old home of the Sidney family at Penshurst. Not all of this was time off, though. Tours of the provinces were not just about holidaying. They offered him an opportunity to escape, certainly, but also to show his face to friends and supporters outside of London. His visit also afforded him time at Olantigh, Sawbridge's seat in Kent, no doubt to plan the SSBR's next moves. On 19 August, he hosted a dinner at his lodgings in Tunbridge Wells, the party including an ensign from the 3rd Regiment, the outfit that had been involved in the St George's Fields massacre. From there he returned to the coast and the fashionable resort of Brighthelmstone (Brighton), before heading back to London.[59]

Wilkes remained in semi-retreat at Fulham until the second week of September when he presided at the sessions at Guildhall and the Old Bailey. On 27 September there was a lively Common Council when Wilkes led moves to censure the City Recorder, Sir James Eyre, for his failure to turn out in May when the City's remonstrance had been presented to the king. In spite of the effort, Wilkes and his party were outvoted and Eyre escaped.[60] The following month, he took a leading role in opposing a decision taken by Trecothick to permit Navy press gangs to operate in the City. Trecothick had announced the decision to work with the Admiralty on the issue at a Court of Common Council on 12 October. He clearly felt he had done enough to protect the City's privileges by securing guarantees that freemen and their servants would not be taken up. Wilkes was unimpressed and responded that Magna Carta had been suspended. Realizing he had miscalculated, Trecothick subsequently joined other magistrates, Wilkes among them, in releasing some of those who had been pressed, and secured an agreement that only seamen should be forced into service. Wilkes was perfectly alive to the Navy's need to recruit new hands. To sweeten the pill, he proposed that bounties should be offered to any sailors willing to volunteer at the Guildhall, a policy that was adopted and managed to settle affairs until the present recruiting crisis was over.[61]

Wilkes's issues were not simply with members of the Corporation, like Trecothick. Already by the autumn of 1770, what unity there had ever been within the SSBR was beginning to fracture. At the heart of this were competing visions for what the society should be about, which had been accelerated by Wilkes's release. There was also a simple personality clash between Wilkes and Horne: both very much alpha males. For as long as he had remained in prison Wilkes had been constrained (literally). Now he was free, the tensions between him and Horne were impossible to disguise. Horne wanted the society to be transformed into a much broader campaigning organization. Wilkes was still intent on ensuring that paying off his debts and maintaining him in the style to which he had become accustomed remained a central goal of the group. However, it would not be fair to suggest that this was all that he thought the SSBR should be about. Ever mindful of the best way to achieve a splash, on

30 October he proposed at a meeting of the society that the MPs should be instructed to impeach Prime Minister Lord North. It is perhaps notable that he had dined that day at Appleby's, close to Parliament, with the familiar trio of John Churchill, William Ellis (a fellow Beefsteak) and Trevanion.[62] Although the Society willingly adopted Wilkes's plan, the proposal was objected to by Sawbridge, who was closely allied to Horne. Sawbridge proposed instead that the MPs should present the king with a Remonstrance, calling for Parliament to be dissolved and a new general election to be held. Wilkes was unimpressed and his criticism of the tactic was borne out when it was received with scant interest by the king on 7 November. A fortnight later the City followed suit, with their new Lord Mayor, Brass Crosby, doing the honours.[63]

Wilkes's suggestion that North should be impeached was interesting on two levels. It formed part of a calculated Wilkite tactic of encouraging constituents to offer instructions to their MPs. This fitted with what he had set out in his appeal to the electors of Aylesbury from his exile. According to this model, MPs were delegates, in contrast to the vision outlined most famously by Burke where they used their best judgment to represent their constituents. In 1769, electors from the City, Middlesex and Westminster had all instructed their MPs to protest against Wilkes's expulsion. Wilkes may have been a chameleon in many regards but on this point he was remarkably consistent. His papers included a copy of an engagement he signed along with his fellow MP in 1774.[64] Ten years later, he attended a meeting of Middlesex freeholders in which he once again underscored the importance of MPs bowing to the will of the people who voted them in.[65]

The idea of impeachment was interesting because it had not been employed for a long time. The last person to be impeached had been Lord Lovat in 1747, as one of the Scots peers arrested for supporting the Jacobites in the 1745 Rebellion. Otherwise, the mechanism had been used against the earl of Macclesfield, for corruption, in 1725, and Dr Sacheverell in 1710. Sawbridge dismissed the process as archaic – and pointless, when North commanded majorities in both Houses. Wilkes no doubt expected any impeachment attempt to fail, but that would not have been the point. He made no secret of his deep distrust of North, who had succeeded Grafton as prime minister earlier in the year. As he put it in the first of his letters in response to Horne, during their highly public falling out: 'I think him a weak, wicked and despotic minister, and that, from the two important posts he now fills, he must be considered as the ostensible prime minister, and the chief instrument of the tyranny we groan under at home and in the colonies.'[66]

The prospect of impeaching the Prime Minister, forcing members of the House of Lords to receive articles complaining of his conduct in a formal setting, and the prospects for widespread coverage in the press must have been very tempting. It would keep the story running and hold up other parliamentary business. Wilkes understood the potential impact such an action might have, but men like Sawbridge would not have calculated in the same way.

One of the immediate consequences of these latest disagreements was that the split between Wilkes and Horne finally came out into the open. Horne had long been resentful of being side-lined by Wilkes. He probably had good cause. Horne felt that he had done a great deal to help reboot Wilkes's political career. He had played a key role in arranging the logistics at Brentford for the Middlesex polls and undoubtedly contributed to the committee organization behind the scenes. As a parson he was unable to stand for Parliament himself, so Wilkes's campaigns had allowed him to live vicariously through his one-time hero, even giving him the opportunity of speaking to voters alongside Wilkes.[67]

What followed was a lively campaign in the press in which each man did his utmost to throw the most dirt. The opening salvo was fired by Horne in a letter to the *Public Advertiser*, in which he set out his side of what had happened at the Westminster freeholders meeting. Wilkes had been chairman of the meeting and objected to 'several gross misrepresentations' in the piece, so published a rejoinder, dated from his house in Prince's Court on 7 November. Horne insisted that it was owing to him alone that Wilkes had been rescued from extremis, that he had found him an outlaw without friends and managed to turn his fortunes around. Wilkes responded in kind, arguing that before he had taken Horne up, the parson had been a nobody. It was only the friendship of John Wilkes that had made him worth anything at all. Over a number of weeks, the press was full of their letters haranguing each other. Horne published details of Wilkes's debts, how much his house was worth and how many servants he had. Wilkes responded as he knew best, taking down the allegations made against him article by article.[68]

Unsurprisingly, while neither man emerged particularly well from the episode, it was Wilkes who came out on top. His followers had long shown a striking willingness to accept his foibles. They knew him as an indebted libertine, who always sailed close to the wind, and forgave him for it. Horne was much the less likeable of the two, and he was never going to win in this kind of contest. Ultimately, though, it accelerated the splintering of the SSBR. In April 1771, the society divided, with Horne, Sawbridge and Glynn, who had gradually distanced himself from Wilkes and found a place in Horne's camp, withdrawing to form a new Constitutional Society. Wilkes and his immediate followers remained to continue the SSBR in his image. Spotting an opportunity to make a profit out of the spat, Wilkes went on to publish the correspondence.

The Printers' Case (1771)

It was set against this internecine feuding that the members of the SSBR were to score their greatest success in a struggle with the Commons over reporting parliamentary business. It was then considered a breach of privilege for the content of debates to be published in the press. In reality, Parliament's attitude to publication of proceedings was inconsistent. There had been long periods earlier in the century when detailed information about debates had been published. Entrepreneurial journalists like Ebenezer Timberland and the Huguenot Abel Boyer had made their careers publishing information that stemmed from Parliament. Every so often, one or other of the Houses took exception to their offerings, but it was really only from the 1740s onwards that a serious effort was made to crack down on the practice.

The Wilkes affair, unsurprisingly, reignited interest in the political process, and by the 1760s printers were regularly summoned before Lords and Commons to be reprimanded, fined and occasionally given short prison sentences. That it was not just the Commons is clear from the fact that in February 1770 the earl of Sandwich and the 2nd Earl Gower moved in the Lords for William George Edmunds, printer of the *Middlesex Journal* (a Wilkite organ) to be seized for publishing the formal protests lodged in the Lords on 2 February. In May, Sandwich was at it again, this time complaining of William Oxlade of the *London Packet*. Sandwich was joined by the 6th earl of Denbigh, an influential courtier, who lodged a similar complaint against John Miller of the *London Evening Post*.[69] Wilkes seems to have planned a response by having a satire printed lampooning the earl of Pomfret, who was well known for being quick to take offence.[70]

It was, however, to be in the Commons that the SSBR's campaign was to begin. In the spring of 1771, Wilkes and Morris worked together to concoct an attack on the Commons' efforts to guard their privacy, for which they also secured the SSBR's support and that of Lord Mayor Crosby. They persuaded several printers, among them Wheble of the *Middlesex Journal*, Roger Thompson of the *Gazetteer* and John Miller, the man previously complained of by Denbigh, to defy Parliament and continue printing information on debates. Miller had form on thumbing his nose at Parliament. He had managed to evade the Lords' messengers since the earlier effort to secure him and had never bothered to attend at the bar as ordered. True to form, on 12 March Colonel George

Onslow (known as Cocking George and not to be confused with his cousin, Wilkes's supporter) complained in the House that several papers had been printing parliamentary proceedings. The Commons duly summoned each man to appear before them to answer a case for breach of privilege. Guided by Wilkes and Morris, Wheble released a statement declaring the summons to be illegal as the Commons was not a court of law. He then allowed himself to be arrested by his own servant, Edward Carpenter, who brought Wheble before Wilkes, Richard Oliver and Lord Mayor Crosby on 14 March to claim the bounty that had been placed on Wheble's head. The three sitting magistrates released Wheble, arguing that he was a freeman of the City, the case against him neither a felony nor breach of the peace, and Carpenter not an authorized officer of the peace. Wheble then turned the tables on Carpenter by charging him with assault. The same day that all of this was happening with Wheble, a messenger of the Commons, William Whittam, attempted to arrest Miller. A constable, located conveniently close to Miller, then arrested Whittam for assault, who was hauled again before Wilkes, Oliver and Crosby. Perhaps suggestively, Wilkes's diary for the day noted that he dined at the Mansion House along with Lord Mayor Crosby, a Reverend Mr Evans and Reynolds: he may have been keen to have Reynolds' legal advice for what was to come.[71]

The 14th of March 1771 was a busy day when it came to breaches of parliamentary privilege. Wheble, Thompson and Miller were not the only people in the Commons' sights. The Commons' Journals for the day recorded that several other printers had also been ordered to attend, among them Woodfall and Henry Baldwin, printer of the *St James's Chronicle*. Unlike the three detailed by Wilkes and his associates, Baldwin did appear before the House and declared himself sorry for printing the debates. He undertook that he would obey the House's ruling 'though it would be attended with the Ruin of his Paper'. He was then reprimanded on his knees. After him, three more printers were summoned to the bar, Thomas Evans, Thomas Wright of the *Whitehall Evening Post*, and Samuel Bladon of the *General Evening Post*.[72]

On the 18th, the Commons returned to the business, citing their order of the 14th for Miller to be arrested. Crosby, Oliver and Wilkes's interference was also reported. As Crosby was not to be in his place that day, the House ordered him to appear on the next. An effort by Crosby's supporters to secure him more time to attend was defeated on division by 267 votes to eighty, but the motion for him to attend was rephrased acknowledging that he should be in his place 'if his health permit'.[73] Tellingly, Wilkes was again at the Mansion House that day.[74] On the next, the Commons decided to prod the bear further and summoned John Wilkes, Esquire, Alderman of London, on the 20th. He penned a letter to the Speaker in which he insisted on being summoned as MP for Middlesex.[75] The Commons refused to do so, of course, so after a couple more efforts at restating the order, the Commons eventually let it go.[76]

Crosby was not so lucky. The same day that the Commons issued the order for Wilkes to appear, Crosby was back in his place. Following some brief interactions he pleaded ill health and was allowed to withdraw again. In the end, it was not until 25 March that the Commons was finally able to turn its attention properly to Crosby and Oliver (who had also been summoned for the 20th along with Wilkes). Crowds flocked to the lobby with labels in their hats marked, Crosby, Wilkes, Oliver and Freedom of the Press.[77] During that sitting, on a division of 170 to thirty-eight, Oliver was ordered to the Tower for his contempt. Wilkes meanwhile was at the King's Arms in nearby Bridge Street along with other members of the Lord Mayor's committee, doubtless assessing their next moves.[78] Two days later Crosby was sent to join Oliver in the Tower, following a very similar vote of 202 to thirty-nine.[79]

The affair transformed Crosby and Oliver into folk heroes, much as Wilkes had been during his earlier period in the Tower. There were prints and commemorative wares produced in their honour, such as a glazed earthenware bowl created in Lambeth, inscribed simply Crosby And Oliver 1771.[80] Although Wilkes escaped being sent back to the Tower, one print satire depicted him along with Crosby and Oliver in their cell, the three of them being presented with addresses from Cardigan, Carmarthen and Pembroke by Sir Watkin Lewes.[81] Wilkes certainly did not neglect his companions. On the 28th, the day after Crosby had been sent to his new lodgings, Wilkes was there in the Tower and he continued to visit on numerous occasions through to 3 May, shortly before Crosby and Oliver were finally released.[82]

Wilkes and his associates had succeeded in pitting the power of the City against the Commons, whipping up the by now familiar crowd to protest against Parliament's high-handedness. The Commons also scored a particularly egregious own goal by ordering the Lord Mayor's clerk before them and having the orders relating to Whittam's arrest expunged from the minutes. Infuriated by recent transactions, on 1 May Chatham rose to his feet in the Lords complaining of the Commons' behaviour. Strikingly, he now characterized them as a mob.[83] The whole cemented Wilkes's reputation among the crowd. Equally, it demonstrated his keen grasp of *Realpolitik*. There was only so much the Commons could do against him as a non-member if he refused to co-operate; and their interference in the life of a corporate body, like the City of London, had proved woefully misjudged.

Crosby and Oliver remained in the Tower until Parliament was prorogued on 8 May. They left it to predictable rejoicing.[84] For Wilkes it was also a particularly busy day. There was a dinner at the Mansion House, while in the evening he was at the Red Hart in Shoe Lane with the Lombard Troop, before heading to a supper with the Common Council at the Three Tuns in Smithfield.[85] During their time in the Tower, Crosby and Oliver had been fêted by the City but also visited by grandees like Temple. On their release, both men, along with Wilkes, were awarded silver 'loving cups' by the City. Crosby's was valued at £200; Wilkes's and Oliver's £100.[86] Wilkes's was decorated at his own request with an engraving depicting the assassination of Julius Caesar and a verse from Charles Churchill: 'May every Tyrant feel The Keen deep searchings of a Patriots steel.'[87] Wilkes also received a certificate from Dublin, thanking him for his 'steady perseverance in the cause of liberty'.[88] Above all, the stunt had paid off. Although the Commons did not relinquish its demand for debates to remain secret for well over a century, in effect no more efforts were made to restrain papers from publishing them. The Lords held out for a few years more, before finally conceding the point as well.

Wilkes's growing influence within the City was put to the test soon after the release of Crosby and Oliver, when he stood for the office of Sheriff of London. This was a post, it might be remembered, that his father had been suggested for but backed away from. Wilkes was determined that it was to be his as part of his steady progression towards the mayoralty itself. It had initially been intended that he would stand on a joint ticket with Oliver, but Oliver had informed Wilkes from his cell in the Tower that he did not wish to stand with him. Wilkes tried to persuade him that their policies were aligned, but Oliver remained obdurate. The government, meanwhile, hoped that the split in the opposition's ranks would allow their candidates, Kirkman and Samuel Plumbe, to make their way through the middle. Wilkes joined forces with a new partner, Frederick Bull, a wealthy tea merchant and prominent dissenter in the City, and at the close of the poll on 1 July they carried the day convincingly. Oliver, who had persisted in standing alone, secured just 119 votes, while Wilkes and Bull each had well over two thousand, comfortably ahead of the government candidates.[89] The noted bluestocking, Hester Thrale, compared the election of Wilkes and Bull with the consulate of Julius Caesar and Marcus Calpurnius Bibulus, which was dubbed that of Julio et Cesare: 'as poor Bibulus like Bull had no share in the management of publick affairs.'[90] She was being too harsh. Wilkes probably thought little of Bull but, unlike Caesar, he did not have his rival covered in excrement.

As usual, Wilkes's success prompted a demonstration, which was reported in detail by Sir John Fielding. He noted that Wilkes passed through Temple Bar at about ten in the evening accompanied by 'a mob' of around 200 people. Fielding thought they were largely drawn from the lower orders, and many of them boys (by which he may have meant apprentices). Up until this point, he assessed that few householders had felt the need to illuminate their windows. Now as the party passed by, with the crowd hallooing, locals chose to insure themselves against attack by lighting candles in their windows all the way down the Strand. Having seen Wilkes home, the crowd turned its attention to Downing Street but was held back by the magistrates accompanied by a detachment of soldiers and peace officers, who made a stand to protect Lord North in Number Ten. Deciding that it was not the evening for a major altercation, the crowd limited its activities. A few windows were broken as they dispersed around Charing Cross, and they were able to pluck a prisoner from the hands of some constables before the evening was through.[91]

Following his election, Wilkes allowed himself another of his tours of the south-east in July and August.[92] There were also a number of day trips. Some of them, one suspects, must have been deliberately intended to invite comment. On 25 July he went to Windsor to watch the Garter procession, when the Prince of Wales (the future George IV) was installed. Always able to inveigle his way into high society, Wilkes managed to snatch a conversation with the earl of Pembroke. The king noticed and called Pembroke over to find out with whom he had been talking. Pembroke's response was 'One that Your Majesty should know much better than I.'[93]

Not everything went Wilkes's way in 1771. For the mayoral election that autumn he miscalculated badly, and the government was able to exploit the divisions between Wilkes's SSBR and Horne's Constitutional Society, now closely allied with Shelburne. Wilkes had hoped to engineer Crosby's re-election but his scheme fell apart when former Lord Mayor William Bridgen, who was supposed to work in combination with Crosby, refused to co-operate. The pseudonymous *Junius* had encouraged Wilkes to lay aside factionalism and support Sawbridge, who was standing with Shelburne's backing. Wilkes declined, suggesting that Sawbridge had become 'the absolute dupe of Malagrida's gang' (Malagrida being a derogatory nickname for Shelburne).[94] Horne's associates also refused to work with Wilkes, thereby enabling the government candidate William Nash to secure the election, just as *Junius* had predicted would be the case.[95]

In mid-October, Wilkes's reputation underwent a further beating. While his decision to undertake his magisterial duties seriously broadly played in his favour, on 16 October he found himself presiding at the execution of 18-year-old Mary Jones, who had been convicted for shoplifting. Her husband had been press-ganged and the young woman had found herself without means. The sight of the radical 'friend of liberty' calmly watching a young person's life snuffed out did him no favours whatsoever. It is perhaps telling that his diary entry for the day makes no mention of the event, merely noting a dinner at home without any company. He must have known that this was not what liberty was supposed to look like.[96]

Much more positively, during his shrievalty reforms were proposed for executions, barring the presence of soldiers in an effort to make the events less of a spectacle. He also proposed at the end of his term further reforms that would limit the number of people condemned to execution for committing lesser crimes. Working with Bull, he made a point of recommending improvements in the conditions at Newgate and that prisoners should not be expected to plead before the courts while still shackled.[97] There were other ways in which he attempted to use his office to make some fairly obvious statements. Stung by Horne's accusations that he was too pro-French, he forbade French wine during his shrievalty. In an effort to make justice more transparent, he opened up the galleries of the Old Bailey for free.[98] Unsurprisingly, he could not avoid attracting some criticism from his mother: still as powerful an influence on his life as when he was a child. Noticing that he had been spending far too much time at the house of a notorious courtesan, she wrote to upbraid him for parking his official chariot outside while he was paying his visit.[99] It seems to have been less the knowledge that her son visited prostitutes that worried her as the fact that he allowed himself to be driven there in his official carriage.

For the rest of the year, Wilkes's life followed a familiar pattern. There were days spent at the Mansion House undertaking his duties as alderman and sheriff, as well as time at one or other of his numerous clubs and societies. Family also remained important. On 15 December 1771, for example, he was with his brother in St John's Square and on days when he could not face seeing anyone else, there was always time for Polly.[100]

That winter, he set out on what was to become a regular visit to Bath, leaving London on Christmas Eve. A retreat to Bath for the festive season by no means meant complete removal from City affairs, though. One of his keen supporters, Watkin Lewes, was there, as were the Bulls. On 2 January 1772 he travelled to Bristol, accompanied by Bull and Lewes, where he was entertained at a dinner in honour of the 'Friends of Freedom'. He was back at Prince's Court in time for Epiphany and on 7 January presiding at the Guildhall.[101]

Wilkes's daily regime in 1772 continued in similar vein. Having failed to inspire a printer to take on the Lords in the way he had the Commons – a plan that had been discussed in print between him and *Junius* – he concentrated on his duties in the City. In June, Wilkes returned to the south coast and on the 8th set out for the Isle of Wight with three companions. He had visited the island for the first time while an officer of the Buckinghamshire militia and always liked the place. His visit clearly made an impression as he was back there in July, following a busy month back in London, presiding at the sessions and attending numerous dinners with the usual clubs and societies. The middle of August found him undertaking a pilgrimage to Brixham, the site of William of Orange's landing in 1688. Wilkes told Polly he was 'ready to fall on my knees on the sacred spot; and could scarcely leave the holy steps on which he landed to rescue a wretched people from slavery and the Stuarts.'[102] It is easy to dismiss this as mere hyperbole but Wilkes was in earnest here. He viewed himself very much as a product and inheritor of the 'Glorious Revolution'. For men of his generation much political discourse was framed in 17th-century terms and he viewed his struggle with George III and his administrations as on a par with previous struggles against the Stuarts. If there was a central core to Wilkes's 'political philosophy', it was all founded on the idea of 1688 and the revolution's role in underpinning English liberty.

All of this was gearing up for Wilkes's first attempt on the mayoralty. Unsurprisingly, then, from the beginning of September onwards Wilkes was busy attending dinners hosted by his own livery company, but also the Colts of the Committee of City Lands, the Artillery Company and the SSBR. Wilkes was one of two 'patriot' candidates, the other being James Townsend. They were opposed by aldermen Thomas Hallifax and John Shakespear, backed by the Court, as well as an independent, Sir Joseph Bankes (who was only to secure two votes). Although Wilkes headed the poll with 2,301 votes, followed closely by Townsend with 2,278, their opponents demanded that the election be subjected to scrutiny. The king and Lord North kept a close eye on what was going on in the City. North assured George that a number of Wilkes's votes were illegal: 'The strange ragged forces whom he brought up today were such as were never seen at any poll before, except at his own.'[103] Wilkes's party were clearly live to such criticism and ready with their own response. It was noted that at least one voter had been turned away for appearing drunk.[104] Meanwhile, four liverymen complained that 'a set of riotous, insolent, and audacious men', hired for the purpose, had tried to stop them from polling for Wilkes and Townsend.[105] Despite North's optimism, the scrutiny merely confirmed the result. Wilkes and Townsend were consequently presented to the court of aldermen as candidates for the mayoralty. At this point, though, Wilkes's campaign stalled, when the court decided to elect Townsend.

Edmund Burke was convinced that even though he had lost, Wilkes had still achieved something extraordinary. Just two years after his release from gaol, and four after being rejected by the City as their MP, he had only narrowly failed to become Lord Mayor. Despite this, Wilkes was clearly infuriated at being frustrated in his ambitions. The Lord Mayor's procession that year was characterized with bad-tempered rioting, at least some of it stirred up by Wilkite supporters. In March 1773, Wilkes was able to make Townsend's position thoroughly uncomfortable by drawing up a new City remonstrance calling for a dissolution of Parliament and for the removal of some of the king's ministers. Townsend was forced to present it at Court, while Wilkes himself declined to attend. He explained, 'I am not used to go into any gentleman's house who does not wish to see me.'[106]

The Mayoralty (1773-4)

Through all of his concentration on City politics, Wilkes had not lost sight of his Middlesex seat, nor of opportunities to embarrass the government whenever possible. He was not the only one fretting about the county. Early in 1772 the king wrote to North responding to an application by Luttrell to take the Chiltern Hundreds (the formula for resigning a seat). George described it as 'too absurd to give any credit to it'.[107] Luttrell raised the issue again in May, quite bizarrely insisting that he resign his seat in Wilkes's favour.[108] Needless to say, the administration refused his request.[109] At the same time, Wilkes continued to insist he was the true MP for Middlesex. Thus, on 26 April he presented himself at Westminster in response to a call of the House, even though some papers had suggested he would not.[110] He had been encouraged to do so by sheriffs Lewes and Oliver, who had made a point of summoning him rather than Luttrell. Unsurprisingly, Wilkes was denied entry by the parliamentary authorities. The same day that he was turned away from Parliament, the Commons dealt with a motion for Wilkes to be called before them so that he could complain about not being granted a certificate confirming his election. It was rejected, though the minority, 124 against 227, pointed to just how many MPs remained uncomfortable about the way in which Wilkes had been deprived of his seat.[111] Wilkes shrugged off the rebuff. There was a dinner with his ally, Watkin Lewes, and a supper in Goodge Street with MP Miles Peter Andrews before attending a masquerade at the Haymarket.[112]

Wilkes stood for Mayor again in 1773. This time he paired with Frederick Bull, his former shrieval running mate. Once again, Wilkes headed the poll, with Bull coming in second; and once again, the aldermen chose to elect the second-choice candidate rather than accept Wilkes. Bull then had further success in December at the by-election triggered by the death of Sir Robert Ladbroke, a former Lord Mayor. Standing on a platform largely derived from SSBR policies, Bull asserted the importance of 'the restoration of the American liberties' on the hustings, underscoring the Wilkites' identification of their cause with that of the colonies.[113] Tellingly, Lord North had written to the king soon after Ladbroke's death expressing his concern that attempting to stop Wilkes on this occasion would be 'fruitless'. This was because even though North reckoned most of the livery were not allies of Wilkes, they lacked the 'zeal' to undergo a stormy election on this occasion. The king concurred. He would have loved to have prevented Bull's election but also thought it best not to interfere.[114]

Coinciding with his second tilt at the mayoralty, Wilkes had become involved with his next long-term mistress, Marianne Genevieve Charpillon (or Charpillion), one of London's better-known courtesans. She counted Casanova among her former lovers and had, in fact, brought an action against Casanova for assault, which had resulted in him being gaoled. An unfavourable assessment described her as 'the breadwinner of a family of bawds and harpies living in Denmark Street' in Soho.[115] By the time Wilkes met her, Charpillon was in her early thirties (she was about fifteen years his junior). She made her first appearance in his diaries on 24 September 1773 as one of a party at the Old Swan in Chelsea, the others including Chase Price and John Churchill. Over the next few days her name recurred frequently and by the beginning of November, Wilkes had set her up in lodgings at 30, Titchfield Street.[116] Their relationship would endure for some years, though as John Sainsbury has observed, by then Wilkes was effectively settled into a pleasant domesticity with Polly running his household: something Charpillon would find particularly trying.[117] The remainder of the year showed Wilkes juggling his mistress's household, his own at Prince's Court presided over by Polly, and occasional forays to his family in St John's Square. Christmas 1773 summed this up as well as any other. Christmas Eve was spent with Polly at Prince's Court; Christmas Day in St John's Square with Heaton Wilkes, his family, and a cousin, Sophia Nesbitt; Boxing Day was with Charpillon in Titchfield Street.[118]

The next year began much as had the last and Wilkes's daily routine persisted as before. Meetings with political clubs were interspersed with the familiar round of a man of fashion. Thanks to the SSBR he was settled financially, enabling him to indulge in things like a visit to the newly opened Pantheon on Oxford Street at the end of January. A book of twelve tickets covering the season cost six guineas: far out of the reach of most of Wilkes's supporters.[119] In the late summer, there was a health scare. Wilkes was confined to bed with a severe fever, sufficiently alarming for Edward Gibbon to remark on it in his correspondence. He noted Wilkes was 'dangerously ill' and that society would thereby 'lose much amusement'.[120] Wilkes set out on one of his familiar trips around the south coast, seeking a cure. It was, after all, important that he was fighting fit for two contests on the horizon.[121]

Towards the end of the summer, *The Middlesex Journal* reported what it was sure it would please its readers that a coalition had been agreed on among the radical factions in the City. Sawbridge had agreed to 'scratch' for Wilkes and it was therefore assumed that they would stand together.[122] The press had indicated previously that Wilkes was becoming frustrated by his lack of success to date and that if he failed again, he might choose to seek new opportunities across the Atlantic.[123] Bolstered by these more promising developments, though, in mid-September Wilkes was back at the London Tavern meeting with the SSBR, planning for the elections to come. That it was not just the mayoralty that was at stake, but the forthcoming parliamentary elections, too, was made plain in a piece in the press two days later.[124] That evening, there was a meeting of the City livery at the Half Moon Tavern. One attendee criticised Sawbridge, saying he looked on the City like a great plum pudding and only wanted a slice of it, before proposing Wilkes and Bull as joint candidates. Another wanted Wilkes and Sawbridge to stand together but was 'much hissed'. Finally, after over two hours, which seems to have included some fisticuffs and mutual exchange of insults, the meeting endorsed Wilkes and Lord Mayor Bull as their candidates.[125] As part of the plan, Bull agreed to step aside should he beat Wilkes to first place. A good deal of pressure was then exerted on Sawbridge in the coming days not to interfere with the arrangement. He eventually agreed not to mount a challenge. His 'candid' behaviour was praised, though it was widely supposed that it was all part of a deal between him and the Wilkites that would hand him the mayoralty next time around, as well as one of the City seats in Parliament.[126]

As a reminder that the mundanities of existence continued, on 21 September Wilkes was reported to have taken his place on the bench at Bow Street to see some members of the 'Barnet Gang', who were suspected of having robbed him some time back. As it happened, their appearance was postponed and there was no resolution that day.[127]

On 29 September, nominations opened for the mayoral candidates at Guildhall. Sawbridge made it clear that he had decided not to run, but there were plenty of other aldermen proposed. Some fared better than others. For Alderman Hallifax there was 'hooting' but no hands held up for him; Alderman Shakespear was greeted with hissing and hooting. There was some support for the two ministry candidates, Sir James Esdaile and Brackley Kennett. The last was a wine merchant, generally believed to have started out as a waiter in a tavern.[128] Esdaile had been noted canvassing for support several days before, but one paper noted dismissively that 'his own interest is confined to a single Porter Club.'[129] For Wilkes, there were all the hands that had not shown for Esdaile and predictable 'shouts and huzzas'.[130] At the close of the poll a week later, Wilkes was first with 1,957 votes, Bull second and Esdaile and Kennett substantially adrift.

On 8 October, John Wilkes, former outlaw, convicted felon, in debt up to his eyeballs before being bailed out by the SSBR, was elected Lord Mayor of London. Only two voted against him.[131] His success was also a remarkable moment for the Joiners' Company, Wilkes being the first member of the company to become Lord Mayor. Over the next two decades two more Joiners would be elected Lord Mayor: both of them Wilkites.[132] In 1774, the Joiners celebrated their new-found prominence by spending £56 15s. 6d. on a set of banners for the Lord Mayor's day. There was also the usual expenditure on a stand, 'whifflers' etc.[133]

Under a fortnight later, Wilkes was able to crown this success with re-election to Middlesex. Parliament had been dissolved just a day after the mayoral nominations had opened, giving little time for Wilkes to prepare for this new contest. One paper reported that the dissolution, earlier than required, had actually been a mistake, based on a misunderstanding between North and the king. George, it was said, had reacted badly to news of Wilkes's success in the City and declared he would 'dissolve this Bill of Rights'. North was believed to have misheard him and thought he was asking for Parliament to be dissolved.[134] It is a nice story, but unlikely to be true. In any event, a county meeting was held on 26 September when Wilkes and Glynn (the sitting Member) were selected. They both signed up to a series of reforms outlined by the SSBR. These included reducing the length of parliaments and franchise reform. Wilkes was disappointed, though, that the meeting had been relatively poorly attended. Lord North reported to the king that few of those attending had been freeholders, and 'all of them of the lowest sort of the people'.[135] Wilkes blamed the weather for the unsatisfactory turnout.[136]

After everything that had gone before the king and North were determined to try to stop Wilkes from being returned all over again. Strenuous efforts were made to persuade anyone with a chance to stand. One of those approached was James Clitherow, Blackstone's brother-in-law, but he left no room for doubt about the scale of the challenge. He insisted that no one would be willing to stand: 'The only possible way of our succeeding will be to wait and see if, from the division amongst the faction, any gentleman not connected with Government will step forth, and in that case to give him our assistance.' Any government-backed candidate would be 'infallibly defeated'.[137]

Champion of English Freedom

A second possible entrant, Sir Charles Raymond, proved just as unwilling. Consequently, on 20 October Wilkes and Glynn were able to stage a procession from the City to Brentford where they were both chosen without contest. There was further success in the City elections, which saw three candidates endorsed by Wilkes – Sawbridge, Hayley and Bull – returned, along with Richard Oliver, even though Oliver had been abused by the crowd for refusing to sign up to the reform programme agreed by the others. The only one of Wilkes's favoured candidates not to make it through was Crosby. Two ministry candidates, William Baker and John Roberts, were also defeated. In the other London seats there were mixed results. Sir Joseph Mawbey chose not to contest Southwark again, trying, and failing, to be returned for Surrey instead. He was, though, elected at a by-election the following year. One of the Southwark seats went to Nathaniel Polhill, standing as a Wilkite. The other went to Henry Thrale, husband of Hester Thrale, who was probably suspicious of the radicals. At Westminster, the poll books indicate that Wilkes voted for Viscount Mountmorres and his old associate, Humphrey Cotes.[138] Mountmorres came third with a respectable 2,533 votes. Poor Cotes limped in fifth, with just 125. Cotes may have felt let down in spite of Wilkes wasting a vote on him and the experience may have contributed to their final falling out. When Wilkes later offered him the opportunity to supply the wines to the Mansion House during his mayoralty, Cotes refused.[139]

For Wilkes himself, the election was a considerable achievement. A decade after first being expelled from Parliament, he was back in the House of Commons and Lord Mayor to boot. Thanks to the SSBR, there was a programme of reform to argue for at Westminster. The question was whether the fractious alliance of City radicals would hold – and what Wilkes would make of this new opportunity.

10

Lord Mayor of London, MP for Middlesex and City Chamberlain

(1774–1779)

Arcui meo non confido

The government was heartily disappointed by Wilkes's election as Lord Mayor. There seems to have been some discussion about whether the election might be refused, but wiser heads counselled that it was better to allow it to go forward rather than risk turning him into *King of the City* for *life*.[1] Consequently, Wilkes made his way from the Guildhall on 3 November accompanied by Crosby, Lewes and Hayley as well as the two sheriffs, to the residence of Lord Chancellor Apsley in Great Russell Street to be acknowledged formally. Wilkes travelled in a brand-new coach, in black Japan, pulled by two cream-coloured geldings sporting blue and silver tassels. The coach was embellished with the family motto: *Arcui meo non confido*: I trust not in my bow. This was derived from *Psalm* 44, vi: 'For I will not trust in my bow, neither shall my sword save me.' It took them around an hour and a quarter to make the journey of just under two miles. On arrival, Apsley made them wait a while longer before joining them in the drawing room. There was then a brief ceremony. Glynn, as Recorder of London, made a speech indicating the City's choice of Wilkes and highlighting his qualities. Apsley made a briefer one in return and then took Wilkes by the hand, wishing him well in his new duties. A gold loving cup went round along with various cakes. After about ten minutes, Apsley clearly felt he had done his bit and left them to it. The cup then went round again, before Wilkes and his party made their way back to the City, through a crowd of several hundreds.[2] The day was completed with a celebratory dinner at Joiners' Hall.[3]

Lord Mayor of London

The cold welcome from the government may not have been particularly surprising, but it was not only from the Court that Wilkes faced challenges in his new role. He faced a divided corporation, not least among the radicals. Many of them were deeply suspicious of him, even though he had been successful in detaching Sawbridge from other members of the Constitutional Society. In advance of the election, the two had reunited and both campaigned on a platform drawn up by the SSBR, which included the question of constituencies issuing instructions to their representatives in Parliament.[4] It was a point on which Edmund Burke took a completely different view, as he made clear in his speech to his own voters in Bristol.[5] As a sign of the challenge ahead, just a few days after his triumph at Middlesex, Wilkes's candidate for Alderman of Bridge Ward, William Neate, was defeated by John Hart, a member of the Skinners' Company. It was a tight election and a scrutiny revealed that Neate had actually won, but Hart was sworn in by the Court of Aldermen and it was not until 1 May 1776 that the election was finally voided by King's Bench.[6]

Wilkes's own supporters were not always a source of joy and comfort to him, either. He found it hard – or rather could not be bothered – to disguise his contempt for some of the less refined of them. At the dinner celebrating Bull's election as mayor the year before, there had been the famous exchange with Burke, after Burke drew him up for ridiculing his allies. Burke informed Rockingham of their conversation: 'I hinted to him [Wilkes] jestingly that his friends by being such were too respectable not to be treated with a little decorum. Oh, says he, I never laugh at my friends, but these are only my followers.'[7] On other occasions, Wilkes referred to his colleagues dismissively as 'fat-headed turtle-eating aldermen'.[8]

If he was the supreme master of making the press work for him, Wilkes also faced opposition from the organs supporting the government. A letter to the editor of the *Morning Post* highlighted various unsuitable new MPs returned at the general election. Wilkes headed the list, of course, followed by a barker from Monmouth Street, a former waiter at Arthur's, who had been caught stealing, a footman and pimp to a courtesan, and a dancing master.[9] The letter no doubt exaggerated, but it shows that in some quarters there was general apprehension about the state of the new Parliament. It was not just Wilkes; the general quality of MP was going to the dogs. Wilkes had his defenders, of course.

Another paper carried a letter objecting to the latest rantings of one of his critics, noting 'The stale dirt which *Britannicus* so plentifully throws at Mr Wilkes, is of such a hackneyed kind, that the best return it deserves is sovereign contempt.'[10]

The Lord Mayor's Day procession a few days after the swearing in before Apsley saw Wilkes in full regalia proceed along with the other aldermen, his own livery company and that of the Salters, from Guildhall to the river, where some of the party went by water to Westminster and then back to the City. According to one paper, there was such a crush that some of the liverymen had their gowns torn off their backs. There were also unfortunate, but for the period all too common, accidents. At least one person was run over by a carriage; and perhaps as many as six drowned when their boat was overset trying to get in close to the bank to see the show.[11] The Joiners' accounts noted that as there was no barge large enough for them they had to process on foot.[12] By contrast, the Grocers were able to show off their new barge, the *Royal Charlotte*, hailed in the press as the grandest and most magnificent of its kind in Europe.[13] The banquet that followed was suitably lavish, but it was noted that a number of courtiers chose not to attend.[14]

More positively, there were newspaper reports that Wilkes had received an unexpected gift of £1,000 from his estranged wife, with her best wishes on his new office. Whether this was the case is not clear. What is more certain is that from the off Wilkes set about putting in place significant reforms. The Old Bailey was to be refigured, the Lord Mayor's parlour improved, and changes made at the Mansion House for the accommodation of poor people applying for passes.[15] Whatever the administration's concerns about Wilkes cementing his role as a dangerous force in the City, much about his mayoralty demonstrated his genuine desire to implement change for the better. There were initiatives to improve animal welfare; efforts to curb the numbers of road traffic accidents; and a concerted policy of fixing the price of basic foodstuffs. Bakers who adulterated their flour were fined.[16] Wilkes's interest in responding to animal cruelty continued beyond his term of office. While sitting as a justice at the Guildhall in the winter of 1775, he heard a case brought by William Langford against a carman named Thomas White, who was accused of 'misbehaving himself and maliciously whipping' Langford's horses. The case was found against White and a marginal comment noted that Wilkes also ordered two shillings to be awarded to 'a poor boy', presumably for providing evidence against White.[17] Other types of disorderly behaviour also exercised him. On the very day of the Lord Mayor's procession it was reported that he wished to initiate a scheme tackling the pickpockets who exploited the crowds congregating at executions.[18] Ironically, a later image of Wilkes by Robert Dighton showed him as part of a tightly packed crowd attending the Westminster election of 1788, and having his own pocket picked.[19]

The day after the festivities that had seen him welcomed into his new office, Wilkes fell sick and spent the next week confined to barracks in Prince's Court.[20] The excitement of the past few days had evidently been too much for him. By 17 November he was well enough to spend time with Charpillon at her house in Great Titchfield Street. Their relationship would be strained during his mayoralty as she was determined to be visible as his 'lady mayoress'. Wilkes was equally clear that this would not be the case. A radical and libertine he may have been, but Wilkes had a clear sense of what was appropriate. A professional courtesan, and a foreign one at that, was an unsuitable consort. Besides, he had a ready-made lady mayoress in the form of Polly, and she was to fulfil the role with some aplomb.

Shortly after Wilkes had recovered from his illness, his attention became divided between his duties in the City and the new Parliament, which opened on 29 November. On that day, the *Public Advertiser* printed its Political Catechism for 1774. This comprised a series of questions and answers touching on hot topics of the moment. Heading them were a series of points lampooning the public's support for Wilkes.

> Question. What is the cause of the public? Answer. To keep up the consequence, and fill the pockets of John Wilkes.
> Question. Who are the Friends of Freedom? Answer. All those who suffer Mr Wilkes to lead them by the nose, and to put his fingers in their purses whenever he thinks proper.[21]

The 29th was a busy day for Wilkes. Before 10am he, along with the City MPs, were sworn in as new Members of Parliament. He appears to have amused himself with contemplating proposing Robert Mackreth to stand as Speaker, knowing it would upset the king. Mackreth was one of the unsuitable new MPs who had featured in the newspaper report. He had previously been a waiter and billiard marker at Arthur's Coffee House (forerunner of White's Club) before making his fortune. Did Wilkes ever seriously intend to put Mackreth forward? It would have been like him to tease the possibility while never meaning to do anything about it. Besides, he would have enjoyed the effect on Mackreth quite as much as that on the government. Whether ever seriously contemplated, the scheme was soon shelved and the sitting Speaker, Sir Fletcher Norton, was allowed to retain his place unchallenged.[22] That afternoon Wilkes was back in the City presiding over the disputed election for the new alderman of the ward of Bridge Within. He refused to accept John Hart's demand to be sworn in, but he was overruled by the Court of Alderman. Asked to propose a motion accusing himself of violating the rights of the freemen he replied, 'I thank God, I am not quite idiot enough to put that question.'[23]

December 1774 and January 1775 found Wilkes dividing his time between Prince's Court, convenient for Parliament, and the Mansion House, with occasional forays further afield to Richmond. On 22 January there was a dinner at the Mansion House attended by d'Eon, along with Domenico Angelo, proprietor of the famous fencing and riding academy to which Wilkes had entrusted the education of his son John Smith, as well as the familiar figures of Churchill and Polly.[24] Where Wilkes had been careful as sheriff to avoid accusations of preferring French wines, as Lord Mayor he was subject to criticism for the French company that was found there. He seems to have been alive to the criticism, though, and when Jack Smith appeared fresh from his French sojourn, Wilkes seems to have been concerned by his transformation into a 'Frenchified' petit maître.[25] However, if the company on 22 January appeared to show the poorer side of the Lord Mayor – a questionable French contact and a foreign fencing master – one held just uner a month later has been seen as a moment when he turned a corner and began to be accepted as far more respectable. On this occasion the guest list included half a dozen bishops, including the archbishop of Canterbury.[26] On a later occasion, Bishop Terrick of London rejected an opportunity to dine at the Mansion House with Wilkes. He pleaded business for refusing, but may well have been reluctant to socialize with someone out of step with his own views.[27]

The presence of the bishops at the Mansion House at this point is interesting, as it came not long after Wilkes had risen in the Commons to speak for the first time since his re-election. The occasion, on 26 January, was a debate on the annual observance of the execution of Charles I, which was objected to by Viscount Folkestone, who argued that the commemoration was a reflection on the 1688 revolution.[28] Folkestone even went so far as to suggest the event was blasphemous. Wilkes was the fifth person to weigh in. He started out by saying that he was in favour of the day being marked, but that it should not be a day of prayer and fasting. Rather, it should be 'celebrated as a festival', marking a day when the king, 'a determined enemy of the liberties of his country' who had 'murdered' thousands, had been justly brought to account. When the division was called, the original motion was carried comfortably by 138 to fifty, but Wilkes had reminded the administration of his presence with a characteristic speech, cheekily wrong-footing his hearers by appearing to agree to the motion but then subverting the original idea with a clarion call for liberty.[29]

On 6 February, he spoke again. This time the topic was a debate on an address to the king on the American crisis. He warned of the likelihood of civil war if the ministry did not alter course, querying 'whether justice is on our side'. Wilkes was in uncompromising mood as he set out his objections.

> The Address now reported from the Committee of the whole House appears to be unfounded, rash, and sanguinary. It draws the sword unjustly against America; but before administration are suffered to plunge the nation into the horrors of a civil war, before they are permitted to force Englishmen to sheath their swords in the bowels of their fellow subjects, I hope this House will seriously weigh the original ground and cause of this unhappy dispute.

Along with the injustice of the cause, as he saw it, Wilkes also feared that current policy would drive the Americans to despair and terminate any hopes of a negotiated settlement. In conclusion, there was a sanguinary warning of his own:

> I hope the just vengeance of the people will overtake the authors of these pernicious counsels, and the loss of the first province of the empire be speedily followed by the loss of the heads of those ministers who advised these wicked and fatal measures.[30]

Wilkes was far from the only person warning of the dangers of goading America, but his rebuke underlined his keen insight. Two years later, following Burgoyne's surrender, he advocated repealing the Declaratory Act (1766) and he would go on to urge the administration to recognize American independence.[31]

Just over a fortnight later, Wilkes was on his feet again, but this time for a much more personal issue. Now the motion was his own, and it was the first of several attempts he was to make at having the resolution regarding his expulsion from Parliament expunged from the Journals. The House was particularly full that day. By three o'clock the place was packed and orders were given for strangers and peers' sons not to be admitted, though it was not until quarter past four that Wilkes finally rose.[32] As was so often the case, Wilkes equated his own position with that of the people in general. It was, he insisted, something that affected 'the very vitals of the constitution' as well as reiterating his view that MPs were delegates of their constituents. He rounded off with a plea: 'I feel, I deeply feel the wounds given to the constitution. They are still bleeding, and this House only can heal them, as well as restore the constitution to its former state of purity, health, and vigour.'[33]

Wilkes was seconded, unsurprisingly, by Glynn, before a number of other MPs piled in. Colonel Onslow, the man Wilkes had provoked over printing debates, was an opponent, as was Charles James Fox, still at this point a government supporter, who declared that he thought the expulsion had been 'a right measure'. There were various pernickety corrections to Wilkes's facts, which elicited further remarks by Wilkes. The debate rounded off with an ill-timed intervention by the hot-headed Welsh MP, Charles Van, who accused Wilkes of blasphemy. Wilkes called him to order and had the resolution read out again, at which the chamber descended into laughter. This seems to have been a typical response to Van, who was known for his somewhat unhinged contributions. He was a determined enemy of America, considering it Carthage to Britain's Rome. Only a few months before, Van had advocated setting light to the forests of Massachusetts as a punishment.[34]

Once everyone had got over Van's latest performance, the result was an unsurprising defeat for Wilkes. The number voting with him, however, 171, indicated the strength of support for him. Edward Gibbon offered a slightly different perspective. He noted that he sat by Wilkes in the debate, who spoke 'well and with temper; but before the end of the debate fell fast asleep.'[35] Long hours divided between the Mansion House and Westminster were clearly taking their toll.

Over the next few years, Wilkes delivered numerous significant orations in the Commons. It was a far cry from the early days when he struggled to be noticed. Could he actually be heard, though? An anecdote by Henry Angelo, Domenico's son, from just a few years later noted that as Wilkes had lost so many teeth, 'it required particular attention to understand him, so imperfect was his articulation.'[36] Even when he had been younger and in better physical shape, Wilkes had always lisped badly. Whatever the limitations of his ability to enunciate, though, he had great presence and appears to have put on a spirited performance. This alone was not enough, so to ensure that his points were clearly understood he was usually careful to make sure that his speeches were available to be read in print as well. This was the opinion of Nathaniel Wraxall:

> In the House of Commons he was not less an actor than at the Mansion House or at Guildhall. His speeches were full of wit, pleasantry, and point, yet nervous, spirited, and not all defective in argument. They were all prepared before they were delivered; and Wilkes made no secret of declaring that, in order to secure their accurate transmission to the public, he always sent a copy of them to William Woodfall before he pronounced them...[37]

Wraxall's assessment was borne out by another anecdote, which claimed that during one lengthy but utterly indistinct oration he was begged to wind up but insisted on persisting. He pointed out that the speech had to be delivered as it was already in the newspapers.[38]

Two days after his failed attempt to have his expulsion expunged, Wilkes quit London for a few days to appear at the Cricklade by-election.[39] A previous by-election, held just after Christmas, had been declared void, so there was now a new opportunity for a Wilkite candidate. Samuel Petrie, a close associate and City of London merchant, had determined to try his hand and persuaded Wilkes to appear to help further his cause. Wilkes was not impressed by Petrie's chances. Writing to Polly, he likened Petrie's quest to that of Don Quixote tilting at windmills.[40] His hunch was right and unfortunately for Petrie, the town was not fertile ground. After less than an hour on the stump, Wilkes turned to Petrie and declared 'Sam, Wilkes and liberty will not do here; I see it must be hard money.' Petrie ended up with just six votes.[41]

After his return from Cricklade, Wilkes seems not to have travelled far beyond the bounds of London for the remainder of his mayoralty. His attention was clearly fixed on the duties of office, which he undertook with commendable dedication, though he occasionally complained about the burden and clearly looked forward to laying it down. This was all of a piece with Wilkes. There was the constant quest for recognition, accompanied by rapid loss of interest and resentment at the burdens of fame. Writing to Boswell in August 1775, he referred to 'the hurry of the life I am doomed to pass till November.'[42] There was also the familiar hectic round of entertainments. His diaries are full of a series of dinners with a host of acquaintances between coffee shops close to Westminster and grand occasions at the Mansion House. When not sharing a turtle with his fellow aldermen, he pressed on with his reforms in the City. One cause close to his heart was that of the debtors; he was also hypocritically active in curbing the numbers of prostitutes.[43] There were splendid formal entertainments, the crowning glory being the Easter Ball of 17 April. One mark of distinction, as Trench observes, seems to have been that Wilkes, or Polly, was able to ensure that at these great feasts the food actually reached the table when still hot.[44]

The cause of America

Besides his enlightened social and economic policies within the City, Wilkes used his time as Lord Mayor to highlight the situation in America. His own cause had resonated across the Atlantic; his struggle against the government equated with their own.[45] London helped redouble the relationship between Wilkes and America. Indeed, Wilkes was almost certainly involved in sending funds to the Americans.[46] There was already a rich seam of support for America in the City, not a little thanks to the numbers of merchants there with interests across the Atlantic. This, of course, included members of Wilkes's own family. There was his sister Mary, with her business interests in Boston, while his nephew Charles was to settle in America working for a bank. These sorts of trans-Atlantic careers were not uncommon. Several prominent London merchants had been born or lived in America, adding to the close bonds between the two. In 1773, William Lee and Stephen Sayre, both American-born and closely associated with Wilkes and the SSBR, had been elected sheriffs.[47] In January 1775, George Hayley presented the Commons with a petition from merchants trading with America and in February the Common Council offered thanks to Chatham for his conciliatory efforts and to the members of both Houses who were opposing the government over America.[48]

Early in April, following an address by Wilkes, the Livery voted a remonstrance (composed by Arthur and William Lee).[49] It complained about the likely results of the government's actions on trade, as well as lamenting the likely loss of life. Although the king felt obliged to receive the remonstrance, he made plain his disquiet at its apparent encouragement of rebellion and resolved not to accept any more like it. He did, though, acknowledge that Wilkes himself was well behaved on the occasion. It was the beginning, perhaps, of George III's gradual, grudging change of attitude towards Wilkes. While he could not abide Wilkes's present political stance, he could not help admitting that his manners were faultless.[50]

Further indications of the City's stance on the deteriorating relations between America and the mother country were in evidence over the summer. Wilkes's fellow Beefsteak, the earl of Effingham, received a vote of thanks after he resigned his commission, so he could not be sent to fight.[51] His gesture came as matters were rapidly building to a head, concluding with the Proclamation of Rebellion at the end of August. In the City, its formal announcement was muted and Wilkes deliberately made things difficult for the officials involved. He then took advantage of the next mayoral election to make his own stance clear by reading out a letter from John Hancock, requesting that the City help to broker a peaceful resolution. Over the next few weeks, a series of addresses were composed protesting against the war. Wilkes's final speech, stepping down from the mayoralty, was used as a further opportunity to lambast the government.[52]

The autumn of 1775 witnessed a success for Wilkes in securing the unopposed return of Sawbridge to succeed him as Lord Mayor. However, it also saw his pro-American position increasingly under pressure as loyal addresses whipped up support for the king and government. Dinners at the Mansion House in his final months continued to feature a mix of people. The author Beaumarchais was present more than once, as was the inevitable d'Eon. The contact with Beaumarchais may well have gone well beyond a shared interest in literature. Beaumarchais was soon to be active in facilitating the transfer of arms and money via France to the American rebels and there is good reason to think that Wilkes was up to his ears in these transactions.[53] When the ministry was at last forced to offer peace terms to the Americans, Wilkes was open in questioning how sincere the government truly was.[54] On 8 November there was the farewell dinner, at which Wilkes bowed out and Sawbridge was formally ushered in. Wilkes's diaries noted, perhaps wryly, that the dinner was held 'at the joint expence of the two Mayors'. While there was much for him to celebrate, Wilkes exited as Lord Mayor heavily in debt once again. His official allowances had been just under £5,000 but, as Trench notes, he had managed to spend over £8,000. He would have to find ways to balance the books once more.[55]

One particularly galling point for Wilkes had occurred just before the end of his mayoralty. On 10 October Wilkes had received a letter from his firm supporter, John Barnard, informing him that Jane Barnard had confessed all to him about their affair. Barnard had recently rewritten his will, leaving Wilkes £8,000 as well as a collection of prints and items from his library. Jane Barnard's confession threatened to deny Wilkes this very welcome windfall. A series of meetings ensued, with Wilkes rejecting Jane Barnard's confession as the ramblings of someone suffering from a form of breakdown. He also denied an accusation that he had on one occasion taken her by force, throwing her on to a sofa and raping her. Nothing of this episode is creditable to Wilkes. His attitude towards Jane Barnard was brutal and he was very obviously motivated almost entirely by concern about his promised £8,000. It is a reminder that the libertine world he inhabited had a very nasty edge to it and that Wilkes, who spoke of liberty, definitely regarded his female companions as little more than playthings. Barnard was not the most acute of observers and was derided by contemporaries as a foolish old miser. On this occasion, though, he was not taken in and a new will was drawn up leaving Wilkes nothing.[56]

No longer Lord Mayor, Wilkes's focus shifted back to Parliament. This is reflected in the diaries in the preponderance of occasions when he noted dining back at Prince's Court, or, occasionally, 'in the room over the House of Commons'.[57] He was able to command a degree of support there, though it was something short of a 'party'. Both he and Sawbridge launched attacks on Lord George Germain, the new secretary of state responsible for American affairs. He had been court-martialled for cowardice following the battle of Minden (1759), and never managed to live it down. Wilkes's group then supported Richard Oliver's motion that those responsible for the administration's American policies should be named. As Wilkes's backers on this occasion amounted to a round dozen, Wilkes dubbed them his 'twelve apostles'.[58]

That he had not given up on the City, though, was demonstrated both by his continued dedicated service as a justice and by his concerted effort to secure election to the lucrative post of City Chamberlain, responsible for administering London's finances. As a justice, Wilkes had to oversee a range of cases, many of them relatively petty. On 11 December 1775, for example, he was in the chair deputising for Bull. Among those brought before him were a woman charged with stealing a pewter pot, another woman accused of uttering (distributing) counterfeit money, and a man who had been arrested for carrying a piece of timber 'at an unseasonable hour in the night'. The first woman was discharged as no felony was proved against her; the second was remanded to Wood Street Compter to await trial at the next assizes. The man was handed over to a Middlesex constable, as it was determined the wood had been stolen in Middlesex and thus outside of the City's jurisdiction.[59]

The Chamberlaincy, though, was Wilkes's real target. In effect a job for life,[60] he hoped that this would set his finances back on an even keel and free him from worry. The only problem was convincing the incumbent, Sir Stephen Janssen, to agree to retire. Wilkes had raised the issue while still mayor and in November wrote to Janssen, promising to carry on his work, but explaining in refreshingly honest terms precisely why he needed the position:

> After being harassed for so many years, I cannot but earnestly desire to arrive in a safe post, and acquire an honourable independence by a continuance of services in the best way I am able.[61]

Janssen agreed to Wilkes's proposal, but unfortunately, plenty in the City felt that Wilkes was hardly the ideal candidate to manage London's finances. An anonymous letter to the *Morning Chronicle* reminded the paper's readers of Wilkes's track record. His financial conduct relating to the Foundling Hospital was noted, as was his behaviour towards his wife. His refusal to accept a place while at the same time petitioning for the governorship of Canada was also dredged up.[62] Unwilling to sit by and let Wilkes take on such a responsible position, a rival was found to oppose him.

Benjamin Hopkins was a former MP as well as being a director of the Bank of England. Although he had rebelled in Parliament on occasion, he was generally reckoned a safe government supporter and was certainly resolutely anti-Wilkes. Just how divided the City was on the issue was indicated by the bad-tempered meeting held at the Half Moon Tavern in Cheapside convened to nominate candidates to replace Janssen. At half past six, a party of Hopkins' friends tried to take over the meeting and impose their choice of chairman. Wilkes's supporters fought back and nominated their own. There was then confusion as other potential chairmen were suggested. After an hour of this, Wilkes's man, Saxby (a linen draper) was finally ushered into the chair and Wilkes and Hopkins nominated formally. Early indications suggested at that point that Wilkes commanded a substantial majority.[63] When the polls opened on 20 February 1776, Wilkes sportingly offered to expend a portion of his salary as chamberlain discharging the debts he had ramped up during his mayoralty. His diaries noted him at the Paul's Head in Cateaton Street with the election committee from then until the 24th and again on the 26th and 27th.[64] Despite the early lead, by the close of polls on 27 February, Hopkins had outstripped Wilkes by more than 100 votes. A print satire from the time depicts Hopkins being chaired as the new Chamberlain, while Wilkes sits to the side pointing to a scroll reading 'Alas, how unstable the affections of a Mob'. He is comforted by a weeping Bull (shown anthropomorphically as a bull wearing his aldermanic gown), while a woman bearing a cap of liberty on a staff is drenched in urine from a chamber pot poured from an upper window. One of Hopkins' supporters flourishes a banner with the slogan 'Hopkins for ever, down with Wilkes & Liberty'.[65]

Wilkes resolved not to take this lying down and tried again that summer, but he should not have bothered. Hopkins secured 2,869 votes and Wilkes just 1,673. Subsequent challenges further damaged Wilkes's reputation and this was reflected in increasingly poor showing in the polls. In 1778, he could only manage 287 votes. It was only Hopkins' death in 1779 that finally opened the way for Wilkes at last to secure the office he had coveted for so long.[66]

Parliamentary Reform

At the 1774 general election, both Wilkes and Glynn had stood for Middlesex on a programme advocated by the SSBR. One of the central features of the reform agenda was addressing the question of the franchise and on 21 March 1776, Wilkes rose in his place to argue in favour of significant changes to the electoral system. The speech demonstrated once more Wilkes's grasp of detail, but also his eye for the bigger picture. A growing population meant that the Britain of the 1770s was less well represented than during Anne's reign.⁶⁷ Numbers of constituencies, which may well have been significant centuries before, retained MPs even if their populations had all but disappeared. Cornwall, in particular, was over-represented. New, burgeoning industrial towns like Birmingham, on the other hand, were yet to achieve representation at all. It was this fundamental imbalance that Wilkes sought to address. 'This House is at this hour composed of the same representation it was at [Charles II's] demise, notwithstanding the many and important changes which have since happened.' Parliament, he argued, no longer properly reflected the will of the people, even if there was no such thing as corruption and bribery associated with its Members' returns.

Turning to specifics, Wilkes suggested that the south of the country consisted of about five million people, but that a key division in 1741, alluding here to the fall of Walpole, had been decided, in effect, by no more than 5,723 people. Many of these, he underlined, were from the numerous Cornish boroughs. He highlighted the craziness of places like Gatton and Old Sarum (the latter a Pitt family seat, of course), desolate places with barely any inhabitants at all, retaining MPs. As was so often the case, Wilkes was not being entirely original here. By highlighting the imbalance in the system, he was echoing what had been said before him by Beckford in 1761. On that occasion, Beckford had highlighted the absurdity that the City of London paid a huge proportion of the nation's taxes but returned just four MPs.⁶⁸ Wilkes's plan, however, went beyond a simple redistribution of seats. He intended a raft of changes, including disfranchisement, stamping out of corruption, and offering the vote to more among the lower and middle ranks:

> The disfranchising of the mean, venal, and dependent boroughs would be laying the axe to the root of corruption and treasury influence, as well as aristocratical tyranny. We ought really to guard against those, who sell themselves, or whose lords sell them... I wish, Sir, an English parliament to speak the free, unbiassed sense of the body of the English people, and of every man among us, of each individual, who may justly be supposed to be comprehended in a fair majority...

To achieve this, Wilkes advocated extending the franchise to 'the meanest mechanic, the poorest peasant and day labourer' as they, quite as much as the wealthy, were subject to the laws of the land. 'Some share therefore in the power of making those laws, which deeply interest them, and to which they are expected to pay obedience, should be reserved even to this inferior, but most useful, set of men.'⁶⁹

This was a truly radical programme and the effort was, of course, unsuccessful. No one, least of all Wilkes himself, expected it to be adopted.

It is even questionable whether he truly believed everything he was advocating. There was also the nice point about him laying into those who relied on aristocratic patrons. Not so long before, he had been just such a man. If he was ambivalent, why then did he bother? It seems fair to say that having signed up to the SSBR's programme, he had felt obliged as a delegated MP to argue the case. But there was more to it than that. There was an obvious resonance between what Wilkes declaimed on that day in the Commons and what he had said all those years before in Westminster Hall when arguing for his liberty. Then he had stated that, quite as much as being concerned with the rights of the upper echelons, 'what touches me more sensibly' were the needs 'of all the middling and inferior Classes of People, who stand most in Need of Protection'.[70] Once again, Wilkes had identified himself as their champion, as a man who came from just such a middling sort background. It is also striking that just a few years later an address to the freeholders of Middlesex contained the line: 'The idea of an equal and adequate representation was, several years ago, proposed, and ably supported in the House of Commons, by that intelligent and inflexible assertor of English Liberties, Mr Wilkes.' He clearly enjoyed that, as he kept a copy and underlined that section.[71] If he was equivocal about reform, he was determined to remain a champion of liberty. Besides, Wilkes's attempt, along with that of others like Horne Tooke and Christopher Wyvill, did have an impact. It was not just in America that questions were being asked about the British constitution. On the continent, many were beginning to question whether the much-vaunted British freedoms were everything they were cracked up to be.[72]

Two months after his unsuccessful effort to secure Parliament's support for reform, Wilkes was invited to dinner by his friends the Dillys at their house in the Poultry. What might on the face of it have appeared just one of a number of such events was the more extraordinary as it was the occasion that finally brought him together with his longstanding critic, Samuel Johnson. Boswell, friends with both, had been eager to get them together for some time. The Dillys' invitation for 15 May prompted him to suggest that they ask Johnson, too. This elicited a horrified reply from Edward Dilly: 'not for the world… Dr Johnson would never forgive me.' It speaks much that the concern was all about how the querulous Johnson would react. Wilkes, it was assumed, would have taken the whole thing in his stride. Boswell insisted that he would be able to work it, and he would take the blame for any ill feeling. On that basis, the Dillys allowed him to broach the matter with Johnson and Boswell managed to propose the party in such a way that Johnson was unable to refuse, leaving all in readiness for the Wednesday to come.

On the day in question there was a brief hiatus as Johnson had forgotten the engagement and already ordered his dinner at home.

Boswell managed to sweet-talk Johnson's landlady out of the meal she had prepared for him and Johnson was hurried into his clothes. On arrival, they found Arthur Lee there ('Too, too, too' muttered Johnson) and then Johnson enquired after 'the gentleman in lace'. That was Wilkes. According to Boswell, Johnson was so stunned he had to retreat to a window seat with a book for a few moments to compose himself. This rather inauspicious start was improved hugely by Wilkes's behaviour at the dinner table. Sitting himself next to Johnson, he strained himself to be helpful, offering a masterclass in carving to tempt Johnson to the best cuts, portions of stuffing and gravy and other delicacies.[73] Carving was a gentlemanly skill and true proficiency was much lauded.[74]

Aside from his prowess as a carver of roast meat, Wilkes also managed to charm Johnson with his knowledge of literature and the theatre. But it was over their disdain for the Scottish landscape that they really bonded. Wilkes allowed himself an extended monologue on the absurdities of the climax to Shakespeare's *Macbeth*. How could Birnam Wood ever have marched to Dunsinane, when Scotland was notoriously barren of vegetation? By the end of the evening, if not fast friends, much of the ice had been melted, and on his return home Johnson was heard praising the quality of Wilkes's company.[75]

That summer, Wilkes's health took a turn for the worse and in July he quit London for a holiday on the south coast. He rallied during the first few days, reporting to Polly the day after his arrival in Brighton, 'The feverish heat is greatly diminished, and the sea air I think already is salutary to me.' He was eager for her to join him there and detailed some 'very good apartments' he had seen, which were available until early August. He left it to her to decide whether she would come, travelling with Catherine Molyneux, wife of the King's Lynn MP Crisp Molyneux, with whom the Wilkes family were on close terms.[76] He insisted 'three as good-humoured people, so disposed to be happy, seldom meet.' He was to be disappointed, so rather than taking on the large well-furnished rooms in Brighton, he retreated to his 'old little cabin' up on the cliffs, which he had for a weekly rent of a guinea.[77] Denied his daughter's company, he sent her a present of rabbits and chickens. He had hoped to include some lobsters for Mrs Molyneux, but the weather had been rough and the fishermen refused to go out. He had no patience with their caution, mocking their cowardice as well as their apparent identification with Methodism:

> The cowardly, methodistical fishermen have not dared to venture out these three days. It is very extraordinary, that the heresy of methodism has infected almost all the seafaring people here, and has made them cowards as well as simpletons. I remain however sound in the faith, and

will keep to my good orthodox mother, the Church of England, to the last moment of – its legal establishment.[78]

It was quite a departure for the scion of a non-nonconformist household, who had once had an Arian for a tutor. Unsurprisingly, John Wesley was equally critical of Wilkes. He objected to 'the mercurial elusive rake' and all he appeared to stand for.[79]

A week after arriving, Wilkes noted in his diary that his fever had returned. He detailed the medicine he was taking to treat himself, largely based around 'Dr James's powder', which he took in currant jelly along with drinking 'great quantities of baum tree'. It was not until early August that his health improved, but he hoped nonetheless that the holiday was providing him with 'a stock of health for the next winter, to follow dutifully all the claims which my good friends the freeholders of Middlesex have on me in Parliament.' From Portsmouth he sent Polly a gift of two hams, asking that one of them should be sent on to Charpillon: a rare mention of his mistress in his correspondence with his daughter.[80]

The new parliamentary session, which opened on 13 October 1776, found Wilkes once again on his feet denouncing the administration's American policies. In his speech against the Address, he argued that the Americans did not seek independence. They merely wanted to be treated on the same terms as the mother country. The following month, there was another opportunity to voice his support for the Americans and criticism of the ministers, when Richard Oliver moved an address to the king to tackle misgovernment. However, by this point Wilkes's position was beginning to change. His speech insisting that the Americans did not really seek independence came after the Declaration of Independence of 4 July 1776, after all, and represented his own wishful thinking as much as anything else. Wilkes's position had always been that a fair policy to America would result in an end to conflict. He did not wish to see the colonies go their own way. Indeed, his immediate response to the Declaration had supposedly been: 'I will never give up the supremacy of Great Britain.'[81] This was a line to which the king himself might not have objected. He always opposed the war, though, and never believed that Britain would be able to win.

The year 1776 had been a taxing one for Wilkes in many ways. Cut loose from the mayoralty, he no longer had to put up with the endless entertainments at the Mansion House, but he had also lost the financial security that went with it. He had spoken with spirit in favour of reform and attacked the ministry over the worsening situation in America, but in neither case was he heeded. In November, there was also a reminder of his old lost friend Churchill, when Dr Andrew Kippis approached him for assistance in composing Churchill's entry for his *Biographia Britannica*. Wilkes ended up writing a significant part of the article on Churchill, as well as sections on the life of Baxter.[82]

Wilkes quit the parliamentary session a few days early, setting out on 7 December for another much-needed holiday at Bath. Christmas Day was spent at Alfred House, home of Catharine Macaulay, republican writer and sister of his London associate and occasional rival, Sawbridge. Macaulay had been one of those to send Wilkes money while he was in King's Bench and they had several acquaintances in common, including Thomas Birch, who had co-sponsored Wilkes's membership of the Royal Society, and Edward Dilly. Thomas Wilson, with whom Macaulay and her daughter lived, had been Wilkes's successor as master of the Joiners' Company. Despite that, Wilkes's relations with her were never entirely straightforward. He disapproved of some of her political opinions; she of his libertinism.[83] Shortly after his return from the Christmas break, there was what was to be in retrospect a significant meeting, when Wilkes was invited to dine with the Reverend William Dodd (known as the Macaroni Parson). This seems to have been Wilkes's and Dodd's second meeting, after coming across one another just a few weeks before at the Dillys'.[84] It was also to be the last. In February, Dodd was arrested and subsequently condemned to death for forging a bond. In spite of a spirited campaign backed by, among others, Samuel Johnson, Dodd went to the gallows.[85]

Back in Parliament, Wilkes remained a thorn in the government's side for the remainder of the session. In February 1777 he spoke out against the bill for suspending *Habeas Corpus*, concluding his address with a line from Terence, '*Homo sum, humani nihil a me alienum puto.*'[86] In April, he attracted the king's displeasure again, by querying demands for the Civil List debts to be paid in a lengthy and detailed speech. The following month, he weighed in once more, this time backing a proposal that the king's brothers, the dukes of Cumberland and Gloucester, should be allotted more from the Civil List: both, as Thomas has pointed out, had made injudicious mésalliances.[87] Quite as important, though, was another oration, delivered on 28 April. This was prompted by the sale of the fabulous Walpole art collection. Ever since his earlier association with the Society of Artists, Wilkes had remained a champion of the fine arts and the prospect now of such a collection being lost to the nation was something that troubled him.

> The British Museum, Sir, possesses few valuable paintings, yet we are anxious to have an English school of painters. If we expect to rival the Italian, the Flemish, or even the French school, our artists must have before their eyes the finished works of the greatest masters.[88]

Wilkes envisaged the British Museum becoming the home of a 'national gallery' and seconded Burke's motion for the Museum's grant to be increased from £3,000 to £5,000.[89] It is a crucial reminder that Wilkes's vision of patriot politics was not just about personal liberty (though it was that in spades). It was also a more hifalutin conception of the importance of the country, one 'saved' from 'slavery' by the 1688 Revolution and a place where arts and manufactures should be permitted to flourish.

If Wilkes's political trajectory continued to be combative against king and administration, his emotional life was no less turbulent. On 11 May 1777, his diary recorded one in a long series of dinners at Prince's Court with Polly, followed by supper with Charpillon, a Madame Topin and the Maryland merchant, Tommy Lee, now MP for Wilkes's old seat of Aylesbury. It made no reference to the fact that this was also the day when he and Charpillon indulged in what was to be their last blazing row. The next day, he wrote to tell her that their relationship was at an end.[90]

Bath and the Chamberlaincy

Relieved of the demands of his mistress, Wilkes permitted himself much-needed breaks on the south coast that summer and autumn. In December he made his way to Bath for the Christmas holidays once more. He was again suffering from some minor ailment and dosing himself with 'the *beaume*'.[91] He announced his arrival to Polly: 'Just arrived in this city, and to be seen without loss of time at the *Bear*, in Cheap Street, an *Alderman* of London, alive.' Unable as ever to hide his conceit, he concluded 'He is thought by many good judges the greatest curiosity in this city – except himself.'[92] After his pub dinner, he settled into lodgings at Number 5, Gallway's Buildings, presided over by a Miss Temple. These were not his usual digs, but he found them 'warm and spacious'.[93] He dubbed his hostess 'a perfect Huncamunca', comparing her to the amorous and rather overweight character in Henry Fielding's *Tom Thumb*.[94]

Bath was full of company for the holidays, though Wilkes was underwhelmed by the quality. He wrote of one ball, attended by 500 people, 'no female danced half so well as the little Grace of Prince's Court.'[95] At another, he was distinguished by assisting the master of ceremonies in the Upper Assembly Rooms, an event attended by 'a well-dressed crowd of near 900 persons'.[96] If he missed his daughter, Wilkes was certainly not alone as swathes of politicians and other grandees of all sorts had descended on the city. So many political figures in a relatively confined space seems to have made Bath a hotbed of political gossip. 'The rage of politics is, I think, more violent at Bath than even at London, and nothing is talked of but America.'[97]

Away from Westminster, Wilkes had other things on his mind. On 10 January 1778, just a few days before he was set to leave, his head was turned by meeting Maria Stafford, who was recently separated from her husband. Probably for the first time since his affair with Corradini, Wilkes found himself head over heels. The timing was somewhat awkward as it seems likely that only a matter of days before this meeting, he had embarked on another liaison.[98] This was with the daughter of a Wiltshire farmer, Amelia Arnold, whom Wilkes established in rooms in Bath. She was very different to his usual long-term mistresses, a much steadier influence and ultimately to become effectively his second wife. For the time being, though, she was very much eclipsed by Stafford and the other society women around her. Indeed, Wilkes now in his fifties, may have been experiencing something of a mid-life crisis. The same trip saw him salivating over a Miss Rian, whom he mentioned in a letter to Polly as 'the most beautiful woman at Bath'.[99]

Wilkes seems genuinely to have lost his head over Maria Stafford, though. Within days of their meeting he was musing on the possibility of them marrying, though by March this had been watered down to a less appealing offer for her to become his new *maîtresse en titre*.[100] Unusually, he contrived an excuse to head to Bath again in April 1778 so he could be with her. A few days before setting out, he had sent her a love poem just before heading into a committee of the House of Commons examining the not particularly romantic Basingstoke navigation bill.[101] He had also moved in the Commons for a bill to prevent 'the dangerous and unconstitutional practice' of awarding money to the Crown without parliamentary consent. The matter stood no chance of being adopted and when the House divided, it was rejected seventy-one to forty.[102]

Wilkes's April meeting with Stafford went equally badly. Oddly, he seems to have tried to encourage Polly to join him on the trip, but she declined the offer. He found Bath 'very thin for the spring season', but of course that was not why he was there. He found Maria Stafford in poor health. Had she not been, she would have left Bath before he arrived to avoid an unwelcome confrontation. In the event, they did meet, and he managed to persuade her to accompany him to a concert, wearing a rose that he had brought for her. She was, however, advised by her friends of the social stigma she would suffer should she agree to his proposal to become his mistress. By the middle of April, she had written demanding the return of her letters and brought the infant affair to a conclusion. Wilkes made no mention of any of this to Polly, of course. He limited himself to confiding more palatable details of his stay, like a tedious evening drinking tea at the Lower Assembly Rooms with 'an old tabby dowager', or making light of himself, 'the greatest fop at Bath, or the most perfect *macaronissimo* of the age'.[103] He may have hidden it from Polly, but Wilkes was genuinely thrown by the rejection describing himself as 'the most unhappy man at Bath'.[104] He remained in the city until 2 May, perhaps hoping that Stafford might change her mind. While there, he visited Bristol and on his return met with his old supporter, New York-born Henry Cruger, who was one of the city's MPs. As he wound his way back towards London, Wilkes indulged in some more tourism, admiring Longleat, Fonthill and the duke of Bolton's seat at Hackwood.[105]

Wilkes's madcap rush after Maria Stafford rather disguised the fact that he was at the same time carrying on his relationship with Amelia Arnold. On 20 October 1778, he became a father again, when Amelia gave birth to a daughter, Harriet. Wilkes duly established the new family in a house at Kensington Gore, close enough to be visited regularly, far enough away not to impede on his life in London. It is striking that Arnold's first mention in his diaries does not occur until 1 August 1782. There is a break in the run of the diaries between July 1779 and July 1782, bar a fragmentary set of records for the Christmas season of 1779-1780, but it is still noticeable that he did not bother to include her for the first two years of their relationship. It is the more remarkable as Arnold and Harriet were to become, along with Polly, Wilkes's mainstay in the final years of his life.

Fatherhood did nothing to interrupt Wilkes's routine. Christmas 1778 found him back at Bath.[106] On Boxing Day there was another party at Alfred House, though things were very different there than they had been during his previous visit. There had recently been a scandal in the Macaulay Wilson household, over Catharine Macaulay leaving Wilson for a man under half her age. Wilson read out a letter from Macaulay written on the day of her marriage, which Wilkes thought 'indecent, insolent, mean, fawning, threatening, coaxing, menacing, and declamatory'. Denied his hoped-for bequest from John Barnard, Wilkes seems to have believed there might be a financial windfall from Wilson. He made a point of being attentive to Wilson, listening to him unburdening himself about Macaulay, dubbed 'the *modern Messalina*'.[107] He was to be disappointed again.[108]

Among the party at Alfred House over Christmas was at least one other Member of Parliament: David Hartley, MP for Hull, who was also a fellow Leiden alumnus.[109] He was famed as a bore, and notorious for the tediousness of his lengthy speeches.[110] Like Wilkes, though, he was closely concerned with settling the conflict with America and earlier in 1778 Hartley had travelled to France to negotiate, unofficially, with Benjamin Franklin and the French foreign minister, the comte de Vergennes. If uninspiring, then, Hartley was thought of as an honest broker and certainly would have had much to say – at wearisome length – that would have interested Wilkes, who always made the most of such meetings. Away from the funereal Wilson household, Wilkes also found time to attend 'a most superb ball' in the Upper Assembly Rooms. He regaled Polly with details of the sets, and how 'the minuets are now danced three deep, so that they are finished in an hour and a half.'[111]

Given that Wilkes's finances remained somewhat precarious, he may have been keen to spend such lengthy stints at Brighton or Bath, as he could live more cheaply there than in the capital. He was not alone among his family in struggling to get by. Neither of his brothers were faring well. As Cash has shown, the family enterprise had gone under and Heaton had tried in vain to diversify. Israel was managing no better. In business terms, Mary Hayley was by far the most enterprising of the siblings. Wilkes, meanwhile, remained afloat largely through handouts from friends and admirers. His 1777 Bath jaunt had been funded, in part, by Polly's generosity. Indeed, she was now much wealthier than her father, thanks to her inheritance of a significant portion of the Mead estate.[112]

The annual pilgrimage came to an end on 16 January and by the following day Wilkes was back in London in time for a promised meeting with the Middlesex freeholders. That autumn, another tie with the past was cut with the death of Serjeant Glynn on 16 September 1779. He had been in ill health for some years and had been said only to have managed to second Wilkes's 22 February 1775 motion on the question of the Middlesex election with great difficulty. Glynn's death left a vacant seat in Parliament. The man lined up for the seat was George Byng, a Rockingham Whig and at that point MP for Wigan. He applied to Lord North to enable him to resign Wigan and stand for Middlesex. North refused. As a result, a stopgap candidate was settled on to keep the seat warm for Byng until the 1780 general election.[113]

If the death of Glynn brought one old pairing to an end, just a few weeks later Wilkes was thrown a helpful lifeline. In November, the City Chamberlaincy became vacant once more. Promptly, Wilkes announced his intention of standing again, and this time he offered to employ half of the returns towards paying off his (still unsettled) bills as mayor. He was opposed by a Court-backed candidate, William James, and the government machine cranked into motion, portraying Wilkes as a profligate who should not be trusted with the post. Other papers responded on his side, arguing for his consistency as a friend to liberty.[114] On the 22nd, the election came on at Guildhall. Wilkes reported to Polly an overwhelming show of support for him ('Certainly above 100 to 1') but James demanded the contest be put to a formal poll nevertheless.[115] The result was a landslide for Wilkes, reversing the embarrassment of his final effort against Hopkins. At the close he had 2,343 votes; James could only muster 371. As Wilkes reported triumphantly to Polly, James 'is retired *sans tambour ou trompette*'.[116] Wilkes was sworn in ten days later. He would retain the office for the remainder of his life. It gave him financial security as well as securing him his place in the City. As he put it himself, 'It is a post adequate after payment of my debts to every wish I can form at fifty-three; profit, patronage and extensive usefulness with rank and dignity.'[117]

It must have been with a lighter heart that Wilkes set out for Bath a few days before Christmas. He was still there at the end of January 1780, reporting back to Polly the rival entertainments of the two Assembly Rooms. Brereton was said to have had 750 revellers at his ball a few days before; Dawson expected 1,300 at his next event.[118] On 2 February, Wilkes exchanged one crowded room for another when he appeared at the packed meeting in Westminster Hall in support of Charles James Fox as the prospective candidate for Westminster in the coming general election. It was a remarkable transformation. Fox's father had been one of Wilkes's principal bogeymen for his alliance with Bute, and Fox had taken up the cudgels in defence of the family honour. Horace Walpole even recalled a public breakfast having been laid on at the Fox London residence, Holland House, to celebrate Luttrell's victory over Wilkes in 1769. Fox, though, had now changed his spots and adopted the cause of the radicals. He and Wilkes were never to be comfortable bedfellows, but for the time being the alliance seemed amicable enough.[119] At the ensuing election in October, the alliance was cemented when Wilkes plumped for Fox, choosing not to lodge his second vote.[120]

In spite of his support for the coming man, Fox, by now Wilkes's outlook had altered. He no longer had the same axe to grind that he had in 1768 or even in 1771. A secure position in the City and a seat in Parliament had taken some of the edge off him. Indeed, one correspondent of the duke of Portland's commented in January 1780 that Wilkes would no longer make trouble in London and that it was said Wilkes thought 'patriotism too dangerous for a Chamberlain'.[121] Less inclined to pursue some of his former radical schemes, leisure became an increasingly important part of his existence. He stole another trip down to Bath in May. He then wound his way home via Chepstow, Gloucester and Oxford, having made a detour to Bristol and taken the opportunity of a brief hop across the Severn into Wales. His letters to Polly charting the journey were peak Wilkes in pastoral vein.[122] All of that was about to be blown apart by the most serious rioting the country had seen in decades. Wilkes's response to the Gordon Riots would change his relations with many of his old supporters for good and set him on a new course.

11

From the Gordon Riots to Respectability

(1780–1787)

A quondam friend of Liberty.

On 8 June 1780, Wilkes scribbled a hurried note to Polly from his post in the churchyard of St Sepulchre's, not far from the old Mead family residence. He assured her that he was there 'with a good party of horse and foot' along with armed locals, and that the rioters were 'so intimidated, that we shall have no business but rest on our arms'. He planned to remain there until five or six in the morning.[1]

The reason for Wilkes finding himself surrounded by troops in the middle of the night was that London (along with several other cities) was at that point transfixed by the 'Gordon Riots'. On 2 June, Lord George Gordon, the 29-year-old son of the 3rd duke of Gordon, and MP for Ludgershall (Buckinghamshire), had presented a petition from the Protestant Association calling for the repeal of the Catholic Relief Act. Gordon was an eccentric character, most famously depicted by Charles Dickens in *Barnaby Rudge*. He had spent eight years in the Navy before being elected to Parliament in 1774, but then seems to have waited almost four years to trouble Parliament with a speech. When it came, in April 1778, it was characteristically strident. He appealed to Lord North to 'call off his butchers and ravagers from the colonies', urging the prime minister 'to turn from his wickedness and live; it was not yet too late to repent.'[2] News of the intervention reached Wilkes in Bath, where he was attempting to salvage his relationship with Maria Stafford. He asked of Polly who the 'Lord – Gordon' was, who had 'attacked Lord North in so unwarrantable a manner'? Gordon had used words such as 'villainous', which even Wilkes considered to be unparliamentary.[3]

Wilkes had an opportunity of meeting the young firebrand twice in 1778, both times at dinners hosted by Sir Robert Clayton, the Rockinghamite MP for Bletchingley.[4] Gordon was a striking individual, with later criminal records noting him as five feet eleven, with sandy hair and a sallow complexion.[5] Wilkes would have had little time for his angry anti-Catholic views, though. This was in contrast to his colleague, Bull, who was closely aligned with the Protestant Association, and Nathaniel Polhill, the Wilkite MP for Southwark, whose only known speech in Parliament was to second Gordon's motion for Parliament to accept the Association's petition.[6] Gordon had been elected the Association's president in November 1779. The following May he announced that he would present their petition on Friday 2 June and invited supporters to descend on London to accompany the procession. By then, he had become a familiar bore in Parliament, subjecting his colleagues to lengthy fulminations. On one occasion he emptied the chamber by insisting on reading out a pamphlet in its entirety. The next day, he read it again. He was not a subtle man. Although substantial efforts were made by Gordon and the Association's organizers to ensure that the day of the presentation should be orderly, many feared that gathering so many people together was asking for trouble. A print satire from the period shows a well marshalled procession outside Westminster Hall bearing the huge petition, containing an estimated 44,000 signatures.[7] Very quickly, though, order broke down and that afternoon members of both Lords and Commons found themselves besieged in their chambers.[8]

There followed the first of several nights of general lawlessness in the capital. One of the most celebrated chroniclers of the riots in London was Ignatius Sancho, formerly enslaved, but who had been taken into service by the Montagus and ultimately established himself as a shopkeeper and composer of country dances. He was until recently believed to have been the first black Briton to have voted in an election. On 6 June, the day Lord Mansfield's House in Bloomsbury Square was attacked, he addressed a letter to his friend, John Spink, offering 'a very imperfect sketch of the maddest people – that the maddest times were ever plagued with'.[9]

Response to the Gordon Riots

For the first few days the rioters were able to act almost with impunity. As the disorder persisted over the weekend and into the following week, other causes were tacked on. Many of those involved were small tradesmen and artisans, along with the usual apprentices and day labourers, some at least taking advantage of the breakdown in law and order to make a noise, loot or protest about their own particular concerns.[10] That they were able to do so was largely due to the wholly inadequate response to the crisis both from the government and the authorities in London. Lord North was personally courageous in the face of an attack from rioters in Downing Street, but he was less assured dealing with the larger crisis.[11] Lord Mayor Brackley Kennett was also unable to rise to the occasion. As the rioters began targeting prisons, some of those who had been locked up found themselves back on the streets.

Reluctance to do more was in part due to weakness, coupled with a belief that it would all blow itself out over the weekend. There was also, however, considerable sympathy for the anti-Catholicism of the Protestant Association within the City of London. Only on 31 May the Court of Common Council resolved to request the City MPs to support the bill repealing the Relief Act.[12] Normally an uncompromising friend of religious tolerance, Wilkes's own attitude to all of this had been ambiguous. He had kept away from the meeting of the Common Council that had composed a petition against the 1774 Quebec Act, which granted religious toleration to Catholics in the former French province, but then argued against it in Parliament. Wilkes then supported Savile's 1778 Relief Act, not sharing some radicals' concerns that it should be viewed in the same terms as the Quebec Act.[13] He did not, however, speak out against the Common Council's 31 May resolution.[14] There seems no reason to doubt that his own broad, consistent, view was in favour of toleration, but he was willing to play the politician when necessary.

By 5 June, with the violence showing no signs of abating Wilkes attended a meeting of the Court of Aldermen at Guildhall, along with the Lord Mayor and other aldermen. Next day, there was another meeting but still no sign of the authorities restoring control. That evening, Newgate was set alight. Finally, on 7 June Wilkes effectively took command of the situation and insisted on the Lord Mayor getting a grip. An order was made for the *Posse Comitatus* to be raised and the soldiers in the City were brought under the sheriffs' control. It was certainly long overdue. Key landmarks continued to be attacked, including King's Bench prison, where Wilkes had been resident for almost two years. That evening, he found himself stationed with a file of soldiers guarding the Bank of England. According to his diaries the troops fired six or seven times on parties of rioters, killing two outside the Bank and several others in Pig Street and Cheapside.[15]

The next day, Wilkes was in his place in the Commons when the City petition supporting repeal of the Relief Act was presented. He was then back on duty with the troops, stealing a moment to write to Polly. In the course of the evening, various people were arrested and despatched to the City compters (prisons) and on 9 June, there was a breakthrough when Gordon was arrested. Over the next few days Wilkes was fully occupied officiating as a justice and giving orders to the soldiers overseeing workmen, who were beginning the task of clearing up the City and constructing new prisons.[16] There was, almost inevitably, a degree of irony in some of Wilkes's duties. The day after Gordon's arrest, for example, he helped to disperse a mob in Fleet Street outside the premises of the radical printer, William Moore, where he seized various treasonable papers. Moore was formerly associated with the *North Briton*. He was examined the next day and later committed to the Wood Street compter for publishing two seditious and treasonable papers: *England in Blood* and *The Thunderer*.[17] The latter's 8 June edition had congratulated the Protestant Association for preventing ministerial tyranny.[18] Moore had form for spreading incendiary conspiracy theories. He had previously published a paper called *The Whisperer*, which claimed Catholics intended to assassinate the king and were responsible for setting fire to the dockyards in Portsmouth.[19] Brought before Wilkes, Moore refused to co-operate and sign his examination. Wilkes, though, was happy that he had secured proof that Moore had also been involved in the assault on Lord Mansfield's house. He reported to Polly that on the morning the house was sacked, Moore 'gave a glass of wine to a man, telling him *that* was Lord Mansfield's wine'.[20]

The events of June 1780 altered Wilkes's reputation in London for good and his response to them formed a key episode in his career. Taking up printers like Moore must have seemed particularly hypocritical. The greatest irony was that general warrants were employed to seize some of the protesters. Many of those engaged in the rioting may well have thought of themselves as 'his' people, protesting against aristocratic corruption as much as fear of so-called 'Popery'. It is striking that symbols the Wilkites had appropriated from the Tories and Jacobites – blue cockades, for example – and other very Wilkite tactics, such as the chalking of slogans on people's property, had been adopted by the Gordon rioters. Tellingly, on the day the petition was presented to Parliament, some in the crowd left the main group and celebrated outside Wilkes's house.[21]

These, however, were very different forms of public disobedience to those associated with Wilkes. It was not infrequently remarked that Wilkite 'mobs' were fairly good-humoured. The Gordon rioters were anything but, and armed patrols continued for some time afterwards.[22] Several died in the violence and a number of people were convicted and hanged for their role in the disturbances. Gordon himself was tried for treason. Wilkes's defence of the Bank of England showed that he had recognized that this was a moment of profound importance and the City could not bear such violent lawlessness. He was a far more intelligent and much more subtle man than Gordon and his political antennae much more acutely attuned. Wilkes was appalled by Gordon's people and their violent display of anti-libertarianism. It was a moment for choosing sides and Wilkes made his choice in favour of the City and order, in the name of liberty and the constitution. For him there was no contradiction in making that decision. What is more, it was not just Wilkes whose attitudes were affected by the violence of the Gordon Riots. Other radicals, too, were forced to rethink their tactics and the dangers inherent in inciting the mob.[23] Wilkes's relationship with the crowd would never be the same again and it would mark the beginning of his steady transformation into a respectable civic figure. It would take another few years and the emergence of Pitt the Younger, though, before Wilkes would fully throw his lot in with the Court.

Three months after the country had been wracked by the anarchy of the riots, Parliament was dissolved as the government tried to catch the opposition on the hop. At the general election, Wilkes was returned, unchallenged, in Middlesex, along with the Rockinghamite George Byng, who had hoped to secure the seat on Glynn's death the previous year. Post-Gordon, Wilkes's selection had not been without opposition and was greeted in more muted terms than his previous, joyful elections. There were newspaper reports that he was no longer committed to the cause of liberty and was dedicating too much attention to being Chamberlain. A livery meeting held not long after the riots had been suppressed had been fairly hostile, with at least one person shouting 'No Popish Chamberlain' at him.[24] A freeholders' meeting held a couple of days before the poll also showed that Wilkes could no longer expect the degree of support he once had. His candidature was opposed by Thomas Draper, who objected to him silently allowing the Relief Act to pass, opposing the protestant petitions, and for his treatment of Bull in the Commons. Wilkes had criticized Bull for walking arm-in-arm with Gordon and allowing City constables to wear blue cockades (symbols of support for the Association).[25] Wilkes defended himself, insisting that he wished to see an end to all persecution and that he had acted according to his best judgment. He blamed his constituents for failing to offer instructions to their Members and concluded that he wished to see 'the old language of Representatives revived, "I dare not decide on such an important matter, until I have consulted my constituents."'[26]

Draper's objections were not enough to encourage anyone to stand against Wilkes, but it was noted in the press that on the day of the poll Wilkes's speech on the hustings did not receive 'those warm bursts of applause' his previous orations had. Quite the reverse, according to one paper he was met with cries of 'No Wilkes', 'No Popery', and 'No dinners at Richmond'. His chairing was also rather peremptory. He was carried straight to the Castle inn, while Byng was chaired all round the town.[27] With the memory of the Gordon Riots still fresh in everyone's mind, how candidates had behaved back in June was a live issue for the voters. Wilkes was castigated for his lack of support for the Protestant

Association, others for their apparent quiescence during the rioting. A few days before the poll for London, one newspaper carried a letter rebutting claims that Sawbridge had taken no part in the defence of the City, while pointing out that Nathaniel Newnham (another City MP) had been conspicuous by his absence.[28] Despite this, Sawbridge lost his seat, Newnham survived. Sawbridge then regained his place a month later following the death of Alderman Kirkman. Aside from the details of such personal contests, the overall result was disappointing for the government. It lost around half a dozen seats when it had hoped to pick up possibly as many as thirty.[29]

Elder Statesman

Wilkes was to serve another decade in Parliament but something undoubtedly had changed in the wake of Gordon. Indeed, many lives of Wilkes effectively write him off from this point.[30] This would seem to be a mistake, though. True, he became steadily more respectable and his concerns apparently more mundane. In August 1780, about the worst he was able to report to Polly was the minor domestic crisis prompted by his valet returning home roaring drunk after a night on the town. Wilkes was never much interested in drinking to excess and was repelled on this occasion by 'the most disgusting of all human figures, a man metamorphosed into a stupid brute'.[31] However, it is possible to see in this latter part of his career more than a mere winding down. Rather, it might be viewed as just such another reinvention as he had managed on several occasions before. No longer a rabble rouser, he morphed steadily into an elder statesman, perfecting a life just as full of interest and variety as his old, rebellious self. At times, there was an elegiac quality to it. He turned once more to his unfinished autobiography and began tinkering with it.[32] There is more to the final Wilkes than his own, much quoted epitaph of 'Exhausted Volcano' suggests, but he clearly also had half an eye on how he might be viewed by posterity and wanted to be sure that he had said his own piece first.

Wilkes had not yet given up on criticizing the government for its handling of the American War, though. On 27 November, he responded to a motion in the House thanking the British commanders, Clinton and Cornwallis for their service. Rising to his feet after North's brief intervention, he insisted he could not support something that suggested approbation of the American war, a conflict he considered 'unfounded in principle, and fatal in its consequences to this country'. While acknowledging Cornwallis's military qualities, 'which dazzle in my countryman as they did in Julius Caesar', he could not thank the commanders for their actions against the Americans having, as he put it, 'bathed them in their blood'.[33] However, the war was coming towards an end and British successes in 1780 and 1781 proved to be a false dawn. Cornwallis's surrender at Yorktown in 1781 caught the administration completely by surprise and was followed by three months of instability within the ministry. On 22 February 1782, the government survived a motion to bring the war to an end by a single vote. Five days later, a slightly amended motion, for the 'offensive war' to be halted, was carried by the opposition by nineteen. George III finally gave way and allowed North to resign the following month.[34]

The day after North's resignation, Wilkes quit the capital for another Bath jaunt. He was very aware of quitting the scene at a particularly interesting time and begged Polly to send him all the news. He arrived to find Bath thinly populated, though more company was anticipated the following week.[35] Over the next few days the shape of the new administration began to take shape. Reflecting the tensions within the new ministerial alliance, Wilkes understood Rockingham to be 'the nominal' and Shelburne 'the efficient' minister. He made no reference to Fox's role in this triumvirate.[36]

Wilkes had never had any time for North and certainly did not lament his removal. Besides, his replacement with a new administration headed by Rockingham offered Wilkes new opportunities. He sent Rockingham hearty felicitations. He also petitioned to be appointed Receiver General of the Land Tax for Middlesex, a post that had previously been held in conjunction with the Chamberlaincy. When he found out that taking the place would require him to resign from the Commons, though, Wilkes retracted the application.[37] In any case, he had another, more important, ambition in view. He hoped that the new administration would allow him finally to achieve his long-seated desire of having his expulsion of February 1769 expunged from the Commons' Journals. Wilkes made sure, then, that he beat back from Bath in time to be in his place immediately after the Easter recess, thinking it 'imprudent' to be away at such a crucial juncture.[38]

On 3 May, he rose once again to revive his motion for expunging the offending passages, opening with a paean to the new administration, 'the friends and favourites of the people'. As ever, he equated his situation with that of the electorate in general. This was a case, he argued, touching the fundamental rights of the people to elect their own representatives. Previous efforts had been stymied by the 'machinations of power in the hands of wicked men'. Now he hailed the 'present auspicious moment' that offered an opportunity for this great wrong to be righted.[39] He was seconded by Byng, who stressed that it was not so much to a new Treasury bench, but a new House that he now looked to pass a motion 'in which the rights of the subject and the freedom of election were materially concerned'. In spite of their temporary alliance in 1780, Fox spoke against, as he had done before. When it came to the vote, though, Wilkes at last secured what he had so long wished for in a relatively thin House, by 115 votes to forty-seven.[40] As the *Morning Chronicle* put it: 'This long-contested Question, is therefore at length popularly decided.'[41]

Having at last achieved his ambition, Wilkes spent the remainder of the year following a by now familiar routine. There were dinners with political supporters and at one or other of his clubs, the Beefsteaks being a favourite. He also kept up his round of the livery halls. Frequently, he was to be found with the Joiners, but also with the Fishmongers. In the summer, there was the regular meeting of the Middlesex freeholders and over the Christmas holiday the usual retreat to Bath.[42]

To accompany Wilkes's new more respectable reinvention, there was a new likeness to capture the moment. Strikingly, it was a double portrait of Wilkes and Polly by the fashionable portraitist, Johann Zoffany. It was not the first time Zoffany had 'captured' Wilkes. In about 1770, he had painted a man in a parti-coloured masquerade costume, clasping a Wilkes mask in one hand.[43] It seems not, however, to have been until 1795 that the two found time to socialize, Wilkes's diary entry for 23 March 1795 recording a dinner with the well-known collector, Charles Townley, Zoffany and a few others.[44] Zoffany's new work was intended as a far more respectful and realistic image than the previous one. Horace Walpole caught a glimpse of it back in 1779 when it was still in the artist's studio and commented that it was 'horridly like'. The painting finds Wilkes and Polly caught in a fanciful landscape with the sea just in view in the background. Wilkes is sitting, gazing up at his daughter standing beside him. He is clothed in his habitual dress of a colonel of militia: blue uniform coat with red facings, buff-coloured waistcoat and breeches, black boots and a black hat in one hand. In the other he grasps Polly's uncovered left hand. She is in a pink and green dress, festooned with bows, her powdered hair piled high and decorated with flowers. At their feet lies Zoffany's own pet spitz, Roma. It is a fanciful portrait but a telling one for all that. It is perhaps one of the most realistic likenesses of Wilkes, even though by capturing Wilkes staring up at Polly, Zoffany had succeeded in disguising the extent of his strabismus.[45] It also reveals an important truth about Wilkes. This is not just that he was a devoted father, but that he and Polly were a partnership. This had been demonstrated most tellingly during his tenure as Lord Mayor when she was his Lady Mayoress. It would continue to be the case for the rest of his life.

While Zoffany was busy showing off his masterpiece of paternal devotion, there was yet another change at the top. The king had never fully reconciled himself to the new administration and was constantly on the lookout for ways to supplant his current ministers. He was, unsurprisingly, unenthused by their programme, which included reform as well as bringing to an end the American war. While Rockingham was nominally prime minister, power really lay between the two secretaries of state: Shelburne and Fox. Unfortunately, the pair could not abide one another and the way their responsibilities were distributed allowed for disagreements and divisions to get out of hand. As Foreign Secretary, Fox was in charge of overseeing negotiations with the French and Spanish; as Home and Colonial Secretary, it was left to Shelburne to negotiate with the Americans. They both sent agents to Paris and did all in their power to undermine one another. Fox pressed for accepting American Independence unconditionally, while Shelburne worked behind the scenes for a deal that only accepted independence on conditions. With matters still unresolved between them, Rockingham died, throwing the ministry into crisis. Fox resigned and Shelburne became the new Prime Minister.[46]

Wilkes had stood for Middlesex on a joint platform with the Rockinghamite Byng, but the end of Rockingham's administration found Wilkes quietly opting to back Shelburne's new administration. Given his poor relations with Shelburne's supporters in the city during the 1770s this may appear an odd choice, but his relations with Fox were never much better. Besides, as Wraxall observed, there was always 'a strong element of constitutional loyalty' in Wilkes. Even when he had been protesting against the king and Bute in his most objectionable terms in the 1760s, Wilkes's case had always been for upholding the constitution. It was the king's ministers, he feared, who were endangering it. This line echoed that of one of his former supporters, the duke of Bolton. In May 1764, Bolton was in the frame for a job in government and it was likely in response to an approach that he wrote to the duke of Newcastle:

> I shall ever be ready to support Revolution Principles with my poor Endeavours, & Fortune, which there is little merit in doing when I am convinced it is the only service that can secure us against Ministers who are yet unpunish'd (I might say more) for daring to violate both the Liberty and Property of the subject.[47]

The letter might have been written by Wilkes. Also, Shelburne was ostensibly a supporter of reform, though he was later to retreat from his apparent undertakings on the issue.[48] Taking all of this into account, Wilkes's decision to back Shelburne's ministry seems a little less perplexing. On 9 August he had a meeting with the new Prime Minister.[49] The same day, there was what would once have been thought an impossible sight, Wilkes present at the king's levée, when he was reported to have had a 'long conference with the king'.[50]

When Shelburne's peace preliminaries finally came to be debated by both Houses on 17 February 1783, Wilkes seems not to have troubled the copyists with an intervention, though he held firm to the ministry by voting for the peace. His only contribution to proceedings had occurred a few days earlier when there was a debate in the Commons on Lord Newhaven's motion to publish the articles, so the public might have a chance to digest them. William Pitt, chancellor of the exchequer and the effective leader in the lower chamber, argued against publishing. There was a set-to between Pitt and Fox and Newhaven was urged to withdraw his motion, which he refused to do. Wilkes then stood up and caused Pitt some embarrassment by pointing out that the Lords had already ordered the articles to be published.[51] Clearly, the ministers in the upper chamber had failed to let Pitt know what they intended to do. In the 17 February division, the ministry prevailed in the Lords but only by 13 votes. It was defeated in the Commons by 205 votes to 224, precipitating the inevitable fall of Shelburne's unlucky government.[52] Shelburne remained in post while the details of the new administration were cobbled together and at the beginning of April the new government took possession. Headed, nominally, by the duke of Portland, it was commonly known as the Fox-North coalition, and it came to be viewed as one of the most cynical alliances in British parliamentary history.

An End to Opposition

Although the coalition's agenda was one Wilkes might have been expected to endorse, he was no friend of Fox and pretty determinedly opposed to North. Consequently, he chose to oppose the government. By doing so, he merely confirmed what some satirists believed, that politics had been turned on its head. 'Wonders, Wonders, Wonders & Wonders', a satire produced in 1783, showed a number of prominent politicians, all of them formerly avowed enemies, greeting one another in friendship. In the foreground Shelburne, Denbigh and Fox are grouped together. Off to one side, there is a personification of Britannia shaking hands with America. On the far right Wilkes and the king clasp hands, Wilkes insisting: 'Your M[ajest]y has been long deceived/And at your Subjects was much griev'd.' To this the king responds: 'Enough! my Fault I own, my Subject Loyal,/And you much love, 'pon my Word Royal.'[53] Similar prints the following year hailed this new unlikely coalition of Wilkes and the king, one of them a supposed plan for a celebratory medal featuring the king and Lord Thurlow with Wilkes crammed in between them.[54]

From the Gordon Riots to Respectability

One of the central policies pursued by the coalition was reforming administration of the East India Company. It was this measure that brought Wilkes to his feet in the Commons once more on 8 December 1783, to give one of his most spirited interventions. Three days before, he had been present at a dinner at Fishmongers' Hall in company with the Southwark MP, Sir Richard Hotham, who was a supporter of the bill.[55] Hotham had written *A Candid State of Affairs Relative to East India Shipping* some years before, so Wilkes might well have been interested to discuss the measure with him.[56] He was an early participant in the debate, expressing several objections to the bill, not least the 'indecent haste' with which it was being rushed through Parliament. His second, substantive point, could have come from Pitt the Younger himself. It was a detailed analysis of the state of the East India Company's finances, down to the numbers of ships expected to bring goods to port. Rather than in dire financial straits, as the coalition suggested was the case, Wilkes contested that it was in fact in a much rosier condition. It was only the 'harpy claws' of the coalition that was eager to grasp the company's wealth. Wilkes saw the bill as an effective disfranchisement, offering him an obvious opportunity to draw parallels with his own case in Middlesex. He painted the coalition as an unscrupulous administration only too willing to infringe the country's liberties:

> Not a corporation in the kingdom, not a charter, not the great Charter of our liberties, not a deed, not a contract, not a document, not a security, no species of property, can be safe against bold, violent unprincipled men acting thus in the plenitude and wantonness of power.[57]

While insisting, disingenuously, that he had no particular dislike of either of the coalition's leaders, Wilkes spelled out the reasons for his aversion to the coalition:

> I dread the monstrous, unnatural union of such incongruous, discordant particles, because they could only be brought to coalesce for the division of the public spoils, and the sharing of all power among themselves, to the destruction of the public liberty, and the independency of this House.[58]

This was another cry against faction, of the sort Wilkes had made before in the *North Briton*.

Fox's India bill proved to be the catalyst for the coalition's fall from power. Although the bill passed the Commons, the king made it clear that he expected the Lords to reject it. George delegated to Earl Temple (nephew of Wilkes's old patron) the task of informing members of the Upper House that anyone voting for the India bill should be considered 'his enemies'. On the 17th the Lords dismissed the bill at second reading and the following day the king demanded that Fox and North hand over their seals of office.[59] He entrusted the new administration to William Pitt the Younger, Chatham's twenty-four-year-old son. The Foxites mocked the decision. They were confident that Pitt was too green and that as he lacked a majority in the Commons, he would be unable to govern. It would be a 'mince pie administration' that would not last the Christmas season. Wilkes chose to back Pitt.

Wilkes's daily routine at this point betrayed little anxiety at the events going on around him and on 10 December he was present at a meeting of the Anacreontic Society (named after the Greek poet, Anacreon, who was famed for composing verses celebrating earthly pleasures).[60] This was apparently the only time he attended. Possibly he did not enjoy the long evening rounded off by renditions of catches and bawdy songs.[61] For all his libertine past, Wilkes now preferred a quiet dinner over a busy glee club. In the meantime, the ministry's fate still hung in the balance. The day before the Lords' crucial vote, he dined in rooms over the House of Commons. He then marked the beginning of Pitt's government with a dinner at Goldsmiths' Hall.[62]

Unusually, Wilkes did not undertake his usual Christmas jaunt to Bath. He may have been unwilling to vacate London while the new administration bedded in. It was an event at the end of February 1784, though, that really identified him as one of Pitt's key new supporters. On 28 February Wilkes took a leading role at an event held at Grocers' Hall when Pitt was honoured with the freedom of the City. In one sense, Wilkes's involvement was simply following form, as it fell to him as City Chamberlain to administer the oath. For many, though, Wilkes's role was much more than ceremonial. To them, it represented his final act of apostasy as the old radical finally embraced the government of the day. It was marked in several print satires. One, 'Plum Pudding BILLY in all his Glory' showed a gaunt and haggard version of Wilkes, staggering under the weight of a chamber pot, while a seated Pitt receives a plum pudding, garnished with a leek, from Sir Watkin Lewes.[63] Another, 'Master Billy's Procession to Grocers' Hall', has Pitt being drawn in a carriage procession through the streets of London. Capering ahead of the group is Wilkes, distributing coins to the crowd under a banner marked 45.[64]

Over the next few years, Wilkes continued to feature in satires showing him as one of Pitt's principal cheer-leaders. Age was by now catching up on him and he was portrayed as an increasingly decrepit figure: emaciated and balding. There were also more stylized versions of him, exaggerating his jaw, or melding his face into an ovaloid shape. Many clearly saw his shift from opposition radical to government supporter as a fundamental – and cynical – betrayal. Wilkes seems never to have sought a title, but at least two prints showed him queueing up for a peerage. In one, Pitt the Younger stands to one side, doling out coronets from a stash on a table next to him. Fourth back in the queue is Wilkes with a speech bubble declaring 'I'll thank you even for a barony.'[65] Yet, while many of the satires show him as a subservient courtier in Pitt's entourage, others point to him remaining doggedly on the fringes. In the 'National Assembly', he is depicted as an ape, sitting on the bar of the House of Lords, away from the main group around Pitt.[66] He is similarly marginalized in 'The Return to the Political Ark' showing parliamentarians queueing to enter Noah's ark.[67] Thus, there was frequently an acknowledgment that he remained at heart an independent, even if he was increasingly distanced from his former radical origins.

One factor that allowed Wilkes to keep a measure of distance from the administration was that the City chamberlaincy had finally given him the financial independence he had always craved. That was not to stop him accepting a substantial sum from the king's own fighting fund to help offset the expenses of the 1784 general election. However, even after doing so, and effectively returning to Parliament for his final session there as a government supporter, he made a point (as Thomas notes) of retaining his seat on the opposition benches. This determined refusal to toe the line completely was underscored by an assessment made in advance of the general election. Jack Robinson cautioned the ministry from relying on Wilkes *in toto*:

> Mr Wilkes's support of any government is very uncertain, because the safety of his situation depends on his watching as he calls it all administrations and having no particular connection with any, but taking the side of all popular questions.[68]

This, of course, not only referred to Wilkes's radicalism but also to his insistence that constituents ought to be able to convey instructions to their representatives. Robinson's view echoed an editorial in the *London Evening Post* from 1779, arguing in favour of Wilkes's election as City chamberlain:

> There is no man that had added more uniformity to principle than Mr Wilkes. He has been an active friend of the public for these sixteen years past, during which he has never, in any one action of his life, deserted for a moment the popular cause.[69]

One consequence of Wilkes's acceptance of ministerial assistance for his election expenses was that for the first time since 1769, he faced a contest in Middlesex. Shortly before the general election came on, his long-estranged wife, Mary, died. Her loss elicited only the slightest of entries in his diary.[70] The following year, there was the rather more significant loss for Wilkes of his mother. Both he and Polly were bequeathed items from Sarah Wilkes's art collection. The significance of these should not be discounted, but more importantly still for Wilkes, he also inherited property in Enfield, further underpinning his financial position. His mother requested that he would pass the profits on to his brother, Heaton, who had always struggled, but Wilkes clearly took an interest in cultivating the area.[71] It is notable that in the 1784 election, forty-five (that magic number) Enfield voters polled for Wilkes out of a possible eighty-one.[72] Wilkes was fortunate to inherit the Enfield estate when he did, as a few years later he was to be mightily disappointed when Thomas Wilson's death did not translate into the kind of cash bonus he had been reckoning on for himself and Polly.[73]

The same day that his wife died, there was a meeting of Middlesex freeholders at the Mermaid in Hackney to settle the candidates for the ensuing election. There were three: Wilkes, his new partner, William Mainwaring, and the other sitting member, George Byng, with whom Wilkes had divided over the Fox-North coalition. Each appeared on the balcony, while the freeholders crammed onto the bowling green beneath. Wilkes and Mainwaring were received enthusiastically. According to one paper, Byng was greeted 'with great coolness', encouraging the other two that they should be likely to prevail. Other accounts suggested that each received decent shows of hands and an effort to declare Wilkes and Mainwaring the winners was rejected by Byng's partisans, who insisted on a poll. Byng then spoiled his chances by refusing to sign up to the freeholders' programme of reform.[74]

On 22 April, Wilkes found himself once again on the hustings at Brentford Butts. The day before he had been at Wood's Hotel in Covent Garden with members of the Westminster Committee, and two of the candidates, Lord Hood and Sir Cecil Wray, whom he voted for as a Westminster constituent.[75] The Westminster election proved one of the most notorious of the period. His own return for Middlesex was less so, but by no means assured. His opponent's lieutenants alleged that he had been a poor attender in the Commons in the previous Parliament, only tending to turn out for the big set-piece events.[76] Just how much had changed from the glory days of Wilkes and Liberty was indicated by the fact that he struggled to drum up the same degree of support from wards where previously he had been completely secure. That said, he retained his encyclopaedic head for details, explaining to Polly how one voter, John Decker, had proved crucial to his success. Byng's people had queried Decker's right to vote, only for the sheriffs to find in Wilkes's favour. That, Wilkes informed Polly, 'would have determined many others'.[77] Curiously, there seems no evidence of a John Decker featuring in the poll book. In the event, Mainwaring came first and Wilkes nudged past Byng by sixty-six votes. Wilkes was back in the House, but more than ever detached from his original base. It was to be a very different final stint in Parliament as he settled in to supporting Pitt and the king against more radical voices.

Just how far Wilkes had come from his days as a rabble-rousing instigator of opposition is made clear in his letter to Polly on 17 May, in which he was able to report with satisfaction how he had 'carried Mr Mainwaring to the Cockpit at Whitehall, as one of the Minister's friends'. There they heard the king's speech read out in preparation for the session ahead. It might be said that Wilkes had come full circle and that rather than a final betrayal, it was actually a kind of homecoming. He had entered Parliament and combatted the ministry of the day in the *North Briton* on behalf of Pitt the Elder. Now he was to enjoy his final period in Parliament as a supporter of Pitt the Younger. He certainly demonstrated considerable pleasure watching the young prime minister growing into his role. In one letter to Polly, he observed: 'Mr Pitt is greatly improved as an orator. He has more smoothness and grace, more Attic laugh and easy irony, without the sharpness and gall of the last session.'[78] As Pitt's administration grew more assured during the summer of 1784, Wilkes continued to resist efforts to dislodge him from supporting the government. In July, he informed Polly he had been busy in Parliament over the Navy and Victualling bills, refusing attempts to win him back to the opposition. Wilkes had a personal interest in the measure, as he had invested in Navy stock. What was being proposed was 'not so advantageous as we flattered ourselves with obtaining' but he still thought it a good return both for himself and the City.[79]

One should also remember that Pitt came to government as someone with a history of promoting reform. Many of his close friends and relatives were active in reform movements, in particular that associated with the reverend Christopher Wyvill. Pitt had raised the issue in the Commons in May 1782 and again a year later. Soon after his victory in the 1784 election more concrete plans were being discussed with Wyvill and he would ultimately propose a reform measure to Parliament in April 1785.[80] All of this helps explain Wilkes's choice, though it is difficult to avoid the conclusion that the experience of Gordon and opposition to Fox-North had left him few other options other than to support Pitt, or find himself in an increasingly lonely place on the backbenches.

That Wilkes was willing to stand up for Pitt in a social setting, too, was apparent from an incident over the summer of 1784. In June, he attended a dinner with a group including Captain Morris, who offered a rendition of his latest hit, *The Baby and the Nurse*, a satire on the king and Pitt. In it, Pitt, 'a troublesome Brat', is spoiled to keep him quiet, while showing early ambitions to be an MP, watching with delight a Parliament man 'toss'd in air' during his chairing. Wilkes was asked whether this was not indeed 'the wittiest song in the world'. Always ready with a rejoinder, Wilkes concurred, bar one. Morris' attack on Fox-North, *The Coalition*, he insisted, was better and forced him to perform that, too. After, he noted with satisfaction, 'The tables were turned, and the Coalition laughed at all evening.'[81] There was a less successful event a month later, when Wilkes hosted a small group at Prince's Court, among them Peter Labilliere, an Irish-born former army officer. Quite why Wilkes spent so much time in his company is a bit of a mystery, as they seem not to have agreed on much. On this occasion, Labilliere, 'more mad and slovenly than ever', turned on Wilkes for agreeing to support Pitt. According to his correspondence with Polly, Wilkes refused to offer a response.[82]

Given all of this, it is striking that it was not until January 1785 that Wyvill, founder of the Yorkshire Association, finally made an appearance in Wilkes's diaries. The timing was surely no coincidence, as the same month Pitt contacted Wyvill assuring him of his commitment to reform. It was, however, to be the only occasion Wyvill was to grace Prince's Court with his presence, so perhaps it was not much of a success.[83] A few months later, Pitt offered his reform bill to the Commons, which Wilkes undoubtedly supported, though he seems not to have bothered to speak. There were a number of points that resembled Wilkes's own previous reform proposal. The county franchise was to be expanded, by admitting copyholders with property worth an annual rental of forty shillings. Thirty-six rotten boroughs were to be abolished and new seats established in more deserving places. Bribery and corruption were to be tackled. Without the king's support, though, the bill was doomed and Pitt never bothered the chamber with such a full set of proposals for reform of the electoral system again.[84]

A month after the failure of the reform bill, there was to be another first for Wilkes when he was invited to Bowood, seat of the marquess of Lansdowne (as Shelburne had become).[85] The invitation arrived while he was enjoying one of his regular vacations at Bath. He had found lodgings at Mr Hartford's, where he embellished his newly decorated apartments with some of his own prints, and attended a rout hosted by Lady Conyngham, showing off his new embroidered French waistcoat (a gift from Polly).[86] The summons to Bowood seems to have been inspired by Lansdowne's old supporter (and sometime fierce critic of Wilkes) Colonel Isaac Barré, but Wilkes was evidently delighted by the 'flattering reception' he received there. He thought 'the chateau' (as he termed it) 'truly magnificent' but the layout 'extremely inconvenient'.[87] He was back there during the winter and as that visit also featured his old friend Lord

Abingdon, it was presumably rather more convivial than the awkward meeting with Wyvill.[88]

Wilkes appears to have spent the middle years of the 1780s enjoying time with an expanding group of acquaintance. His focus on London remained keen, but as he became steadily distanced from his old life, he seems to have sought out company from the higher gradations of society. He had already established good relations with members of the nobility like Abingdon and successful military figures like Lord Rodney. The Enfield property may explain references to time spent with a Mr Dance, likely (Sir) Nathaniel Dance, an East India Company officer, who had settled there. He also increasingly found himself associating with foreign diplomats like Count Nesselrode and the bibliophile Count Reviczky. He seems to have particularly delighted in spending time with collectors like Charles Townley, and artists like Sir Joshua Reynolds.[89]

As he had before when first taking up his role as a City magistrate, he took his duties as chamberlain seriously. His continued focus on the City is reflected in the long round of dinners at Livery halls and with various other London societies. The Society he seems most to have relished attending, though, was the Beefsteaks and on 25 February 1786 he noted attending their fiftieth anniversary dinner. Meetings with the Middlesex freeholders were also regular occurrences, one taking place at the Folly House in Blackwall, a place renowned for its whitebait.[90] Later that month, he officiated as one of the stewards for a meeting of the governors of St Thomas's Hospital and in August he dined with the East India Company directors.[91] Wilkes clearly relished his combined roles of charitable citizen and a man keen to keep his finger on the pulse of trade and imperial concerns.

Domestically, he had also at last acquired a set-up that seemed to suit him very well. The residence in Prince's Court was very much his and Polly's abode. While she was away, he kept her up-to-date about the smaller domestic details. In the summer of 1784, there had been a new servant taken on, a 'new Thomas', who was 'very attentive' but 'exceedingly awkward'.[92] Two and a half miles west, there was the cosy little residence he had established for Maria Arnold and their daughter, Harriet. Wilkes alternated between these two addresses, keeping the two households separate but connected in a way that had never been the case with his other long-term mistresses. It is not too much to say that after the violent exertions of combatting Lord George Gordon, securing re-election in 1780 and again in 1784, Wilkes seems at last to have arrived at a safe harbour. The final decade of his life would see him reinvent himself once again. No longer the radical demagogue, he would find new expression as a patriot in retirement, emulating both classical precedent and his old acquaintance Voltaire at Ferney. Now in his sixties, Wilkes would at last have time to cultivate his garden.

12

A Patriot in Retirement

(1787–1797)

Il faut cultiver notre jardin.

On 18 May 1787, Wilkes's diaries noted that he had dined that day in St James's Place with Mr and Mrs Hastings and a few others.[1] This was Warren Hastings, the disgraced governor general of Bengal, who had been impeached by the Commons just over a week before, accused of a series of crimes while in office in India. His trial before the Lords, from February 1788 until his eventual acquittal seven years later, would dominate much political discourse. Wilkes seems first to have come across him in 1785 and he was to prove a firm supporter.[2] Oddly enough, given the number of run-ins Wilkes had had with him, another of Hastings' old friends was Lord Mansfield: yet another example of Wilkes's circle overlapping with people with whom he had locked horns.[3] On 9 May, the day before the Commons resolved to submit their impeachment articles, Wilkes had been one of those to speak for Hastings. It was one of his last orations in the chamber and found him once more on form, drawing parallels between Hastings' case and that of the classical governor of Sicily, Verres, who had already been mentioned by others speaking in the debate.[4]

He noted dining that day in the committee room over the House of Commons in company with three other MPs: John Courtenay, Philip Francis and Lord Duncannon.[5] The last was father of Lady Caroline Ponsonby, later to marry Prime Minister Viscount Melbourne, but best known for her scandalous affair with Lord Byron. Wilkes's choice of companions is interesting. All three were opposed to Hastings and, in the course of the debate, Courtenay delivered a notorious harangue, insulting the Westminster MP Lord Hood and Wilkes, as well as casting aspersions on the king. He was later to retract the words he used against

A Patriot in Retirement

Hood but an apology from him for his other utterances proved more difficult to extract.[6]

What does it say about Wilkes that he chose to dine in such company? This was no accident of tables. Courtenay and Wilkes may have been political opponents, but they were also mutual friends of Boswell.[7] Indeed, Courtenay's assault on Wilkes in the debate may well have been a case of joshing rather than anything more hostile. That said, Courtenay did not appear in the diaries again for another seven years, so perhaps on this occasion he overstepped the mark.[8] Nevertheless, like so much else with Wilkes, there is a sense of ambiguity around his behaviour here. He remained a solid supporter of Hastings throughout the trial, but that did not mean he had to cut everyone who disagreed with him on the issue. The private and public man could remain distinct.

Wilkes's activities around the Hastings trial are an important reminder that even in his last few years in Parliament, he was perhaps not quite as absent as his detractors liked to suggest. The month before the Hastings business came on, he was noted in the press taking a very close interest in a divorce bill concerning William Fawkener and his estranged wife Georgiana Anne Poyntz, who had eloped with one of Fox's inner circle, Hon. John Townshend (a younger son of Marquess Townshend). Wilkes was said to have 'looked remarkably keen through the whole examination'.[9] That he was willing to turn out for even less charged business is suggested by letters to Polly in February 1789. One concerned the disputed Colchester by-election. Wilkes explained that the matter would take up all of the Commons' attention until after six in the evening, so he would not be able to send her any more parliamentary news until the end of the week.[10] The same month, he was 'much taken up' with a dispute involving Sir William Gibbons who wished to enclose land in Stanwell. Wilkes hoped that he would be able to bring together 'the discordant parties' and concluded, with more than a touch of raillery, that he was 'now a great parliamentarian'.[11] It was all a long way from the heady days of Wilkes and Liberty.

Another matter to take up Wilkes's attention in his final years in the House was the crisis in the winter of 1788 precipitated by the king's descent into what was then thought of as madness. The contrast between Wilkes of the *North Briton* and this apparently new, concerned courtier could not be starker. Print satires that had once shown him as the scourge of the king and his entourage, now showed Wilkes clawing for favours. One, 'The New Peerage or Fountain of Honor', depicted the king on a pedestal, blowing bubbles turning into coronets. Gathered around him are a host of court hangers-on eager to be ennobled, among them Wilkes, hands clasped in prayer and the word 'Turncoat' embroidered on his collar.[12]

Wilkes's new-found affection for a man he had once so derided was an about-face his contemporaries struggled to comprehend. That said, some of the information he enjoyed passing on to Polly had more of the gossip magazine about it than serious constitutional insight. This included the intelligence that the royal fishmonger had sent two 'chicken turbot' to Windsor to tempt the king's appetite, which were 'approved and relished'.[13] There was more serious stuff as well. Wilkes was by now a steady adherent of Pitt the Younger, so was happy to turn out to show his support when necessary. Pitt's 20 November address to the Commons was approved by Wilkes as having been delivered 'with much dignity and grace'. Meanwhile, Wilkes kept a close eye on proceedings, advising Polly of the intense 'political caballing' and of the odds being stated by some in favour of Fox carrying his point about the projected regency. Wilkes remained confident that Pitt would prevail.[14]

Wilkes's letters to his daughter help to confirm that his final few years in Parliament lacked the fire of his earlier career, but are suggestive, nonetheless, of a man who was still deeply committed to his life as a politician. It is all too easy to assume that Wilkes's final decade was a period of relatively little interest. He had achieved financial security and made his peace with the king. He had scant patience with the direction taken by the new generation of radical politicians, and he would be disgusted by the violent turn that was taken by the French Revolution. This is the more ironic, given his earlier fulminations against tyrannous monarchs; his avowed dislike of aristocracy; and the fact that he may have been a correspondent of revolutionaries like Marat.[15]

As with so much else about Wilkes, though, even in the way that he stepped back from political engagement, there was symbolism. While it is true to say that there was always a tension between the private and public man, he was well aware that he was simply too notorious to step quietly into the shadows. Retirement for him was thus arguably just as much a conscious statement as his previous political campaigns. Like the best Roman senator of classical times, retreating to his estates and to the contemplation of art and literature did not need to mean giving up. On the one hand, it was something due to him after his labours. On the other, it was the fulfilment of an Arcadian idyll that said as much about liberty as any other of his causes. Besides, even now that he was on good terms at Court, he had still not made his peace with the Stuarts. On 31 January 1788, one newspaper reported that the Commons had that year chosen not to attend St Margaret's for the annual sermon commemorating the execution of Charles I the day before. It was observed, however, that Wilkes, 'who never liked the measure, observed the day at home, as usual'.[16]

Sandown Cottage

In 1788, Wilkes's annual routine changed. In May he set out for a flying visit to Bath, as he had done on so many occasions before, but this would be the last time he would make the journey westwards. Later that month, he quit London again, this time heading to Southampton where he boarded a vessel commanded by Captain Harris and thence to the Isle of Wight. Thirty years or more after first setting eyes on the island, Wilkes had hit on it as his preferred retreat. On the 30th, he looked over 'Sandam Cottage', which he noted in his habitually precise manner lay 8½ miles from Newport. He dined there with the owner, Colonel James Barker, both that day and the next, before starting on his journey back.[17] The purpose of this brief foray was to finalize arrangements for him renting what he was to refer to as his 'villakin'. The term was not his own. Hogarth also referred to his 'villakin' at Chiswick.[18]

Wilkes's papers contain a cutting advertising 'A snug Retreat' in the Isle of Wight, previously occupied by 'a Person of Fashion'.[19] It was, presumably, this advertisement that had led Wilkes to his latest acquisition. The dates certainly work. Negotiations for securing the lease on the desirable little seaside cottage and garden were hammered out while Wilkes was in Bath just a few days after the notice was posted.[20] Sandown was to become of huge importance to him, a place where he could play out his Arcadian fantasy, complete his writing projects and, above all, spend time away from the hurly-burly of London life. As a 19th-century guide to the Isle of Wight put it, it was here that Wilkes 'spent the evening of his days'.[21] When in residence, he eschewed his fashionable city garb and posed as a bumpkin. One witness described him as 'perfectly Arcadian; instead of a crook, he walked about his grounds with a hoe, raking up weeds and destroying vipers.'[22] For the next nine years he would repeat the journey, often several times a year, finding great solace in his little slice of perfect English countryside.

By investing in this idealized portion of rural England, Wilkes was following a fashionable trend. Cottages were very much in vogue as practical establishments that required a small household to run them and offered to the busy politician, merchant or businessman the opportunity for fresh air and time out from their hectic routines. The Isle of Wight was particularly favoured, so while Wilkes may have been seeking solitude there, he was surrounded by plenty of others who had all determined to do the same.[23]

Wilkes's frequent sorties back and forth from Westminster and Kensington to the Isle of Wight were not only about him living out a pastoral ideal. Life had dealt him a fair number of knocks and it seems clear that now in his early sixties his health was fairly delicate. This is not that surprising. He had endured a stay in the Tower of London, never an especially salubrious place; almost two years confined to King's Bench; and he had been shot. Life on his island retreat offered him peace and good living while he battled his regular agues. He had the opportunity of gentle exercise: long walks and undemanding riding. In mid-September 1788 he informed Polly cheerfully that he had enjoyed making his way from Ryde to the cottage astride a Welsh pony 'and found myself benefited by the exercise'.[24] This was a far cry from the intrepid horseman cautioned by Baxter all those years ago. Not long after, though, he complained of being 'so oppressed with one of my crying colds, that I can scarcely see to thank you for your letter.'[25] He remained, however, charmed with his new acquisition, and indulged in some rather saccharine verses in imitation of the Welsh poet John Dyer's *Grongar Hill*:

> Ever charming, ever new,
> The landscape never tires the view,
> The verdant meads, the river's flow,
> The woody vallies warm and low,
> The windy summit, wild and high,
> Roughly rushing on the sky...[26]

Wilkes introduced Polly to the island in August, but it seems not to have been until the winter that he took Maria Arnold over with him.[27] Sandown may have been intended as a retreat from Wilkes's duties in the City, but here, as in London, he maintained a separation of his households. Polly was indulgent towards her father's new family, but the two rarely overlapped.

One of Wilkes's London acquaintances with whom he did enjoy sharing Sandown was the French writer and numismatist, Jean-Jacques Barthélemy. Barthélemy subsequently became one of Wilkes's regular circle, both in Prince's Court and at events attended by Mademoiselle D'Eon (as the former Chevalier was now noted by Wilkes) and the likes of the artists Richard and Maria Cosway, and Sir Joshua Reynolds. Having introduced Barthélemy to Sandown, Wilkes told Polly he was 'more and more charmed with my fellow traveller' and was truly sorry by the thought of his imminent departure.[28] Barthélemy spoke to Wilkes's interests as a scholar and book collector and no doubt had some influence on his growing library at Sandown.

A Patriot in Retirement

As was always the case with Wilkes, there was another side to this apparent pastoral idyll. He made the acquaintance of the island's principal landowner, Sir Richard Worsley, bt., who had been elected MP for Newport (Isle of Wight) the same year that Wilkes had re-entered Parliament for Middlesex. Like Wilkes, Worsley was a libertine scholar. By a strange coincidence, he also shared with Wilkes frustrated ambitions for the embassy at Constantinople.[29] Worsley had become notorious for his behaviour towards his wife, Seymour Fleming, their marriage ending in divorce following Lady Worsley's much publicized affair with another of the island's landowners, George Bissett. Wilkes had a habit of gravitating towards people like Worsley. It was also entirely characteristic that Wilkes was able to strike up friendships with both Worsley and Bissett, who also resided on the island, even though the two carefully avoided one another.[30]

When Wilkes took the cottage at Sandown, Worsley was only recently returned from an extended grand tour, having quit England in April 1783. Wilkes had, though, visited Worsley's seat, Appuldurcombe, on one of his previous visits to the island.[31] Worsley's long absence meant that he had not been re-elected in 1784 but clearly identified himself with Pitt as in December 1788, amid rumours that Pitt might be displaced, he confided to Wilkes that were that to happen, 'we shall both lose a friend.'[32] The two, thereafter, were often to be found in each other's company and Wilkes's diaries also log his steady socializing with other locals within his milieu.[33]

Wilkes may have been following a trend by settling on an island cottage, but in other respects what he set about doing at Sandown was more personal. He had always enjoyed gardening. The grounds of Prebendal House in Aylesbury had been a particular delight for him. Now at last he was able to indulge once more in horticultural pursuits. His papers contain numerous press cuttings for nurseries and imaginative new inventions for greenhouses and cloches. In his typically meticulous fashion, snippets from the press were pasted into his papers with advertisements, such as one for 'curious cherry trees' and another for 'curious flowers' sourced from the marquess of Buckingham's gardener, William Woodward.[34] His efforts were soon rewarded and on 30 April 1790 he was able to write to his daughter describing the current state of the floral display: 'We have violets, primroses, and cowslips in great abundance; and our peach, apple, and apricot trees are in full bloom, and perfume the air.'[35] Just over a year later he had the satisfaction of observing 'The primroses and cowslips, to which I paid so much attention last year, have rewarded me by their superior beauty and fragrance in the present.'[36] Five years after first taking on the house and garden, Wilkes was unable to hide his pride in his achievement: 'This little spot is in high beauty, and the gardener has exerted himself to have every thing in very great order. The progress of vegetation since the last year is truly astonishing, and we are in a wilderness of sweets.'[37]

The garden was not restricted to flowers. Wilkes ordered in seeds so that he could add Dutch kale and Brussels sprouts to the kitchen garden and in summer 1792 he recorded consuming at dinner 'very fine asparagus and brocoli [sic] from our own kitchen garden'.[38]

As well as flowers, fruit and vegetables, Wilkes developed an extensive menagerie including Chinese pigs and a variety of exotic fowl.[39] He also delighted in more mundane birdwatching. In August 1790 he related to his daughter how '30 blackbirds were yesterday morning on the large cherry-tree near the bed-rooms in the garden. I hope they will hail your arrival in their sweetest notes.' The following year he noted that the blackbirds had decimated his cherries, but seemed unbothered.[40] The blackbirds may have been welcome to devastate his crop, but Wilkes was unsentimental about his rare breed pigs. Proud to note that they 'go on very prosperously' he assured Polly he would 'soon make a sacrifice of some of them to you, for they seem very delicate.'[41]

The garden also offered Wilkes space to proclaim his patriot credentials. In a sense, what he created there was a kind of miniature Stowe, a place full of symbolism and it was one that was visited frequently.[42] Rather than stone temples of concord and busts of British worthies, though, Wilkes limited himself to three more modest edifices. He constructed two pavilions, made of a revolutionary new type of canvas. One he dubbed his Tuscan room and filled it with a collection of prints and vases from his travels. In May 1790, he reported to his daughter that he had 'now disposed of all my Tuscan vases, with several prints from Sir Richard Worsley' in the space, as a result of which he had 'now completed all I wish for Sandham Cottage, and shall not have any farther idea for the place, but preserving a rural neatness.' A subsequent letter of August 1791 offers a glimpse of what some of these were. In it he asked Polly to have packed up 'directly and carefully' prints of 'the Queen and Princess Royal'; 'the Old Man and Child in his Arms'; 'Laocoon'; 'Seven ovals of Hampden'; and 'King William'. These subjects embraced several Wilkite themes: the Revolution, classical antiquity, and his latter-day adherence to the royal family.[43] The other pavilion was dubbed the temple of filial piety – an acknowledgment of his affection for and debt to his daughter.

The third of the features Wilkes made room for was a monument constructed, according to some sources, in imitation of the tomb of Petrarch. In this case it was a Doric wooden column surmounted by an alabaster urn, which he had been given years before by Winckelmann. This rather bizarre structure was dedicated to his old friend and former collaborator, Charles Churchill. Wilkes had never forgotten him and now, at last, he was able to construct a memorial to his fallen comrade. The original concept seems to have been for a memorial comprising 'an ice house below, and a library above', for which he received a quotation of £349 19s. 6d.[44] In true Wilkite fashion, what was eventually constructed was much more than a mere monument. It also doubled up as a wine store. Wilkes had earned a reputation for being (unpatriotically) fond of French wines during his tenure as Lord Mayor, but the range of his tastes is indicated in a note attached to the diary for May 1788. Here, he recorded sending to Sandown Castle from the Bugle in Newport: 'Port 12 bottles, Madeira 6, Sherry 12, Brandy 3, Rum 6, Strong beer 12, Table beer 12, Porter 12'; in all 75 bottles. The capacity of the garden monument is hinted at by a subsequent note appended to the diary for 1791 which recorded that he had left there 15 bottles of Madeira, 12 of Cyprus, six bottles of port, eight of sherry, four of claret, 22 bottles of Champagne, three of Calcavello, one of fleur d'Orange, three more Clarets from Bath, two more Madeiras from Bath, five bottles of cider, 36 of porter, 24 of Burton ale, six of rum and two bottles of brandy – in all 149 bottles.[45] Churchill would definitely have appreciated the joke.

Wilkes's existence on the Isle of Wight may have been in part Arcadian, in part patriarchal, but it was also scholarly. He had long sought for a place where he could concentrate on his numerous writing projects. Much of his private time was given over to producing translations and compositions often derived from classical authors. To assist him in these endeavours, he established a sizeable library in his cottage. One of Wilkes's greatest regrets back in 1764 had been the loss of his first collection. Since his return he had laboured to rebuild it and both Prince's Court and Sandown boasted eclectic collections that reflected Wilkes's broad and sometimes surprising tastes.[46] These included volumes in Greek, Latin, French and English and a variety of dictionaries. Among the English volumes were Blackstone's Commentaries. Wilkes's close association with a number of prominent naval men was reflected in his possession of Kippis's *Life of Captain Cook* and Campbell's *Lives of the British Admirals*, while his well-known interest in travel was covered by Mrs Piozzi's *Travels in France, Italy, and Germany*. A desire to acquire some background on his new surroundings (as well as flatter an eminent neighbour) was suggested by the inclusion of a copy of his neighbour Sir Richard Worsley's *History of the Isle of Wight*, published the year before Worsley's divorce.[47]

There were also a number of practical volumes, clearly geared towards Wilkes's rural seclusion. These included several books of ornithology, among them William Thompson's *New and Complete Bird Fancier*, as well as the no doubt invaluable 1777 octavo edition of the *Complete Vermin-Killer*. In July 1791 he asked his daughter to send him 'in the next parcel, Dr Trusler's Garden Companion, price one shilling. Byfield and Hawksworth can get it.'[48] The year before, reasonably enough given his new Panglossian existence, he had informed his daughter 'I have been of late deeply read in Voltaire.'[49] Wilkes's eagerness to share his passion with his children is also indicated by the addition to the collection of volumes intended for the children's market, such as the 1786 duodecimo publication of *The Natural History of Birds from Facts*.[50]

With his time divided between Sandown and his duties as City Chamberlain, Wilkes increasingly became a symbol and less an active participant in the causes he continued to support. This much is clear from a letter written in early May 1790 to his daughter from his villakin, in which he complained, 'Every part of this little island is frantic about electioneering, except Appledurcombe Park and Sandham Cottage, where we talk of better things.'[51]

The lack of activity at Appuldurcombe is ironic given that Worsley was once more seeking re-election, though as the effective owner of one seat at Newtown, he was in no danger of failing at the poll. For Wilkes, though, the whole purpose of his Isle of Wight villa was as a haven from his obligations in the City and his activities as a Member of Parliament. Indeed, so removed had he become from his role as MP for Middlesex by the dissolution of 1790, that when he made the sea-crossing back to the mainland a month later to be in London in time for the meeting at the Mermaid at Hackney, he faced a significant challenge. This had come on sooner than he had originally predicted. In December 1788, he had been heartened by Pitt carrying a key motion with a majority of sixty-four and had concluded Parliament would 'die a natural death in May 1791'.[52] It would likely have made no difference to his chances of re-election as his constituents had become increasingly frustrated with their absentee Member. Their attitude was a far cry from the winter of 1781 when they had agreed a vote of thanks for Wilkes and his partner MP 'for their diligent attendance in Parliament'. Wilkes had a copy with the relevant section underlined pasted into one of his volumes of newspaper cuttings.[53] Now, confronted with the likelihood of defeat, he withdrew from the contest and thus from the House of Commons. When Parliament opened that autumn, for the first time since 1774 there was no John Wilkes on the benches.

Wilkes may not have regretted overmuch his final retirement from frontline politics and increasing concentration on his island retreat, but not everyone saw it that way. In January 1791 a letter to the *Public Advertiser* insisted: 'As a Middlesex man, I regret we have him [Wilkes] not in this Parliament; he shewed there could be no foundation for the Impeachment [of Warren Hastings], and that the way to prevent injustice and consequent disgrace, would be to get rid of the whole by putting it off for six months.'[54]

A Patriot in Retirement

Wilkes's change of tack does not necessarily imply a loss of interest, but his role at Sandown points to how he viewed this latest manifestation of his campaign for personal liberty. Gone perhaps was Number forty-five and his insolent teasing of the ministry of the day. In its place was a no less significant demonstration of patriotic retirement and benevolence.

Grosvenor Square

Around the same time that he was negotiating for the lease of Sandown, Wilkes had also begun looking around for a new London residence. Prince's Court had served him well since his release from prison but he was keen now to establish himself in more fashionable quarters. This was in keeping with his increasingly respectable image and the roll-call of aristocrats with whom he increasingly spent his time. That said, it is notable that none of his near neighbours in Grosvenor Square, where he was eventually to settle, appear in the diaries, so perhaps he was not quite able, at the end, to make that final transition from City Patriot to noble host.

It took Wilkes well over a year to source a house suitable for his needs. In January 1789 he expressed his frustration about delays in settling the matter, alluding to problems over the seller's title to one property. He resolved to 'cut the Gordian knot' and withdraw from the bargain.[55] At another point there was the prospect of a house in Downing Street, which he was alerted to by Heaton, but he concluded that 'no such thing exists.'[56] It is a tantalizing prospect, that at the end, Wilkes could have been the Prime Minister's near neighbour.

The house Wilkes hit on eventually, Number 35, Grosvenor Square, was not the finest property in the area. It was old, dating from 1728, and had 'low storeys and other drawbacks'. The most recent long-term occupier appears to have quitted the place in 1785, which also suggests that buyers were reluctant to take it on. Wilkes set about making improvements, the most obvious being a new set of windows for the parlour. They included large panes of engraved plate glass, designed by Polly. As ever, Wilkes proved unable to resist indulging his daughter. When they were shattered during rioting in the 1790s, he proved equally accommodating. Wilkes understood all too well that he had once incited such vandalism, so it was only to be understood that he might now become a victim to similar outrages.[57]

What the new house did offer him was the opportunity for more space to expand his library. It was not just his own renowned collection that needed housing. A report in the press around the time of the move, lauding Polly as 'the most accomplished woman in England', referred to her fine collection of French and Italian volumes. When the two collections were brought together, as it was assumed could not be far off, it would constitute 'the most select and curious library in the kingdom'.⁵⁸ Indeed, it is one of the great losses of the period that after Wilkes's death, his library was dispersed and as Polly was to die unmarried, hers, too, must have gone the same way. One of the most splendid private collections amassed by two middling-sort bibliophiles was lost.

At the opening of 1791, the year in which Wilkes was finally able to settle into his new surroundings in Grosvenor Square, the *Public Advertiser* published a selection of 'Extraordinary Characters, and Circumstances, of the Present Times'. Among them were Fox's coalition with North; Sheridan arguing for national economy and, in reference to Warren Hastings' impeachment, 'A Battle (of Hastings) lasting three years'. Also included on the list was the at one time unbelievable attendance of 'Mr Wilkes at Court'.⁵⁹ The same month, another paper reported that a recently published anonymous work, *A Sketch of the Reign of George the Third, from 1780, to the close of the year 1790*, was 'generally among the fashionable circles ascribed to the pen of Mr Wilkes'.⁶⁰

To call Wilkes's final years a retirement would therefore be to overlook what for him continued to be a particularly creative period. He remained an active figure in the City both as alderman and chamberlain, and it was this combination of offices that prompted a renewed challenge to his continuance as chamberlain in June 1791. Facing an unexpected and unwanted contest, Wilkes found himself once again forced to supplicate for votes. Among those approached was his old friend, Dilly, who was asked for his own support and to use his 'interest with his numerous friends of the livery'.⁶¹

The brief scare safely dealt with, Wilkes was able to resume his familiar routine, alternating between Grosvenor Square, Kensington Gore and Sandown. In June 1791 he made the acquaintance of another Wilkes, a Portsmouth ironmonger. Wilkes seems to have been tickled by the coincidence and members of the family, Richard, William David, and Anne, continued to feature in the diaries on occasion for the next few years. That the acquaintance was not just limited to his moments passing through on the way to Sandown is made clear by the fact that invitations were also extended to Sandown itself and to Kensington Gore. If they were not actually family, Wilkes seems to have adopted them into his circle.⁶²

The inclusion of the ironmonger Wilkeses into his social round is a reminder of the breadth of Wilkes's acquaintance by now. He remained on terms with numbers of rising and established politicians in both Houses of Parliament, whilst maintaining a more modest, separate life in Kensington Gore with Maria Arnold. It says much about these different faces of Wilkes that having married an heiress and carried on with exuberant mistresses like Corradini and Charpillon, he was to find contentment with a yeoman farmer's daughter in a solidly 'middle-class' address in Kensington. Three days in February 1794 sum up this split existence as well as any. On 4 February he attended a dinner in Parliament Street attended by Earl Gower and his wife, the countess of Sutherland, the rising star George Canning and Polly. Next day, he was in Great Russell Street with the bishop of Llandaff and on the 6th back in Kensington Gore with Maria Arnold and Harriet.[63] It is no wonder he kept his dining book diaries with such care and annotated his address books so assiduously. Wilkes had at least two and sometimes three lives to lead and was a master at keeping them as distinct as possible.

1797: the final year

On 31 October 1797, Wilkes made a final entry in his diary. It was spare but poignant. It recorded merely that he had dined that day with Polly in Grosvenor Square. There should be no doubting Wilkes's genuine fondness for Maria and Harriet Arnold, or his concern to do his best by John Smith. At one point there had been an idea for Smith to be commissioned into a Hessian cavalry regiment, but there were concerns he might be expected to fight in America. Following further education abroad, the lad was, instead, carted off to a post in India, thanks to Warren Hastings.[64] Wilkes had never got over Charles Churchill's death, and while he took pleasure in the company of the likes of Barthélemy, there was nothing like the rapport between them he had enjoyed with Churchill. Polly, however, was different. From the moment of her birth, she had been a constant in Wilkes's life and far and away the most important person in his packed and hazardous universe.[65]

The year represented a changing of the guard in more ways than one. In February, Britain had been invaded for the last time when a French force landed at Fishguard (Pembrokeshire), just days after the British had devastated a Spanish fleet at the battle of Cape St Vincent. On the continent, Napoleon Bonaparte enjoyed a number of key successes, including the capture of Venice in May. In November, pupils at Rugby staged a rebellion against their headmaster after they were ordered to compensate local tradesmen for their smashed windows.[66]

Several key players who had dominated society and politics left the stage. The first to go, in March, was the old Court gossip, wit, novelist and creator of the gothic fantasy retreat of Strawberry Hill, Horace Walpole, who late in life had succeeded to the earldom of Orford. In July, Edmund Burke, the philosopher of the Rockingham Whigs, followed him and in August Joseph Wright of Derby. The following month, Mary Wollstonecraft, the ground-breaking feminist author, also bowed out.

On 28 October, Wilkes celebrated his seventy-second birthday quietly at Grosvenor Square with Polly. A month later, he undertook what was to be his last significant duty as City Chamberlain. Earlier in the year, the up-and-coming admiral Horatio Nelson had lost his arm in an unsuccessful assault on Tenerife. Although the action did not achieve its aim, Nelson was lauded for his personal bravery and the corporation of London voted to honour him with freedom of the City. It fell to Wilkes to make the presentation to Nelson.[67] He uttered, apparently without irony: 'In your case there is a rare heroic modesty which cannot be sufficiently admired,' before wishing Nelson a long life praised by his country.[68] It was fitting that this was to be Wilkes's last ceremonial appearance. Both were larger than life, they were equally proficient as showmen and loved and disliked in equal measure. There is also the strange coincidence that some years before Wilkes had toured *HMS Victory*, aboard which Nelson was to die eight years later.[69]

Wilkes's health had always been more delicate than his rumbustious lifestyle implied and in mid-December, he was taken seriously ill. A wardmote in Farringdon Without had to be presided over by the Lord Mayor in Wilkes's absence.[70] By the 22nd, his doctors had given up all hope of his recovery.[71] He died during the afternoon of Boxing Day 1797, joining Walpole, Burke, Wright and Wollstonecraft as one of the notable fatalities of the year.[72] It is hard to think of anyone else in the period who Walpole might have enjoyed assessing more, but Wilkes outlasted him, robbing Walpole of what would doubtless have been a rich, if wholly partial, summation.

It is remarkable, given the fact that for so much of his career it was impossible to pick up a newspaper without spotting the name Wilkes in it, that notices in the press were surprisingly brief. All the more so when one considers just how much he had done to enable newspapermen to fill their pages. None could agree on how old he was, with estimates ranging from him being in his seventy-first year to his seventy-fifth.[73] His loss to the City, to which he had dedicated so much of his efforts, was mostly overtaken by the immediate scramble for his offices. Before the breath had left his body reports were abroad of four candidates vying for his chamberlaincy, soon increased to five.[74] Details of his will were printed soon after. An estate in Huntingdonshire worth about £1,200 a year was to go to Polly; £1,000 to Maria Arnold with the Kensington Gore house, and £2,000 to Harriet, along with Sandown. The residue, estimated at £60,000 and her choice from his library, was to go to Polly. There were no particular bequests to either of his brothers, Heaton, who survived until 1803, or Israel, who lived on until 1805. Nor was there any mention of his sister Mary Hayley (since remarried to Patrick Jeffrey), who was by then resident in Bath. It is surprising in some ways, as his family had always been important to Wilkes. Heaton in particular had been a loyal and long-suffering support for his more famous brother, rewarded with a marginal, easily missed walk-on part in one of the many print satires from 1763.[75] Mary did not need his money, but Heaton and Israel might well have been glad of a helping hand. What the will did do was emphasize that for all of his protestations to the contrary, Wilkes still regarded himself above all as a champion of liberty. He left clear instructions that a plaque should be erected noting his burial spot, with a simple inscription: 'John Wilkes: A Friend to Liberty'. It represented his final statement on how he wished to be remembered and what he still believed his essential legacy ought to be.[76]

As with so much else in Wilkes's life, things were not so straightforward. Wilkes believed he was parting the world a wealthy man, but his finances were in as much of a muddle as they had ever been, and it turned out that he died possessed of nothing like the sums reported. It fell to Joseph Paice to inform Polly and Harriet that their inheritance was so much less than they had expected.[77] Wilkes did not quite die destitute, as had once looked very likely, but he had certainly continued to live far beyond his means.

Wilkes may have wished to have 'Wilkes and Liberty' carved in stone, but given the numbers who had once marched the streets calling out his name, his funeral on Thursday 4 January 1798 proved to be a distinctly low-key affair. In his will he had made provision for six poor but honest local men to be given mourning suits and a guinea each to act as his pallbearers.[78] There was a modest cortège comprising the hearse, three mourning coaches and two more coaches carrying family members. This rather small procession made the short journey from his house in Grosvenor Square to the Grosvenor Chapel just around the corner, where his remains were to be buried.[79] It made a stark contrast with that of Burke just a few months earlier. Burke's pallbearers had been some of the most prominent men in the country.[80]

After it was all over, Polly retuned to Grosvenor Square, which was now hers. She was not to enjoy it for very long. On 11 March 1802 she was due to host a rout but, complaining of stomach cramps, retired to bed. In the middle of the night, she rang for a servant to call a doctor. The physician had barely got past the door when she died.[81] Before then, Polly had overseen auctioning off much of her father's collection and had almost certainly destroyed a significant portion of his papers. The engraved silver cup, one of the iconic items awarded to him by the City in his fight with Parliament over the printers' case, was bequeathed to her cousin Dinah Baker. The task fell to William Rough, who married Harriet after Wilkes's death, to make a first attempt at publishing a life, along with a selection of correspondence. He repeated the inaccurate date of birth, and also managed to get the name of Wilkes's father wrong. Wilkes would, no doubt, have approved.[82]

Epilogue

On 2 January 1798, the *Morning Chronicle* published a sketch of Wilkes's life. The author made clear that the newspaper's scope simply did not permit a full appreciation of Wilkes's career. In common with so many others, though, the writer concluded that the final twenty years had been markedly different from the first fifty of dissipation. This was not least because Wilkes increasingly found himself part of the establishment against which he had once rebelled. Polly was noted in the press as one of the ladies attending the queen's drawing rooms, and it was not unheard of for Wilkes himself to be seen at Court.[1]

Wilkes's progress was catalogued from the moment he exploded onto the stage in the early 1760s by the print satirists and it was not long before his distinctive face, a gift for any caricaturist, was widely known. How he was represented evolved over the years, and by the end of his life he was frequently shown in a much more stylized manner. Certain iconographical devices almost always featured: the strabismus and the cap of liberty. Both were adapted, though, as Wilkes's career developed from libertine hellraiser to radical friend of reform and ultimately Court hanger-on. One print from 1784 depicting the campaign for Middlesex as a horse race showed Wilkes out ahead, bearing the cap of liberty on a pole, but astride a horse wearing a crown, making clear that he was now riding in the king's colours.[2] Of course, Wilkes would have argued that he had always campaigned as a friend of the king. A medal from 1768 supported this notion, sporting a profile of Wilkes on one side and on the reverse the legend: 'A Friend to Liberty to his King and to his Country'.[3]

Of course, there was always more to Wilkes than his political life. His letters and diaries make all too plain just how important his private world was to him and how successful he was in regulating his various personas. As well as Wilkes the radical and Wilkes the family man, there was Wilkes the scholar and patron of the arts. He had always delighted in showing off his talents as a classicist of no mean ability. This had begun early on with his rather pompous lectures to his brothers. His political sentiments were similarly laced with classical allusions, quite as much as with his most favoured recourse to comparisons with the Civil Wars. In the final phase of his life, he was at last able to settle to producing editions of classical authors. As Wraxall noted, even in the 'serene evening of life' he remained 'a votary to pleasure'.[4] 1788 saw his edition of the Roman poet Catullus.[5] In 1790, he produced for private circulation an edition of the Greek philosopher Theophrastus.[6]

In understanding Wilkes, appreciating the role of the City of London in his life is crucial. Although groomed to become a gentleman of ease in a pleasant market town, when he needed to rebuild his political fortunes, he returned to his original stamping ground. He was not the first to recognize London's potential. By turning his attention to Middlesex, too, Wilkes was not an innovator. Under Walpole, Middlesex had been on occasion a keenly fought battleground. But unlike former opposition politicians like George Cooke (at one point Wilkes's partner in Middlesex), Wilkes was able to capitalize on the changing demography of the county. When Cooke had originally stood against the Walpole ministry he failed to rally to his side the kinds of small freeholders – shopkeepers and artisans – that Wilkes was so expert in inspiring. Wilkes was also able to take advantage of the fact that since Cooke's time, their numbers had increased significantly. In 1750, these 'lesser' men had comprised around a fifth of the electorate. By 1768 it has been estimated that they constituted nearer sixty per cent of it.[7]

This, surely, is the key to Wilkes. If not necessarily always an innovator, he was an absolute expert in testing limits in ways others could not. Wraxall concluded that it was circumstances alone that allowed Wilkes's rise to prominence: 'Neither his wit, his talents, nor his courage could have raised him to political eminence if he had not been singled out for severe, not to say unconstitutional, prosecution.'[8] This seems slightly mean-spirited. Arthur Beardmore, editor of *The Monitor*, had experienced very similar proscription to Wilkes, but Wilkes saw the opportunity of pushing the issue to its limits in a way that Beardmore did not. Where Wilkes was able to capitalize on his situation was by making his case that of the whole nation. He exploited the national economic malaise of the 1760s, the concerns of striking labourers and unemployed apprentices, trumpeting his concerns that the liberties of the people secured by Magna Carta and the Glorious Revolution were in peril. When the establishment sought to suppress him, it was seeking to suppress everyone else as well. Whether he truly believed his own propaganda or not, Wilkes was consistent in his message and always viewed himself as walking in the footsteps of the likes of John Hampden. Wilkes may have wanted 'A Friend to Liberty' to be his epitaph, but if anyone had called him a second Hampden, he would have been every bit as content.

If the City of London was central to Wilkes's career, Westminster was no less important to him, and he continues to haunt the place. His portrait, by Edge Pine, hangs in one of the tea rooms, reminding members of his presence and when June Mendoza was commissioned to paint the interior of the Commons during Margaret Thatcher's premiership, she included a scattering of historic Members watching from the gallery. Among them was a ghostly John Wilkes. He also continues to be referred to with striking regularity in Parliament. Referencing the Edge Pine portrait, MP John Grogan observed in the October 2018 debates on the future of BBC Parliament, how looking at it had reminded him that 'the reporting of this place has never been straightforward.' As recently as January 2023, Ruth Cadbury, MP for Brentford, referred to Wilkes as 'a radical journalist with a flair for words and a sharp tongue'.[9] There has even been an early day motion calling for Wilkes to be commemorated each year. Given the causes with which he was involved, freedom of the press, the rights of electors to choose their own representatives and the case for reform of the franchise, it is perhaps not so very surprising that MPs from a variety of political backgrounds should have had recourse to Wilkes's example.

The same might be said of those who have studied the man. The first edition of Wilkes's letters edited by Rough appeared in 1804 but they proved, to many, disappointing. Lady Bessborough thought them 'very trifling' and written in 'a pert, vulgar style'. There was nothing of weight, just 'jocular accounts of his ague, and household arrangements'. The accompanying memoir was even worse: 'very ill written and telling literally nothing'.[10] Some years later, the parliamentary expert Thomas Erskine May penned a brief biographical entry as part of a series. He noted that Wilkes's 'manners were elegant and conversation pleasing and witty' but (like Wraxall) was in no doubt that Wilkes was the beneficiary of governments making a number of unforced errors: 'Neither his character nor his talents would have raised him to political eminence; but the impolitic and illegal measures of his opponents was hereafter to make him the idol of the people.'[11]

Wilkes's importance in crucial periods in George III's reign was made more than clear, though, when it was an engraving of him that was used as a frontispiece for the 1859 edition of Horace Walpole's journal published by Richard Bentley, rather than of the author himself.

It was some time before Wilkes was accorded a full-length biography. There was a joint life of Wilkes and William Cobbett in 1870 and then a two-volume life of Wilkes eighteen years later. Since then, a further dozen biographies or comparative studies of Wilkes have been produced, three of them in 1962.[12] It is no surprise that so many different aspects of Wilkes's character have been highlighted and his story treated by authors from a variety of angles and traditions. He has attracted the attention of Marxist and socialist authors, as well as those of a more conservative persuasion. Most recently, he has been portrayed as both 'the father of civil liberty' and a multi-faceted libertine.

What many of these point to is Wilkes's ability to reinvent himself.[13] He was the distiller's son from Clerkenwell who became Baxter's muse, lord of the manor of Aylesbury and chief propagandist for Pitt the Elder. He embraced radical politics, experienced the life of an enlightenment man on the continent and took on the weight of the establishment by returning to test the constitution to its limits. As such, he was not alone and there are parallels to be drawn with contemporaries like Charles Lucas, 'the Irish Wilkes'.[14] Wilkes, though, knew how to capitalize on his predicament in ways others simply did not. He became a celebrity politician, revelling in the adulation of the crowd. As champion of a free press and a reforming Mayor, he used the independence of London to its full potential, before recognizing that the fury of Gordon needed to be resisted and employing his military training to defend London's institutions. Wilkes was frequently self-obsessed and never tired of seeing his name in print, carefully squirrelling away press cuttings that mentioned him and his utterings.[15] His final phase as courtier, Arcadian and translator were all of a piece with the fastidious man who progressed through life taking full advantage of all that the period offered. Horace Walpole was perhaps nearest the mark in dubbing him a 'phoenix'.

Wilkes's statue in Fetter Lane proclaims him as a Champion of English freedom, a quotation derived from Gladstone.[16] So often, it was his own personal liberty that was in question. His talent, though, was to see where this correlated with wider concerns and make his issues those of the public at large. In his final decade, he underwent a final transformation as the cause of radicalism was taken over by people with rather different agendas. Wilkes will remain a contested figure. Yet, as a man of extraordinary pertinacity and genuine courage, he remains relevant and fascinating. As he suggested, immodestly, at the opening of his own autobiography:

> It is the certain fate of all men, who have eminently distinguish'd themselves on the great theatre of the world, that their private actions will likewise become the subjects of enquiry, and the little anecdotes of their lives be eagerly sought after, and nicely scrutiniz'd.[17]

Endnotes

Abbreviations

Add. MS	Additional Manuscript
BL	British Library
Bleackley, *Wilkes*	Horace Bleackley, *Life of John Wilkes* (London, 1917)
Cash, *Wilkes*	Arthur Cash, *John Wilkes: The Scandalous Father of Civil Liberty* (New Haven and London: Yale University Press, 2006)
CJ	*Journals of the House of Commons*
Cobbett	*Cobbett's Parliamentary History of England : from the Norman conquest in 1066 to the year 1803* (36 vols., London: T.C. Hansard, 1806-1820)
Correspondence	*The Correspondence of the Late John Wilkes with his Friends Printed from the Original Manuscripts in Which are Introduced Memoirs of his Life*, ed. John Almon, 5 vols (London, 1805)
EHR	*The English Historical Review*
Dell, *Aylesbury Years*	Alan Dell, *John Wilkes, The Aylesbury Years (1747-1763): His Collected Letters to his Agent, John Dell* (Buckingham: Buckinghamshire Papers no. 17, 2008)
HMC	Historical Manuscripts Commission
Hants. Archs.	Hampshire Archives and Local Studies
HLQ	*Huntington Library Quarterly*
HP Commons 1754-90	*The History of Parliament: the House of Commons 1754-1790*, ed. Sir Lewis Namier and John Brooke (London: Secker and Warburg, 1985)
JBS	*Journal of British Studies*
JECS	*Journal of Eighteenth-Century Studies*
LJ	*Journals of the House of Lords*

Endnotes

LMA	London Metropolitan Archives
LWL	Lewis Walpole Library, Farmington, Connecticut
NLS	National Library of Scotland
ODNB	Oxford Dictionary of National Biography
PA	Parliamentary Archives
PRONI	Public Record Office of Northern Ireland
RO	Record Office
Sainsbury, *Libertine*	John Sainsbury, *John Wilkes: The Lives of a Libertine* (Aldershot, 2006)
Thomas, *Liberty*	P.D.G. Thomas, *John Wilkes: A Friend to Liberty* (Oxford: Oxford University Press, 1996)
Trench, *Patriot*	Charles Chevenix Trench, *Portrait of a Patriot: A Biography of John Wilkes* (Edinburgh and London: William Blackwood & Sons, 1962)
TNA	The National Archives, London
UNL	University of Nottingham Library
VCH	Victoria County History
Walpole Correspondence	*The Yale edition of Horace Walpole's correspondence* (48 vols., New Haven: Yale University Press, 1937-1983)
Wilkes Churchill Corresp.	*The Correspondence of John Wilkes and Charles Churchill*, ed. Edward H. Weatherly (New York: Columbia University Press, 1954)
Wilkes Letters	*Letters from the Year 1774 to the Year 1796, of John Wilkes Esq. Addressed to his Daughter, the Late Miss Wilkes*, 4 vols. (London: 1804)
Wilkes MSS	Wilkes Manuscripts, William L. Clements Library, University of Michigan
WMQ	*William and Mary Quarterly*

Introduction

1. PRONI, D2707/A2/4/7.
2. John Brooke, *King George III* (London, 1972), 144.
3. Katrina Navickas, 'The Contested Right of Public Meeting in England from the Bill of Rights to the Public Order Acts', *Transactions of the Royal Historical Society*, 6th series, xxxii (2022), 201.
4. *North Briton*, xxxii.
5. *Daily Courant*, 28 March 1734.
6. *North Briton*, xxvi.
7. https://johnsonsdictionaryonline.com/views/search.php.
8. *North Briton*, xxxvi.
9. *North Briton*, xxx.
10. *North Briton*, i.

11. *North Briton*, xlv.
12. D.H. Robinson, *The Idea of Europe and the Origins of the American Revolution* (Oxford: Oxford University Press, 2020), 270.
13. https://johnsonsdictionaryonline.com/views/search.php; Sainsbury, *Libertine*, xxiii.
14. Declan Kavanagh, 'John Wilkes's "Closet": Hetero Privacy and the Annotation of Desire in An Essay on Woman', in Ana de Freitas Boe and Abby Coykendall, eds. *Heteronormativity in Eighteenth-Century Literature and Culture* (Abingdon: Routledge, 2016), 77-94.
15. *Correspondence of Adam Ferguson*, ed. Vincenzo Merolle (2 vols., 1995), i. 80.
16. James L. Clifford, *Hester Lunch Piozzi (Mrs Thrale)* (rev. edn. Oxford, 1968), 73, 156.
17. Matthew McCormack, *The Independent Man: Citizenship and Gender Politics in Georgian England* (Manchester: Manchester University Press, 2005), 110.
18. *North Briton*, xxxiii, xxxiv.
19. Sainsbury, *Libertine*, 227-31.
20. *North Briton*, xliii.
21. Freya Gowrley, *Domestic Space in Britain, 1750-1840* (London: Bloomsbury, 2022), 75.
22. David Brion Davis, *The Problem of Slavery in the Age of Revolution* (Oxford: Oxford University Press, 1999), 501; Gabriel Banat, *The Chevalier de Saint-Georges: Virtuoso of the Sword and Bow* (New York: Pendragon Press, 2006), 280-1, 286; Jeffrey R. Kerr-Ritchie, Rebellious Passage: The Creole Revolt and America's Coastal Slave Trade (Cambridge: Cambridge University Press, 2019), 216; Elisabeth Grass, 'The House and Estate of a Rich West Indian: Two Slaveholders in Eighteenth-Century East Anglia', in *Politics and the English Country House, 1688-1800*, ed. Joan Coutu, Jon Stobart and Peter N. Lindfield (Montreal and Kingston: McGill-Queen's University Press 2023), 202; https://www.ucl.ac.uk/lbs/person/view/2146649831.
23. BL, Add. MS 30865A, f. 5.

Chapter One

1. *John Wilkes, Patriot, An Unfinished Autobiography*, ed. R. des Habits (Harrow: William F. Taylor, 1888), 6.
2. BL, Add. MS 30865A, f. 1.
3. In 1752 England finally abandoned the Julian and embraced the Gregorian calendar.
4. Most authorities agree on 1725. Arthur Cash suggested a middle date of 1726, based on an announcement for the sale of the Aylesbury estate in 1764. P.D.G. Thomas speculated that the 1727 date may have been intended as a posthumous joke or 'some kind of vanity'. As he noted, Wilkes's younger brother, Heaton, *was* born in 1727 and certainly knew it to be wrong. Thomas, Liberty, 1; Cash, *Wilkes*, 398-9; Louis Kronenberger, *The Extraordinary Mr Wilkes* (London:

Endnotes

New English Library, 1974), 3; Raymond Postgate, *That Devil Wilkes* (London: Dobson Books, 1956), 1.
5. *Autobiography*, 9.
6. Postgate, *That Devil Wilkes*, 1.
7. A document relating to this branch of the Wilkes family is bound at the beginning of a volume of Wilkes's correspondence in the British Library. Add. MS 30867, f. 3.
8. Luke Wilkes was appointed a groom of the Withdrawing Wardrobe on 10 June 1660. He was then promoted Yeoman on 1 August 1662, holding the place until the beginning of 1674. Bucholz, *Database of Court Officers*.
9. TNA, PROB 11/344/59, will of Luke Wilkes, 14 January 1674.
10. Postgate, *That Devil Wilkes*, 1.
11. *St James's Chronicle or the British Evening Post*, 1-3 January 1765.
12. Sainsbury, *Libertine*, 2.
13. William H. Rideing, *Young Folks' History of London* (Boston: Estes and Lauriat, 1884), 452. The crest was a crossbow, hence the motto.
14. Cash, *Wilkes*, 5.
15. Patrick Dillon, *The Much-lamented Death of Madam Geneva: the Eighteenth-century Gin Craze* (London: Review, 2002), 9.
16. Sainsbury, *Libertine*, 2.
17. PA, HL/PO/JO/10/1/511/1358.
18. https://www.distillers.org.uk/about/whos-who/masters-through-the-ages/.
19. Dillon, *Madam Geneva*, 6, 9-10.
20. Peter Earle, *The Making of the English Middle Class: Business, Society and Family Life in London 1660-1730* (Berkeley and Los Angeles: University of California Press, 1989), 256.
21. M. Dorothy George, *London Life in the Eighteenth Century* (London: Penguin, 1992), 41-42.
22. *Survey of London, xlvi: South and East Clerkenwell*, 118-21.
23. *Daily Journal*, 23 January 1731.
24. *Lloyd's Evening Post*, 18-21 Aug. 1758.
25. *Daily Post*, 1 May 1728.
26. *Daily Advertiser*, 24 September 1745.
27. Sainsbury, *Libertine*, 2.
28. Cash, *Wilkes*, 398 n.3.
29. Trench, *Patriot*, 3.
30. Jerry White, *London in the Eighteenth Century: A Great and Monstrous Thing* (London: Bodley Head, 2012), 115; Dorothy George, *London Life in the Eighteenth Century*, 41.
31. *Life and Letters of George Berkeley*, ed. Alexander Campbell Fraser (Oxford: Clarendon Press, 1871), 287.
32. Cash, *Wilkes*, 6.
33. Sainsbury, *Libertine*, 2.

34. Walpole is normally accounted the first British Prime Minister. He had emerged as such in 1721 and remained in power until he was forced from office in early 1742.
35. In the 18th century the City of London had four MPs, unlike most English constituencies which normally had two. For the list of electors see *Daily Journal*, 31 October 1727.
36. *HP Commons 1715-54*, i. 280-1, 435; ii. 21, 326, 341.
37. *Autobiography and Correspondence of Mary Granville, Mrs Delany, with interesting reminiscences of King George III and Queen Charlotte*, ed. Lady Llanover (3 vols, London: Richard Bentley, 1862), i. 163.
38. *London Daily Post and General Advertiser*, 7 June, 14, 18, 19 July, 13 September 1739.
39. *Daily Gazetteer*, 19 April 1738; *London Evening Post*, 13-15 June 1738.
40. *Daily Post*, 26 June 1738.
41. Emily Cockayne, *Hubbub: Filth, Noise & Stench in England* (New Haven and London: Yale University Press, 2007), 21.
42. TNA, PROB 11/362/50, will of John Heaton, 24 December 1679.
43. PA, HL/PO/JO/10/1/408/87.
44. TNA, PROB 11/804/292, will of John Heaton, 14 August 1753.
45. Jerry White, *London in the Eighteenth Century*, 512.
46. *Post Man*, 8-11 January 1704, quoted in Jenny Uglow, *Hogarth* (London: Faber, 1997), 20.
47. *Sussex Archaeological Collections*, x. 211; BL, Add. MS 32735, f. 217.
48. Cash, *Wilkes*, 6.
49. Wilkes MSS, 1, f. 2.
50. Wilkes MSS, 1, ff. 15, 20.
51. Sainsbury, *Libertine*, 5.
52. For more on Mary Wilkes see Amanda Bowie Moniz, 'A Radical Shrew in America', http://commonplace.online/article/a-radical-shrew-in-america/.
53. Quoted by Kronenberger, *Extraordinary Mr Wilkes*, 4; Charles Robert Leslie and Tom Taylor, *Life and Times of Sir Joshua Reynolds: with notices of some of his cotemporaries* (2 vols., London: John Murray, 1865), i. 126-7.
54. Quoted in White, *London in the Eighteenth Century*, 512.
55. White, *London in the Eighteenth Century*, 329.
56. John Gay, *Poems on Several Occasions* (London, 1737), i. 150.
57. Thomas Almeroth-Williams, *City of Beasts: How animals shaped Georgian London* (Manchester: Manchester University Press, 2019), 74, 80.
58. *Whitehall Evening Post*, 15-18 December 1750.
59. Robert O. Bucholz and Joseph P. Ward, *London: A Social and Cultural History, 1550-1750* (Cambridge: Cambridge University Press, 2012), 163.
60. Hannah Greig, *The Beau Monde Fashionable Society in Georgian London* (Oxford: Oxford University Press, 2013), 1-7.
61. Bucholz and Ward, *London*, 130-31.

Endnotes

62. *Remembrancer*, 24 February 1750.
63. See measuringworth.com.
64. *Daily Courant*, 18 October 1725.
65. *Daily Post*, 20 October 1725.
66. Bucholz and Ward, *London*, 128.
67. Andrew C. Thompson, *Britain, Hanover and the Protestant Interest, 1688-1756* (Woodbridge: Boydell, 2006), 60.
68. Andrew C. Thompson, ' "Oh that glorious first of August!" The Politics of Monarchy and the Politics of Dissent in Early Hanoverian Britain', in *Negotiating Toleration: Dissent and the Hanoverian Succession, 1714-1760*, ed. Nigel Aston and Benjamin Bankhurst (Oxford: Oxford University Press), 79-95.
69. Julie Farguson, *Visualising Protestant Monarchy: Ceremony, Art and Politics after the Glorious Revolution (1689-1714)* (Woodbridge: Boydell, 2021), 154, 168-9, 173.
70. Hannah Smith, *Georgian Monarchy: Politics and Culture, 1714-1760* (Cambridge: Cambridge University Press, 2006), 67-8; Ragnhild Hatton, *George I* (New Haven and London: Yale University Press, 2001), 260.
71. Smith, *Georgian Monarchy*, 69.
72. John Brooke, *King George III* (London: Constable & Co., 1972), 89.
73. According to Postgate, Wilkes's education 'was conditioned partly by his father's desire that he should be a gentleman, partly by his mother's that he should be a dissenter of unimpeachable morals'. Postgate, *That Devil Wilkes*, 2.
74. Worsley's death was reported in the press in December 1767 as having occurred in the Tower-House where he had run his Academy 'for young gentlemen': *Public Advertiser*, 31 December 1767.
75. A Gordon and R. Webb, 'Israel Worsley', *ODNB*.
76. Sainsbury, *Libertine*, 6.
77. BL, Add. MS 30,867, f. 4, cited in Cash, *Wilkes*, 8.
78. Declan Kavanagh, *Effeminate Years: Literature, Politics, and Aesthetics in Mid-Eighteenth-Century Britain* (Lewisburg: Bucknell University Press, 2017), xxix.
79. Wilkes MSS, 1, f. 4.
80. *VCH Oxfordshire*, vii. 212-13.
81. Wilkes MSS, 1, f. 1.
82. Wilkes MSS, 1, f. 3.
83. *Autobiography*, 10.
84. Cash, *Wilkes*, 10; *Records of the Honourable Society of Lincoln's Inn. Admissions, 1420-1790* (2 vols., London: Lincoln's Inn, 1896), i. 425.
85. Sainsbury, *Libertine*, 5-6.
86. Cash, *Wilkes*, 10.
87. Jonathan Swift, *Gulliver's Travels*, eds. Peter Dixon and John Chalker (London: Penguin, 1985), 53.

88. Jeremy Black, *The British Abroad: The Grand Tour in the Eighteenth Century* (Stroud: Alan Sutton, 1992), 289.
89. Kees van Stien, 'A Medical Student at Leiden and Paris: William Sinclair 1736-38: part 1', *Proceedings of the Royal College of Physicians Edinburgh*, xxv (1995), 301.
90. Wilkes MSS 1, f. 12.
91. Nicholas Carlisle, *Collections for a History of the Ancient Family of Bland* (London: 1826), 51-52; *CJ* xviii. 328.
92. Wilkes MSS, 1, f. 10.
93. van Stien, 'A Medical Student at Leiden', 295, 300.
94. *Diaries*, xv.
95. Alexander Carlyle, *Autobiography of the Rev. Dr. Alexander Carlyle, Minister of Inveresk, containing memorials of the men and events of his time* (Boston: Ticknor and Fields, 1861), 168, 176. The others were Charles Townshend, (Sir) James Johnstone and William Dowdeswell.
96. *Correspondence*, i. 9-10.
97. *HP Commons 1754-90*, iii. 540-8.
98. *HP Commons 1715-54*, ii. 333-5.
99. Cash, *Wilkes*, 14-15.
100. Carlyle, *Autobiography*, 160.
101. Carlyle, *Autobiography*, 168.
102. Carlyle, *Autobiography*, 168-9; Cash, *Wilkes*, 13. After Wilkes had returned home, Baxter wrote to him from Spa, which he noted as 'the place where I was first made happy in your acquaintance'. BL, Add. MS 30867, f. 23.
103. *Berkeley's Principles and Dialogues: Background Source Materials*, ed. C.J. McCracken and I.C. Tipton (Cambridge: Cambridge University Press, 2000), 193.
104. GEC, *Complete Peerage*.
105. Quoted in Keith Thomas, *In Pursuit of Civility: Manners and Civilization in Early Modern England* (London and New Haven, Yale University Press, 2018), 211.
106. BL, Add. MS 30892, f. 83.
107. Carlyle, *Autobiography*, 169-70.
108. Quoted in Cash, *Wilkes*, 14.
109. Cash, *Wilkes*, 14.
110. BL, Add. MS 30867, f. 41.

Chapter Two

1. *Correspondence*, i. 22-23, cited in Cash, *Wilkes*, 18.
2. Postgate, *That Devil Wilkes*, 3.
3. Sainsbury, *Libertine*, 83.
4. V.E. Lloyd Hart, *John Wilkes and The Foundling Hospital at Aylesbury* (Aylesbury: HM&M, 1979), 53.

Endnotes

5. Sainsbury, *Libertine*, 83-84.
6. BL, Add. MS 30867, ff. 8, 11.
7. Cash, *Wilkes*, 16.
8. Wilkes was originally commissioned into the Buckinghamshire militia in 1759 as a captain, later being promoted colonel.
9. Christopher Duffy, *The '45: Bonnie Prince Charlie and the Untold Story of the Jacobite Rising* (London: Cassell, 2003), 298. Andrew Thompson has argued, on the other hand, that 'the danger to London was probably minimal': Andrew C. Thompson, *George II* (London and New Haven: Yale University Press, 2011), 166.
10. *The Correspondence of The Dukes of Richmond & Newcastle 1724-1750*, ed. Timothy J. McCann (Sussex Record Society 73, 1984), 193.
11. Duffy, *The '45*, 306-8.
12. Paul Kleber Monod, *Jacobitism and the English people, 1688-1788* (Cambridge: Cambridge University Press, 1989), 114.
13. *Richmond Newcastle Correspondence*, ed. McCann, 197.
14. Dell, *Aylesbury Years*, 1.
15. Robin Eagles, *Francophilia in English Society 1748-1815* (Basingstoke: Macmillan, 2000), 138.
16. Black, *The British Abroad*, 56.
17. LMA, SC/GL/NOB/C/1078/41.
18. BL, Add. MS 30867, f. 14.
19. Cash, *Wilkes*, 17-18.
20. Kronenberger, *Extraordinary Mr Wilkes*, 5.
21. Sainsbury, *Libertine*, 9-10.
22. Dell, *Aylesbury Years*, 1.
23. Eveline Cruickshanks, 'Ashby v. White: the case of the men of Aylesbury, 1701-4, in *Party and Management in Parliament 1660-1784*, ed. Clyve Jones (Leicester: Leicester University Press, 1984), 88, 97-98.
24. This is according to Israel Wilkes's will. TNA, PROB 11/862/393. John Sainsbury suggests the amount was £350 with 'a promise of more to come'. Sainsbury, *Libertine*, 12. Arthur Cash suggests the sum was £450. Cash, *Wilkes*, 18.
25. John Sainsbury, 'John Wilkes, Debt, and Patriotism', *JBS* xxxiv (1995), 169.
26. Sainsbury, *Libertine*, 12; BL, Add. MS 30867, f. 23.
27. Sainsbury, *Libertine*, 12.
28. Sainsbury, *Libertine*, 13.
29. *Correspondence*, i. 17.
30. Sainsbury, *Libertine*, 16.
31. Cash, *Wilkes*, 18.
32. *Correspondence*, i. 13-14.
33. *HP Commons 1754-90*, i. 215. It is the only borough described as 'squalid' by the History of Parliament.
34. ie before the Great Reform Act of 1832.

35. Cash, *Wilkes*, 23.
36. As an Irish earl, Inchiquin was entitled to stand for the House of Commons as his title did not confer a seat in the British House of Lords.
37. Thomas, *Liberty*, 4; Cash, *Wilkes*, 29.
38. James Collett-White, *How Bedfordshire Voted, 1735-1784: The Evidence of Local Documents and Poll Books*, Bedfordshire Historical Record Society 90 (Woodbridge: Boydell, 2012), 67-68.
39. John Potter, successively royal chaplain, bishop of Oxford (1715-37) and archbishop of Canterbury (1737-47).
40. Robin Eagles, 'Thomas Potter', *ODNB*.
41. There is no authenticated likeness of Potter, but he is generally believed to be the 'handsome candidate' who stares out of Hogarth's Election: An Entertainment, on the left hand side beneath an orange banner, submitting to being caressed by an elderly woman. A sketch of Potter, drawn by himself, and included in one of his many letters to Wilkes certainly is far from flattering. BL, Add. MS 30867, f. 92.
42. Cash, *Wilkes*, 29-30.
43. BL, Add. MS 30867, f. 50.
44. BL, Add. MS 30867, ff. 59-60.
45. BL, Add. MS 30867, ff. 66-67.
46. BL, Add. MS 30867, f. 94. The sketch was attached to a letter from Spa of 25 July 1753. Add. MS 30867, f. 92.
47. *Correspondence*, i. 18.
48. Dell, *Aylesbury Years*, 6.
49. BL, Add. MS 30867, f. 99.
50. Dell, *Aylesbury Years*, 6.
51. BL, Add. MS 30867, ff. 75-76; Aubrey Newman, 'Leicester House Politics, 1750-60, from the papers of John, second earl of Egmont' (*Camden Miscellany* xxiii, 4th series 7), 126.
52. *VCH Buckinghamshire*, iii. 2.
53. BL, Add. MS 30892, f. 36.
54. Cash, *Wilkes*, 22.
55. Dell, *Aylesbury Years*, 9.
56. It is not clear what Dyson's connection with Leeson was but he later owned estates in Buckinghamshire, which may be how Leeson came across him. He later played a key role in devising the administration's proceedings against Wilkes over the Middlesex election. See *HP Commons 1754-90*, ii. 371-3.
57. TNA, PROB 11/816/212.
58. *Correspondence*, i. 40-43.
59. Sainsbury, *Libertine*, 87-88.
60. *Public Advertiser*, 14 January 1761; https://www.justincroft.com/book/4120/armstrong-john/a-day-an-epistle-to-john-wilkes-of-aylesbury-esq/.
61. Cash, *Wilkes*, 24; Ian Campbell Ross, *Laurence Sterne: A Life* (Oxford: Oxford University Press, 2001), 226.

Endnotes

62. https://www.laurencesternetrust.org.uk/sterne/life-and-times/key-dates/.
63. BL, Add. MS 30867, f. 95.
64. Dell, *Aylesbury Years*, 6.
65. *London Gazette*, 29 Jan.-2 Feb. 1754.
66. Walter Arnold points out that this was not the first society of beef steaks, and that others also co-existed with this one, including one founded in Dublin in 1748, which included a solitary female member, Peg Woffington. Walter Arnold, *The Life and Death of the Sublime Society of Beef Steaks* (London: Bradbury, Evans & Co., 1871).
67. Arnold, *Sublime Society of Beef Steaks*.
68. Arnold, *Sublime Society of Beefsteaks*.
69. Elections took place across a number of days and even weeks. Contested results often meant that there were then re-runs later in the year or into the next. It was not unheard of for seats to take years to settle and for MPs to be turfed out mid-term if the Committee for Elections voided their original election.
70. This made Potter a multi-millionaire in modern terms. See measuringworth.com.
71. Dell, *Aylesbury Years*, 7.
72. BL, Add. MS 30867, f. 74.
73. Sainsbury, *Libertine*, 49; Dell, *Aylesbury Years*, 7.
74. Dell, *Aylesbury Years*, 7.
75. *Correspondence*, i. 23.
76. Sainsbury, *Libertine*, 49.
77. Lewis Namier, *The Structure of Politics At the Accession of George III* (London: St Martin's Press, 1968), 124.
78. Barrington held an Irish peerage which meant he was not entitled to a seat in the Lords at Westminster, but was free to stand for the Commons instead.
79. Frank O'Gorman, *Voters, Patrons and Parties: the unreformed electorate of Hanoverian England, 1734-1832* (Oxford: Oxford University Press, 1989), 115.
80. Sainsbury, *Libertine*, 45.
81. Sainsbury, *Libertine*, 46.
82. There have only ever been two pairs of father and son Prime Ministers: William Pitt the Elder (as earl of Chatham) and his younger son, William Pitt the Younger; and their relations, George Grenville and his youngest son, William Grenville, Lord Grenville.
83. George Bickham, *The Beauties of Stow (1750)*, ed. George B. Clark (The Augustan Reprint Society, Los Angeles, 1977), ii.
84. Cited in Jemima Hubberstey, ' "For the Owner I am Convinced Has Neither Much Taste or Genius": Jemima Marchioness Grey's Accounts of the Gardens at Stowe and Hagley', *JECS* xliv (2021), 298.
85. BL, Add. MS 30877, f. 1.
86. *Correspondence*, i. 24.
87. Cash, *Wilkes*, 41.

88. *Correspondence*, i. 25.
89. *Correspondence*, i. 26.
90. *London Evening Post*, 25-27 April 1754.
91. *London Evening Post*, 27-30 April 1754.
92. *HP Commons, 1754-90*, i. 348-9.
93. BL, Add. MS 30867, ff. 99-100.
94. *London Evening Post*, 27-30 Apr. 1754.
95. *Correspondence*, i. 27.
96. Sainsbury, *Libertine*, 50.
97. Cash, *Wilkes*, 44; George Rudé, *Hanoverian London 1714-1808* (Berkeley and Los Angeles: University of California Press, 1971), 55.

Chapter Three

1. *London Chronicle*, 7-9 July 1757; *London Evening Post*, 7-9 July 1757.
2. John Sainsbury, 'John Wilkes, Debt and Patriotism', *JBS* xxxiv (1995), 169.
3. Max Skjönsberg, *The Persistence of Party: Ideas of Harmonious Discord in Eighteenth-Century Britain* (Cambridge: Cambridge University Press, 2021), 209, 212.
4. Dell, *Aylesbury Years*, 14-15.
5. Paul Langford, *Public Life and the Propertied Englishman 1689-1798* (Oxford: Oxford University Press, 1991), 294.
6. Namier, *Structure of Politics*, 11-12.
7. H. Trevor Colbourn, 'A Pennsylvania Farmer at the Court of King George: John Dickinson's London Letters 1754-56', *Pennsylvania Magazine of History and Biography* 84:4 (1962), 421.
8. R.E.M. Peach, *The Life and Times of Ralph Allen of Prior Park* (London: D. Nutt, 1895), 159-60.
9. Peach, *Ralph Allen*, 162.
10. Sainsbury, 'John Wilkes, Debt, and Patriotism', 169.
11. Trench, *Patriot*, 12, 32-33.
12. Concluded by the Treaty of Aix la Chapelle in 1748.
13. Geoffrey Holmes and Daniel Szechi, *The Age of Oligarchy: Pre-Industrial Britain 1722-1783* (London: Longman, 1993), 241; Warwickshire County RO, CR4141/7/216/1, Lord Brooke to Edward Willes, 7 September 1757.
14. Linda Colley, *In Defiance of Oligarchy: The Tory Party 1714-60* (Cambridge: Cambridge University Press, 1982), 173.
15. Brendan Simms, *Three Victories and a Defeat: The Rise and Fall of the First British Empire* (London: Penguin, 2008), 416.
16. W.A. Speck, *Stability and Strife: England 1714-1760* (London: Edward Arnold, 2nd edn. 1980), 260.
17. *The memoirs & speeches of James, 2nd Earl Waldegrave 1742-1763*, ed. J.C.D. Clark (Cambridge: Cambridge University Press, 1988), 146.
18. Holmes and Szechi, *Age of Oligarchy*, 258; Thompson, *George II*, 267-9.

Endnotes

19. Pitt was the secretary of state, but the nominal 'Prime Minister' as first lord of the treasury, was the duke of Devonshire.
20. Thompson, *George II*, 259-60.
21. *Waldegrave memoirs*, ed. Clark, 79-84.
22. Dell, *Aylesbury Years*, 18.
23. *Richmond Newcastle Correspondence*, 121, 123.
24. Cash, *Wilkes*, 45.
25. Dell, *Aylesbury Years*, 18.
26. Cash, *Wilkes*, 46.
27. Dell, *Aylesbury Years*, 19.
28. Peach, *Ralph Allen*, 163.
29. Dell, *Aylesbury Years*, 18-19.
30. Namier, *Structure of Politics*, 58.
31. Arthur Cash suggests that this was because Willes had been offered a post in the administration. If this was so, no office was forthcoming and it was not until 1766 that he was appointed solicitor general by Pitt (by then elevated to the Lords as earl of Chatham). Cash, *Wilkes*, 46.
32. Dell, *Aylesbury Years*, 20.
33. *Richmond Newcastle Correspondence*, 61.
34. Trench, *Patriot*, 18.
35. Cash, *Wilkes*, 51-52.
36. BL, Add. MS 30877, f. 5.
37. Robert Gibbs, *A History of Aylesbury* (Aylesbury, 1885), 220.
38. Trench, *Patriot*, 19.
39. *London Chronicle*, 9-11 August 1757.
40. *Public Advertiser*, 11 August 1757.
41. Arthur Cash suggests that Wilkes moved to Great George Street towards the end of 1758, but he was in residence for at least a year before this, as both the *Survey of London* and a series of letters to Dell bear out. Cash, *Wilkes*, 53-54; Dell, *Aylesbury Years*, 20-21.
42. *Survey of London: Volume 10, St. Margaret, Westminster, Part I: Queen Anne's Gate Area* (London, 1926), 34-41, 46-48.
43. Paul Seaward, ' "A Sense of Crowd and Urgency"? Atmosphere and Inconvenience in the Chamber of the Old House of Commons', in *Space and Sound in the British Parliament, 1399 to the Present: Architecture, Access and Acoustics*, ed. J.P.D. Cooper and Richard A. Gaunt (*Parliamentary History* xxxviii, 2019), 105.
44. *The London Letters of Samuel Molyneux, 1712-13*, ed. P. Holden (London Topographical Society: 172, 2011), 43.
45. Seaward, 'A Sense of Crowd and Urgency', 103.
46. Edward Hatton, *A New View of London* (2 vols, London, 1708), ii. 629.
47. Seaward, 'A Sense of Crowd and Urgency', 112-13.
48. BL, Add. MS 30877, f. 13.
49. BL, Add. MS 30877, f. 14.

50. Heneage Finch, 3rd earl of Aylesford. The title Lord Guernsey was merely a courtesy and before succeeding to his father's earldom he was MP for Leicestershire and then for Maidstone.
51. *Lloyd's Evening Post*, 2-4 November 1757.
52. *CJ* xxviii. 23.
53. *CJ* xxviii. 28.
54. *CJ* xxviii. 31; *LJ* xxix. 212; Cash, *Wilkes*, 50.
55. N.A.M. Rodger, *The Insatiable Earl: A Life of John Montagu, 4th Earl of Sandwich* (London: HarperCollins, 1993), 85.
56. More properly, the Knights of St Francis of Medmenham.
57. Namier, *Structure of Politics*, 124.
58. *CJ* xxviii. 38.
59. *CJ* xxviii. 39.
60. *CJ* xxviii. 41.
61. Dell, *Aylesbury Years*, 21.
62. History of Parliament archive, Newdigate Diary.
63. *LJ* xxix. 594.
64. *LJ* xxix. 603.
65. *LJ* xxix. 639.
66. *LJ* xxix. 680.
67. *LJ* xxx. 153; Cash, *Wilkes*, 51.
68. For more on the practice of reporting political news see *Scribal News in Politics and Parliament, 1660-1760*, ed. Robin Eagles and Michael Schaich (*Parliamentary History* xli, pt. 1, 2022).
69. *Chesterfield Letters*, ed. Roberts, 378.
70. BL, Add. MS 30877, f. 2.
71. Cash, *Wilkes*, 42.
72. *The Letters of David Hume, vol. 1, 1727-1765*, ed. J.Y.T. Greig (Oxford: Oxford University Press, 1932), 194-5.
73. Trench, *Patriot*, 15.
74. Dell, *Aylesbury Years*, 23.
75. *London Evening Post*, 26-28 July 1759.
76. *London Chronicle*, 7-10 Apr. 1759.
77. *Public Advertiser*, 16 July 1759.
78. For more on this see Jonathan Conlin, 'High Art and Low Politics: A New Perspective on John Wilkes', *HLQ* lxiv (2001), 360, and Donna T. Andrew, *Philanthropy and Police: London Charity in the Eighteenth Century* (Princeton, 1989).
79. Dell, Aylesbury Years, 24.
80. Lloyd Hart, *John Wilkes and the Foundling Hospital at Aylesbury*, 63.
81. Jenny Uglow, *Hogarth*, 632.
82. Uglow, Hogarth, 633.
83. Conlin, 'High Art and Low Politics', 359, 361.

Endnotes

84. Lloyd Hart, *John Wilkes and the Foundling Hospital at Aylesbury*, 48.
85. N.A.M. Rodger has suggested: 'The subject is unfortunately one which attracts cranks and repels scholars'. Rodger, *The Insatiable Earl*, 80. Wendy Frith, 'Sexuality and Politics in the Gardens at West Wycombe and Medmenham Abbey', *in Bourgeois and Aristocratic Encounters in Garden Art, 1550-1850*, ed. Michel Conan (Washington: Dumbarton Oaks, 2002), 285-9.
86. Cash, *Wilkes*, 35.
87. Geoffrey Ashe, *The Hell-Fire Clubs: A History of Anti-Morality* (Stroud: Sutton, rev. edn. 2000), 120-22.
88. Cash, *Wilkes*, 32.
89. Sainsbury, *Libertine*, 101.
90. Ashe, *The Hell-Fire Clubs*, 144-5.
91. Langford, *Public Life and the Propertied Englishman*, 81.
92. Trench, *Patriot*, 26.
93. According to the terms of the 1716 Septennial Act, parliaments lasted for seven years. The act had been forced through by the Whigs shortly after George I's accession as a way of cementing their hold on power and to deny the Tories any opportunity of an earlier poll.
94. Dell, *Aylesbury Years*, 33.
95. *Correspondence*, i. 52-53.
96. Trench, *Patriot*, 29.
97. Willes's decision to try his hand at Bridgwater in Somerset instead proved not to be the right one. Although he joined forces with one of the sitting Members, Robert Balch, and was backed by George Bubb Dodington, both were defeated and neither sat in Parliament again.
98. Cash, *Wilkes*, 57-8.
99. Trench, *Patriot*, 31.
100. *Correspondence*, i. 53.

Chapter Four

1. Dell, *Aylesbury Years*, 34.
2. Dell, *Aylesbury Years*, 21.
3. William Warburton, *Letters from a late Eminent Prelate to one of his Friends* (London: T. Cadell and W. Davies, 2nd edn. 1809), 289.
4. *Public Advertiser*, 2 February 1761; *Whitehall Evening Post*, 31 January-3 February 1761.
5. *Lloyd's Evening Post*, 6-9 Feb. 1761.
6. TNA, PROB 11/873.
7. *Public Advertiser*, 16 February 1761.
8. Sainsbury, *Libertine*, 10.
9. Sainsbury, *Libertine*, 3; Cash, *Wilkes*, 17.
10. *Daily Post*, 1 May 1728; *Public Advertiser*, 28 May 1761.
11. Cash, *Wilkes*, 24. Cash accidentally calls Wilkes's cousin, Robert.

12. Dell, *Aylesbury Years*, 34.
13. Porter left Constantinople in May 1762 and the following year was appointed minister at Brussels but resigned the position after just two years finding it too expensive to maintain. 'Porter, Sir James', *ODNB*.
14. Sainsbury, *Libertine*, 57-58. Chevenix Trench has the order the other way around, suggesting Wilkes tried for the Board of Trade first and then for Constantinople. Trench, *Patriot*, 53.
15. Dell, *Aylesbury Years*, 34.
16. John Brooke, *George III*, 85.
17. *Leeds Intelligencer*, 15 September 1761.
18. *Letters of Horace Walpole*, ed. C.B. Lucas (London: Simpkin, Marshall Hamilton, Kent & Co., c.1900), 323-4.
19. *Letters of Horace Walpole*, 325; *Derby Mercury*, 18 September 1761; Samuel Lodge, *Scrivelsby, The Home of the Champions, with some account of the Marmion and Dymoke families* (2nd edn. London, 1894), 189.
20. Paul Langford, *A Polite and Commercial People: England 1727-1783* (Oxford: Oxford University Press, 1989), 342.
21. Brooke, *George III*, 74.
22. Sainsbury, *Libertine*, 58.
23. Cash, *Wilkes*, 61; Horace Walpole, *Memoirs of the Reign of King George the Third*, ed. Sir Denis Le Marchant (4 vols., London; Richard Bentley, 1845), i. 91-92.
24. James Smith Stanley, Lord Strange, heir to the earldom of Derby.
25. *The Devonshire Diary: William Cavendish Fourth Duke of Devonshire Memoranda on State of Affairs 1759-1762*, eds. Peter D. Brown and Karl W. Schweizer (Camden 4th series, xxvii: London 1982), 151.
26. He had previously contributed essays to a couple of newspapers. Sainsbury, *Libertine*, 60.
27. Cash, *Wilkes*, 62.
28. *Observations on the Papers Relative to the rupture with Spain* (1762), 52.
29. Trench, *Patriot*, 54.
30. *An Answer to the Observations on the Papers Relative to the rupture with Spain...* (1762); *A Full Exposition of a Pamphlet entitled, Observations on the Papers Relative to the rupture with Spain...* (1762)
31. BL, Egerton MS 2136, f. 29; Cash, *Wilkes*, 62.
32. Dodd was also MP for Reading and a follower of Newcastle. He was acquitted.
33. *London Chronicle*, 17-20 April 1762.
34. *Private Letters of Edward Gibbon (1753-1794)*, ed. Rowland E. Prothero (London: John Murray, 1896), i. 50n.
35. Glover was known as 'Dodington's trumpeter'. He had at one point fallen out with Pitt and the Grenvilles, but by the accession of George III his political position had shifted again. He admired Bute but Dodington was convinced he would not support him. *HP Commons, 1754-90*, ii. 504-5.
36. NLS, Saltoun MS 17499, f. 64.

Endnotes

37. *London Chronicle*, 5-8 June 1762.
38. Cash describes Churchill as 'the most heteroclite parson and the most celebrated poet of the time'. Cash, *Wilkes*, 66.
39. Jenny Uglow, *Hogarth*, 680-1.
40. Conrad Brunstrom, ' "Be Male and Female Still": An ABC of Hyperbolic Masculinity in the Eighteenth Century', in *Presenting Gender: Changing Sex in Early-Modern Culture*, ed. Chris Mounsey (London: Associated University Presses, 2001), 44.
41. Cash, *Wilkes*, 66.
42. Jenny Uglow, *Hogarth*, 635.
43. Cash, *Wilkes*, 66-67.
44. Thomas, *Liberty*, 19.
45. Cash, *Wilkes*, 67-68.
46. Thomas, *Liberty*, 19.
47. *North Briton*, no. I, 5 June 1762.
48. Simms, *Three Victories and a Defeat*, 512.
49. BL, Add. MS 32960, f. 83; from a transcript in the History of Parliament archive. Bolton was not alone. Henry Bilson Legge referred to Bute merely as 'the Scotchman', while Newcastle called him 'the Scotch Chief'. Add. MS 32960, ff. 337, 361.
50. Simms, *Three Victories and a Defeat*, 512.
51. T.C.W. Blanning, *The Culture of Power and the Power of Culture: Old Regime Europe 1660-1789* (Oxford: Oxford University Press, 2002), 326.
52. Later in his career Wilkes would be compared with other great revolutionary figures of the 17th century. Along with Hampden there were also John Pym, John Lilburne and Algernon Sydney. Linda Colley, *Britons: Forging the Nation 1707-1837* (New Haven and London: Yale University Press, 1992), 111.
53. Trench, *Patriot*, 84; *Diary, Reminiscences, and Correspondence of Henry Crabb Robinson, Barrister at Law*, ed. Thomas Sadler (London: Macmillan, 3 vols, 1869), iii. 110.
54. *North Briton*, no. 2, 12 June 1762.
55. Cash, *Wilkes*, 72; *Wilkes Churchill Corresp.*, 3.
56. *Wilkes Churchill Corresp.*, 4-5, 11.
57. *Wilkes Churchill Corresp.*, 13-14.
58. *Wilkes Churchill Corresp.*, 14-15; Uglow, *Hogarth*, 666-7.
59. LMA, CLC/521/MS00214, f. 90, Wilkes to [Kearsley], 29 August [1762].
60. Uglow, *Hogarth*, 665-6.
61. LMA, CLC/521/MS00214, f. 96, Wilkes to [Kearsley], 18 October [1763].
62. Uglow, *Hogarth*, 668.
63. *Wilkes Churchill Corresp.*, 16.
64. *North Briton*, no. 17, 25 September 1762.
65. Uglow, *Hogarth*, 668-71.
66. Thomas, *Liberty*, 22.

67. John Cannon, *Aristocratic Century*, 28.
68. Robin Eagles, '"I Have Neither Interest nor Eloquence Sufficient to Prevaile": The Duke of Shrewsbury and the Politics of Succession during the Reign of Anne', *electronic British Library Journal*, article 11 (2015).
69. The 1764 edition of the *North Briton* gives the date as 22 August.
70. *North Briton*, no. 12, 21 August 1762.
71. Cash, *Wilkes*, 81; Millingen, *History of Duelling*, ii. 67.
72. *Wilkes Churchill Corresp.*, 17.
73. Stephen Banks, *A Polite Exchange of Bullets: The duel and the English Gentleman 1750-1850* (Woodbridge: Boydell Press, 2010), 245.
74. Millingen, *History of Duelling*, ii. 69-75.
75. Sainsbury, *Libertine*, 73.
76. *Chatham Correspondence*, ii. 192-3.
77. *Wilkes Churchill Corresp.*, 19.
78. Barnard was the son of former lord mayor of London and long-serving MP for London, Sir John Barnard.
79. Cash, *Wilkes*, 84-5; Sainsbury, *Libertine*, 124-5.
80. *Wilkes Churchill Corresp.*, 23.
81. BM 1868,0808.4245.
82. BM 1868,0808.4242.
83. *The Grenville Papers – being the correspondence of Richard Grenville, Earl of Temple and the Rt Hon George Grenville*, ed. W.J. Smith (John Murray: London, 3 vols, 1852-3), ii. 5.
84. *Grenville Papers*, ii. 7.
85. Cash, *Wilkes*, 85.
86. *Grenville Papers*, ii. 3, 4, 7.
87. *Wilkes Churchill Corresp.*, 34-35.
88. Cash, *Wilkes*, 89.
89. Cash, *Wilkes*, 92.
90. *Grenville Papers*, ii. 7.
91. *The Correspondence of John Campbell MP, with His Family, Henry Fox, Sir Robert Walpole and the Duke of Newcastle, 1734-71*, ed. J.E. Davies (*Parliamentary History: Texts & Studies* 8, 2013), 251-2.
92. Devonshire was prime minister from November 1756 to June 1757. According to Elaine Chalus, he had been appointed by George II 'without having been asked'. Elaine Chalus, 'Duke of Devonshire', in *The Prime Ministers*, ed. Iain Dale (London: Hodder and Stoughton, 2020), 30-31.
93. Brooke, *George III*, 97-98.
94. Oxford History Centre, J xxvi/b/4.
95. Langford, *Polite and Commercial People*, 344-9.
96. *Devonshire Diary*, cited in Langford, *Polite and Commercial People*, 347.
97. Pitt the Elder had a rural retreat at Hayes in Kent, now a suburb of Bromley and within easy striking distance of central London. *Wilkes Churchill Corresp.*, 35-36.

Endnotes

98. Brooke, *George III*, 99, 101; Cash, *Wilkes*, 93.
99. *Wilkes Churchill Corresp.*, 36-37. Sandwich was – like Wilkes – a friend of the actor David Garrick. Rodger, *The Insatiable Earl*, 87.
100. *Wilkes Churchill Corresp.*, 37-39.
101. *North Briton*, xxxiii.
102. *Correspondence of John, Fourth Duke of Bedford*, ed. Lord John Russell (London: Longman, Brown, Green and Longmans, 3 vols, 1843), iii. 202.
103. Perry Gauci, *William Beckford: First Prime Minister of the London Empire* (London and New Haven: Yale University press, 2013), 115-16.
104. *Wilkes Churchill Corresp.*, 45.
105. *Wilkes Churchill Corresp.*, 46.
106. Thomas, *Liberty*, 25.
107. BL, Add. MS 32947, f. 246.
108. *Wilkes Churchill Corresp.*, 49-51.
109. Dell, *Aylesbury Years*, 35.
110. Sainsbury, *Libertine*, 23.
111. *Wilkes Churchill Corresp.*, 51-52.
112. Thomas, *Liberty*, 26.
113. *Correspondence*, ii. 23-24.
114. Oxford History Centre, J xxvi/b/4.
115. Brooke, *George III*, 101.
116. *HP Commons 1754-90*, ii. 539.
117. Brooke, *George III*, 101-2.
118. Cash, *Wilkes*, 97; Thomas, Liberty, 26.
119. *The Jenkinson Papers 1760-1766*, ed. N.S. Juncker (London: Macmillan, 1949), 147.
120. Cash, *Wilkes*, 98.
121. Oxford History Centre, J xxvi/b/4.
122. *North Briton*, xlv; Cash, *Wilkes*, 100.
123. John Heneage Jesse, *George Selwyn and his Contemporaries, with memoirs and notes* (4 vols., London: Richard Bentley, 1843-4), i. 218.
124. Norman S. Poser, *Lord Mansfield: Justice in the Age of Reason* (Montreal and Kingston: McGill-Queen's University Press, 2013), 248.
125. Thomas, *Liberty*, 28-29; Trench, *Patriot*, 99-103.

Chapter Five

1. *Correspondence*, ii. 25.
2. H.T. Dickinson, *Liberty and Property: Political Ideology in Eighteenth-Century Britain* (London: Weidenfeld and Nicolson, 1977), 210.
3. Thomas, *Liberty*, 28.
4. LMA, CLC/518/MS02892, State of Facts relative to Mr Wilkes.
5. TNA, TS 11/923; *State Trials*, xix. 1002-1030.
6. TNA, SP 37/2/66, examination of Dryden Leach, 2 May 1763.

7. TNA, SP 37/2/64.
8. TNA, SP 37/2/68, 70.
9. Cash, *Wilkes*, 103.
10. Trench, *Patriot*, 101.
11. TNA, SP 37/2/62-63, examination of Richard Balfe, 29 April 1763.
12. LMA, CLC/521/MS00214, f. 105, Wilkes to Kearsley, 26 July [1762].
13. Poser, *Lord Mansfield*, 248.
14. BL, Add. MS 32955, f. 460: transcript from the History of Parliament archive.
15. Thomas, *Liberty*, 28-29.
16. Cited in Trench, *Patriot*, 102.
17. Trench, *Patriot*, 103.
18. *Letters from George III to Lord Bute, 1756-1766*, ed. Romney Sedgwick (London: Macmillan, 1939), 232-3.
19. Cash, *Wilkes*, 104.
20. Oxford History Centre, Jxxvi/b/4.
21. *Letters from George III to Lord Bute*, 232-3.
22. John Wilkes, *A Letter to the Worthy Electors of the Borough of Aylesbury in the County of Buckinghamshire*, in *Correspondence*, iii. 104.
23. Cash, *Wilkes*, 104-5; Kronenberger, *Extraordinary Mr Wilkes*, 38.
24. *General Evening Post*, 30 April-3 May 1763.
25. *Correspondence*, ii. 93-94. See also Jonathan Conlin, 'Wilkes, the Chevalier D'Eon and "the Dregs of Liberty": An Anglo-French Perspective on Ministerial Despotism, 1762 – 1771', *E.H.R.* cxx (2005), 1251-88; and Jonathan Conlin, 'Faire le Wilkes': the Chevalier D'Eon and the Wilkites, 1762-1775, in S. Burrows, J. Conlin, R. Goulbourne, & V. Mainz, eds., *The Chevalier d'Eon and his Worlds: Gender, Espionage and Politics in the Eighteenth Century* (Continuum, 2010), 45-56.
26. Cash, *Wilkes*, 106-7; Trench, *Patriot*, 106-7.
27. *Letter to the Worthy Electors of Aylesbury*, iii. 104.
28. *Letters from George III to Lord Bute*, 232-3.
29. Kronenberg, *Extraordinary Mr Wilkes*, 39.
30. Kronenberg, *Extraordinary Mr Wilkes*, 40.
31. Rodger, *Insatiable Earl*, 98.
32. GEC.
33. Trench, *Patriot*, 108-10.
34. *Letters from George III to Lord Bute*, 232-3.
35. Poser, *Lord Mansfield*, 249.
36. NLS, MS 16728, ff. 123-4, James Stuart Mackenzie to Milton, 30 April 1763.
37. *Gazetteer and New Daily Advertiser*, 28 February 1765; *London Evening Post*, 23-26 March 1765.
38. *LJ* xxxiii. 125.
39. *Lloyd's Evening Post*, 13-15 April 1763; *Gazetteer and London Daily Advertiser*, 26 May 1763.

Endnotes

40. Dorothy George, *London Life in the Eighteenth Century*, 291.
41. Charles Powlett, 5th duke of Bolton, was a rather tragic figure. A close associate of Temple, in the summer of 1765 he committed suicide for no one knew what reason. It happened in the same house (the same room even) where the 2nd earl of Scarbrough had shot himself some years before.
42. Kronenberger, *Extraordinary Mr Wilkes*, 42.
43. *Letters from George III to Lord Bute*, 232-3.
44. *London Chronicle*, 5-7 May 1763.
45. BL, Add. MS 30877, f. 21.
46. *Lloyd's Evening Post*, 2-4 May 1763.
47. *Public Advertiser*, 4 May 1763.
48. Trench, *Patriot*, 113.
49. *HP Commons 1754-90*, ii. 506.
50. *Public Advertiser*, 4 May 1763.
51. Trench, *Patriot*, 113.
52. *Lloyd's Evening Post*, 2-4 May 1763.
53. NLS, MS 16728, ff. 128-9, Stuart Mackenzie to Milton, 3 May 1763.
54. *Public Advertiser*, 4 May 1763.
55. NLS, MS 17499, f. 84.
56. Kronenberger, *Extraordinary Mr Wilkes*, 42-43.
57. *Lloyd's Evening Post*, 2-4 May 1763.
58. *Lloyd's Evening Post*, 2-4 May 1763.
59. *Gazetteer and London Daily Advertiser*, 5 May 1763.
60. *Public Advertiser*, 5 May 1763.
61. *Gazetteer and London Daily Advertiser*, 7 May 1763.
62. Thomas, *Liberty*, 31; Dickinson, *Liberty and Property*, 210-11.
63. Thomas, *Liberty*, 31.
64. *Boswell's London Journal*, 253.
65. Paul Kleber Monod, *Jacobitism and the English People, 1688-1788* (Cambridge: Cambridge University Press, 1989), 231.
66. For more on this see Sainsbury, 'John Wilkes, Debt, and Patriotism', *JBS* xxxiv (1995), 181.
67. Paddy Bullard, *The Oxford Handbook of Eighteenth-Century Satire* (Oxford: Oxford University Press, 2019), 363; see also Anna Clark, *Scandal: The Sexual Politics of the British Constitution* (Princeton: Princeton University Press, 2004), Ewan Fernie, *Shakespeare for Freedom: Why the Plays Matters* (Cambridge: Cambridge University Press, 2017) and David Francis Taylor, *The Politics of Parody: A Literary History of Caricature, 1760-1830* (New Haven: Yale University Press, 2018), 117.
68. *Boswell's London Journal*, 261, 266.
69. Uglow, *Hogarth*, 675-6.
70. *HMC Townshend*, 397.
71. BM 1891,0511.156.

72. BM 1997,0323.31.
73. BM 1868,0808.4186.
74. Uglow, *Hogarth*, 675-8.
75. *Wilkes Churchill Correspondence*, 59.
76. John Brewer, *The Pleasures of the Imagination: English Culture in the Eighteenth Century* (London: Harper Collins, 1997), 302-3.
77. George C. Williamson, *Life and Works of Ozias Humphry, RA* (London, 1918), 298, 309.
78. Conlin, 'High Art and Low Politics', 361-2.
79. *Derby Mercury*, 6 May 1763; *Public Advertiser*, 7 May 1763.
80. *HP Commons 1754-90*, ii. 367.
81. Wilfrid Prest, *William Blackstone: Law and Letters in the Eighteenth Century* (Oxford: Oxford University Press, 2008), 148, 185.
82. *Wilkes Churchill Corresp.*, 56.
83. *Correspondence*, ii. 26.
84. BL, Add. MS 30877, ff. 26-27.
85. *Public Advertiser*, 27 July 1763.
86. Cash, *Wilkes*, 136-7; Thomas, *Liberty*, 36.
87. *St James's Chronicle or the British Evening Post*, 28-30 July 1763.
88. *Lloyd's Evening Post*, 5-8 August 1763.
89. *Wilkes Churchill Corresp.*, 59, 62.
90. Cash, *Wilkes*, 138.
91. LMA, CLC/518/MS14176/1.
92. Egremont died on 21 August.
93. *Wilkes Churchill Corresp.*, 63, 71.
94. *Wilkes Churchill Corresp.*, 55.
95. *Grenville Papers*, ii. 155.
96. Lance Bertelsen, 'The Education of Henry Sampson Woodfall, Newspaperman', in Anthony W. Lee, *Mentoring in Eighteenth-Century British Literature and Culture* (Abingdon: Routledge, 2016), 158-9.
97. TNA, TS 11/879.
98. Wilkes's contacts included an MP called 'Mr Walkub', possibly Charles Walcot, George Onslow, Humphrey Cotes, Lords Temple, Cornwallis, Petre and Verney, Sir William Stanhope and Lord Harry Paulet. *Grenville Papers*, ii. 155-60.
99. Rodger, *Insatiable Earl*, 101-2.
100. *Grenville Papers*, ii. 151-3.
101. Thomas, *Liberty*, 37-38.
102. Peach, *Life and Times of Ralph Allen*, 189-90.
103. LMA, CLC/521/MS00214, f. 96, Wilkes to Kearsley, 18 October [1763].
104. Cash, *Wilkes*, 126-36.
105. LMA, SC/GL/NOB/C/1078/41.
106. Details of how Curry came to hand over the copy is dealt with in Thomas, *Liberty*, 38-39; Cash, *Wilkes*, 136-42; and Sainsbury, *Libertine*, 153.

Endnotes

107. Sainsbury, *Libertine*, 154.
108. TNA, KB 7/6.
109. Rodger, *Insatiable Earl*, 99.
110. *Diaries*, 206.
111. William C. Lowe, 'Peers and Printers: The Beginnings of Sustained Press Coverage of the House of Lords in the 1770s', *Parliamentary History* vii (1988), 242.
112. Sainsbury, *Libertine*, 154.
113. Cited in Thomas, *Liberty*, 41.
114. *HP Commons 1754-90*, ii. 291.
115. Thomas, *Liberty*, 41.
116. *George III Correspondence*, ed. Fortescue, i. 63.
117. NLS, MS 16728, ff. 178-9, Stuart Mackenzie to Milton, 20 October 1763.
118. Thomas, *Liberty*, 39.
119. *LJ* xxx. 413-14.
120. *LJ* xxx. 414.
121. *CJ* xxix. 668.
122. Peach, *Life and Times of Ralph Allen*, 192, 194.
123. Peach, *Life and Times of Ralph Allen*, 192.
124. *CJ* xxix. 668.
125. Thomas, *Liberty*, 41-42.
126. *George III Correspondence*, ed. Fortescue, i. 54.
127. Sainsbury, *Libertine*, 159.
128. *HP Commons 1754-90*, iii. 75.
129. Richard Hurd, *The Works of the Right Reverend William Warburton, D.D., Lord Bishop of Gloucester* (XIII) (London, 1841), 227-9.
130. Poser, *Lord Mansfield*, 250.
131. Stephen Farrell, 'Divisions, Debates and 'Dis-ease': the Rockingham Whig Party and the House of Lords, 1760-1785' (Cambridge PhD thesis, 1993), 154.
132. Cobbett, xv. 1346-51.
133. Cited in Farrell, 'the Rockingham Whig Party and the House of Lords', 155.
134. Sainsbury, *Libertine*, 77.
135. Thomas, *Liberty*, 43.
136. William Prideaux Courtney, *Parliamentary Representation of Cornwall to 1832* (London, 1889), 350.
137. Peach, *Life and Times of Ralph Allen*, 191.
138. Hurd, *Works of the Right Reverend William Warburton*, 226, 230.
139. *Oxford Journal*, 19 Nov. 1763.
140. *Correspondence*, ii. 19-21.
141. *George III Correspondence*, ed. Fortescue, i. 59-60. Warburton had also reported that Wilkes had been struck twice. Hurd, *Works of the Right Reverend William Warburton*, 226.
142. Warwickshire County RO, Lucy pprs. L6/1360 William Dobson to George Lucy, 17 November 1763.

143. *George III Correspondence*, ed. Fortescue, i. 59-60.
144. *Correspondence*, ii. 27-8.
145. PRONI, D2924, Colonel Bate to Moira, 19 November 1763.
146. NLS, MS 16728, ff. 190-1, Stuart Mackenzie to Milton, 25 November 1763.
147. *Correspondence*, ii. 28-9.
148. Peach, *Life and Times of Ralph Allen*, 197.
149. LMA, SC/GL/NOB/C/1078/41.
150. *Grenville Papers*, ii. 185-6.
151. *Correspondence*, ii. 33-35.

Chapter Six

1. *Grenville Papers*, ii. 188-9.
2. *Grenville Papers*, ii. 249-50.
3. Cited in Eagles, *Francophilia in English Society*, 72; *Correspondence*, iii. 124.
4. *Correspondence*, iii. 126-7.
5. *Correspondence*, ii. 35-36.
6. Mary Lou Lustig, *Privilege and Prerogative: New York's Provincial Elite* (Madison, Teaneck: Associated University Presses, 1995), 153-4.
7. *Grenville Papers*, ii. 185.
8. Trench, *Patriot*, 168.
9. *CJ* xxix. 675.
10. BL, Add. MS 30886, f. 6.
11. Peach, *Life and Times of Ralph Allen*, 195.
12. *CJ* xxix. 697.
13. *CJ* xxix. 709.
14. Andrew Millar, Thomas Cadell, Charles Shaw, John Williams, Anne Balfe, Thomas Davis, Jonathan Scott, Samuel Jenings, George Savile Carey, John Bagnall, Benjamin Burd and James Hoey. *CJ* xxix. 710.
15. NLS, MS 16524, Andrew Fletcher to Lord Milton, endorsed 21 January 1764; *HP Commons 1754-90*, iii. 639.
16. *Correspondence*, ii. 37. Chevenix Trench remarks that Wilkes used Samuel Martin, also in Paris at the time, as his messenger. The two met cordially and Martin even went so far as to undertake to stay out of the way 'to avoid even a colour of suspicion that he is capable of appearing against Mr Wilkes'. Trench, *Patriot*, 168.
17. *Correspondence*, ii. 41-43; LMA, CLC/518/MS02892/2. The name appears as Dufouare in the Commons Journals.
18. *Correspondence*, ii. 38-40.
19. BL, Add. MS 30886, f. 17.
20. *Correspondence*, ii. 18; *CJ* xxix. 721-2.
21. NLS, MS 16732, ff. 154-5.
22. *Correspondence*, ii. 41-43.
23. *Correspondence*, ii. 45-47.

24. Thomas, *Liberty*, 49.
25. BL, Add. MS 30886, f. 6.
26. *HP Commons 1754-90*, iii. 639.
27. *Correspondence*, ii. 51.
28. *Correspondence*, ii. 48-50.
29. *Correspondence*, ii. 52.
30. *Correspondence*, ii. 49-55.
31. *Correspondence*, ii. 54.
32. Thomas, *Liberty*, 57-58.
33. BL, Add. MS 30866, f. 3.
34. Cited in Eagles, *Francophilia in English Society*, 105.
35. *Correspondence*, ii. 56-57.
36. *HMC Lothian*, 249.
37. *Correspondence*, iii. 57-58, 125.
38. *HMC Fortescue*, i. 109.
39. *Correspondence*, ii. 57-59.
40. *Correspondence*, ii. 156.
41. *Correspondence*, ii. 60-61.
42. Carol Merriam and John Sainsbury, eds., 'The Life of John Wilkes', *Studies in Voltaire and the Eighteenth Century* 6 (2008), 270. Arthur Cash assumed the 'young one' in this case to be Corradini's child. Cash, Wilkes, 202.
43. *Correspondence*, ii. 56.
44. *VCH Buckingham*, iii. 13-14.
45. Sainsbury, *Libertine*, 216.
46. Thomas, *Liberty*, 58.
47. BL, Add. MS 30886, f. 12. The letter followed a lengthy screed written earlier in the month in which he had demanded materials from the Lords' proceedings against him. Add. MS 30866, f. 10.
48. *Correspondence*, ii. 70-77.
49. *Correspondence*, ii. 36.
50. *Wilkes Churchill Corresp.*, 83.
51. Campbell Ross, *Laurence Sterne*, 305, 308-9.
52. *Wilkes Churchill Corresp.*, 79.
53. *Wilkes Churchill Corresp.*, 80.
54. *HP Commons 1754-90*, ii. 429.
55. Derbyshire RO, D239 M/F 8244, Wilkes to Fitzherbert, 10 September 1764.
56. *Wilkes Churchill Corresp.*, 85-86.
57. Trench, *Patriot*, 175.
58. Trench, *Patriot*, 169.
59. Merriam and Sainsbury, 268; Alan Charles Kors, *D'Holbach's Coterie: An Enlightenment in Paris* (Princeton: Princeton University Press, 1976), 101-2; Daniel Gordon, *Citizens without Sovereignty: Equality and Sociability in French Thought 1670-1789* (Princeton: Princeton University Press, 1994), 141.

60. Kors, *D'Holbach's Coterie*, 302; Laura Nicoli, *The Great Protector of Wits: Baron d'Holbach and his Time* (Leiden: Brill, 2022), 31.
61. Kors, *D'Holbach's Coterie*, 105, 109.
62. Sainsbury, *Libertine*, 120.
63. BNF, MS Francaise 11359, Maraire to Sartine, 8 June 1764. My thanks to Jonathan Conlin for this reference.
64. Merriam and Sainsbury, 270, 288, 289.
65. Merriam and Sainsbury, 290; Sainsbury, *Libertine*, 120-1.
66. Trench, *Patriot*, 175-6.
67. Merriam and Sainsbury, 289.
68. Christopher Hibbert, *The Grand Tour* (London: Methuen, 1987), 165; Sainsbury, *Libertine*, 122.
69. Merriam and Sainsbury, 288.
70. Merriam and Sainsbury, 291; BL, Add. MS 30865B, f. 16.
71. John Noorthouck, *A New History of London Including Westminster and Southwark* (1773), 443.
72. *Wilkes Churchill Corresp.*, 86-87, 92.
73. *Correspondence*, ii. 82.
74. *Wilkes Churchill Corresp.*, 88-89; *Correspondence*, ii. 86.
75. *Wilkes Churchill Corresp.*, 91.
76. Merriam and Sainsbury, 292; Sainsbury, *Libertine*, 121.
77. *Correspondence*, iii. 86-87.
78. *Correspondence*, iii. 87.
79. *Correspondence*, iii. 130.
80. Merriam and Sainsbury, 293.
81. *Correspondence*, ii. 53.
82. BL, Add. MS 30865B, f. 20.
83. Cash, *Wilkes*, 180; Merriam and Sainsbury, 271.
84. *Correspondence*, ii. 91.
85. Beinecke Library, GEN MSS 89, C3088, Wilkes to Boswell, 27 April 1765.
86. Cash, *Wilkes*, 180.
87. *Correspondence*, ii. 89, 93.
88. Cash, *Wilkes*, 181-2.
89. *Correspondence*, ii. 100.
90. Ian McIntyre, *Garrick* (London: Penguin, 1999), 349.
91. *Correspondence*, ii. 107, 126.
92. BL, Add. MS 30865B. For a recent edition, see Merriam and Sainsbury, passim.
93. Cash, *Wilkes*, 182.
94. Merriam and Sainsbury, 294-5.
95. Merrian and Sainsbury, 294.
96. Merriam and Sainsbury, 295-297.
97. *Correspondence*, ii. 131; Merriam and Sainsbury, 297-9.
98. Merriam and Sainsbury, 298; BL, Add. MS 30865B, f. 31.

99. Merriam and Sainsbury, 302-3.
100. *Correspondence*, ii. 153.
101. David Constantine, *Fields of Fire: A Life of Sir William Hamilton* (London: Weidenfeld and Nicolson, 2001) 25-26.
102. *Correspondence*, ii. 170.
103. *Correspondence*, ii. 148, 150-1.
104. Cash, *Wilkes*, 184-5.
105. Hibbert, *Grand Tour*, 192.
106. *Correspondence*, ii. 144.
107. Hibbert, *Grand Tour*, 189; Merriam and Sainsbury, 300-1; *Correspondence*, ii. 162-5.
108. Cash, *Wilkes*, 188-9.
109. Sainsbury, *Libertine*, 122-3.
110. Bedfordshire Archives, Wrest papers, L 30/17/2/17, Frederick Robinson to his sister, Anne, December 1771.
111. W.M. Elof, *The Rockingham Connection and the Second Founding of the Whig Party* (Montreal and Kingston: McGill Queen's University Press, 1996), 30.
112. *Correspondence*, ii. 176-8.
113. Merriam and Sainsbury, 305-8.
114. J. Patrick Lee 'The English Translations of Voltaire's La Pucelle', in *British-French Exchanges in the 18th Century*, eds. K.H. Doig and D. Medlin (Newcastle: Cambridge Scholars, 2007), 19.
115. *Correspondence*, ii. 184.
116. Trench, *Patriot*, 196-197.
117. BL, Add. MS 30869, ff. 22-23.
118. *Gazetteer and New Daily Advertiser*, 18 April 1766. *The Plain Dealer* was by William Wycherley, *The Deuce is in him* by George Colman the Elder.
119. *London Evening Post*, 22-24 April 1766.
120. *Gazetteer and New Daily Advertiser*, 3 May 1766.
121. *London Evening Post*, 10-13 May 1766; *Public Advertiser*, 14 May 1766.
122. *Lettres inédites de Suard a Wilkes*, ed. Gabriel Bonno (University of California Publications in Modern Philosophy, xv. 1932), 257.
123. BL, Add. MS 30877, ff. 56-57.
124. BL, Add. MS 30869, f. 33.
125. *Public Advertiser*, 16 May 1766.
126. BL, Add. MS 30897, f. 55.
127. *St James's Chronicle or the British Evening Post*, 29-31 May 1766.
128. Thomas, Liberty, 60-64; *London Evening Post*, 5-7 June 1766.
129. Elof, *The Rockingham Connection*, 30.
130. *HP Commons 1754-90*, ii. 435; Cash, *Wilkes*, 196.
131. LMA, MS 31900, Wilkes to Mr Becket, 7 August 1766.
132. BL, Add. MS 30869, f. 78.

133. Alexander Stephens, *Memoirs of John Horne Tooke* (2 vols., London: J. Johnson and Co., 1813), i. 69, 83.
134. *Gazetteer and New Daily Advertiser*, 1 November 1766; *London Evening Post*, 30 October-1 November 1766.
135. Thomas, *Liberty*, 64-65.
136. Cash, *Wilkes*, 198.
137. Thomas, *Liberty*, 66-67.
138. *Walpole Correspondence*, iii. 322.
139. Thomas, *Liberty*, 67.
140. *St James's Chronicle or the British Evening Post*, 17-19 September 1767.
141. Cash, *Wilkes*, 198-9.
142. Cash mistakenly identified Baker as one of the London MPs. He was actually MP for Plympton Erle.

Chapter Seven

1. In his correspondence with his daughter, Wilkes asked to be written to as Fitzosborne. Almon, *Correspondence*, iii. 228.
2. *Correspondence*, iii. 227; Cash, *Wilkes*, 202-3; Thomas, *Liberty*, 69.
3. *Cited in HP Commons 1754-90*, iii. 640.
4. Thomas, *Liberty*, 69.
5. https://founders.archives.gov/documents/Franklin/01-14-02-0072; https://founders.archives.gov/documents/Franklin/01-13-02-0214.
6. *Lloyd's Evening Post*, 9-11 March 1768; *Public Advertiser*, 14 March 1768.
7. Earle, *Making of the English Middle Class*, 251-2. Earle presents a table indicating the Distillers as one of a minority of companies still largely made up of practitioners of the trade, which may be why Wilkes did not join them.
8. *Gazetteer and New Daily Advertiser*, 11 March 1768.
9. Charlotte Young, *Join Loyalty and Liberty: A History of the Worshipful Company of Joiners and Ceilers* (Stroud: Amberley, 2021), 213.
10. *Public Advertiser*, 14 March 1768.
11. Young, *Join Loyalty and Liberty*, 39.
12. Young, *Join Loyalty and Liberty*, 210; *Gazetteer and New Daily Advertiser*, 14 March 1768.
13. *Gazetteer and New Daily Advertiser*, 12, 14 March 1768.
14. Cited in Young, *Join Loyalty and Liberty*, 211.
15. *WILKES and FREEDOM: A New Ballad* (1768). My thanks to Kendra Packham for making me aware of this.
16. Langford, *Polite and Commercial People*, 375.
17. *Gazetteer and New Daily Advertiser*, 11 March 1768.
18. Thomas, *Liberty*, 72.
19. *St James's Chronicle or the British Evening Post*, 12-15 March 1768.
20. *Lloyd's Evening Post*, 14-16 March 1768.
21. *Gazetteer and New Daily Advertiser*, 17 March 1768.

Endnotes

22. *Public Advertiser*, 19 March 1768.
23. *Public Advertiser*, 17 March 1768.
24. *St James's Chronicle or the British Evening Post*, 22-24 March 1768.
25. *St James's Chronicle or the British Evening Post*, 22-24 March 1768.
26. Hants. Archs. 9M73/G395/15.
27. John Sainsbury, 'John Wilkes, Debt, and Patriotism', *JBS*, xxxiv (1995), 166.
28. BL, Add. MS 32893, f. 283.
29. *Lloyd's Evening Post*, 25-28 March 1768.
30. Langford, *Polite and Commercial People*, 375.
31. *Lloyd's Evening Post*, 25-28 March 1768.
32. Blanning, *The Culture of Power and the Power of Culture*, 329.
33. https://ecppec.ncl.ac.uk/case-study-constituencies/middlesex/election/Mar-1768/.
34. https://spitalfieldslife.com/2019/11/16/the-mile-end-assembly/.
35. *Lloyd's Evening Post*, 30 March-1 April 1768.
36. BL, Add. MS 30895, f. 59.
37. BL, Add. MS 30877, f. 68.
38. For much more on the nature of Wilkes's support see G. Rudé, *Wilkes and Liberty. A Social Study of 1763 to 1774* (Oxford: Oxford University Press, 1962).
39. Thomas, *Liberty*, 73.
40. *Public Advertiser*, 6 April 1768.
41. Hants. Archs. 9M73/G329/2, Edward Hooper to James Harris, 7 April 1768.
42. Thomas, *Liberty*, 74.
43. *Public Advertiser*, 28 March 1768.
44. *Lloyd's Evening Post*, 30 March-1 April 1768.
45. *Gazetteer and New Daily Advertiser*, 29 March 1768.
46. Cash, *Wilkes*, 211.
47. https://ecppec.ncl.ac.uk/case-study-constituencies/middlesex/election/Mar-1768/. These figures are in contrast to those in *HP Commons 1754-90*, i. 331, which give the tallies as: 1,297, 827 and 802 respectively. Other figures were reported in the contemporary press, Peter Moore, *Life, Liberty and the Pursuit of Happiness: Britain and the American Dream 1740-1776* (London: Chatto and Windus, 2023), 259.
48. Thomas, *Liberty*, 75.
49. Cash, *Wilkes*, 211.
50. *Gazetteer and New Daily Advertiser*, 30 March 1768.
51. Michael J. Franklin, *Orientalist Jones; Sir William Jones, Poet, Lawyer and Linguist, 1746-1794* (Oxford: Oxford University Press, 2011), 132.
52. *The North Briton From No I to No XLVI Inclusive: with several useful and explanatory notes...* (1769), appendix lii.
53. One might compare this with the phenomena of 'mock elections' that often ran hand-in-hand with formal polls. See Hillary Burlock, 'Mock Elections', https://ecppec.ncl.ac.uk/features/mock-elections-the-political-participation-of-non-voters/.

54. W.M. Elofson, *The Rockingham Connection and the Second Founding of the Whig Party*, 55.
55. *Cavendish's Debates*, i. 19.
56. PRONI, T3019/5729, Waite to Wilmot, 9 April 1768.
57. PRONI, D924, Colonel Bate to Sir John Rawdon, 30 April 1768.
58. George Rudé, *Ideology and Popular Protest* (Chapel Hill and London: University of North Carolina Press, 1980), 143.
59. *Gazetteer and New Daily Advertiser*, 29 March 1768.
60. Hants. Archs. 9M73/G329/2, Hooper to Harris, 7 April 1768.
61. *Gazetteer and New Daily Advertiser*, 4 April 1768.
62. Hants. Archs. 9M73/G329/2, [Hooper] to Harris, 7 April 1768.
63. *Public Advertiser*, 4 April 1768.
64. https://ecppec.ncl.ac.uk/case-study-constituencies/middlesex/election/Mar-1768/.
65. TNA, SP 37/7, f. 63.
66. Hants. Archs. 9M73/G341/5.
67. James E. Bradley 'The British Public and the American Revolution', in H.T. Dickinson, *Britain and the American Revolution* (Abingdon: Routledge, 1998), 132.
68. Cash, *Wilkes*, 213.
69. Merrill Jensen, *The Founding of a Nation: A History of the American Revolution 1763-1776* (Indianapolis/Cambridge: Hackett, 1968), 317.
70. PRONI, T3428/1/9, Townshend to de Grey, 9 April 1769.
71. Langford, *Polite and Commercial People*, 374-5.
72. Cited in Langford, *Polite and Commercial People*, 378.
73. *Autobiography and Political Correspondence of Augustus Henry, Third Duke of Grafton*, ed. W.R. Anson (1896), cited in P.D.G. Thomas, 'The House of Commons and the Middlesex Elections of 1768-1769', *Parliamentary History* xii (1993), 234.
74. *Gazetteer and New Daily Advertiser*, 4 April 1768; *Lloyd's Evening Post*, 4-6 April 1768.
75. Hants. Archs. 9M73/G235/18, George Harris to James Harris, 12 April 1768.
76. *Gazetteer and New Daily Advertiser*, 18 April 1768.
77. Poser, *Lord Mansfield*, 252.
78. Langford, *Polite and Commercial People*, 379.
79. Hants. Archs. 9M73/G325/19, George Harris to James Harris, 22 April 1768.
80. Poser, *Lord Mansfield*, 252.
81. *Political Register* (1768), ii. 373.
82. Cited in Cash, *Wilkes*, 217.
83. Paul Langford has noted that the government hoped to follow the precedent of John Ward, who had been expelled in 1726, but, as Langford observed, he was a very different character to Wilkes, so it was 'a highly inappropriate parallel'. Langford, *Polite and Commercial People*, 378-9.
84. Cash, *Wilkes*, 222.

85. R. Leslie-Melville, *The Life and Work of Sir John Fielding* (London: Lincoln Williams, 1934), 180.
86. John Noorthouck, *A New History of London* (1773), 444-5; Langford, *Polite and Commercial People*, 380; Thomas, *Liberty*, 82-83, 247; Cash, *Wilkes*, 222-3; Jerry White, *London in the Eighteenth Century*, 525.
87. BM 1915,0313.112.
88. BM Y,4.561.
89. Brewer, 'The Wilkites and the law', 132.
90. Cash, *Wilkes*, 227.
91. Brewer, 'The Wilkites and the law', 134.
92. *Cavendish's Debates*, i. 20.
93. Thomas, *Lord North*, 24-25.
94. Margarette Lincoln, *Trading in War: London's Maritime World in the Age of Cook and Nelson* (New Haven; Yale University Press, 2018), 45.
95. Poser, *Lord Mansfield*, 253-4.
96. Hants. Archs. 9M73/G314/28, Thomas Harris to James Harris, 23 June 1768.
97. Thomas, *Liberty*, 86. Richard Rigby thought the demand had been for £20,000. *Bedford Correspondence*, iii. 409.
98. Hants. Archs. 9M73/G314/27, Thomas Harris to James Harris, 14 June 1768.
99. Langford, *Polite and Commercial People*, 379.
100. TNA, KB 33/5/7; Poser, *Lord Mansfield*, 255.

Chapter Eight

1. Thomas, *Liberty*, 110.
2. Joanna Innes, *Inferior Politics: Social Problems and Social Policies in Eighteenth-Century Britain* (Oxford: Oxford University Press, 2009), 238.
3. Joanna Innes, 'The King's Bench Prison in the Later Eighteenth Century: law, authority and order in a London debtors' prison', in *An Ungovernable People: the English and their law in the seventeenth and eighteenth centuries*, ed. John Brewer and John Styles (New Brunswick; Rutgers University Press, 1980), 265-6.
4. Moore, *Life, Liberty and the Pursuit of Happiness*, 278.
5. *Correspondence*, v. 44-45. This was the former Kitty Hyde, daughter of the 4th earl of Clarendon and 2nd earl of Rochester. She had previously been forbidden George II's court for petitioning on behalf of John Gay.
6. *Wilkes Letters*, i. 111.
7. Brewer, *Party Ideology and Popular Politics*, 177.
8. Sainsbury, *Libertine*, 123-6.
9. *Correspondence*, v. 65.
10. LMA, SC/GL/NOB/C/1078/41.
11. Cited in Conlin, 'High Art and Low Politics', 365.
12. Holger Hoock, *The King's Artists: The Royal Academy of Arts and the Politics of British Culture 1760-1840* (Oxford: Oxford University Press, 2003), 149-50.

13. To Miss Wilkes, On Her Birthday, 1768, *Wilkes Letters*, i. 201.
14. John Brewer, 'The Wilkites and the Law, 1763-74: a study of radical notions of governance', in *An Ungovernable People*, ed. Brewer and Styles, 131.
15. John Sainsbury, 'The Pro-Americans of London, 1769-1782', *WMQ* xxxv (1978) 426.
16. H.T. Dickinson, *Britain and the American Revolution*, 11.
17. Cash, *Wilkes*, 228-33.
18. P.D.G. Thomas, *Lord North* (London: Allen Lane, 1976), 25.
19. *Wilkes Letters*, i. 87.
20. Norman S. Poser, *The Birth of Modern Theatre: Rivalry, Riots, and Romance in the Age of Garrick* (London and New York: Routledge, 2019), 90.
21. Thomas, *Liberty*, 90-91.
22. Hants. Archs. 9M73/G1242/16, James Harris to James Harris, 15 November 1768.
23. J. Wright, *Sir Henry Cavendish's Debates of the House of Commons, during the thirteenth parliament of Great Britain, commonly called the unreported parliament: to which are appended illustrations of the parliamentary history of the reign of George the Third: consisting of unpublished letters, private journals memoirs, &c.* (2 vols., London: Longman, 1841-43), i. 46-48.
24. Gauci, *William Beckford*, 166.
25. *Cavendish's Debates*, i. 66-67.
26. Thomas, *Liberty*, 92-93.
27. Hants. Archs. 9M73/G1242/18, James Harris to James Harris, 29 November 1768.
28. PA, HL/PO/1/151.
29. https://ecppec.ncl.ac.uk/case-study-constituencies/middlesex/election/Dec-1768/. *HP Commons 1754-90*, i. 331 gives the figures and 1,548 votes to 1,272. Thomas, Liberty, 88, gives the figures as 1,542 to 1,278.
30. *Correspondence of Edmund Burke, volume II (1768-1774)*, ed. Lucy Sutherland (Cambridge: Cambridge University Press, 1960), 21-22; John Noorthouck, *A New History of London* (1773), 448-9.
31. Thomas, *Liberty*, 94.
32. *HP Commons 1754-90*, iii. 114.
33. Brooke, *George III*, 150.
34. LWL, MSS 38, box 1, folder 41, James Erskine to Lord Townshend, 25 January 1769.
35. *The Papers of John Hatsell, Clerk of the House of Commons*, ed. Peter J. Aschenbrenner and Colin Lee (Camden Fifth Ser. 59, Cambridge, 2020), 29-30.
36. Thomas, *Liberty*, 94-95.
37. PA, HL/PO/RO/1/131, ff. 3, 6.
38. Thomas, *Liberty*, 109.
39. TNA, PRO 30/8/62, f. 141, Temple to Lady Chatham, no date.
40. Thomas, *Liberty*, 96-98.

Endnotes

41. LWL, MSS 38, box 1, folder 41, James Erskine to Lord Townshend, 4 February 1769.
42. *The Diary of Sylas Neville 1767-1788.* ed. Basil Cozens-Hardy (Oxford: Oxford University Press, 1950), 61-62.
43. Gauci, *William Beckford*, 172.
44. TNA, PRO 30/8/62, f. 155, Temple to Lady Chatham, 16 February 1769.
45. Hants. Archs. 9M73/266/8, James Harris to James Harris, 27 February 1769.
46. PRONI, T3019/5909, Wilmot to MacCartney, 17 March 1769.
47. Thomas, *Liberty*, 99-100.
48. TNA, SP 37/7, f. 19.
49. *HP Commons 1754-90*, i. 333.
50. LWL, MSS 38, box 1, folder 41, James Erskine to Lord Townshend, 1 April 1769.
51. Hants. Archs. 9M73/G1242/22, James Harris to James Harris, 18 April 1769.
52. Thomas, *Liberty*, 102.
53. Hants. Archs. 21M57/C2/3, Elizabeth Griffith to Charles Agar, 7 April 1769.
54. Hants. Archs. 9M73/G1242/22, James Harris to James Harris, 18 April 1769.
55. *Campbell Correspondence*, ed. Davies, 312-13.
56. James E. Bradley, 'Parliament, Print Culture and Petitioning in late Eighteenth-Century England', in *The Print Culture of Parliament 1600-1800*, ed. Jason Peacey (*Parliamentary History* xxvi, 2007), 97.
57. *Correspondence of Edmund Burke, volume II (1768-1774)*, 70.
58. Thomas, *Liberty*, 103-6.
59. John Brewer, *Party Ideology and Popular Politics at the Accession of George III* (Cambridge: Cambridge University Press, 1976), 172.
60. Brewer, *Party Ideology and Popular Politics*, 178. See also *The adventures, Voyages, and Travels, of Two famous candidates, In Search of Discoveries towards the North Pole. (to the Tune of Wilkes's Wriggle.)* (Newcastle, 1774). My thanks to Kendra Packham for this reference.
61. Lars Tharp, *Hogarth's China: Hogarth's Paintings and 18th-Century Ceramics* (London: Merrell Holberton, 1997), 107.
62. *Wilkes Letters*, i. 112.
63. BM 1868,0808.4438.
64. John Noorthouck, *A New History of London Including Westminster and Southwark* (1773), 430.
65. Brewer, 'The Wilkites and the Law', 138.
66. Brewer, 'The Wilkites and the Law', 131.
67. Frank O'Gorman, *Voters, Patrons and Parties*, 291.
68. Langford, *Polite and Commercial People*, 386. John Brewer estimated the number of signatures slightly lower, at 55,000. Brewer, *Party Ideology and Popular Politics*, 179.
69. *Campbell Corresp.* ed. Davies, 313.
70. Brewer, *Party Ideology and Popular Politics*, 178.

Chapter Nine

1. *Independent Chronicle*, 23-26 February 1770.
2. Brewer, 'The Wilkites and the law', 135.
3. LMA, SC/GL/NOB/C/1078/41.
4. *London Evening Post*, 14-17 Apr. 1770.
5. LWL, MSS Misc. Box 72, folder 52, Wilkes to Reynolds, 3 October 1768. My thanks to Hillary Burlock for this reference.
6. *Diaries*, 3.
7. Trench, *Patriot*, 273.
8. Bleackley, *Wilkes*, 249.
9. *London Evening Post*, 19-21 April 1770.
10. Frederick Reynolds, *The Life and Times of Frederick Reynolds by Himself* (2 vols., London, 1826), i. 21, 26-27.
11. *Diaries*, 3.
12. Cash, *Wilkes*, 266.
13. *Diaries*, 3.
14. Patrick Woodland, 'The House of Lords, The City of London and Political Controversy in the Mid-1760s: The Opposition to the Cider Excise Further Considered', *Parliamentary History* xi (1992), 62-63.
15. Fitzmaurice, *Life of William Earl of Shelburne* (2 vols., London: Macmillan, 1912), i. 460.
16. Walpole, *Memoirs of George III*, iv. 195.
17. Gauci, *William Beckford*, 183.
18. Moore, *Life, Liberty and the Pursuit of Happiness*, 308-10.
19. Young, *Join Loyalty and Liberty*, 213.
20. Thomas, *Liberty*, 116.
21. *Private Letters of Edward Gibbon*, ed. Prothero, i. 93.
22. LMA, SC/GL/NOB/C/1078/41.
23. *Correspondence*, iv. 30.
24. Brewer, 'The Wilkites and the law', 136.
25. Bleackley, *Wilkes*, 273.
26. *Bedford Correspondence*, iii. 411-12.
27. Hants. Archs. 9M73/G341/17, 5 May 1770.
28. *Diaries*, 3.
29. *Correspondence*, iv. 25.
30. Gauci, *William Beckford*, 183; Walpole, *Memoirs of the Reign of King George III* (4 vols, Yale 2000), iv. 160.
31. Thomas, *Liberty*, 117.
32. Gauci, *William Beckford*, 180.
33. *Diaries*, 4.
34. *Court and City Register or Gentlemen's Complete Annual Calendar, For the Year 1775*. Among the party was John Fox, a member of the Grocers' Company.
35. Brewer, 'The Wilkites and the Law', 139.

Endnotes

36. Trench, *Patriot*, 274.
37. Brooke, *George III*, 153.
38. Cash, *Wilkes*, 272; *Walpole Correspondence*, xxiii. 193. My thanks to Hillary Burlock for drawing my attention to this reference.
39. *Craftsman or Say's Weekly Journal*, 2 March 1771.
40. *Diaries*, 6-7.
41. Thomas, *Liberty*, 119.
42. *Correspondence*, iv. 44.
43. *Diaries*, 5; Cash, *Wilkes*, 272.
44. *Diaries*, 7.
45. *Correspondence*, iv. 44, 49.
46. *Wilkes Letters*, i. 204.
47. Gauci, *William Beckford*, 185-6, 189.
48. Gauci, *William Beckford*, 188.
49. *Correspondence*, iv. 56.
50. *HP Commons 1754-1790*, iii. 557.
51. *Diaries*, 7.
52. *Diaries*, 7.
53. Young, *Join Loyalty and Liberty*, 214.
54. *Diaries*, 9.
55. Young, *Join Loyalty and Liberty*, 214.
56. John A. Graham, *Memoirs of John Horne Tooke Together with his Valuable Speeches and Writings...* (New York, 1828), 60-61; Prest, *William Blackstone*, 268-70.
57. *Diaries*, 9.
58. Trench, *Patriot*, 276.
59. *Diaries*, 10-11.
60. *Diaries*, 12.
61. Thomas, *Liberty*, 120-1.
62. *Diaries*, 13.
63. Thomas, *Liberty*, 123.
64. BL, Add. MS 30895, f. 51.
65. Paul Kelly, 'Constituents' Instructions to Members of Parliament in the Eighteenth Century', in *Party and Management in Parliament 1660-1784*, ed. Clyve Jones, 180-1.
66. *The Controversial Letters of John Wilkes, Esq. The Rev. John Horne, And Their Principal Adherents* (1771), 6.
67. Stephens, *Memoirs of John Horne Tooke* (1813), i. 94-95.
68. *Controversial Letters of Wilkes, Horne, And Their Principal Adherents*, passim.
69. Lowe, 'Peers and Printers', 245.
70. Michael McCahill, *The House of Lords in the Age of George III (1760-1811)* (*Parliamentary History Texts and Studies* 3, Chichester: Wiley, 2009), 173.
71. *Diaries*, 18.

72. *CJ* xxxiii. 258-9.
73. *CJ* xxxiii. 263-4.
74. *Diaries*, 18.
75. *Wilkes Letters*, i. 116.
76. *CJ* xxxiii. 269, 275, 283.
77. *London Evening Post*, 23-26 March 1771.
78. *Diaries*, 18.
79. *CJ* xxxiii. 286-9.
80. BM, 1969,0302.1.
81. BM, 1880,0911.1058.
82. *Diaries*, 18-20.
83. Cobbett, xvii. 220-224.
84. *General Evening Post*, 7-9 May 1771.
85. *Diaries*, 20.
86. *Morning Chronicle*, 25 September 1772; *Memoir of Brass Crosby Esq. Alderman of the City of London and Lord Mayor, 1770-1771* (1829), 50.
87. Wilkes's cup is now lost. It seems last to have been used at the annual dinner of the Poulters' Company on 29 June 1881. LMA, SC/GL/NOB/C/1078/41; *Correspondence*, v. 63-64, 113.
88. Cash, *Wilkes*, 285.
89. Thomas, *Liberty*, 144-5.
90. *THRALIANA, The Diary of Mrs Hester Lynch Thrale (later Mrs Piozzi) 1776-1809*, ed. KC Balderston (2 vols., Oxford; Oxford University Press, 1951), i. 143.
91. R. Leslie-Melville, *The Life and Work of Sir John Fielding*, 199-200.
92. *Diaries*, 23.
93. Cited in Trench, *Patriot*, 291.
94. Sainsbury, *Libertine*, 198.
95. Thomas, *Liberty*, 145-6.
96. *Diaries*, 27.
97. Trench, *Patriot*, 293-4.
98. *Correspondence*, iv. 172.
99. Trench, *Patriot*, 295.
100. *Diaries*, 29.
101. *Diaries*, 29-31.
102. *Correspondence*, iv. 111-12.
103. Kronenberger, *Extraordinary Mr Wilkes*, 142.
104. *London Evening Post*, 3-6 October 1772.
105. *Bingley's London Journal*, 3-10 October 1772.
106. Trench, *Patriot*, 301-3.
107. Georgian Papers Online (http://gpp.rct.uk., January 2022): RA, GEO/MAIN/1243.
108. Georgian Papers Online (http://gpp.rct.uk., January 2022): RA, GEO/MAIN/38045.

109. Georgian Papers Online (http://gpp.rct.uk., January 2022): RA, GEO/MAIN/38046.
110. *Morning Chronicle*, 20 April 1773.
111. *Diaries*, 51; *George III Correspondence*, ed. Fortescue, ii. 476.
112. *Diaries*, 51.
113. Sainsbury, 'Pro-Americans', 431-2.
114. *George III Correspondence*, ed. Fortescue, iii. 20.
115. Leslie-Melville, *Life of Sir John Fielding*, 207, 212.
116. *Diaries*, 58-59.
117. Sainsbury, *Libertine*, 29.
118. *Diaries*, 61.
119. Brewer, *Pleasures of the Imagination*, 400.
120. *Diaries*, 63, 68.
121. *Letters from the Year 1774*, i. 1.
122. *Middlesex Journal*, 8-10 September 1774.
123. *St James's Chronicle, or the British Evening Post*, 30 June-2 July 1774.
124. *Middlesex Journal*, 13-15 September 1774.
125. *Morning Chronicle*, 16 September 1774.
126. *Adams's Weekly Courant*, 27 September 1774.
127. *Public Ledger*, 22 September 1774.
128. Alfred Beaven, *Aldermen of the City of London* (2 vols., London: Eden Fisher, 1908-13), ii. 200.
129. *Public Advertiser*, 21 September 1774.
130. *Public Advertiser*, 30 September 1774.
131. Thomas, *Wilkes: a Friend to Liberty*, 152.
132. Sir Watkin Lewes in 1780 and Richard Clark in 1784.
133. Henry Laverock Phillips, *Annals of the Worshipful Company of Joiners of the City of London* (London, 1915), 67.
134. *St James's Chronicle or the British Evening Post*, 29 September-1 October 1774.
135. *George III Correspondence*, ed. Fortescue, iii. 133-4.
136. Thomas, *Liberty*, 153.
137. *HP Commons 1754-90*, i. 334.
138. https://ecppec.ncl.ac.uk/case-study-constituencies/westminster/election/Oct-1774/. Not, for Mountmorres and Viscount Mahon: *HP Commons 1754-90*, i. 336.
139. Trench, *Patriot*, 320.

Chapter Ten

1. *Craftsman or Say's Weekly Journal*, 5 November 1774.
2. *Public Advertiser*, 4 November 1774; *Craftsman or Say's Weekly Journal*, 5 November 1774.
3. *Diaries*, 72.
4. Max Skjönsberg, *Catharine Macaulay: Political Writings* (Cambridge: Cambridge University Press, 2023), 145.

5. *Mr Edmund Burke's Speeches at his arrival at Bristol and at the conclusion of the Poll* (1774), 14-16.
6. Beaven, *Aldermen of the City of London*, i. 61-62.
7. Burke, *Correspondence*, ii. 483.
8. Sainsbury, *Libertine*, 208.
9. *Morning Post*, 7 November 1774. No one appears listed in the *History of Parliament* for the relevant election who fits the description of former Dancing Master.
10. *Morning Chronicle*, 4 November 1774.
11. *Daily Advertiser*, 10 November 1774.
12. Laverock Phillips, *Accounts of the Worshipful Company of Joiners*, 67.
13. *Daily Advertiser*, 10 November 1774.
14. Trench, *Patriot*, 310.
15. *Daily Advertiser*, 10 November 1774.
16. Trench, *Patriot*, 315.
17. *Summary Justice in the City: A Selection of Cases Heard At the Guildhall Justice Room 1752-1781*, ed. Greg T. Smith (London Record Society XLVIII, 2013), 73.
18. *Morning Chronicle*, 9 November 1774.
19. Museum of London, 50.69.
20. *Diaries*, 72-73.
21. *Public Advertiser*, 29 November 1774.
22. Trench, *Patriot*, 310.
23. *Public Advertiser*, 30 November 1774.
24. *Diaries*, 75.
25. Trench, *Patriot*, 305.
26. *Diaries*, 76; Trench, *Patriot*, 314.
27. BL, Add. MS 30871, f. 247. I am grateful to Nicholas Dixon for this reference.
28. Jacob Pleydell Bouverie, heir to the earldom of Radnor.
29. *Cobbett*, xviii. 183-4.
30. *Cobbett*, xviii. 234-40; Thomas, *Liberty*, 165.
31. Moore, Life, *Liberty and the Pursuit of Happiness*, 415.
32. *Craftsman or Say's Weekly Journal*, 25 February 1775.
33. *The Genuine Interesting Speech of the Right Hon. Lord Mayor Upon the Very Important Subject of the Middlesex Elections, Delivered on Wednesday, Feb. 22, 1775, in the House of Commons* (London, 1775), 2.
34. *HP Commons 1754-90*, iii. 572.
35. *Cobbett*, xviii. 358-77.
36. *Reminiscences of Henry Angelo, with memories of his late father and friends...* (2 vols., 1830), i. 56-57.
37. *Historical and the Posthumous Memoirs of Sir Nathaniel William Wraxall 1772-1784* (5 vols, 1884), ii. 48-49.

Endnotes

38. Trench, *Patriot*, 312.
39. *Lloyd's Evening Post*, 27 February-1 March 1775.
40. *Wilkes Letters*, i. 5.
41. *HP Commons 1754-90*, i. 409.
42. Beinecke Library, GEN MSS 89, C3091, Wilkes to Boswell, 10 August 1775.
43. Thomas, *Liberty*, 155.
44. Trench, *Patriot*, 313.
45. David Scott, *Leviathan: The Rise of Britain as a World Power* (London: Harper Collins, 2013), 416.
46. Sainsbury, 'Pro-Americans', 436-7.
47. Sainsbury, 'Pro-Americans', 431.
48. Thomas, *Liberty*, 166.
49. Sainsbury, 'Pro-Americans', 434.
50. Thomas, *Liberty*, 167.
51. Trench, *Patriot*, 318.
52. Thomas, *Liberty*, 169.
53. Sainsbury, 'Pro-Americans', 437.
54. P.D.G. Thomas, *Lord North* (London: Allen Lane, 1976), 109.
55. Trench, *Patriot*, 321-2, 376-9.
56. Cash, *Wilkes*, 325-7.
57. *Diaries*, 87.
58. *HMC Carlisle*, 311; *HP Commons 1754-90*, iii. 225.
59. *Summary Justice in the City*, ed. Greg T. Smith, 71-72.
60. The actual terms were 'during good behaviour'. Percy Hetherington Fitzgerald, *Life and Times of John Wilkes, MP, Lord Mayor of London, and Chamberlain* (1888), 235.
61. Cited in Thomas, *Liberty*, 156.
62. *Morning Chronicle*, 20 February 1776.
63. *Chester Chronicle or Commercial Intelligencer*, 19 February 1776.
64. *Diaries*, 90-91; Thomas, *Liberty*, 157.
65. BM 1868,0808.10076.
66. Thomas, *Liberty*, 157-8.
67. Frank O'Gorman, *Voters, Patrons and Parties*, 179.
68. Gauci, *Beckford*, 102.
69. *The Eighteenth Century Constitution: Documents and Commentary*, ed. E.N. Williams (Cambridge 1960), 215-17; Cobbett, xviii. 1287.
70. Moore, Life, *Liberty and the Pursuit of Happiness*, 183.
71. BL, Add. MS 30895, f. 110.
72. Paul Langford, *Englishness Identified: Manners and Character 1650-1850* (Oxford: Oxford University Press, 2000), 269.
73. Boswell, *Life of Johnson*, ii. 46-49.

74. Keith Thomas, *In Pursuit of Civility: Manners and Civilization in Early Modern England*, 51-52. See also Rory Muir, *Gentlemen of Uncertain Fortune*, 209. I am grateful to Rory Muir for pointing out this reference.
75. Boswell, *Life of Johnson*, ii. 49-55.
76. Elisabeth Grass, 'The House and Estate of a Rich West Indian', 202.
77. *Wilkes Letters*, i. 13-16, 17.
78. *Wilkes Letters*, i. 19.
79. G.J. Barker-Benfield, *The Culture of Sensibility: Sex and Society in 18th-century Britain* (Chicago and London: University of Chicago Press, 1992), 75.
80. *Wilkes Letters*, i. 21, 26, 27, 29-30, 33-34.
81. Thomas, *Liberty*, 170.
82. *Correspondence*, v. 70-71.
83. *The Correspondence of Catharine Macaulay*, ed. Karen Green (Oxford: Oxford University Press, 2020), 14-15, 104-5; Max Skjönsberg, *Catharine Macaulay: Political Writings*, 163.
84. *Diaries*, 101, 104.
85. Stefka Ritchie, *The Reformist Ideas of Samuel Johnson* (Newcastle: Cambridge Scholars, 2017), 146, 178-85.
86. Cobbett, xix. 27-34. 'I am a man: I deem nothing pertaining to men foreign to me'. Richard A. Bauman, *Human Rights in Ancient Rome* (London and New York: Routledge, 2000), 1.
87. Thomas, *Liberty*, 182-3; Cobbett, xix. 108-22, 226.
88. Cited in Thierry Morel, 'Houghton Revisited: An Introduction', in *Houghton Revisited: The Walpole Masterpieces from Catherine the Great's Hermitage* (London, 2013), 32.
89. Conlin, 'High Art and Low Politics', 357-8, 369-72.
90. *Diaries*, 108. Cash suggests that Wilkes may have been eager to end the relationship as he could no longer afford to keep her. Cash, *Wilkes*, 337.
91. *Wilkes Letters*, i. 39-40, 45.
92. *Wilkes Letters*, i. 46-47.
93. *Diaries*, 116.
94. Diaries, 309-10; *Wilkes Letters*, i. 48.
95. *Wilkes Letters*, i. 51.
96. *Wilkes Letters*, i. 54.
97. *Wilkes Letters*, i. 69.
98. Sainsbury, *Libertine*, 35; Barbara White, 'Love, Gossip and Diversion: John Wilkes in Bath', *Bath History* xiv (2016), 42.
99. *Wilkes Letters*, i. 60, 66.
100. White, 'Love, Gossip and Diversion', 40.
101. Green, *Some Bath Love Letters*, 26-27.
102. Thomas, *Liberty*, 184.
103. *Wilkes Letters*, i. 79, 81, 83, 85.
104. White, 'Love, Gossip and Diversion', 41.

105. *Diaries*, 120-1.
106. *Wilkes Letters*, i. 112-13.
107. *Wilkes Letters*, i. 115, 130.
108. Cash, *Wilkes*, 334-5.
109. *Diaries*, 128.
110. *HP Commons 1754-90*, ii. 592-3.
111. *Wilkes Letters*, i. 130.
112. Cash, *Wilkes*, 337-9; *Wilkes Letters*, i. 42-43.
113. *HP Commons 1754-90*, ii. 168.
114. Cash, *Wilkes*, 351.
115. *Wilkes Letters*, i. 171.
116. Cash, *Wilkes*, 352. Wilkes's own figures were that he had secured 2,332 votes to James's 370. *Wilkes Letters*, i. 172.
117. Trench, *Patriot*, 337.
118. *Wilkes Letters*, i. 201.
119. L.G. Mitchell, *Charles James Fox* (Oxford: Oxford University Press, 1992), 34-35.
120. https://ecppec.ncl.ac.uk/case-study-constituencies/westminster/election/Oct-1780/.
121. UNL, Pw F 2750, R. Champion to duke of Portland, 11 January 1780.
122. *Wilkes Letters*, i. 202-11.

Chapter Eleven

1. *Wilkes Letters*, i. 212.
2. *HP Commons 1754-90*, ii. 513.
3. *Wilkes Letters*, i. 86.
4. *Diaries*, 122, 123.
5. See https://www.londonlives.org/.
6. Cash, *Wilkes*, 361; *HP Commons 1754-90*, iii. 306.
7. Ian Haywood and John Seed, 'Introduction', in *The Gordon Riots: Politics, Culture and Insurrection in Late Eighteenth-Century Britain*, ed. Ian Haywood and John Seed (Cambridge 2012), 2. Arthur Cash suggests a much larger number. Cash, *Wilkes*, 361.
8. Robin Eagles, ' "Got together in a riotous and tumultous manner": Crowds and the Palace of Westminster, c.1700-1800', *JECS* xliii (2020), 349-50.
9. Quoted in Brycchan Carey, ' "The Worse than Negro barbarity of the populace": Ignatius Sancho witnesses the Gordon riots', in *The Gordon Riots*, ed. Haywood and Seed, 144.
10. Haywood and Seed, 'Introduction', 5.
11. Thomas, *Lord North*, 125.
12. *Diaries*, 277. Wilkes recorded a fuller than usual set of diary entries covering the period of the riots, starting on 31 May and running to 28 June.
13. Nicholas Rogers, *Crowds, Culture, and Politics in Georgian Britain* (Oxford: Oxford University Press, 1998), 157.
14. Sainsbury, *Libertine*, 170-1.

15. *Diaries*, 278-9.
16. *Diaries*, 279-85.
17. *Diaries*, 280-2.
18. Rogers, *Crowds, Culture, and Politics*, 162n.
19. Colin Haydon, ' "Popery at St. James's": the conspiracy theses of William Payne, Thomas Hollis, and Lord George Gordon', in *Conspiracies and Conspiracy Theory in Early Modern Europe from the Waldensians to the French Revolution*, ed. Barry Coward and Julian Swann (Abingdon: Routledge, 2004), 189.
20. *Wilkes Letters*, i. 214.
21. Sainsbury, *Libertine*, 171.
22. PRONI, T3429/2/7.
23. Gerald Newman, *The Rise of English Nationalism: A Cultural History 1740-1830* (London: Weidenfeld and Nicolson, 1987), 209.
24. Thomas, *Liberty*, 192.
25. *Cobbett*, xxi. 702.
26. *Lloyd's Evening Post*, 11-13 September 1780.
27. *General Evening Post*, 12-14 September 1780; *Gazetteer and New Daily Advertiser*, 15 September 1780.
28. *Gazetteer and New Daily Advertiser*, 13 September 1780.
29. Thomas, *Lord North*, 126.
30. Trench, *Patriot*, 345-69; Postgate, *That Devil Wilkes*, 223-37.
31. *Wilkes Letters*, i. 216-17.
32. Cash, *Wilkes*, 365-6.
33. *Cobbett*, xxi. 891-5.
34. Thomas, *Lord North*, 128-32.
35. *Wilkes Letters*, i. 234, 237, 238.
36. *Wilkes Letters*, i. 244, 247.
37. Thomas, *Liberty*, 192.
38. *Wilkes Letters*, i. 244, 246.
39. *Cobbett*, xxii. 1407-9.
40. *General Advertiser and Morning Intelligencer*, 4 May 1782.
41. *Morning Chronicle*, 4 May 1782.
42. *Diaries*, 142-3.
43. Johann Zoffany, A Gentleman in Masquerade Costume. See Conlin, 'Wilkes, the Chevalier D'Eon and 'the Dregs of Liberty', 1251–88.
44. *Diaries*, 248.
45. Arthur Cash thought that Zoffany had also been rather generous in shrinking both Wilkes's and Polly's chins. Cash, *Wilkes*, 340.
46. Mitchell, *Charles James Fox*, 48-52.
47. BL, Add. MS 32959, f. 65, Bolton to Newcastle, 24 May 1764.
48. John Cannon, 'Lord Shelburne's Ministry, 1782-3: "A Very Good List"', in *An Enlightenment Statesman in Whig Britain: Lord Shelburne in Context, 1737-1805* (Woodbridge: Boydell, 2011), 161, 164.

Endnotes

49. *English Chronicle*, 8-10 August 1782.
50. Thomas, *Liberty*, 193; *Morning Chronicle*, 10 August 1782.
51. Cobbett, xxiii. 359-61.
52. Cannon, 'Lord Shelburne's Ministry', 170-1.
53. BM 1851,0901.108.
54. BM 1868,0808.5286: 'The New Coalition'; 1868,0808.5289: 'The grand coalition medal, struck in base metal gilt.'
55. *Diaries*, 155.
56. *HP Commons 1715-54*, ii. 643.
57. Cobbett, xxiv. 20.
58. Cobbett, xxiv. 22-23.
59. Brooke, *George III*, 253.
60. *Diaries*, 155.
61. Stella Achilleos, 'The *Anacreontea* and a Tradition of Refined Male Sociability', in *A Pleasing Sinne: Drink and Conviviality in 17th-Century England*, ed. Adam Smyth (Cambridge: Cambridge University Press, 2004), 22-23; *Recollections of R.J.S. Stevens: an organist in Georgian London*, ed. Mark Argent (Carbondale and Edwardsville, 1992), 24-28; Ian Newman, 'Becoming Institutional: The Case of the Anacreontic Society', in *Institutions of Literature 1700-1900: The Development of Literary Culture and Production*, ed. Jon Mee and Matthew Sangster (Cambridge: Cambridge University Press, 2022), 101-4.
62. *Diaries*, 155.
63. BM J,2.118.
64. BM 1851,0901.179.
65. BM J,2.88.
66. BM 1868,0808.5907.
67. BM 1868,0808.5974.
68. Cited in Thomas, *Liberty*, 196.
69. *London Evening Post*, 11 November 1779.
70. *Diaries*, 158.
71. Trench, *Patriot*, 349; Cash, *Wilkes*, 379; Diaries, 188.
72. https://ecppec.ncl.ac.uk/case-study-constituencies/middlesex/election/Apr-1784/.
73. *Wilkes Letters*, iii. 125.
74. *Gloucester Journal*, 5 April 1784; *Morning Herald*, 5 April 1784.
75. https://ecppec.ncl.ac.uk/case-study-constituencies/westminster/election/May-1784/.
76. Thomas, *Liberty*, 195.
77. *Wilkes Letters*, iii. 5.
78. *Wilkes Letters*, iii. 11, 23.
79. *Wilkes Letters*, iii. 82-83.
80. Jennifer Mori, *William Pitt and the French Revolution 1785-1795* (Edinburgh: Keele University Press, 1997), 21-24.
81. *Wilkes Letters*, iii. 46-47.

82. *Wilkes Letters*, iii. 106; *Diaries*, 163.
83. *Diaries*, 169.
84. Mori, *William Pitt and the French Revolution*, 24-26.
85. *Wilkes Letters*, iii. 121.
86. *Wilkes Letters*, iii. 119, 122.
87. *Wilkes Letters*, iii. 127-8.
88. *Diaries*, 173, 181.
89. *Diaries*, 169, 191.
90. *Diaries*, 183, 187.
91. *Diaries*, 188.
92. *Wilkes Letters*, iii. 112.

Chapter Twelve

1. *Diaries*, 196.
2. *Diaries*, 180.
3. Poser, *Lord Mansfield*, 173-5.
4. Chiara Rolli, *The Trial of Warren Hastings: Classical Oratory and Reception in the Eighteenth-Century England* (London: Bloomsbury, 2019), 116.
5. Frederick Ponsonby, Viscount Duncannon, later 3rd earl of Bessborough.
6. *HP Commons 1754-90*, ii. 262.
7. Richard B. Sher, *Making Boswell's Life of Johnson: an author publisher and his support network* (Cambridge: Cambridge University Press, 2023), 13; Robert Zaretsky, *Boswell's Enlightenment* (Cambridge MA and London: Harvard University Press, 2015), 198.
8. *Diaries*, 239.
9. *World and Fashionable Advertiser*, 4 April 1787.
10. *Wilkes Letters*, iii. 326.
11. *Wilkes Letters*, iii. 323.
12. BM, 1868,0808.5665.
13. *Wilkes Letters*, iii. 234.
14. *Wilkes Letters*, iii. 239, 245-6.
15. *The Chevalier d'Eon and his Worlds*, ed. Burrows, Conlin and Goulbourne, 223.
16. *World*, 31 January 1788.
17. *Diaries*, 208.
18. Hesketh Hubbard, 'William Hogarth, the Founder of English Painting', *Journal of the Royal Society of Arts*, lxxx (1932), 440.
19. BL, Add. MS 30866, f. 166.
20. Beinecke Library, OSB MSS File 16120, Wilkes to William Sharp, 14 May 1788; *St James's Chronicle or the British Evening Post*, 1-3 May 1788.
21. *Topographical and Historical Guide to the Isle of Wight* (1840), 188.
22. Cash, *Wilkes*, 388.
23. John Broad, 'Permanence and Impermanence in Housing Provision for the Eighteenth-Century Rural Poor in England', in *Investing in the Early Modern*

Endnotes

  Built Environment: Europeans, Asians, Settlers and Indigenous Societies, ed. Carole Shammas (Leiden and Boston: Brill, 2012), 112-13; Freya Gowrley, *Domestic Space in Britain*, 81.
24. *Wilkes Letters*, iii. 221.
25. *Wilkes Letters*, iii. 225.
26. *Wilkes Letters*, iii. 221-2.
27. *Diaries*, 211, 214-5.
28. *Wilkes Letters*, iv. 3.
29. *HP Commons 1754-90*, iii. 659.
30. Hallie Rubenhold, *Lady Worsley's Whim: An Eighteenth-Century Tale of Sex, Scandal and Divorce* (London: Chatto and Windus, 2008), 220.
31. *Diaries*, 97.
32. *HP Commons 1754-90*, iii. 659, citing BL, Add. MS 30873, f. 146.
33. *Diaries*, 217; *London Chronicle*, 26-29 April 1788.
34. BL, Add. MS 30866, ff. 167-9.
35. *Wilkes Letters*, iv. 23.
36. *Wilkes Letters*, iv. 66.
37. *Wilkes Letters*, iv. 139.
38. *Wilkes Letters*, iv. 105.
39. Gowrley, *Domestic Space in Britain*, 73-74.
40. *Wilkes Letters*, iv. 48, 85.
41. *Wilkes Letters*, iv. 16.
42. Gowrley, *Domestic Space in Britain*, 81.
43. *Wilkes Letters*, iv. 33, 102.
44. BL, Add. MS 30866, f. 168; Cash, *Wilkes*, 388.
45. *Diaries*, 225.
46. BL, Add. MS 30893.
47. BL, Add. MS 30893, f. 18.
48. *Wilkes Letters*, iv. 87.
49. *Wilkes Letters*, iv. 20.
50. BL, Add. MS 30893, f. 21.
51. *Wilkes Letters*, iv. 26.
52. *Wilkes Letters*, iii. 263.
53. BL, Add. MS 30895, f. 3.
54. *Public Advertiser*, 15 January 1791.
55. *Wilkes Letters*, iii. 301, 304-5.
56. *Wilkes Letters*, iii. 321.
57. *Survey of London*, xl. 148-9.
58. A.M.W. Stirling, *Macdonald of the Isles: a Romance of the Past and Present* (London: John Murray, 1913), 114.
59. *Public Advertiser*, 8 January 1791.
60. *Gazetteer and New Daily Advertiser*, 24 January 1791.
61. Beinecke Library, GEN MSS 89, C3099, Wilkes to Dilly, 21 June 1791.

62. *Diaries*, 223, 225, 228, 230, 241, 252, 253, 254, 259, 262, 271, 274.
63. *Diaries*, 235.
64. Trench, *Patriot*, 329, 348-9.
65. Julia Zucchetti, 'The "Redeeming Feature" of John Wilkes' Life: A Study of Polly' (McGill University MA, 2022).
66. Matthew Adam, *Teaching Classics in English Schools 1500-1840* (Newcastle: Cambridge Scholars, 2015), 75.
67. *Models of Familiar Letters, in English, French, and Italian; with numerous examples of classical and commercial letters and topics for the exercise of students*, ed. David Blair (London, 1814), 154.
68. *Lloyd's Evening Post*, 27-29 November 1797; *General Evening Post*, 28-30 November 1797.
69. *Diaries*, 23.
70. *Lloyd's Evening Post*, 20-22 December 1797.
71. *General Evening Post*, 21-23 December 1797.
72. *Lloyd's Evening Post*, 25-27 December 1797.
73. *Lloyd's Evening Post*, 25-27 December 1797; *General Evening Post*, 26-28 December 1797; *London Evening Post*, 26-28 December 1797.
74. *General Evening Post*, 21-23 December 1797; *Lloyd's Evening Post*, 25-27 December 1797.
75. BM 1868,0808.4324. *Daniel in the Lion's Den*. Heaton Wilkes features on the right of the design, holding a sheet with Magna Carta written on it and complaining at not being allowed to visit his brother in the Tower.
76. *London Packet or New England Post*, 27-29 December 1797.
77. *Correspondence*, v. 94-97.
78. *Correspondence*, v. 92.
79. *London Chronicle*, 4-6 January 1798.
80. Conor Cruise O'Brien, *The Great Melody: a thematic biography of Edmund Burke* (London: Sinclair-Stevenson, 1992), 591.
81. *Correspondence*, v. 102.
82. *Wilkes Letters*, i. 10.

Epilogue

1. *Times*, 24 Nov. 1797.
2. BM, 1868,0808.5261.
3. BM, M.4741.
4. *Historical and the Posthumous Memoirs of Sir Nathaniel William Wraxall 1772-1784 (5 vols.,, 1884)*, ii. 49.
5. *Caius Valerius Catullus. Recensuit Iohannes Wilkes, Anglus* (1788).
6. Θεοφραστου Χαρακτηρες ἠθικοι. *Johannes ... Wilkes ... recensuit (Theophrasti ... capita duo hactenus anecdota quae ... edidit J. C. Amadutius* (1790); *The Letters of Sir Joshua Reynolds*, ed. John Ingamells and John Edgcumbe (Yale, 2000), 209-10

Endnotes

7. Nicholas Rogers, *Whigs and Cities: Popular Politics in the Age of Walpole and Pitt* (Oxford: Oxford University Press, 1989), 205, 214.
8. *Wraxall Memoirs*, i. 331.
9. Hansard, 648: column 57WH; 726: column 450.
10. *Lord Granville Leveson Gower (first Earl Granville) Private Correspondence 1781-1821*, ed. Castalia Countess Granville (2 vols., London; Murray, 1917), i. 484.
11. PA, ERM/18/1.
12. *The life and political writings of John Wilkes* (Birmingham, 1769); J.S. Watson, *Biographies of John Wilkes and William Cobbett* ... (Edinburgh and London, 1870); P.H. Fitzgerald, *The Life and Times of John Wilkes, M.P., Lord Mayor of London and Chamberlain* (2 vols., 1888); Alexander Meyrick Broadley, *Brother John Wilkes, M.P.; alderman, chamberlain and lord mayor of London, as freemason, 'Buck', 'Leech', and 'Beefsteak'* (1914); Horace William Bleackley, *Life of John Wilkes* (1917); Owen Aubrey Sherrard, *A Life of John Wilkes* (London: George Allen and Unwin, 1930); Raymond Postgate, *That Devil Wilkes* (1956); Ian R. Christie, *Wilkes, Wyvill and Reform: The Parliamentary Reform Movement in British Politics, 1760–1785* (1962); Charles Chevenix Trench, *Portrait of a Patriot: a biography of John Wilkes* (1962); George Rudé, *Wilkes and Liberty: A Social Study of 1763 to 1774* (1962); Hyman Shapiro, *John Wilkes and Parliament* (London: Longman, 1972); Louis Kronenberger, *The Extraordinary Mr Wilkes* (1974); P.D.G. Thomas, *John Wilkes: A Friend To Liberty* (1996); John Sainsbury, *John Wilkes: the Lives of a Libertine* (2006); Arthur H. Cash, *John Wilkes: The Scandalous Father of Civil Liberty* (2006).
13. Penelope J. Corfield, *The Georgians: The Deeds and Misdeeds of 18th-Century Britain* (London and New Haven: Yale University Press, 2022), 197.
14. PRONI, T3019/5723, 5774.
15. BL, Add. MS 30895.
16. G.O. Trevelyan, *The Early History of Charles James Fox* (New York: Harper and Brothers, 1881), 140. The earliest notice has Gladstone suggesting that Wilkes deserved to be 'ranked amongst the very first of the champions of English freedom'. See the *Hastings and St Leonard's Times*, 9 February 1878. My thanks to Martin Spychal for this reference.
17. BL, Add. MS 30865A, f. 2.

Bibliography

Primary Sources
Manuscript
Bedfordshire Archives
L30/17/2/17 Wrest Park Papers

Beinecke Library, New Haven
GEN MSS 89 Boswell Papers
OSB MSS File 16120

Bibliothèque Nationale Francaise
MS Francaise 11359

British Library, London
Add. 30866, 30867, 30869, 30871, 30873, 30877, 30886, 30892, 30895, 30897 (Wilkes Papers)
Add. 32735, 32893, 32947, 32955, 32959, 32960 (Newcastle Papers)
Add. 41355 (Martin Papers)

Derbyshire Record Office
D239 M/F 8244 (Fitzherbert of Tissington Papers)

Hampshire Archives
9M73 (Harris, Earl of Malmesbury Papers)
21M57 (Agar Family Papers)

History of Parliament Trust, London
Newdigate Diary (copy in the 1715-1754 archive)

Lewis Walpole Library, Farmington, Connecticut
MSS 38, box 1, folder 41
MSS Misc. box 72, folder 52

Bibliography

London Metropolitan Archives
CLC/518/MS02892
CLC/518/MS14176/1
CLC/521/MS00214
MS 31900
SC/GL/NOB/C/1078/41

National Library of Scotland
MS 16524
MS 16728
MS 16732
MS 17499 (Saltoun)

Oxford History Centre
J xxvi/b/4 (Diary of Viscount Villiers)

Parliamentary Archives
ERM/18/1
HL/PO/JO/10/1/408/87
HL/PO/JO/10/1/511/1358
HL/PO/RO/1/131

Public Record Office of Northern Ireland
D2924 (Rawdon Papers)
T3019 (Wilmot Papers)
T3428 (Walsingham Papers)
T3429 (Hotham Papers)

The National Archives, London
KB 7/6 King's Bench Papers
KB 33/5/7 King's Bench Papers
PRO 30/8 Chatham Papers
PROB 11/344/59 will of Luke Wilkes
PROB 11/362/50 will of John Heaton
PROB 11/635/375 will of Jeremiah Dyson
PROB 11/804/292 will of John Heaton
PROB 11/816/212 will of Matthew Leeson
PROB 11/862/393 will of Israel Wilkes
PROB 11/1302 /42 will of John Wilkes
PROB 11/1372 /123 will of Mary (Polly) Wilkes
SP 37/2/62-3, 64, 66, 68, 70
SP 37/7
TS 11/879
TS 11/923

University of Nottingham Library
PwF 2750 (Portland Papers)

Warwickshire County Record Office
L6/1360 (Lucy Papers)

William L. Clements Library, Ann Arbor
Wilkes MSS

Newspapers and Periodicals
Aberdeen Press and Journal
Adams's Weekly Courant
Aris's Birmingham Gazette
Bingley's London Journal
Chester Chronicle or Commercial Intelligencer
Court and City Register or Gentleman's Complete Annual Calendar, For the Year 1775
Craftsman or Say's Weekly Journal
Daily Advertiser
Daily Courant
Daily Gazetteer
Daily Journal
Daily Post
Derby Mercury
Gazetteer and London Daily Advertiser
Gazetteer and New Daily Advertiser
Gloucester Journal
Independent Chronicle
Leeds Intelligencer
Lloyd's Evening Post
London Chronicle
London Daily Post and General Advertiser
London Evening Post
London Packet or New England Post
Middlesex Journal
Morning Chronicle
Morning Post
North Briton
Oxford Journal
Political Register (1768)
Public Advertiser
Public Ledger
Remembrancer
St James's Chronicle or the British Evening Post
Whitehall Evening Post
The World
World and Fashionable Advertiser

Printed
The Adventures, Voyages, and Travels, of Two famous candidates, In Search of Discoveries towards the North Pole. (to the Tune of Wilkes's Wriggle.) (Newcastle, 1774)
An Answer to the Observations on the Papers Relative to the rupture with Spain... (1762)
A Full Exposition of a Pamphlet entitled, Observations on the Papers Relative to the rupture with Spain... (1762)
Reminiscences of Henry Angelo, with memories of his late father and friends... (2 vols., 1830)

Bibliography

Beaven, Alfred, *The aldermen of the City of London, temp. Henry III - [1912], with notes on the parliamentary representation of the city* (2 vols., London: Eden Fisher, 1908-1913)

Correspondence of John, fourth Duke of Bedford, selected from the originals at Woburn Abbey, ed. Lord John Russell (3 vols., London: Longman, 1842)

How Bedfordshire Voted, 1735-1784: The Evidence of Local Documents and Poll Books, ed. James Collett-White (Bedfordshire Historical Record Society XC, Woodbridge, 2012)

Berkeley's Principles and Dialogues: Background Source Materials, ed. C.J. McCracken and I.C. Tipton (Cambridge: Cambridge University Press, 2000)

Life and Letters of George Berkeley, formerly bishop of Cloyne, ed. Alexander Campbell Fraser (Oxford: Oxford University Press, 1871)

Bickham, George *The Beauties of Stow (1750)*, ed. George B. Clark (Augustan Reprint Society, Los Angeles, 1977)

Boswell's London Journal, 1762-63, ed. Frederick A. Pottle (New York, London, Toronto, 1950)

Boswell, James, *Life of Johnson*, ed. Sir Sydney Roberts (2 vols., London: J.M. Dent, 1960)

Brettell, Thomas, *A Topographical and Historical Guide to the Isle of Wight: comprising authentic accounts of the antiquities, natural productions and romantic scenery* (London: Leigh & co., 1840)

Correspondence of Edmund Burke, volume II (1768-1774), ed. Lucy Sutherland (Cambridge: Cambridge University Press, 1960)

Mr Edmund Burke's Speeches at his arrival at Bristol and at the conclusion of the Poll (1774)

The Correspondence of John Campbell MP, with his Family, Henry Fox, Sir Robert Walpole and the Duke of Newcastle, 1734-71, ed. J.E. Davies (*Parliamentary History: Texts and Studies* 8, Wiley, 2014)

Carlyle, Alexander, *Autobiography of the Rev. Dr. Alexander Carlyle, Minister of Inveresk, containing memorials of the men and events of his time* (Boston: Ticknor and Fields, 1861)

Caius Valerius Catullus. Recensuit Iohannes Wilkes, Anglus (1788)

Cavendish, Sir Henry, *Sir Henry Cavendish's debates of the House of Commons, [1768-1771]: during the thirteenth Parliament of Great Britain, commonly called the unreported Parliament: to which are appended illustrations of the parliamentary history of the reign of George the Third: consisting of unpublished letters, private journals, memoirs &c* (2 vols., London; Longman, 1841-1843)

Correspondence of William Pitt, Earl of Chatham, ed. John Pitt, earl of Chatham (4 vols., London: John Murray, 1838-40)

Lord Chesterfield's Letters, ed. David Roberts (Oxford: Oxford University Press, 1992)

Cobbett, William, *Cobbett's parliamentary history of England : from the Norman conquest in 1066 to the year 1803* (36 vols., London: T.C. Hansard, 1806-1820)

Journals of the House of Commons

Memoir of Brass Crosby Esq. Alderman of the City of London and Lord Mayor, 1770-1771 (1829)

W. Prideaux Courtney, *Parliamentary Representation of Cornwall to 1832* (London, 1889)

The Devonshire Diary: William Cavendish Fourth Duke of Devonshire Memoranda on State of Affairs 1759-1762, ed. Peter D. Brown and Karl W. Schweizer (Camden 4th series 27, London, 1982)

The Eighteenth Century Constitution: Documents and Commentary, ed. E.N. Williams (Cambridge, 1960)
Correspondence of Adam Ferguson, ed. Vincenzo Merolle (2 vols., London: William Pickering, 1995)
Fitzmaurice, E.G.P., *Life of William Earl of Shelburne* (2 vols., London: Macmillan, 1912)
Gay, John, *Poems on Several Occasions* (London, 1737)
The correspondence of King George the third from 1760 to December 1783: printed from the original papers in the Royal Archives at Windsor Castle, ed. Sir John Fortescue (6 vols., London; Macmillan, 1927-28)
Letters from George III to Lord Bute 1756-1766, ed. R. Sedgwick (London: Macmillan, 1939)
Private Letters of Edward Gibbon (1753-1794), ed. Rowland E. Prothero (London: Murray, 1896)
Autobiography and political correspondence of Augustus Henry, third Duke of Grafton from hitherto unpublished documents in the possession of his family, ed. W.R. Anson (London: John Murray, 1898)
Graham, John A. *Memoirs of John Horne Tooke Together with his Valuable Speeches and Writings...* (New York, 1828)
The Autobiography and Correspondence of Mary Granville (Mrs Delany): with interesting reminiscences of King George III and Queen Charlotte, ed. Lady Llanover (3 vols., London: Richard Bentley, 1862)
Additional Grenville Papers 1763-1765, ed. J.R.G. Tomlinson (Manchester: Manchester University Press, 1962)
The Grenville Papers; being the correspondence of Richard Grenville, Earl Temple, K.G., and the Right Hon. George Grenville, their friends and contemporaries, ed. W.J. Smith (4 vols., London: John Murray, 1852-3)
The Papers of John Hatsell, Clerk of the House of Commons, ed. Peter J. Aschenbrenner and Colin Lee (Camden Fifth Series LIX, Cambridge 2020)
Hatton, Edward *A New View of London* (2 vols., London, 1708)
Historical Manuscripts Commission: The manuscripts of the Earl of Carlisle, [formerly] preserved at Castle Howard (London: H.M.S.O., 1897)
Historical Manuscripts Commission: Report on the manuscripts of the Marquess of Lothian, preserved at Blicking Hall, Norfolk (London: H.M.S.O., 1905)
Historical Manuscripts Commission: Manuscripts of the Marquess Townshend (London: H.M.S.O., 1887)
Hurd, Richard *The Works of the Right Reverend William Warburton, D.D., Lord Bishop of Gloucester (XIII)* (London, 1841)
Howell, T.B., *A complete collection of state trials and proceedings for high treason and other crimes and misdemeanors from the earliest period to the year 1783* (34 vols., London; T.C. Hansard, 1816-28)
The Letters of David Hume, vol. 1, 1727-1765, ed. J.Y.T. Greig (Oxford: Oxford University Press, 1932)
The Jenkinson Papers 1760-1766, ed. N.S. Juncker (London: Macmillan, 1949)
Jesse, John Heneage, *George Selwyn and his Contemporaries, with memoirs and notes* (4 vols., London: Richard Bentley, 1843-4)
The Letters of Sir William Jones, ed. Garland Cannon (2 vols., Oxford: Oxford University Press, 1970)
Lettres inédites de Suard a Wilkes, ed. Gabriel Bonno (University of California Publications in Modern Philosophy, xv. 1932)
Lord Granville Leveson Gower (first Earl Granville) Private Correspondence 1781-1821, ed. Castalia Countess Granville (2 vols., London: Murray, 1917)
Journals of the House of Lords

Bibliography

The Correspondence of Catharine Macaulay, ed. Karen Green (Oxford: Oxford University Press, 2020)

Models of Familiar Letters, in English, French, and Italian; with numerous examples of classical and commercial letters and topics for the exercise of students, ed. David Blair (London, 1814)

The London Letters of Samuel Molyneux, 1712-13, ed. P. Holden (London Topographical Society 172, 2011)

The Diary of Sylas Neville 1767-1788, ed. B. Cozens-Hardy (Oxford: Oxford University Press, 1950)

Noorthouck, John *A New History of London Including Westminster and Southwark* (London, 1773)

Observations on the Papers Relative to the rupture with Spain (1762)

Phillips, Henry Laverock, *Annals of the Worshipful Company of Joiners of the City of London* (London, 1915)

Correspondence of Richard Price, ed. W.B. Peach and D.O. Thomas (3 vols., Cardiff: University of Wales Press, 1983-1994)

Pyle, Edmund, *Memoirs of a Royal Chaplain, 1729-1763: the correspondence of Edmund Pyle, D.D. Chaplain in ordinary to George II, with Samuel Kerrich D.D. vicar of Dersingham, Rector of Wolferton, and Rector of West Newton*, ed. Albert Hartshorne (London: Bodley Head, 1905)

Reynolds, Frederick, *The Life and Times of Frederick Reynolds by Himself* (2 vols., London, 1826)

The Letters of Sir Joshua Reynolds, ed. John Ingamells and John Edgcumbe (New Haven: Yale University Press, 2000)

The Correspondence of the Dukes of Richmond & Newcastle 1724-1750, ed. Timothy J. McCann (Sussex Record Society 73, 1984)

Diary, Reminiscences, and Correspondence of Henry Crabb Robinson, ed. Thomas Sadler (3 vols., London: Macmillan, 1869)

Stephen, Alexander, *Memoirs of John Horne Tooke* (2 vols., London: J. Johnson and Co., 1813)

Recollections of R.J.S. Stevens: an organist in Georgian London, ed. Mark Argent (Carbondale and Edwardsville: Southern Illinois University Press, 1992)

Summary Justice in the City, ed. Greg T. Smith (London Record Society xlviii, 2013)

Swift, Jonathan, *Gulliver's Travels*, ed. Peter Dixon and John Chalker (London: Penguin, 1985)

THRALIANA, The Diary of Mrs Hester Lynch Thrale (later Mrs Piozzi) 1776-1809, ed. K.C. Balderston (2 vols., Oxford: Oxford University Press, 1951)

The Memoirs and Speeches of James, 2nd Earl Waldegrave 1742-1763, ed. J.C.D. Clark (Cambridge: Cambridge University Press, 1988)

Walpole, Horace, *Memoirs of the reign of King George the Third*, ed. Derek Jarrett (4 vols., London and New Haven: Yale University Press, 2000)

Walpole, Horace, *Memoirs of the Reign of King George the Third*, ed. Sir Denis Le Marchant (4 vols., London; Richard Bentley, 1845)

Walpole, Horace, *The Yale edition of Horace Walpole's correspondence* (48 vols., New Haven; Yale University Press, 1937-1983)

Warburton, William, *Letters from a late Eminent Prelate to one of his Friends* (London: T. Cadell and W. Davies, 2nd edn., 1809)

John Wilkes, Patriot, An Unfinished Autobiography, ed. R. des Habits (Harrow: William F. Taylor, 1888)

John Wilkes: The Aylesbury Years (1747-1763) His Collected Letters to his Agent, John Dell, ed. Alan Dell (Buckinghamshire Papers 17, Buckingham, 2008)

The Controversial Letters of John Wilkes, Esq. The Rev John Horne, And Their Principal Adherents (London, 1771)

The Correspondence of the late John Wilkes with his Friends, printed from the original manuscripts, in which are introduced Memoirs of his Life, ed. John Almon, 5 vols. (London, 1805)

The Correspondence of John Wilkes and Charles Churchill, ed. E.H. Weatherly (New York: Columbia University Press, 1954)

The Diaries of John Wilkes 1770-1797, ed. Robin Eagles (London Record Society XLIX, Woodbridge, 2014)

The Genuine Interesting Speech of the Right Hon. Lord Mayor Upon the Very Important Subject of the Middlesex Elections, Delivered on Wednesday, Feb. 22, 1775, in the House of Commons (London, 1775)

Some Bath Love Letters of John Wilkes, Esq., ed. Emanuel Green (Bath, 1918)

Letters from the 1774 to the Year 1796, of John Wilkes Esq. Addressed to his Daughter, the late Miss Wilkes (4 vols., London, 1804)

WILKES and FREEDOM: A New Ballad (1768)

[Wilkes, John], *The Genuine Interesting Speech of the Right Hon. Lord Mayor Upon the Very Important Subject of the Middlesex Elections, Delivered on Wednesday, Feb. 22, 1775, in the House of Commons* (London, 1775)

[Wilkes, John], *Observations on the Papers Relative to the rupture with Spain* (1762)

Θεοφραστου Χαρακτηρες ήθικοι. *Johannes ... Wilkes ... recensuit* (Theophrasti ... capita duo hactenus anecdota quae ... edidit J. C. Amadutius (1790)

Wraxall, Nathaniel, *The Historical and the Posthumous Memoirs of Sir Nathaniel William Wraxall 1772-1784*, ed. Henry B. Wheatley (5 vols., London: Bickers, 1884)

Secondary Literature

Books

Adam, Matthew, *Teaching Classics in English Schools 1500-1840* (Newcastle: Cambridge Scholars, 2015)

Almeroth-William, Thomas, *City of Beasts: How animals shaped Georgian London* (Manchester: Manchester University Press, 2019)

Andrew, Donna T., *Philanthropy and Police: London Charity in the Eighteenth Century* (Princeton N.J.: Princeton University Press, 1989)

Arnold, Walter, *The Life and Death of the Sublime Society of Beef Steaks* (London: Bradbury, Evans & Co., 1871)

Ashe, Geoffrey, *The Hell-Fire Clubs: A History of Anti-Morality* (Stroud: Alan Sutton, rev. edn. 2000)

Aston, Nigel and Campbell Orr, Clarissa, ed., *An Enlightenment Statesman in Whig Britain: Lord Shelburne in Context, 1737-1805* (Woodbridge: Boydell, 2011)

Banat, Gabriel, *The Chevalier de Saint-Georges: Virtuoso of the Sword and Bow* (New York: Pendragon Press, 2006)

Banks, Stephen, *A Polite Exchange of Bullets: The duel and the English Gentleman 1750-1850* (Woodbridge: Boydell, 2010)

Barker-Benfield, G.J., *The Culture of Sensibility: Sex and Society in 18th-Century Britain* (Chicago and London: University of Chicago Press, 1992)

Bauman, Richard, *Human Rights in Ancient Rome* (London and New York: Routledge, 2000)

Black, Jeremy, *The British Abroad: The Grand Tour in the Eighteenth Century* (Stroud: Alan Sutton, 1992)

Bibliography

Blanning, T.C.W., *The Culture of Power and the Power of Culture: Old Regime Europe 1660-1789* (Oxford: Oxford University Press, 2002)

Bleackley, Horace, *Life of Wilkes* (London: John Lane, 1917)

Brewer, J., *Party Ideology and Popular Politics at the Accession of George III* (Cambridge: Cambridge University Press, 1976)

Brewer, J., *The Pleasures of the Imagination: English Culture in the Eighteenth Century* (London, 1997)

Brewer, J. and Styles, John (ed.), *An Ungovernable People: the English and their law in the seventeenth and eighteenth centuries* (1980)

Brooke, John, *George III* (London: Constable and Co., 1972)

Bucholz, Robert O. and Ward, Joseph P., *London: A Social and Cultural History, 1550-1750* (Cambridge: Cambridge University Press, 2012)

Bullard, Paddy, *The Oxford Handbook of Eighteenth-Century Satire* (Oxford: Oxford University Press, 2019)

Carlisle, Nicholas, *Collections for a History of the Ancient Family of Bland* (London, 1826)

Campbell Ross, Ian, *Laurence Sterne: A Life* (Oxford: Oxford University Press, 2001)

Cannon, John, *Aristocratic Century* (Cambridge: Cambridge University Press, 1984)

Cash, Arthur H., *John Wilkes: The Scandalous Father of Civil Liberty* (London and New Haven: Yale University Press, 2006)

Christie, Ian, *Myth and Reality in late Eighteenth-Century British Politics and other papers* (Berkeley and Los Angeles: University of California Press, 1970)

Christie, Ian, *Wilkes, Wyvill and Reform: the parliamentary reform movement in British Politics, 1760-1785* (London: Macmillan, 1962)

Clark, Anna, *Scandal: The Sexual Politics of the British Constitution* (Princeton: Princeton University Press, 2004)

Clifford, James L., *Hester Lynch Piozzi (Mrs Thrale)* (rev. edn. Oxford: Oxford University Press, 1968)

Cockayne, Emily, *Hubbub: Filth, Noise & Stench in England* (London and New Haven: Yale University Press, 2007)

Colley, Linda, *Britons: Forging the Nation, 1707-1837* (London and New Haven: Yale University Press, 1992)

Colley, Linda, *In Defiance of Oligarchy: The Tory Party 1714-1760* (Cambridge Cambridge University Press, 1982)

Constantine, David, *Fields of Fire: A Life of Sir William Hamilton* (London: Weidenfeld and Nicolson, 2001)

Corfield, Penelope J., *The Georgians: The Deeds and Misdeeds of 18th-Century Britain* (London and New Haven: Yale University Press, 2022)

Dale, Iain (ed.), *The Prime Ministers* (London: Hodder and Stoughton, 2020)

Davis, David Brion, *The Problem of Slavery in the Age of Revolution* (Oxford: Oxford University Press, 1999)

Dent, Robert K., *The Making of Birmingham: Being a History of the Rise and Growth of the Midland Metropolis* (Birmingham, 1894)

Dickinson, H.T., *Liberty and Property: Political Ideology in Eighteenth-Century Britain* (London: Weidenfeld and Nicolson, 1977)

Dillon, Patrick, *The Much-lamented Death of Madam Geneva: the Eighteenth-century Gin Craze* (London: Review, 2002)

Duffy, Christopher, *The '45: Bonnie Prince Charlie and the Untold Story of the Jacobite Rising* (London: Cassell, 2003)

Eagles, Robin, *Francophilia in English Society 1748-1783* (Basingstoke: Macmillan, 2000)

Eagles Robin and Schaich, Michael, ed., *Scribal News in Politics and Parliament, 1660-1760* (*Parliamentary History* xli. pt. 1, 2022)

Earle, Peter, *The Making of the English Middle Class: Business, Society and Family Life in London, 1660-1730* (Berkeley and Los Angeles: University of California Press, 1989)

Elofson, W.M., *The Rockingham Connection and the Second Founding of the Whig Party, 1768-1773* (Montreal and Kingston: McGill Queen's University Press, 1996)

Farguson, Julie, *Visualising Protestant Monarchy: Ceremony, Art and Politics after the Glorious Revolution (1689-1714)* (Woodbridge: Boydell, 2021)

Fernie, Ewan, *Shakespeare for Freedom: Why the Plays Matter* (Cambridge: Cambridge University Press, 2017)

Fitzgerald, Percy Hetherington, *The Life and Times of John Wilkes, MP, Lord Mayor of London and Chamberlain* (London, 1888)

Flavell, Julie, *When London was Capital of America* (Yale, 2010)

Franklin, Michael J., *Orientalist Jones; Sir William Jones, Poet, Lawyer and Linguist, 1746-1794* (Oxford: Oxford University Press, 2011)

Gauci, Perry, *William Beckford: First Prime Minister of the London Empire* (London and New Haven: Yale University Press, 2013)

George, M. Dorothy, *London Life in the Eighteenth Century* (London: Penguin, 1992)

Gibbs, Robert, *A History of Aylesbury with its Borough and Hundreds...* (Aylesbury, 1885)

Gordon, Daniel, *Citizens without Sovereignty: Equality and Sociability in French Thought 1670-1789* (Princeton: Princeton University Press, 1994)

Gowrley, Freya, *Domestic Space in Britain, 1750-1840* (London: Bloomsbury, 2022)

Greig, Hannah, *The Beau Monde: Fashionable Society in Georgian London* (Oxford: Oxford University Press, 2013)

Hart, Lloyd, *John Wilkes and the Foundling Hospital at Aylesbury* (Aylesbury: HM&M, 1979)

Hatton, Ragnhild, *George I* (London and New Haven: Yale University Press, 2001)

Haywood, Ian, and Seed, John, *The Gordon Riots: Politics, Culture and Insurrection in Late Eighteenth-Century Britain* (Cambridge, 2012)

Hibbert, Christopher, *The Grand Tour* (London: Methuen, 1987)

Hitchcock, Tim and Shoemaker, Robert, *London Lives: Poverty, Crime and the Making of a Modern City 1690-1800* (Cambridge: Cambridge University Press, 2015)

Holmes, Geoffrey and Szechi, Daniel, *The Age of Oligarchy: Pre-Industrial Britain 1722-1783* (London: Longman, 1993)

Hoock, Holger, *The King's Artists: The Royal Academy of Arts and the Politics of British Culture 1760-1840* (Oxford: Oxford University Press, 2003)

Innes, Joanna, *Inferior Politics: Social Problems and Social Policies in Eighteenth-Century Britain* (Oxford: Oxford University Press, 2009)

Ingram, Robert G., Peacey, Jason and Barber, Alex W. *Freedom of speech, 1500-1850* (Manchester: Manchester University Press, 2020)

Jensen, Merrill, *The Founding of a Nation: A History of the American Revolution 1763-1776* (Indianapolis/Cambridge: Hackett, 1968)

Kavanagh, Declan, *Effeminate Years: Literature, Politics and Aesthetics in Mid-Eighteenth-Century Britain* (Lewisburg: Bucknell University Press, 2017)

Kerr-Ritchie, Jeffrey R., Rebellious Passage: The Creole Revolt and America's Coastal Slave Trade (Cambridge: Cambridge University Press, 2019)

Bibliography

Kors, Alan Charles, *D'Holbach's Coterie: An Enlightenment in Paris* (Princeton: Princeton University Press, 1976)

Kronenberger, Louis, *The Extraordinary Mr Wilkes: His Life and Times* (London: New English Library, 1974)

Langford, Paul, *A Polite and Commercial People: England 1727-1783* (Oxford: Oxford University Press, 1989)

Langford, Paul, *Englishness Identified: Manners and Character 1650-1850* (Oxford: Oxford University Press, 2000)

Langford, Paul, *Public Life and the Propertied Englishman 1689-1798* (Oxford: Oxford University Press, 1991)

Leslie, Charles Robert, and Taylor, Tom, *Life and Times of Sir Joshua Reynolds: with notices of some of his contemporaries* (2 vols., London: John Murray, 1865)

Leslie-Melville, R., *The Life and Work of Sir John Fielding* (London; Lincoln Williams, 1934)

Lincoln, Margarette, *Trading in War: London's Maritime World in the Age of Cook and Nelson* (London and New Haven: Yale University Press, 2018)

Lloyd Hart, V.E., *John Wilkes and the Foundling Hospital at Aylesbury, 1759-1768* (Aylesbury: H.M.&M., 1979)

Lodge, Samuel, *The Home of the Champions, with some account of the Marmion and Dymoke families* (London, 2nd edn., 1894)

Lustig, Mary Lou, *Privilege and Prerogative: New York's Provincial Elite* (Madison, Teaneck: Associated University Presses, 1995)

McCahill, Michael *The House of Lords in the Age of George III (1760-1811)* (*Parliamentary History Texts and Studies* 3, Chichester: Wiley, 2009)

McCracken, C.J. and Tipton, I.C., ed., *Berkeley's Principles and Dialogues: Background Source Materials* (Cambridge: Cambridge University Press, 2000)

McCormack, Matthew, *The Independent Man: Citizenship and Gender Politics in Georgian England* (Manchester: Manchester University Press, 2005)

McIntyre, Ian, *Garrick* (London: Penguin, 1999)

Merriam, Carol, and Sainsbury, John, 'The Life of John Wilkes', *Studies in Voltaire and the Eighteenth Century*, 6 (2008)

Millingen, J.G., *The History of Duelling Including Narratives of the Most Remarkable Personal Encounters that have taken place from the Earliest Period to the Present Time* (2 vols., London: Richard Bentley, 1841)

Mitchell, L.G., *Charles James Fox* (Oxford: Oxford University Press, 1992)

Monod, Paul Kleber, *Jacobitism and the English People, 1688-1788* (Cambridge: Cambridge University Press, 1989)

Moore, Peter, *Life, Liberty and the Pursuit of Happiness: Britain and the American Dream 1740-1776* (London: Chatto and Windus, 2023)

Morel, Thierry, 'Houghton Revisited: An Introduction', in *Houghton Revisited: the Walpole Masterpieces from Catherine the Great's Hermitage* (London, 2013)

Mori, Jennifer, *William Pitt and the French Revolution 1785-1795* (Edinburgh: Keele University Press, 1997)

Namier, (Sir) Lewis, *The Structure of Politics at the Accession of George III* (London: St Martin's Press, 1968)

Namier, Sir Lewis, and Brooke, J. eds., *The History of Parliament: The House of Commons 1754-1790*, 3 vols. (London, 1964)

Newman, Gerald, *The Rise of English Nationalism: A Cultural History 1740-1830* (London: Weidenfeld and Nicolson, 1987)

Nichols, R.H. and Wray, F.A., *The History of the Foundling Hospital* (London, 1935)

Nicoli, Laura, *The Great Protector of Wits: Baron d'Holbach and his Time* (Leiden: Brill, 2022)
O'Brien, Conor Cruise, *The Great Melody: a thematic biography of Edmund Burke* (London; Sinclair-Stevenson, 1992)
O'Gorman, Frank *Voters, Patrons and Parties: The Unreformed Electorate of Hanoverian England, 1734-1832* (Oxford: Oxford University Press, 1989)
Olson, Alison, *The Radical Duke: Career and Correspondence of Charles Lennox third duke of Richmond* (Oxford, 1961)
Peach, R.E.M., *The Life and Times of Ralph Allen of Prior Park* (London: D. Nutt, 1895)
Poser, Norman S., *The Birth of Modern Theatre: Rivalry, Riots, and Romance in the Age of Garrick* (London and New York: Routledge, 2019)
Poser, Norman S., *Lord Mansfield: Justice in the Age of Reason* (Montreal and Kingston: McGill Queen's University Press, 2013)
Postgate, R., *That Devil Wilkes* (London: Dobson Books, 1956)
Prest, Wilfrid, *William Blackstone: Law and Letters in the Eighteenth Century* (Oxford: Oxford University Press, 2008)
Rideing, William H., *Young Folks' History of London* (Boston: Estes and Lauriat, 1884)
Ritchie, Stefka, *The Reformist Ideas of Samuel Johnson* (Newcastle: Cambridge Scholars, 2017)
Robinson, D.H., *The Idea of Europe and the Origins of the American Revolution* (Oxford: Oxford University press, 2020)
Rodger, N.A.M., *The Insatiable Earl: A Life of John Montagu, 4th Earl of Sandwich* (London: HarperCollins, 1993)
Rogers, Nicholas, *Crowds, Culture, and Politics in Georgian Britain* (Oxford: Oxford University Press, 1998)
Rogers, Nicholas, *Whigs and Cities: Popular Politics in the Age of Walpole and Pitt* (Oxford: Oxford University Press, 1989)
Rolli, Chiara, *The Trial of Warren Hastings: Classical Oratory and Reception in the Eighteenth-Century England* (London: Bloomsbury, 2019)
Rubenhold, Hallie, *Lady Worsley's Whim: An Eighteenth-Century Tale of Sex, Scandal and Divorce* (London: Chatto and Windus, 2008)
Rudé, G., *Hanoverian London 1714-1808* (Berkeley and Los Angeles: University of California Press, 1971)
Rudé, G., *Ideology and Popular Protest* (Chapel Hill and London: University of North Carolina Press, 1980)
Rudé, G., *Wilkes and Liberty. A Social Study of 1763 to 1774* (Oxford: Oxford University Press, 1962)
Sainsbury, John, *John Wilkes: The Lives of a Libertine* (Aldershot: Ashgate, 2006)
Scott, David, *Leviathan: The Rise of Britain as a World Power* (London: HarperCollins, 2013)
Shapiro, Hyman, *John Wilkes and Parliament* (London: Longman, 1972)
Sher, Richard B., *Making Boswell's Life of Johnson: an author publisher and his support network* (Cambridge: Cambridge University Press, 2023)
Sherrard, Owen Aubrey, *A Life of John Wilkes* (London: George Allen and Unwin, 1930)
Simms, Brendan, *Three Victories and a Defeat: The Rise and Fall of the First British Empire* (London: Penguin, 2007)
Skjönsberg, Max, *The Persistence of Party: Ideas of Harmonious Discord in Eighteenth-Century Britain* (Cambridge: Cambridge University Press, 2021)
Skjönsberg, Max, *Catharine Macaulay: Political Writings* (Cambridge: Cambridge University Press, 2023)

Bibliography

Smith, Hannah, *Georgian Monarchy: Politics and Culture, 1714-1760* (Cambridge: Cambridge University Press, 2006)

Speck, W.A., *Stability and Strife: England 1714-1760* (2nd edn. London: Edward Arnold, 1980)

Stephens, Alexander, *Memoirs of John Horne Tooke* (2 vols., London, 1813)

Stirling, A.M.W., *Macdonald of the Isles: a Romance of the Past and Present* (London: John Murray, 1913),

Taylor, David Francis, *The Politics of Parody: A Literary History of Caricature, 1760-1830* (New Haven: Yale University Press, 2018)

Tharp, Lars, *Hogarth's China: Hogarth's Paintings and 18th-Century Ceramics* (London: Merrell Holberton, 1997)

Thomas, Keith, *In Pursuit of Civility: Manners and Civilization in Early Modern England* (London and New Haven: Yale University Press, 2018)

Thomas, P.D.G., *Lord North* (London: Allen Lane, 1976)

Thomas, P.D.G., *John Wilkes: A Friend to Liberty* (Oxford: Oxford University Press, 1996)

Thompson, Andrew C., *George II* (London and New Haven: Yale University Press, 2011)

Thompson, Andrew C., *Britain, Hanover and the Protestant Interest, 1688-1756* (Woodbridge: Boydell, 2006)

Trench, Charles Chevenix, *Portrait of a Patriot: A Biography of John Wilkes* (Edinburgh and London: William Blackwood and Sons, 1962)

Trevelyan, G.O., *The Early History of Charles James Fox* (New York: Harper and Brothers, 1881)

Uglow, Jenny, *Hogarth* (London: Faber, 1997)

White, Jerry, *London in the Eighteenth Century: A Great and Monstrous Thing* (London: Bodley Head, 2012),

Williams, Olivia, *Gin Glorious Gin: How Mother's Ruin Became the Spirit of London* (2014)

Williamson, George C., *Life and Works of Ozias Humphry, RA* (London, 1918)

Young, Charlotte, *Join Loyalty and Liberty: A History of the Worshipful Company of Joiners and Ceilers* (Stroud: Amberley, 2021)

Zaretsky, Robert, *Boswell's Enlightenment* (Cambridge MA and London: Harvard University Press, 2015)

Articles

Achilleos, Stella 'The Anacreontea and a Tradition of Refined Male Sociability', in *A Pleasing Sinne: Drink and Conviviality in 17th-Century England*, ed. Adam Smyth (Cambridge: Cambridge University Press, 2004)

Aston, Nigel 'The Court of George II: Lord Berkeley of Stratton's Perspective', *The Court Historian* xiii (2008)

Bertelsen, Lance 'The Education of Henry Sampson Woodfall, Newspaperman', in *Mentoring in Eighteenth-Century British Literature and Culture*, ed. Antony W. Lee (Abingdon; Routledge, 2016)

Bradley, James E. 'Parliament, Print Culture and Petitioning in late Eighteenth-Century England', *The Print Culture of Parliament 1600-1800*, ed. Jason Peacey (*Parliamentary History* xxvi, 2007)

Bradley, James E. 'The British Public and the American Revolution', *Britain and the American Revolution*, ed. H.T. Dickinson (Abingdon: Routledge, 1998)

Brewer, John 'The Wilkites and the Law: 1763-74: A Study of Radical Notions of Governance', *An Ungovernable People: the English and their Law in the*

Seventeenth and Eighteenth Centuries, ed. John Brewer and John Styles (New Brunswick, N.J: Rutgers University Press, 1980)

Broad, John 'Permanence and Impermanence in Housing Provision for the Eighteenth-Century Rural Poor in England', in *Investing in the Early Modern Built Environment: Europeans, Asians, Settlers and Indigenous Societies*, ed. Carole Shammas (Leiden and Boston: Brill, 2012)

Brunstrom, Conrad,' "Be Male and Female Still": An ABC of Hyperbolic Masculinity in the Eighteenth Century', *Presenting Gender: Changing Sex in Early-Modern Culture*, ed. Chris Mounsey (London: Associated University Presses, 2001)

Cannon, John 'Lord Shelburne's Ministry, 1782-3: "a very good list"', in *An Enlightenment Statesman in Whig Britain: Lord Shelburne in Context, 1737-1805*, ed. Nigel Aston and Clarissa Campbell Orr (Woodbridge: Boydell, 2011)

Carey, Brycchan ' "The Worse than Negro barbarity of the populace": Ignatius Sancho witnesses the Gordon Riots', in *The Gordon Riots Politics, Culture and Insurrection in Late Eighteenth-Century Britain* ed. Haywood and Seed

Colbourn, H. Trevor, 'A Pennsylvania Farmer at the Court of King George: John Dickinson's London Letters 1754-56', *Pennsylvania Magazine of History and Biography* lxxxiv (1962)

Conlin, Jonathan, 'Faire le Wilkes': the Chevalier D'Eon and the Wilkites, 1762-1775, *The Chevalier d'Eon and his Worlds: Gender, Espionage and Politics in the Eighteenth Century*, ed. S. Burrows, J. Conlin, R. Goulbourne, & V. Mainz (Continuum, 2010).

Conlin, Jonathan G.W., 'High Art and Low Politics: A New Perspective on John Wilkes', *Huntington Library Quarterly* lxiv (2011)

Conlin, Jonathan, 'Wilkes, the Chevalier D'Eon and 'the Dregs of Liberty': An Anglo-French Perspective on Ministerial Despotism, 1762–1771', *E.H.R.* cxx (2005)

Cruickshanks, Eveline, 'Ashby v. White: the case of the men of Aylesbury, 1701-4', *Party and Management in Parliament 1660-1784*, ed. Clyve Jones (Leicester: Leicester University Press, 1984)

Eagles, Robin, '"Got together in a riotous and tumultous manner": Crowds and the Palace of Westminster, c.1700-1800', JECS xliii (2020)

Eagles, Robin, '"I have Neither Interest nor Eloquence Sufficient to Prevail": the Duke of Shrewsbury and the Politics of Succession during the Reign of Anne', *eBLJ* 11 (2015)

Frith, Wendy, 'Sexuality and Politics in the Gardens at West Wycombe and Medmenham Abbey', *Bourgeois and Aristocratic Encounters in Garden Art, 1550-1850*, ed. Michel Conan (Washington: Dumbarton Oaks, 2002)

Grass, Elisabeth, 'The House and Estate of a Rich West Indian: Two Slaveholders in Eighteenth-Century East Anglia', *Politics and the English Country House, 1688-1800*, ed. Joan Coutu, Jon Stobart and Peter N. Lindfield (Montreal and Kingston: McGill-Queen's University Press 2023)

Haydon, Colin '"Popery at St. James's": the conspiracy theses of William Payne, Thomas Hollis, and Lord George Gordon', in *Conspiracies and Conspiracy Theory in Early Modern Europe from the Waldensians to the French Revolution*, ed. Barry Coward and Julian Swann (Abingdon: Routledge, 2004)

Hubbard, Hesketh, 'William Hogarth, the Founder of English Painting', *Journal of the Royal Society of Arts*, lxxx (1932)

Hubberstey, Jemima '"For the Owner I am Convinced Has Neither Much Taste or Genius": Jemima Marchioness Grey's Accounts of the Gardens at Stowe and Hagley', *Journal for Eighteenth-Century Studies*, xliv (2021)

Bibliography

Innes, Joanna 'The King's Bench Prison in the Later Eighteenth Century: Law, Authority and Order in a London Debtor's Prison', *An Ungovernable People*, ed. Brewer and Styles (1980)

Kavanagh, Declan, 'John Wilkes's "Closet": Hetero Privacy and the Annotation of Desire in An Essay on Woman', *Heteronormativity in Eighteenth-Century Literature and Culture*, ed. Ana de Freitas Boe and Abby Coykendall (Abingdon: Routledge, 2016)

Kelly, Paul, 'Constituents' Instructions to Members of Parliament in the Eighteenth Century', *Party and Management in Parliament 1660-1784*, ed. Clyve Jones (1984)

Lee, J. Patrick, 'The English Translations of Voltaire's La Pucelle', *British-French Exchanges in the 18th Century*, ed. K.H. Doig and D. Medlin (Newcastle: Cambridge Scholars, 2007)

Lowe, William C. 'Peers and Printers: The Beginnings of Sustained Press Coverage of the House of Lords in the 1770s', *Parliamentary History* vii (1988)

Navickas, Katrina, 'The Contested Right of Public Meeting in England from the Bill of Rights to the Public Order Acts', *Transactions of the Royal Historical Society*, 6th series, xxxii (2022)

Newman, Aubrey, 'Leicester House Politics, 1750-1760, from the papers of John, second earl of Egmont', *Camden Miscellany*, xxiii, 4th series 7 (London: Royal Historical Society, 1969)

Newman, Ian 'Becoming Institutional: The Case of the Anacreontic Society', in *Institutions of Literature 1700-1900: The Development of Literary Culture and Production*, ed. Jon Mee and Matthew Sangster (Cambridge: Cambridge University Press, 2022)

Pearson, Robin 'Fire, Property Insurance, and Perceptions of Risk in Eighteenth-Century Britain', in *The Appeal of Insurance*, ed. Geoffrey Clark, Gregory Anderson, Christian Thomann, and J. Matthias Graf von der Schulenberg (Toronto, 2010)

Sainsbury, John, 'John Wilkes, Debt, and Patriotism', *Journal of British Studies* xxxiv (1995)

Sainsbury, John, 'The Pro-Americans of London, 1769 to 1782', WMQ xxxv (1978)

Sainsbury, John and Merriam, Carol 'The Life of John Wilkes', *Studies in Voltaire and the Eighteenth Century vi* (2008)

Seaward, Paul, '"A Sense of Crowd and Urgency"? Atmosphere and Inconvenience in the Chamber of the Old House of Commons', in *Space and Sound in the British Parliament, 1399 to the Present: Architecture, Access and Acoustics*, ed. J.P.D. Cooper and Richard A. Gaunt (*Parliamentary History* xxxviii, 2019)

van Stien, Kees, 'A Medical Student at Leiden and Paris: William Sinclair 1736-38: part 1', *Proceedings of the Royal College of Physicians at Edinburgh* 225 (1995)

Sussex Archaeological Collections, relating to the History and Antiquities of the County, x (1858)

Thomas, P.D.G., 'The House of Commons and the Middlesex Elections of 1768-1769', *Parliamentary History* xii (1993)

Thompson, Andrew C., '"Oh that glorious first of August!" The Politics of Monarchy and the Politics of Dissent in Early Hanoverian Britain', in Nigel Aston and Benjamin Bankhurst, ed. *Negotiating Toleration: Dissent and the Hanoverian Succession, 1714-1760* (Oxford: Oxford University Press, 2019)

White, Barbara 'Love, Gossip and Diversion: John Wilkes in Bath', *Bath History* xiv (2016)

Woodland, Patrick, 'The House of Lords, The City of London and Political Controversy in the Mid-1760s: The Opposition to the Cider Excise Further Considered', *Parliamentary History* xi (1992)

Reference works and web resources

Armstrong, John, *A Day: an epistle to John Wilkes of Aylesbury Esq* (htttps://www.justincroft.com/book/4120/armstrong-john/a-day-an-epistle-to-john-wilkes-of-aylesbury-esq/)

Bucholz, R.O., *The Database of Court Officers: 1660-1837* (https://courtofficers.ctsdh.luc.edu/)

Burlock, Hillary, 'Mock Elections', https://ecppec.ncl.ac.uk/features/mock-elections-the-political-participations-of-non-voters/

https://www.distillers.org.uk

https://ecppec.ncl.ac.uk/

https://founders.archives.gov/documents/Franklin

Georgian Papers Online (http://gpp.rct.uk., January 2022)

https://johnsonsdictionaryonline.com

https://www.londonlives.org/

measuringworth.com

Moniz, Amanda Bowie, 'A Radical Shrew in America' (http://commonplace.online/article/a-radical-shrew-in-america/)

Oxford Dictionary of National Biography

Records of the Honourable Society of Lincoln's Inn. Admissions, 1420-1790 (2 vols., London: Lincoln's Inn, 1896)

https://www.laurencesternetrust.org.uk/sterne/life-and-times/key-dates/.

https://spitalfieldslife.com/2019/11/16/the-mile-end-assembly/.

Survey of London

https://www.ucl.ac.uk/lbs/

Victoria County History: Buckinghamshire

Victoria County History: Oxfordshire

Unpublished University Theses

Farrell, Stephen 'Divisions, Debates and "Dis-ease": the Rockingham Whig Party and the House of Lords 1760-1785' (Cambridge University PhD, 1993)

Zucchetti, Julia 'The "Redeeming Feature" of John Wilkes' Life: A Study of Polly' (McGill University MA, 2022)

Index

Abergavenny, Lord, *see* Nevill
Abingdon, earl of, *see* Bertie
Acts of Parliament
   Catholic Relief Act 213, 215, 217
   Cider Tax 12, 84, 135
   Habeas Corpus 58
   Militia Act 50
   Quebec Act 215
   Westminster Paving Act 22
Ailesbury, earl of, *see* Bruce
Albrighton, Shropshire 15
Aldworth, Richard Neville 86, 115
Alfred the Great 45
Allen, Ralph 50, 52, 105, 107, 111, 113
Allen, William 152, 168
Almon, John 27, 35, 39, 65, 122, 129, 137, 157
America 116, 149, 157, 172, 196, 198-201, 204, 206, 208, 210, 222, 241
   War of Independence 11, 196, 206, 218-19, 221
Anacreontic Society 224
Andrews, Miles Peter 186
Angelo, Domenico 195
Angelo, Henry 197
Anne, Princess Royal 10
Anti-Gallicans, Honourable and Laudable Society of 150
Apsley, Lord, *see* Bathurst
Argyll, duke of, *see* Campbell
Armstrong, John 41
Arnauld, l'Abbé 136
Arnold, Amelia 173, 209, 210, 229, 234, 240-1, 242
Arnold, Harriet 173, 210, 229, 241, 242, 243
Artillery Company 185
Aylesbury 14, 25, 33, 34, 35, 36, 37, 39, 40, 41, 43, 44, 47, 48-49, 50, 52, 53, 54, 56, 57, 60, 61, 65, 66, 67, 68, 74, 75, 97, 102, 122, 123, 124, 138, 145, 147, 149, 177, 208, 247
   Ashby v. White 34
   Prebendal House 25, 34, 40, 41, 47, 235
Augusta, Princess of Wales 38, 69, 73, 104
Austrian Succession, War of 50
Bacon, Anthony 53
Bagshot 78-79, 80
Baker, Dinah 243
Baker, Sir William 138, 190
Baldwin, Henry 180
Balf (Balfe), Lawrence 160
Balfe, Richard 81, 90-91, 92
Bankes, Sir Joseph 185
Barker, Colonel James 233
Barnard, Jane 80, 156, 200
Barnard, John 17, 80, 156, 200, 210, 264n.
Barnard, Sir John 156
Barnet Gang 188
Barré, Colonel Isaac 170, 228
Barrington, William Wildman Barrington, 2nd Viscount 44, 71, 122, 159, 257n.
Barrow, Mr (Keeper of Carriages) 145
Barthélemy, Jean-Jacques 234, 241
Bass, Jack 52
Bate, Colonel 148

Bath 20, 34, 37, 38, 41, 50, 52, 53, 54, 150, 184, 207, 208, 209, 210, 211, 212, 213, 219, 220, 224, 228, 233, 242
  Minuets 'danced three deep' 211
Bathurst, Henry, Lord Apsley 191, 193
Bause, Friederich 100
Baxter, Andrew 'Immateriality' 29, 30, 31, 35, 36, 40, 72, 207, 234, 247
Beardmore, Arthur 104, 245
Beauclerk, James, bishop of Hereford 55
Beaumarchais, Pierre 200
Beckford, Richard 72
Beckford, William 84, 104, 142-3, 159, 172, 174, 203
Bedford, duke of, see Russell
Benson, Thomas, bishop of Gloucester 17
Berkeley, George, bishop of Cloyne 17, 29
Berkeley, Norborne 78, 79, 80
Bernard, Sir Robert 173
Bertie, Willoughby, 4th earl of Abingdon 132, 134, 229
Berwick-upon-Tweed 43-46, 47, 59, 149
Bessborough, countess of, see Ponsonby
Bestley, Mr (Shoemaker) 145
Bibulus, Marcus Calpurnius 182
Birch, Thomas 41, 207
Bissett, George 235
Blackmore, Robert 90, 91, 92
Blackstone, William 101, 175, 189, 237
  'Lawyer Keene' 101
Bladon, Samuel 180
Blake, Mr (Watchmaker) 145
Bland, Hungerford 26
Blantyre, Lord, see Stuart
Blenheim, Battle of 56
Boehm, Edmund 163
Boileau, Nicolas (Boileau-Despréaux) 86
Bolton, duke of, see Powlett
Bonaparte, Napoleon 13, 241
Bossiney, Cornwall 153
Boston Massacre 170
Boswell, James 95, 98, 99, 116, 130, 133, 198, 204-5, 231
Bowood House, Wiltshire 228
Boyer, Abel 179
Boyle, John, 5th earl of Cork and Orrery 55
Brewster, Thomas 41
Bridgen, William 183
Brighton (Brighthelmstone) 176, 205, 211

Bristol 44, 46, 58, 61, 165, 184, 192, 210, 212
British Museum 208
Brixham 185
Brocklesby, Dr Richard 41, 118
Bromwich, Thomas 170
Brooke, James 18
Brooke, John 9, 121
Brown, Matthew 114, 134
Bruce, Thomas, earl of Ailesbury 16
Buckingham, duke of, see Villiers
Bull, Frederick 182, 184, 186-7, 188-9, 190, 192, 201, 202, 214, 217
Burke, Edmund 48, 81, 129, 135, 177, 185, 192, 208, 241, 242, 243
Bute, earl of, see Stuart
Byng, George 211, 217, 226
Byng, Admiral John 50-51
Byron, William Byron, 5th Baron 94
Cadbury, Ruth (MP) 246
Cadette, Dufort 126
Caesar, Gaius Julius 182, 218
Caligula 77
Calvin, John 134
Campbell, Alexander 47
Campbell, Archibald, 3rd duke of Argyll 59
Campbell, John 82
Canning, George 241
Canterbury 102
Canute, King 101
Cape St Vincent, Battle of 241
Carlyle, Alexander ('Jupiter') 28-29
Carpenter, Edward 180
Carpentier, madam (Polly Wilkes's tutor) 85
Carr, Elizabeth 129, 130
Carrington, Nathan 90, 91
Casanova, Giacomo 187
Cash, Arthur 16, 62, 211, 250n.
Catilina, Lucius Sergius (Catiline) 127
Catullus, Gaius Valerius 245
Cave, Edward 19
Cavendish, William, 1st duke of Devonshire 10
Cavendish, William, 4th duke of Devonshire 52, 70, 82-83, 259n.
Cavendish Bentinck, William, 3rd duke of Portland 212, 222
Chapman, Mr (Brewer) 145
Charles I 74, 162, 195, 233
Charles II 11, 14, 203

Index

Charpillon (Charpillion), Marianne Genevieve 187, 194, 206, 207, 240
Chatham, earl of, *see* Pitt
Chaworth, William 94
Chesterfield, earl of, *see* Dormer Stanhope
Chippendale, George 95
Christian, Matthew 148
Churchill, Charles 63, 72, 75-76, 78, 79, 80-82, 83-86, 87, 90, 92, 99, 100, 102-4, 111, 122, 125, 126, 128-30, 132, 182, 206-7, 236-7, 241
  An Epistle to William Hogarth 100
  'The Bruiser' 72, 100
  Wilkes's monument to him on the Isle of Wight 236-7
Churchill, John 143, 166, 168, 173, 177, 187, 195
Cibber, Colley 22
Cider tax 12
Clarke, George 160
Clayton, Sir Robert 214
Clinton, Henry 218
Clitherow, James 189
Clive, Robert 85
Cliveden 24
Cobbett, William 246
Cobham, Viscount, *see* Temple
Colchester 231
Collibee, Edward Bushell 53
Collins, Arthur 19
Colman, George 126
Colts of the Committee Lands 185
Compton, Spencer, earl of Wilmington 55
Constantinople 67, 120, 123, 134, 235, 262n.
Conyngham, Ellen Conyngham, countess of 228
Cooke, George 70, 144, 146-7, 160, 245
Cooper, Sir Grey 161
Coram, Thomas 60
Cork and Orrery, earl of, *see* Boyle
Cornelys, Teresa 173
Cornwallis, Charles Cornwallis, Marquess 218-19
Corradini, Gertrude 127-8, 131-3, 209, 240
Cosway, Maria 234
Cosway, Richard 234
Cotes, Humphrey 114, 115, 116, 118, 119-20, 121, 122, 123-4, 126, 128-30, 137, 140, 169, 190
Courtenay, John 230-1

Cromwell, Oliver 162
Crosby, Brass 177, 179, 180-2, 183, 190, 191
Croydon, Surrey 102
Cruger, Henry 210
Cumberland, Henry duke of 207
Cumberland, William Augustus, duke of 51, 100
Curry, Michael 106, 108, 111, 158, 268n.
Cust, Peregrine 87
Cust, Sir John 108, 118
Dance, Sir Nathaniel 229
Darly, Matthias 114, 152
Dashwood, Sir Francis, Baron le Despenser 24, 60, 63, 70, 175
Decker, John 226
Deffand, Marie Anne de Vichy-Chamrond, du 137
De Grey, William (attorney general) 149, 150
Delany, Mary 17
Delaval, Edward 44
Dell, John 39, 40, 42, 43, 48, 52-53, 54, 58, 59, 61, 65, 66-68, 85
Delval, John 44, 45, 46, 47
Denbigh, earl of, *see* Feilding
D'Eon de Beaumont, Charles Chevalier 92, 155, 164, 173, 195, 200, 234
Despenser, Lord, *see* Dashwood
Dettingen, Battle of 68
Devonshire, dukes of, *see* Cavendish
D'Holbach, Paul-Henri Thiry 28, 30, 33, 116, 126
Dickens, Charles 20, 213
  Barnaby Rudge 213
  Great Expectations 20
Dickinson, John 49
Diderot, Denis 126, 147
Dighton, Robert 194
Dilly, Charles 204
Dilly, Edward 204, 207, 240
Dingley, Charles 162
Disney, Frances 15
Disney, Matthew 15
Dixon, Thomas 25
Dobson, William 113
Dodd, Lieutenant-Colonel John 71
Dodd, William (the Macaroni Parson) 207
Dodington, George Bubb (Baron Melcombe) 71
Dormer Stanhope, Philip, 4th earl of Chesterfield 58-59

Douglas, Catherine (Hyde), duchess of Queensberry 156
Douglas, Dr John 70
Douglas, William, 3rd earl of March (4th earl of Queensberry) 106
Dover 86, 102, 114, 117, 121, 135, 136, 175
Dowdeswell, William 28, 31
Draper, Thomas 217
Dryden, John 10
Dufouart, Mr (physician) 118
Dun, Alexander 114
Duncannon, Lord, *see* Ponsonby
Dunning, John 101
Duthy, Mr 73
Dyer, John 234
Dyson, Jeremiah 40, 256n.
Earlom, Richard 156
East India College (Haileybury) 24
East India Company 85, 223, 229
Edinburgh 28, 59
Edmunds, William George 179
Edridge, Mr 169
Effingham, earls of, *see* Howard
Egmont, earl of, *see* Perceval
Egremont, earl of, *see* Wyndham
Ellis, Welbore 57, 65
Ellis, William 177
Enfield 226, 229
Esdaile, Sir James 188-9
Evans, Rev. Mr 180
Evans, Thomas 180
Eyles, Sir John 17
Eyre, Sir James 176
Faden, William 106
Farquhar, George 22
Fawkener, William 231
Feilding, Basil, 6th earl of Denbigh 179, 222
Fermor, George, 2nd earl of Pomfret 179
Fielding, Henry 208
Fielding, Sir John 55, 101, 149, 154, 182-3
Finch, Heneage, Lord Guernsey (3rd earl of Aylesford) 57
Fishguard, invasion of 241
Fitzherbert, William 125, 134, 157
Fitzroy, Augustus, 3rd duke of Grafton 117, 136-7, 149, 150, 151, 153, 157, 158, 159, 164, 177
Fitzroy, Colonel Charles 136
Fleming, Seymour (Lady Worsley) 235

Fletcher, Andrew, Lord Milton 94, 96
Flyte, Lord Sebastian 38
Folkestone, Viscount, *see* Pleydell Bouverie
Forbes, Captain 103
Foundling Hospital, London 60, 101
  Aylesbury Branch 60, 61-62, 123, 146, 201
Fox, Charles James 197, 212, 219, 220, 221, 222, 223-4, 226, 227-8, 231, 232, 240
Fox, Henry, Lord Holland 57, 76, 83, 86-87, 142, 164, 166, 212
France 84, 86-7, 89, 102-4, 106, 114, 116, 117-18, 120, 121, 122, 124, 125, 128, 130, 136, 139, 157, 200, 210
  Calais 86, 114, 118, 130, 131, 156
  Lyons 128
  Paris 29, 85, 86, 89, 102-3, 112, 113, 114, 115-16, 119, 121, 122, 124, 125, 126-9, 132, 134, 135, 136, 137-8, 175, 221
    Hotel de Saxe 113, 122, 123, 134
    Rue St Nicaise 122
  Marseilles 134
  Rouen 46
Francis, Philip 230
Franklin, Benjamin 140, 210
Fraser, Simon, Lord Lovat 99, 177
Frederick, Prince of Wales 23-24, 37, 43, 51, 64
Freeman, John 58
Freeman, Sambrooke 60
Friends of Freedom 184
Garrick, David 19, 76, 126, 131, 157-8
Gascoyne, Bamber 152
Gay, John 21
George I 13, 23, 94
George II 23, 51, 52, 64, 68, 69
George III 10, 11, 24, 64, 67, 68, 69, 82-83, 105, 108, 135, 148, 172, 174, 185, 186, 187, 189, 199, 207, 219, 223, 246
  Coronation 68
George, Prince of Wales (George IV) 183
Germain, Lord George (Viscount Sackville) 200-1
Gibbon, Edward 71, 126, 170, 187, 197
Gibbons, Sir William 231
Glassbach, Christian Benjamin 100
Gloucester, bishop of, *see* Warburton
Gloucester, William Henry, duke of 207
Glover, Richard 71

Index

Glyn, Sir Richard 142
Glynn, John 96, 98, 100, 101, 121, 124, 160, 165, 166, 175, 178, 189, 190, 191, 197, 202, 211, 217
Goodflesh, Mark 58
Gordon, Cosmo Gordon, 3rd duke of 213
Gordon, Lord George 213, 214, 215, 216, 217, 229
   Protestant Association 214
Gordon Riots 212, 213-17
Gordon, William ('Willie') 27
Gower, 2nd Earl, *see* Leveson Gower
Grafton, duke of, *see* Fitzroy
Graves, Mr (surgeon) 118
Green, John 154
Gregory, John 28
Grenville, Anna, Countess Temple 114
Grenville, George 45, 55, 70, 86, 88, 94, 105, 108, 133, 135, 160, 161
Grenville, James 55, 60
Grenville, Richard, 2nd Earl Temple 11, 44, 45, 46, 51, 52, 55, 60, 65, 69, 70, 73, 76, 78, 79, 81, 82, 85, 87, 92, 93, 95, 102, 105-6, 110, 112, 114, 117, 120, 121, 122, 131, 135, 136, 137, 158, 161, 162, 166, 168, 169, 182
Grey, Jemima, Marchioness 45
Grimm, Friedrich-Melchior von 126
Grogan, John (MP) 246
Guernsey, Lord, *see* Finch
Guillam, Samuel 152
Haileybury School 24
Halifax, earl of, *see* Montagu Dunk
Hallifax, Thomas 185, 188
Halsey, Frederick 48-49
Hamilton, Ezeckiel 26, 27
Hamilton, Sir William 132
Hampden, John 54, 74, 101, 236, 246
Hampton Court 23
Hancock, John 199
Hardwicke, earl of, *see* Yorke
Harris, Captain 233
Harris, James 119, 158, 162
Harris, Mr (Wilkes's adjutant) 78-79
Harley, Robert, earl of Oxford 94
Harley, Thomas (Lord Mayor) 142, 143
Hart, John 192, 194-5
Hartford, Mr 228
Hartley, David 210
Hastings, Warren 230-1, 238, 240, 241
Hatsell, John 161
Hatton, Edward 56

Hawkins, Caesar 119
Hayley, George 12, 20, 166, 169, 190, 191, 199
Hayley, Mary 20, 139, 169, 199, 211, 242
Heaton family 15, 18
Heaton, John (grandfather of John) 18
Heaton, John (possible great-grandfather of John) 18
Heaton, John (possible nephew of John) 18
Heberden, Dr 119
Hellfire Club, *see* Medmenham
Herbert, Henry, 10th earl of Pembroke 183
Hertford, earl of, *see* Seymour-Conway
Hertford (town) 24-25, 40
HMS Victory 242
Hogarth, Richard 19
Hogarth, William 12, 20, 32, 42, 61, 72, 76-77, 99-100, 101, 103, 139, 164, 165, 233
   The Times 76
Hood, Samuel Hood, Viscount 226, 230, 231
Hopkins, Benjamin 201-2, 211
Horne, John (later Horne Tooke) 116, 137, 145, 146, 151, 156, 166, 169, 175, 176-8, 183, 184, 204
   Constitutional Society 178, 192
Hotham, Sir Richard 223
Howard, Thomas, 2nd earl of Effingham 70
Howard, Thomas, 3rd earl of Effingham 199
Hume, David 59, 115, 126
Humphry, Ozias 100-1
Hussey, Richard 117
Ichneumon (mythical creature) 11
Immateriality, *see* Baxter
Impeachment 94, 177, 230, 238, 240
Inchiquin, earl of, *see* O'Brien
Isle of Wight 12, 44, 185, 233-4, 237
   Appuldurcombe House 238
   Sandown Cottage (villakin) 233, 235, 237, 238
Italy 128, 129, 130-4
   Bologna 127, 131-2
   Naples 132-4
   Rome 132
Jacobites 10, 26, 31, 32, 77, 84, 93, 98, 99, 122, 144, 165, 177, 216
James II 10, 162

James, William 211
Janssen, Sir Stephen 201
Jeffrey, Patrick (husband of Mary Hayley) 242
Jennings, Samuel 106, 111
Johnson, Samuel 10, 11, 77, 99, 204-5, 207
Jones, Mary 183-4
Jones, Mr 40
Jones, Sir William 147
Jonson, Ben 84
Junius 183, 184
Kauffman, Angelica 134
Kearsley, George 76, 90, 106
Keith, George, 10th Earl Marischal 26
Kennett, Brackley 188, 189, 215
Kent, William 56
Kidgell, John 106, 139
Kippis, Andrew 206
Kirkman, John 218
Kloster Zeven, Convention of 51
Knowles, Admiral Charles 54
Labilliere, Peter 228
Ladbroke, Sir Robert 142, 143, 187
Lamb, William, 2nd Viscount Melbourne 230
Langford, Paul 49, 64, 82
Langford, William 193
Laocoon 236
Le Despenser, Lord, *see* Dashwood
Leach, Dryden 90, 91, 102
Lee, Arthur 157, 199, 205
Lee, George Henry, 3rd earl of Lichfield 77, 81
Lee, Sir William 123
Lee, Thomas (Tommy) 207
Lee, William 199
Leeson, Matthew 25, 26-27, 28-29, 30, 32, 40
Leiden (university) 10, 26, 27, 28, 29, 30, 31, 41, 85, 96, 116, 139, 210
Leighton Buzzard 15
Lennox, Charles, 2nd duke of Richmond 32
Lennox, Charles, 3rd duke of Richmond 103, 134
Leveson Gower, Elizabeth, countess (duchess) of Sutherland 241
Leveson Gower, George Granville, Earl Gower (duke of Sutherland) 241
Leveson Gower, Granville, 2nd Earl Gower (marquess of Stafford) 179

Lewes, Sir Watkin 181, 184, 186, 191, 224
Lichfield, earl of, *see* Lee
Livery Companies of the City of London
  Barber Surgeons, Worshipful Company of 142
  Distillers, Worshipful Company of 15-16, 17, 140
  Fishmongers, Worshipful Company of 141, 220
  Fishmongers' Hall 223
  Grocers, Worshipful Company of 141, 193, 224, 280n.
  Joiners and Ceilers, Worshipful Company of 140-1, 174-5, 189, 193, 207, 220
  Joiners' Hall 175, 192
  Musicians, Worshipful Company of 140
  Poulters, Worshipful Company of 141
  Salters, Worshipful Company of 193
  Skinners, Worshipful Company of 192
Llewellyn, Mr (apothecary at the Westminster Hospital) 123
Lloyd, Robert 63, 72, 130
Locke, John 45
London
  Arthur's Coffee House 192, 194
  Bank of England 201, 215, 216
  Bloomsbury Square 214
  Bow Street 55, 101, 154, 188
  Buckingham House 24
  Carlton House 24
  Clerkenwell 15, 21
  St John's Square 16, 18-19
  Devil Tavern, Temple Bar 151
  Downing Street 55, 183, 215, 239
  Elyzium Row, Fulham 173
  Farringdon Without 170, 242
  Fleet Street 216
  Folly House, Blackwall, renowned for whitebait 229
  Goldsmiths' Hall 224
  Great George Street 52, 55, 68, 72, 78, 88, 89, 91, 98, 99, 101, 105, 106, 114, 120, 169, 259n.
  Great Russell Street 191
  Great Titchfield Street 187, 194
  Grosvenor Square 21, 169, 239, 240, 241, 242, 243
  Guildhall 142, 143, 171, 175, 176, 184, 188, 191, 193, 197, 211, 215

Index

Half Moon Tavern 188
Hyde Park Corner 146
Kensington Gore 210, 234, 240-1, 242
Kensington Palace 23, 24
King's Bench Prison 151, 155, 159, 161, 166, 167, 168, 171, 215, 234
Leicester Square 16
 Leicester House 24, 37, 69
Lincoln's Inn 26, 28, 154
London Tavern 165, 173, 174, 188
Mansion House 168, 171-2, 180, 182, 184, 190, 193, 195, 197, 198, 200, 206
Mermaid Tavern, Hackney 226, 238
Mile End Assembly Rooms 145, 148, 162, 164, 171
Nando's Coffee House 163
Newgate prison 55, 93, 94, 95, 154, 166, 184, 215
Norfolk House 24
Old Bailey 172, 176, 184, 193
Pantheon, Oxford Street 187
Prince's Court 169, 173, 178, 184, 187, 194, 195, 200, 208, 228, 229, 234, 237, 239
 Red Lyon Court 34, 35, 39, 47, 131
St James's Palace 23
St Thomas's Hospital 229
Smithfield 21, 182
 Three Tuns 182
Soho Square 172
 Spitalfields 16, 145, 151
 The Three Tuns 145
 Tower of London 89, 93-94, 95, 96, 97, 105, 153, 164, 181-2, 234
 Wood's Hotel, Covent Garden 226
Louis XV 103
Louis XVI (as Dauphin) 175
Lovat, Lord, *see* Fraser
Lucas, Charles ('the Irish Wilkes') 247
Luttrell, Henry Lawes 153, 163, 164, 172, 173, 186, 212
Lucy, George 113
Lyttelton, George Lyttelton, Baron 110
Macaulay, Catharine 159, 170, 207, 210
Macclesfield, earl of, *see* Parker
Mackender, Mr (Butcher) 145
MacKenzie, James Stuart 94, 96, 108, 113
Mackreth, Robert 194
Macleane, Lauchlin 135
MacQuirk, Edward 160

Magna Carta (Magna Charta) 97, 176, 245
Mainwaring, William 226-7
Mallors, James 58
Manchester, duke of, *see* Montagu
Mansfield, earl of, *see* Murray
March, earl of, *see* Douglas
Marie Antoinette, Queen 175
Marischal, Earl, *see* Keith
Martin, Joseph 160
Martin, Samuel 111-12, 113, 125, 160
Masquerades 173, 186, 220
Mawbey, Sir Joseph 158, 159, 190
May, Thomas Erskine 246
Mayne, William, Baron Newhaven 222
McLoed, Alexander 147
Mead family 14, 25, 130, 131, 213
Mead, John 33
Mead, Mary, formerly Sherbrooke (mother-in-law of Wilkes) 25, 34
Mead, Mary (Wilkes's wife) 14, 25, 31, 32-33, 34, 35, 36, 41, 45, 67, 126, 193, 201, 225-6
Mead, Sir Nathaniel of Gooseshays 33
Mead, Dr Richard 33, 41
Mead, Robert 34
Mead, William 34
Medmenham Abbey 57, 63, 75, 78
 Knights of St Francis of 63-64, 66, 106
Melbourne, Viscount, *see* Lamb
Mendoza, June 246
Meredith, Sir William 117
Mereworth 175
Middlesex 143-6, 147, 148-9, 153, 160, 162, 163, 164, 165, 170, 172, 177, 178, 186, 189, 192, 201, 202, 204, 206, 211, 217, 219, 220, 221, 223, 225, 226, 229, 238, 244, 245
 Brentford 143, 144-6, 148, 163, 178, 190, 226
Millar, Andrew 41, 270n.
Miller, John 179, 180
Milton, Lord, *see* Fletcher
Minorca 51
Mitchell, Thomas (of Perth) 29
Moira, earl of, *see* Rawdon
Molière 86
Molyneux, Catherine 205
Molyneux, Crisp 205
Money, James 90
Monitor, The 72, 73, 81, 104, 245
Montagu, George 68

315

Montagu, George, 4th duke of Manchester 173
Montagu, John, 4th earl of Sandwich 42, 57, 63, 64, 83, 104, 107, 110, 112, 113, 122, 135, 173, 179
  sues for *scandalum magnatum* 107
Montagu Dunk, George, 2nd earl of Halifax 81, 90-91, 93, 99, 101, 104, 105, 112-13, 124, 128, 135, 154
Moore, William 216
Morellet, André 126
Morres, Hervey Redmond, 2nd Viscount Mountmorres 190
Morris, Captain 227-8
Morris, Robert 167, 179, 180
Mortimer, Roger 73, 85
Mosley, Charles 59
Mountmorres, Viscount, *see* Morres
Mountstuart, Lord, *see* Stuart
Mozart, Wolfgang Amadeus 156
Murray, Alexander ('The Tiger Macaroni') 152
Murray, William, earl of Mansfield 110, 122, 128, 150-1, 153, 158, 160, 175, 214, 216, 230
Namier, Sir Lewis 27
Nash, William 183
National Portrait Gallery 56
Neate, William 192
Nelson, Horatio Nelson, Viscount 132, 242
Nesbitt, John 41
Nesbitt, Robert 16, 67
Nesbitt, Sophia 187
Nesselrode, count von 229
Nevill, George, 17th Baron (1st earl of) Abergavenny 168
Neville, Sylas 162
Newcastle, duke of, see Pelham Holles
Newhaven, Lord, *see* Mayne
Newnham, Nathaniel 218
Ninnin, Mr (physician) 118
North Briton 9, 10, 59, 63, 66, 70, 73-77, 80, 81, 83-85, 87, 89, 90, 92, 96, 98, 101, 102, 103, 106, 111, 116, 130, 137, 147, 154, 158-9, 164, 165, 216, 223, 227, 231
  Number 45 10, 87-88, 93, 105, 109, 119, 121, 128, 150
  Ordered to be burned by the common hangman 110
North, Frederick North, Lord 55, 105, 109, 119, 153, 160, 162, 177, 183, 185, 187, 189, 211, 213, 215
Norton, Sir Fletcher 194
Nugent-Temple-Grenville, George, 3rd Earl Temple (marquess of Buckingham) 223, 235
Oatlands 175
Okehampton 49, 50, 52, 53, 54
Olantigh 176
Oliver, Richard 174, 179, 180-1, 182, 186, 190, 201, 206
Onslow, George (ally of Wilkes) 108, 117, 119, 134
Onslow, George ('Cocking George') 175, 179-80, 197
Orange, William IV, Prince of 10
O'Brien, William, earl of Inchiquin 37, 39
Oxford, earl of, *see* Harley
Oxlade, William 179
Ozier, Grace 80
Page, William (Beau) 55
Palmerston, Viscount, *see* Temple
Parker, Thomas, earl of Macclesfield 177
Parliament, *see* Westminster
Parsons, Humphrey 17
Paterson, John 142, 143
Pelham, Henry 37, 51
Pelham Holles, Thomas, duke of Newcastle 19, 32, 33, 37, 45, 46, 47, 51-52, 54, 57, 69, 83, 85, 91, 108, 111, 117, 141, 144, 221
Pembroke, earl of, *see* Herbert
Penshurst 175
Perceval, John, earl of Egmont 39
Perry, Micajah 17
Petrie, Samuel 198
Petty, William, 2nd earl of Shelburne (marquess of Lansdowne) 117, 126, 157, 168, 170, 183, 219, 221-2, 228
Philipps, Alexander 118, 119, 121, 124
Pine, Robert Edge 12, 42, 61, 101, 164, 246
Pitt-Devonshire Ministry 52
Pitt-Newcastle Ministry 54, 83
Pitt, Hester, countess of Chatham 79, 162
Pitt, Thomas, of Boconnoc 49
Pitt, William (the Elder), earl of Chatham 11, 44, 46, 48, 49, 50, 51, 52, 53, 54-55, 57, 58, 67-68, 69, 70, 73, 76, 79, 81, 82, 83, 91, 94, 96, 101, 107, 109-10, 112, 135, 136, 137, 153,

Index

157, 169, 170, 171, 172, 181, 199, 224, 227, 247
Pitt, William (the Younger) 11, 217, 222, 223, 224, 225, 227, 228, 232, 235, 238
  'Mince Pie Administration' 224
Pleydell Bouverie, Jacob, Viscount Folkestone (2nd earl of Radnor) 195
Polhill, Nathaniel 190, 214
Pomfret, earl of, *see* Fermor
Ponsonby, Henrietta, countess of Bessborough 246
Ponsonby, Lady Caroline 230
Ponsonby, William, Viscount Duncannon (2nd earl of Bessborough) 230
Ponton, Daniel 152, 159
Pope, Alexander 44, 86, 106
Porter, James 67
Portland, duke of, *see* Cavendish Bentinck
Potter, John, archbishop of Canterbury 11
Potter, Thomas 10, 37-39, 41-42, 43, 44, 46, 48-50, 52, 53, 54, 55, 57, 63, 66, 72, 75, 106, 107, 120, 130
Powlett, Charles, 5th duke of Bolton 73, 95, 112, 209, 221, 263n., 267n.
Poyntz, Georgiana Anne 231
Pratt, Lord Chief Justice Charles (Lord Camden) 58, 94, 96, 98, 99, 102, 105, 113, 153, 164
Preston, John 149
Price, Chase 187
Proctor, Sir William Beauchamp 144, 146, 147, 149, 160
Quebec 50, 82
Queen Anne 23, 69, 94, 203
Queen Caroline 51
Queen Charlotte 24, 68, 135, 148
Queen Elizabeth I 45
Queen Isabella 73, 84-85
Queensberry, duchess of, *see* Douglas
Rabelais, François 63
Racine, Jean 86
Ramsgate 175
Rawdon, John, earl of Moira 113
Raymond, Sir Charles 190
Revolution of 1688 (Glorious Revolution) 10, 51, 74, 77, 126, 129, 185, 195, 208, 236, 245
Reviczky, Karoly, Count 229
Reynolds, Frederick 168-9
Reynolds, John 168-9, 173, 175, 180
Reynolds, Sir Joshua 20, 229, 234

Rich, John 42
Richardson, William 81
Richmond, dukes of, *see* Lennox
Richmond, Surrey 24, 195, 217
Rigby, Richard 171, 277n.
Roache, Daniel 163
Roberts, John 190
Robinson, Frederick 133
Robinson, John (Jack) 225
Rochester, earl of, *see* Wilmot
Rockingham, marquess of, *see* Watson Wentworth
Rodney, George Brydges Rodney, Baron 229
Roma, Johann Zoffany's spitz 220
Roubiliac, Louis-François 43
Rough, William 165, 243
Royal Academy of Arts 156
Royal Society 33
Rugby School 241
Russell, John, 4th duke of Bedford 44, 60, 84, 86, 103, 115, 171
Ryder, Charles 38
Ryles, William 40
Sacheverell, Henry 177
Sainsbury, John 10, 12, 33, 34, 35, 63, 187
St George's Fields, Massacre of 152, 168, 176
Sancho, Charles Ignatius 214
Sandwich, earl of, *see* Montagu
Sandys, Edwin 172
Savile, Sir George 85, 117, 215
Sawbridge, John 159, 162, 164, 169, 176, 177, 178, 183, 188, 190, 192, 199, 200, 207, 218
Saxby, supporter of Wilkes 202
Sayre, Stephen 199
Seaward, Paul 56
Seven Years War 50, 69
Seymour, Charles, 6th duke of Somerset 93
Seymour-Conway, Francis, earl (marquess) of Hertford 115-16, 119, 132
Seymour, Henry 148
Shakespear, John 185, 188
Shakespeare Club 83
Shakespeare, William 45, 86, 99, 116
  Henry IV 153
  Macbeth 205
Shelburne, earl of, *see* Petty
Sherbrooke, Richard 34

Sheridan, Richard Brinsley 240
Shrewsbury, duke of, *see* Talbot
Sibelius, G. 42
Silva, Isaac Fernandes 50
Smith, Adam 126
Smith, Catherine 123
Smith, John (thief) 16
Smith, John (Wilkes's son) 123, 156, 175, 195, 241
Smith Stanley, James, Lord Strange 159
Smollett, Tobias 41, 54, 67, 72-73, 80
Society of Artists of Great Britain 61, 101, 173, 207
Society of Arts 61
Society of Gentlemen Supporters of the Bill of Rights (SSBR) 165-6, 167, 168, 169, 171, 173, 174, 176, 178-9, 183, 185, 187, 188, 189, 190, 192, 199, 202, 204
Sons of Liberty (Boston) 156
Southampton 233
Southwark 15, 22, 95, 153, 154, 190, 214, 223
Somerset, duke of, *see* Seymour
Spencer, Elizabeth 58
Spencer, Richard 58
Spink, John 214
Spinnage, John 101
Stafford, Maria 209-10, 213
Stanhope, Sir William 65, 133
Stephenson, Sir William 159
Sterne, Laurence 41, 124, 126
  The Life and Opinions of Tristram Shandy 41
Stowe, Buckinghamshire 11, 44, 51, 69, 79, 102, 236
Strahan, William 105, 110, 111, 113
Strange, Lord, *see* Smith Stanley
Straw, Jack 164
Stuart, Charles Edward (Bonnie Prince Charlie) 31, 32, 98
Stuart, John, 3rd earl of Bute 29, 69, 70, 72, 73-74, 75, 76, 82, 83-84, 85, 86-88, 91, 94, 99, 100, 104, 132, 133, 136, 142, 168, 212, 221
  'MacBoote' 99
Stuart, John, Lord Mountstuart (later marquess of Bute) 132
Stuart, Walter, 8th Lord Blantyre 29, 30, 35
Suard, Amélie 126
Suard, Antoine 126, 135, 136, 151, 156
Sublime Society of Beefsteaks 42, 57, 107, 125, 171, 177, 199, 220, 229
Swieten, Gottfried van 156
Swift, Jonathan 26, 86
Talbot, Charles, duke of Shrewsbury 77
Talbot, William Talbot, Earl 68, 77-79, 80, 81, 86, 93, 111, 121, 137, 158
Temple, 2nd Earl, *see* Grenville
Temple, 3rd Earl, *see* Nugent-Temple-Grenville
Temple, Henry, 2nd Viscount Palmerston 103
Temple, Miss ('a perfect Huncamunca') 208
Temple, Richard, Viscount Cobham 44
Tenerife 242
Terence 13, 207
Terrick, Richard, bishop of London 195
Theophrastus 245
Thompson, Roger 179
Thompson, Sir John 17
Thompson, William 237
Thomson, Mr 139
Thornton, Bonnell 99, 104
Thorpe (Wilkes's gardener in Aylesbury) 40
Thrale, Henry 190
Thrale (Piozzi), Hester 11, 182, 190
Thurlow, Edward, Baron Thurow 222
Thynne, Thomas, 3rd Viscount Weymouth (marquess of Bath) 80, 152, 159, 161
Timberland, Ebenezer 179
Topin, Madame 208
Tory Party 10, 11, 51
Townley, Charles 220, 229
Townsend, James 162, 169, 185-6
Townshend, Charles 27-28, 85
Townshend, Charles, 2nd Viscount Townshend 28
Townshend, Charles, 3rd Viscount Townshend 27
Townshend, Hon. George (later Marquess Townshend) 99, 160, 231
Townshend, Hon. John 231
Trail, James (later bishop of Down) 124
Trecothick, Barlow 142, 143, 149, 174, 176
Trench, Charles Chevenix 16
Trott, Thomas 17
Tunbridge Wells 175, 176
Tyler, Wat 164
Tyrwhitt, Thomas 55

Index

Udny, John 127
Utrecht 29, 30, 31
Van, Charles 197
Vanbrugh, John 40
Vergennes, Charles Gravier, comte de 210
Verney, Ralph Verney, 2nd Earl 37
Vignoles family 173
Villiers, George, duke of Buckingham 74
Villiers, George Bussy, Viscount Villiers (earl of Jersey) 82, 86
Voltaire 51, 134, 229, 238
Waldegrave, James, 2nd Earl 51
Walpole, Horace (4th earl of Orford) 68, 93, 122, 126, 137, 149, 171, 212, 220, 241, 242, 246, 247
Walpole, Sir Robert 11, 13, 17, 28, 44, 46, 51, 52, 55, 94, 203, 207, 245
Walsh, John 85, 86
Warburton, Gertrude, formerly Tucker 50
Warburton, Ralph Allen 50
Warburton, William, bishop of Gloucester 29, 50, 107, 110, 112
Watson, James 90, 92
Watson, Richard, bishop of Llandaff 241
Watson, Thomas 44, 46
Watson Wentworth, Charles, 2nd marquess of Rockingham 133, 135, 136, 142, 158, 171, 192, 219, 221
Webb, Philip Carteret 91, 101, 106, 124, 158, 161
Wesley, John 206
West, Miss 168
Westminster 22, 140
  Westminster Abbey 58
  Westminster Bridge 55, 104, 151
  Elections to 12, 34, 44, 46, 48, 49, 52, 65, 87, 142, 144, 160, 163, 165, 188, 190, 194, 198, 217, 257n.
  House of Commons 11, 23, 34, 40, 43, 46, 47, 49, 51, 52, 56-58, 69-70, 71, 82, 83, 84, 85, 91, 105, 108, 109, 110, 111-14, 116, 117-20, 148, 149, 150, 158-9, 160-1, 163, 171, 174, 179-82, 184, 186, 190, 195, 197, 199, 200, 204, 209, 214, 215, 217, 219, 222-3, 224, 226, 227, 228, 230-2, 238, 246
  House of Lords 17, 23, 57, 94, 107, 113, 172, 177, 225
  Palace of 23
  Heaven and Hell 56

St Margaret's 18, 128, 232
Westminster Hall 23, 56, 68, 95-96, 98, 101, 153, 154, 204, 212, 214
Weymouth, Viscount, *see* Thynne
Wheble, John 179, 180
Whig Party 10
  'Old Corps' 51, 126, 133
Whitehead, Paul 42
Whittam, William 180
Wightman, John 18
Wildman, William 136
Wilks (Wilkes), Robert 22
Wilkes, Ann (Nancy) (sister of John) 20
Wilkes, Anne 240
Wilkes, Charles 199
Wilkes, Deborah 16, 67
Wilkes, Edward (of Leighton Buzzard) 14
Wilkes, Edward (great-uncle of John) 15
Wilkes, Heaton (brother of John) 19-20, 57, 92, 123, 131, 136, 166, 169, 187, 211, 226, 239, 242-3, 251n., 292n.
Wilkes, Israel (brother of John) 19-20, 24-25, 26, 67, 72, 140, 211, 242-3
Wilkes, Israel (father of John) 14, 15, 16, 17-18, 19, 25, 34, 45, 61, 66-67
Wilkes, Israel (grandfather of John) 15, 16
Wilkes, Joan 14
Wilkes, John (assumed forebear) 14
Wilkes, John
  Birth 13, 18, 22, 250-1n.
  Education 20, 24-30, 245
  Family of 14-15, 211
  As libertine 10-11, 31, 35, 38, 42, 59, 62, 64, 71, 121, 158, 178, 194, 200, 224, 244, 247
  Elections to Parliament 43-44, 48, 54, 140, 142-7, 150, 162-4, 189-90, 221, 225
  Committee work 57-58
  Governor of the Foundling Hospital 60-62
  Visits Scotland 59
  Buckinghamshire militia 32, 60, 62, 63, 65, 70, 71, 74, 78, 84, 95, 123, 185, 220
  Duels 78-80, 86, 103, 111-12, 117, 121, 125, 137
  The Essay on Woman 44, 50, 106, 109, 128, 139, 150, 154, 158
  Observations on the Papers relative to the Rupture with Spain 70

Writes for *The Monitor* 72
Founds *North Briton* 63, 73-74
Dubbed Marcus Cato 81
Satirised by Hogarth 99
Exile 115-39, 147, 149, 157, 177
Letter to the Worthy Electors of the Borough of Aylesbury 129
Uses alias Osborn 139
'Wilkes and Liberty' 96, 97-102, 126, 135, 138, 144, 147, 149, 153, 156-7, 158, 159, 160, 168, 198, 226, 231, 243
Imprisoned in King's Bench 155-8, 161, 167-8
As Count Belisarius 165
Alderman of Farringdon Without 170
Master of the Joiners' Company 175
Lord Mayor of London 186, 190-1, 193, 194, 198-9, 200, 206
City Chamberlain 201-2, 211, 212
Speaks in favour of parliamentary reform 9, 11, 189, 202-4
As an orator 58, 71, 196, 197, 206, 207
Relations with women 12, 14, 30, 32-33, 35, 80, 85, 102, 125, 127, 187, 200, 205, 208-9, 229, 240
Birdwatcher 35, 175, 236
Book collector 40, 123, 200, 234, 237, 239-40, 242
Patron of the arts 61, 101, 173, 207, 245
Gardener 35, 36, 40-41, 44, 45, 123, 175, 229, 235-6, 237
'a phoenix' 247
Death of 242
Funeral 243
Statue in Fetter Lane 247
Wilkes, Luke 14-15
Wilkes, Mark 14
Wilkes, Mary (sister of John), see Hayley
Wilkes, Mary (Polly, Wilkes's daughter) 12, 14, 35-36, 47, 67, 79, 85-86, 89, 100-2, 113, 114, 121, 122-3, 126, 127, 128, 130-1, 132, 134, 136, 138, 150, 157, 168, 169, 171, 173, 174, 175, 184, 185, 187, 193, 195, 198, 205, 206, 208, 209, 210-11, 212, 213, 215, 216, 218, 219, 220, 226-7, 228, 229, 231, 232, 234, 236, 239, 240, 241, 242-3, 244

Wilkes, Matthew 14
Wilkes, Richard 240
Wilkes, formerly Heaton, Sarah (mother of John) 14, 15, 18, 20, 25, 33, 67, 125, 157, 184, 226, 253n.
Wilkes, Sarah (sister of John, supposed model for Miss Havisham) 20
Wilkes, William David 240
Wilkes's Wriggle 164-5
Wilkite Clubs 165
Willes, Edward 37, 39, 52-53, 65
Willes, John 37, 39, 43, 65
William III 10, 23, 185
Williams, John 165
Wilmington, earl of, *see* Compton
Wilmot, John, 2nd earl of Rochester 11, 35
Wilson, Thomas 207, 210, 226
Winchester 70, 71, 73, 74, 75, 78, 79, 80
Winckelmann, Johann 127, 132, 236
Windsor Castle 23
Witney, Oxfordshire 148
Wolfe, James 50
Wollstonecraft, Mary 241, 242
Wood, Robert 113
Woodfall, Henry Sampson 104
Woodfall, William 94, 180, 197
Woodward, William 235
Worsley, Israel 24
Worsley, John (the elder) 24
Worsley, John (the younger) 24
Worsley, Sir Richard, bt. 235, 236, 237, 238
History of the Isle of Wight 237
Wraxall, Nathaniel 197-8, 221, 245, 246
Wray, Sir Cecil 226
Wren, Sir Christopher 56
Wright, Joseph (of Derby) 241, 242
Wright, Thomas 180
Wyndham, Charles, 2nd earl of Egremont 82, 90-91, 93, 95, 99, 101, 103, 107
Wynn, Sir Watkin Williams 167
Wyvill, Christopher 204, 227, 228, 229
Yalden, Mr 73
Yates, Justice Joseph 154
Yorke, Philip, earl of Hardwicke 85, 91
Yorkshire Association 228
Young, Mr (Baker) 145
Young, Rev. T.O. 99
Zoffany, Johann 220